T0358367

The Chinese Model of Modern Development

This book examines the Chinese model of modern development, reflecting on the historical experience of China's reform, and highlighting theoretical issues that are crucial for understanding the reform in its historical and global contexts. The book brings together scholars, who were either designers of, and active participants in, the reform, or opinion setters in the current debates on the nature and future of the reform, or western scholars whose ideas have had great impact on Chinese intellectuals. Throughout, the book considers the goals of China's reforms and the ways in which these goals may be achieved, the most urgent issues now facing China, and globalization and its impact on China.

Tian Yu Cao studied philosophy at Peking University, was a Fellow of Trinity College, Cambridge, UK, and received his doctorate from Cambridge in 1987. He did post-doctoral research at Northwestern, Harvard and MIT, and is now teaching philosophy of natural and social sciences at Boston University. His research interests include philosophical issues in modernity, postmodernity and globality.

Routledge Studies on the Chinese Economy

Series Editors

Peter Nolan, *University of Cambridge*
Dong Fureng, *Beijing University*

The aim of this series is to publish original, high-quality, research-level work by both new and established scholars in the West and the East, on all aspects of the Chinese economy, including studies of business and economic history.

1 **The Growth of Market Relations in Post-reform Rural China**
A micro-analysis of peasants, migrants and peasant entrepreneurs
Hiroshi Sato

2 **The Chinese Coal Industry**
An economic history
Elspeth Thomson

3 **Sustaining China's Economic Growth in the Twenty-first Century**
Edited by Shujie Yao and Xiaming Liu

4 **China's Poor Regions**
Rural–urban migration, poverty, economic reform and urbanisation
Mei Zhang

5 **China's Large Enterprises and the Challenge of Late Industrialization**
Dylan Sutherland

6 **China's Economic Growth**
Yanrui Wu

7 **The Employment Impact of China's World Trade Organisation Accession**
A. S. Bhalla and S. Qiu

8 **Catch-up and Competitiveness in China**
The case of large firms in the oil industry
Jin Zhang

9 **Corporate Governance in China**
Jian Chen

10 **The Theory of the Firm and Chinese Enterprise Reform**
The case of China International Trust and Investment Corporation
Qin Xiao

11 **Globalisation, Transition and Development in China**
The case of the coal industry
Huaichuan Rui

12 **China Along the Yellow River**
Reflections on rural society
Cao Jingqing, translated by Nicky Harman and Huang Ruhua

13 **Economic Growth, Income Distribution and Poverty Reduction in Contemporary China**
Shujie Yao

14 **China's Economic Relations with the West and Japan, 1949–79**
Grain, trade and diplomacy
Chad J. Mitcham

15 **China's Industrial Policy and the Global Business Revolution**
The case of the domestic appliance industry
Ling Liu

16 **Managers and Mandarins in China**
The building of an international business alliance
Jie Tang

17 **The Chinese Model of Modern Development**
Edited by Tian Yu Cao

The Chinese Model of Modern Development

Edited by Tian Yu Cao

Routledge
Taylor & Francis Group

LONDON AND NEW YORK

First published 2005
by Routledge
2 Park Square, Milton Park, Abingdon, Oxon OX14 4RN

Simultaneously published in the USA and Canada
by Routledge
605 Third Avenue, New York, NY 10017

*Routledge is an imprint of the Taylor & Francis Group,
an informa business*

© 2005 Editorial matter and selection, Tian Yu Cao;
individual chapters, the contributors

Typeset in Times by
Keystroke, Jacaranda Lodge, Wolverhampton

All rights reserved. No part of this book may be reprinted or
reproduced or utilized in any form or by any electronic,
mechanical, or other means, now known or hereafter
invented, including photocopying and recording, or in any
information storage or retrieval system, without permission in
writing from the publishers.

Notice:
Product or corporate names may be trademarks or registered
trademarks and are used only for identification and explanation
without intent to infringe.

British Library Cataloguing in Publication Data
A catalogue record for this book is available from the British Library

Library of Congress Cataloging in Publication Data
A catalog record for this book has been requested

ISBN 13: 978-0-415-34518-7 (hbk)

To Lin Zili
for his original contributions to the Chinese Model

Contents

Contributors   x
Acknowledgments   xii

Introduction: modernization, globalization and the Chinese path   1
TIAN YU CAO

PART I
Socialism: institutional and conceptual innovations   7

1 **We should encourage institutional innovations**   9
   DU RUNSHENG

2 **Imagining alternative modernities**   16
   PERRY ANDERSON

PART II
The historical experience of China's reform   21

3 **Accomplishments and problems: a review of China's reform in the past twenty-three years**   23
   YU GUANGYUAN

4 **The relationship between China's strategic changes and its industrialization and capitalization**   54
   WEN TIEJUN

 5 The historical origin of China's neo-liberalism: another
    discussion on the ideological situation in contemporary mainland
    China and the issue of modernity   61
    WANG HUI

 6 China's economic transition, social justice and democratization
    at the turn of the century   88
    QIN HUI

 7 Theory and practice of the Chinese "market socialism" project:
    is "market socialism" an alternative to liberal globalization?   128
    SAMIR AMIN

PART III
Theoretical deliberations about China's reform   149

 8 Rethinking the relationship between the state and society in
    the age of globalization   151
    ZHU HOUZE

 9 Liberal socialism and the future of China: a petty bourgeoisie
    manifesto   157
    CUI ZHIYUAN

10 Pension funds and responsible accumulation: the choices facing
    China   175
    ROBIN BLACKBURN

11 Ten theses on Marxism and the transition to socialism   188
    DAVID SCHWEICKART

PART IV
Globalization and China's modernization   217

12 China's governance and political development under
    the impact of globalization   219
    YU KEPING

13 Globalization and economic development   238
    CH'U WAN-WEN

14 **What is China's comparative advantage?** 264
LIN CHUN

15 **Globalization and vulnerability: India at the dawn of the twenty-first century** 277
AMIYA KUMAR BAGCHI

16 **Conclusion: the theory and practice of the Chinese model** 293
TIAN YU CAO

Index 318

Contributors

Samir Amin is Director of the Third World Forum, an international organization with its central office in Dakar, Senegal. As a leading critic of capitalism, his work has exercised great influence in China since the early 1970s.

Perry Anderson is Professor in history and sociology at UCLA.

Amiya Kumar Bagchi is a prominent Indian economist. He was a Director of the Centre for Studies in Social Sciences, Calcutta, India, in the 1980s and 1990s, and the Reserve Bank of India Professor of Economics in the same Centre from 1997.

Robin Blackburn is Professor of Sociology at the University of Essex.

Tian Yu Cao teaches philosophy at Boston University.

Ch'u Wan-wen is Deputy Director of the Sun Yat-Sen Institute for Social Sciences and Philosophy, Academia Sinica, Taipei, Taiwan.

Cui Zhiyuan teaches Public Policy and Management at Tsinghua University, Beijing.

Du Runsheng was Director of the Office for Rural Area Policies, under the Secretariat, Central Committee, Chinese Communist Party, from the late 1970s to the early 1990s, and is widely recognized, within and outside of the Party, as the chief designer of the agricultural reform policies; he remains one of the leading voices on various strategic issues facing the Party.

Lin Chun teaches politics at the London School of Economics and Political Science.

Qin Hui is Professor of History at Tsinghua University, Beijing.

David Schweickart is Professor of Philosophy at Loyola University, Chicago. He is also a well-known political economist for trying to provide the notion of a socialist market economy with Marxist justifications.

Wang Hui is Professor of Humanities at Tsinghua University, Beijing, and Editor of *Reading* (a monthly journal).

Wen Tiejun is president and Chief Editor of the journal *Reform in China*, an organ of the State Council Office of System Reform.

Yu Guangyuan was a leading member of the State Council Research Office, a Vice-Minister at the State Commission of Science and Technology, and a Vice-President at the Chinese Academy of Social Sciences from the late 1970s to the mid-1980s. As a leading economist and philosopher, he remains a leading voice in China.

Yu Keping is Deputy Director of the Central Bureau for Translation and Compilation, Central Committee, Chinese Communist Party.

Zhu Houze was former Minister of Propaganda, Central Committee, Chinese Communist Party, in the mid-1980s.

Acknowledgments

This volume is based on a symposium on the Chinese Model of Modern Development, which was held in Hangzhou, China, July 5–7, 2002. In its preparation, Dr. Lin Chun of the London School of Economics and Political Sciences provided great help. At the symposium, Dr. Zhong Xueping of Tufts University and Dr. Ye Weili of the University of Massachusetts at Boston undertook much of the translating. The symposium was partially supported by a grant provided by the Ford Foundation, and logistically supported by Hangzhou University of Commerce. Without this help and support, the meeting could not have proceeded as smoothly as it did. I am sincerely grateful to all those whose help made the symposium possible.

Dr. Yu Keping of the Central Compilation and Translation Bureau could not attend the symposium due to a conflict of schedules; Dr. Lin Chun who attended the symposium did not get the chance to actually speak because the schedule for the meeting was too tight; but their excellent articles, which were submitted in advance and distributed at the symposium, are now included in this volume.

The discussion part of the meeting was transcribed by Miss Feng Ying of the Department of International Politics, Peking University, and edited by Tian Yu Cao.

Credit is due to M.E. Sharpe for its translation of articles written by Chinese scholars, with the exception of those by Dr. Lin Chun and Dr. Cui Zhiyuan, and its initial publication of the translated materials in its journal *The Chinese Economy*. I am deeply indebted to the editor of the journal and to my colleague at Boston University, Professor Joseph Fewsmith, for his help in making all the arrangements. Thanks are also owed to Professor Peter Nolan of Cambridge University for his encouragement, and to Peter Sowden of Routledge for his understanding, encouragement, help and patience. It would be impossible for me to bring this project to completion without their help.

Introduction

Modernization, globalization and the Chinese path

Tian Yu Cao

China's past twenty-three years of reforms have achieved amazing results. Since entering WTO in 2001, China has begun to be integrated into the global market in a comprehensive way. Without a doubt, globalization will also bring various kinds of impact on China's future development. In order to have a better understanding of the situation, a group of scholars gathered in Hangzhou, China, and held a symposium on the Chinese Model of Modern Development. The aim was to explore, in depth, the goals of China's reforms and the ways through which to reach those goals, and to examine the most urgent issues facing China today and the means with which to address them.

The original slogan of China's reform was to achieve the "four modernizations," and, together with political reform, to build a highly civilized, highly democratized, modernized and powerful socialist nation.

What is *modernization*? Sociologists would normally mention secularization, the development in science and technology, industrialization, urbanization and capitalism. Simply put, it is market economy plus democracy. Philosophers, on the other hand, would emphasize rationality (i.e. modernization is a rationalized way of organizing a society, politically, economically and culturally).

What is *rationality*? Roughly speaking, there are two kinds: dogmatic and critical rationality. The former believes that objective truths and universal values can be discovered, and social processes can be controlled and a rational society designed on the basis of that discovery. Statism and planned economy are its incarnations. The latter holds a critical attitude towards various dogmas about truth claims and moral values. It supports tolerant liberalism politically and the market system economically. It believes that the most rational order and structure is the dynamic structure resulting from continuous local interactions and adaptations by numerous rational individuals who are in pursuit of their own self-interests. The libertarian economists also try to justify the "invisible hand" or market rationality by appealing to the idea of self-organization in a non-linear many-body system, and to the scientific and philosophical ideas of the emergence of order out of chaos, which ideas have been popular ever since the time of Freidrich Hayek, Karl Popper and Ilya Prigogine. It is well known, however, that the two types of rationality, though seemingly in opposition and having different domains of application, are in fact complementary to one other.

Historically, modernization has incarnated in capitalism (market and democracy). The nature of capital is expansion: first, expanding within nation-states, having integrated all non-capitalist economic sections, and second, expanding outward; initially there were colonialism and imperialism, now we have globalization.

What is *globalization*? Enthusiasts would quickly point to revolutionary results in science and technology (information, transportation, communication), which have elevated the productive force up to a new level; to the deepening of mutual dependence and the so-called win-win situation. However, socially and economically, globalization, which is characterized by the swift and free movement of transnational financial capital on a global scale and appeared in the 1990s, is none other than a global expansion of the capitalist market in the post-cold war era. Or, more precisely, it is a global expansion of the transnational capital led by that of the U.S.A.

From the Marxist perspective, this new development in capitalism represents huge progress in human history. It has provided an opportunity for underdeveloped nations to enter international division of labor, where they can take advantage of their underdevelopment to develop their national economy, to improve their industrial structure and elevate it to a new level, and to modernize itself. However, just like any other progress brought about by capitalism, the immediate results of globalization are the intensification of exploitation and control of labor by capital; the rapid development of injustice and polarization between the poor and the rich on a global level; the destruction of the ecological system and the alienation of human nature following on from developmentalism and consumerism. What is more, the pressure upon the underdeveloped regions exercised by transnational capital for a suitable investment environment will also seriously impair the welfare of the workers, as well as the environmental protection, economic development and political democratization of these regions. A clear recognition of the danger demands that our government should face the cruel reality, get a clear sense of China's national interests and national goals, have proper policies, and to rely mainly on national industry to both cooperate with and struggle against transnational capital, so that our nation may be rejuvenated.

Some may accuse me of advocating nationalism and opposing globalization. To be sure, globalization is a reality that we must face rather than a process to bypass. However, if, when faced with the powerful and greedy transnational capitalists we do not try to protect our national interests, we will render China under the control of others and the results will be unimaginable. Only by holding firmly to a national stance can we take advantage of globalization for modernizing ourselves.

How can we achieving socialist modernization by participating in capitalist globalization? Facing this paradox, some may argue that modernization is modernization; there is no such thing as whether or not it is socialist or capitalist. Still others may contend that socialism has been proven to be a dead-end and, in order to modernize ourselves, capitalism is the only way to go, and it is also the only way for China to merge into the mainstream of human civilization. According to this argument, Western capitalist modernization is rooted in universal humanity (desire for freedom and autonomy, and instrumental rationality, which is manifested both in the market and in science and technology), and has been brought about by universalizing forces of industry, market and democracy. Consequently, it is universal, inevitable, and thus desirable for China to follow suit.

However, if we examine market and industry, development and progress, and freedom and democracy that comprise the core of Western modernization from the point of view of critical rationality, which itself is part of modernity, we find that developmentalism based upon industry and market was historically compatible with Hitler and Stalin, and may lead to ecological disaster for the human species; democracy is only procedural but not substantial, and thus is detached from the will of the exploited and repressed, and is easily manipulated by those with wealth and power; an individual's freedom realized in the market economy is good for efficiency, but it also entails inequality and injustice. All of this raises the question of searching for an alternative modernity.

Originally, at the beginning of the reforms, the goal was to self-adjust and self-improve socialism, not to develop capitalism. But in order to construct a highly civilized socialist society, China must break away from Stalinist and Maoist frameworks and make theoretical innovations and model selections. The result is the adoption of market socialism. Here, the market is the means for developing a productive force, and the goal is to build socialism. In the context of globalization, participating actively in the integration of a global market with such a firm, socialist-oriented national stance, as a special national actor, is China's path to modernization, or the Chinese model of modern development.

There is a long history in China of seeking an alternative model for modernization: from Sun Yat-Sen, to Jiang Jieshi, to Mao Zedong, and Deng Xiaoping. The reason may be found in China's tradition of egalitarianism (which is manifested in the utopia of universal harmony or socialist ideals) and statism (despotism or the respect paid to a state's economic functions). Liberals in China oppose the concept of a Chinese model, since they believe that it would only serve despotism and reactionary nationalism and would prevent China from merging into the mainstream of human civilization. What is meant by "a Chinese model" here, however, is not based on the so-called traditional cultural values (such as Confucian culture or Asian values), nor is it the same as Maoist socialism. It is a model aiming at humanist socialism.

There are three points worth noting here. First, the possibility of socialism derives from the internal limitations of capitalism. Not only will its inherent developmentalism and consumerism result in incurable ecological and resource problems and social confrontations, which will lead to crises and instability, but the inner logic of capitalist cultural development will also lead to the abandonment of its behavioural norm of exploitation. Second, the essence of socialism is not equalitarianism or equalization but social justice that aims to eliminate exploitation. In this sense, a socialist society is one in which there are no structural confrontations. This is what I mean by humanist socialism. Third, in order to realize socialism, we must make use of the market but we also need to count on the state. Without an effective state apparatus which is responsible for making institutional arrangements for the market, providing it with norms, regulations and constraints so that it will serve the socialist value system, we cannot even begin to discuss the issues relevant here.

Libertarian economists believe that the government's interventions in economic and social affairs are the root causes of corruption and of inefficiency, and thus have to be reduced to a minimum. In fact, the government's economic and social functions, even within the market system, cannot be ignored. This is so not only in the market failure areas, such as education, scientific research, health care and medicine, environmental and ecological system protection, where externalities are involved, but also in the areas of macro-policies, in conceptualizing a "catching-up and surpassing" strategy, in directing investment, social development, income distribution, social security and so on, in making industrial, financial and monetary policies in conjunction with and within the context of globalization, if the state does not perform its normal functions, everything will fall apart, as will the development of a military, cultural, democratic legal system, and a socialist value system.

In turning the state apparatus from the hotbed of corruption into the instrument for building market socialism, the key is to reform it along democratic lines. But what is democracy? Procedural democracy or substantial democracy? Procedural democracy is a must, otherwise there will be no rule of law, only arbitrary rule of personality. But obviously procedural democracy is not enough, for it can be easily manipulated and controlled by the rich and the powerful. To avoid this, we have to have substantial democracy; that is, we have to make political and economic arrangements so that the root causes of unjust distribution of power and wealth may be eliminated. Thus the task of achieving economic democracy.

Some people may object, and argue that economic democracy will invade and limit an individual's property rights and freedom. This is true. This is also why economic liberals do not necessarily want democracy and actually tend to like authoritarianism. On the other hand, procedural democracy may be able to guarantee negative freedom (which in fact involves only human rights), but in and of itself it does not necessarily provide the majority with positive freedom to carry out activities that are more compatible with human nature. Only when substantive democracy based on economic democracy is combined with procedural democracy can citizens' human rights and civil rights and their freedom to carry our various activities that do not impede other people's lives be guaranteed. Here, we have already transcended the boundaries of liberalism or capitalist ideology, and entered the domain of socialism.

Within the twenty-three years of opening up and reform, economic growth and the loosening of political control is an undisputable fact. At the same time, however, exploitation and social injustice have also rapidly developed, constituting yet another undisputable fact. With twenty-three years behind us, are we closer to socialism or further away from it? My impression is that to some people today, socialism as a word has already disappeared. In its place is nationalist developmentalism. How could this change happen? What is its inner logic? It is worth our while to explore these issues.

After twenty-three years of reform, the emergence of a consensus that the establishment and development of a market economy should be the goal of China's reform is a great accomplishment. However, the market is not only a dynamic system full of innovation that can process economic information efficiently, lower transaction costs and increase economic efficiency; historically it has also been an institutional arrangement that the weak have to accept, a closed network of invariant modes of behaviour with structural features of exploitation, competition and instability, together with a social ethos of insecurity, fear and greed. Arguably the market may be viewed as a neutral human institution; if it is guided by a socialist value system, and regulated by a democratic state, it is not impossible for the market to serve socialism. From where we are today, we are still some way from this point; what is more, we still appear uncertain even where to begin.

Today, both the economic and social situation are quite grave. Many things remain unclear. There are different kinds of estimations and assessments. In particular, there are heated debates over the future direction of reform, policy orientations and related theoretical issues. Some on the left believe that the causes of problems lie in the open-door policy and mindless efforts to "connect with the international track." The liberals wish to follow the Western path, insisting that all the troubles are caused by the lack of political reform: there is too much governmental intervention in the economy, which has created a market monopoly based on the power monopoly that is manifest in the formation of sectorial interest groups and regional interest groups, and resulted in a lack of normalcy, maturity and legal infrastructures in the market system, which has provided an institutional warranty for corruption, and led to the loss of state-owned assets, the problems of agriculture, of rural areas and of peasants, social injustice and the demoralizing polarization between the rich and the poor. Where is the way out? Following Western models, developing democracy, perfecting the market system and establishing a comprehensive legal infrastructure? What are the driving forces of this endeavour and what are the resisting forces to it? Is it feasible for China to follow its own path? Is it market socialism with Chinese characteristics or is it a crony capitalism with Chinese characteristics? Is China's next step already fated or does it depend on what people do? In addition to party and governmental officials, rich managers, and scholars and professors, are workers and peasants also included in the "people" who can make a difference? Do they count? Can they also have a say? How can their right to speak be guaranteed?

Problems are deeply rooted, opinions are too widely divided, debates are too heated to form a consensus. However, with the combined efforts of participants, who all intend to promote the prosperity and progress of the Chinese nation and are well prepared for the exchange, the three-day symposium has at least clarified a few important facts and differences, and proposed a few constructive suggestions. Perhaps the publication of both the Chinese edition (in July 2003) and the English edition of the conference volume may give some impetus to further discussions of issues that we were engaged in at the Hangzhou Symposium.

(Adapted from the Opening Address delivered on July 5, 2002)

Part I

Socialism

Institutional and conceptual
innovations

1 We should encourage institutional innovations

Du Runsheng

1 We are still far away from modernization

The modernization of a country must comprise the complete modernization of its economy, politics and culture, and must be the modernization of the whole country. The substantive aspects of modernization are also developed with time. Although the policy of reform and opening has made great progress in China, we still have a long way to go.

- The gross national product per person this year is US$900.00, far below that of developed countries such as the USA, England, France, Germany and Japan.
- The disparity between town and country is growing wider. The income of city dwellers is five times greater than the income of farmers. Only 37.7 per cent of the population live in the city, while the majority live in rural areas. Sixty-three per cent of the population produce food for the consumption of 37.7 per cent of the population. Following Engel's law, when surplus agricultural commodities are too big, farmers' incomes stagnate because it becomes hard to sell grain.
- The average daily income of the whole rural population is lower than US$1.00 (only 6.48 Renminbi); along with the unemployed and part-time working population, they form a large proportion of the low-income nationals who expect social protection and support for the poor.
- The funding of compulsory education has not been stable for some time; the number of illiterate people decreased, and then rose; the number of high school students is less than 25 per cent of adolescents of eligible age to go to high school. These factors affect production and employment.

The government's guidance and services are indispensable in solving these problems. Large amounts of state and private investments are required to promote the economy, which needs more capital investment in order to develop. This requires not only time, but also the creation of new systems and technologies which will benefit future development.

2   The system is more important than technology

Looking at history, at the whole process of social development, we see that it is technological revolutions which promote the development of socially productive forces and further innovate the social system. However, when a social system cannot accommodate the full development of productive forces and bottle-necks occur, it is time to re-establish or improve the system in order to assure sustainable economic development. We can say that the system is more important than technology under these circumstances.

In the past twenty years, our country's basic line of focus has been on building the economy, continually innovating technology and accelerating the development of the national economy. To maintain sustainable and smooth development, we now need to further improve the system and our environment, and to establish social protection.

The function of the system is to provide citizens with a standard of behavior. National modernization depends on the efforts of individuals. In the different historical stages of social development, a good system can embody all that a person depends on: respect, encouragement and guidance. It can allow a person to transform the world outside of him or herself while continually remolding his or her subjective world, to gain command of current knowledge and develop new knowledge, and to have an advantage in manpower capital. We can see that social needs can be advanced and that they can motivate scientific and technological progress through the innovations of the system. Beginning with the fourteenth century, Western Europe went through the Renaissance and the Enlightenment, with society promoting human rights, as well as the notion that state sovereign rights belong to the people. Throughout this time, the ideological bonds of ignorance of medieval religion were broken, and individualism (not selfishness) was fostered, promoting the rise of capitalism and the development of an unprecedented capacity for production. This change symbolized the transformation of the system and played a major role in changing the appearance of the world, but China's situation stagnated for a long time because of the long dominance of feudal autocracy.

Today, China has a government led by the Communist Party which can provide leverage, moving the country into a more favorable position to promote innovation of the system, and to establish a set of more stable democratic and legal rules. This opportunity is so important that we should seize it and move forward in a timely manner. The following are several important systems.

3   Socialism with Chinese characteristics

We want to build socialism with Chinese characteristics, not capitalism with Chinese characteristics. Therefore, we must pay attention to controlling the direction of development and focus on two aspects. The first is to introduce market resources and promote the development of the production force. The second is to give energetic support to the low-income groups both in the cities and the country to improve their economic status and maintain fairness in society. We built socialism in a backward country in the past, and prematurely abandoned the commodity market system and private ownership of means of production, which resulted in great losses for the people. Looking back in history, we were right to pay attention to the innovation of the system, but the arrangement of the system was unrealistic. We acted too fast and made too great a change; also, the economic forms were lacking in variety. People summarized the positive and negative experiences and learned from the mistakes, and changed bad trends into good. The turning point was the Third Plenum of the 11th Central Committee of the Chinese Communist Party (CCP). Deng Xiaoping came up with the theory that the function of socialism is to develop the productive forces, to avoid polarization, and to provide prosperity for all. He did not outline the details of a socialist society in his discussion, but he explained that socialism as a basic system can only be built through the endeavors of several or several dozens of generations. This perspective helps us to gain a better understanding of Marxism, of how socialism develops from an idle dream into reality, and helps us as well to correctly put it into practice.

4 A market economy that can be adjusted and controlled

The introduction of a market economy is one of the substantive details of "socialism with Chinese characteristics." Since the reforms, we have proved with much practice that the market system can be compatible with socialism and that resources adjusted by the market can increase products in order to accommodate the market, and bring prosperity. The prerequisite is that government adjustment and control must be maintained and the policy of non-interference should not be allowed. The market is a competitive and disparate economy that will result in polarization, and it is hard to maintain a balance between efficiency and fairness. The emergence of Western Keynesianism, social democracy, and the third way were all efforts to explore new paths. Therefore, we should standardize the function of the government. We should do some things but also restrain ourselves from doing others. We must learn how to adjust and control the market economy as quickly as possible in order to build socialism with Chinese characteristics. Right now, with the exception of the commodity market which has recently begun, the capital, land and labor markets have many problems and need to be improved. But the main trend of development is positive.

5 The structure of combined property rights

China practiced a complete public economy for more than twenty years, then changed to a system that combined economies in which public ownership is the guiding force and various ownerships coexist. This structure of ownership has more advantages than the structure of single ownership for encouraging many types of investment to play positive roles. The implementation of public ownership as the guiding force reinforces its role and effect. The state can withdraw from competitive sectors and focus its financial resources to invest in big projects such as public products, public welfare, rare products, and protecting the environment, transforming the big rivers, and so on. Among these sectors some can be run by individual proprietorship; some can be operated by proprietary companies; and some can be run by individuals while establishing control mechanisms. We can develop non-governmental enterprises to enlarge the size of the total amount of investments, maintaining flexibility and practicality and emphasizing actual effects. When we withdraw from state enterprises, we must include the masses of workers in the process of reorganizing ownership plans, in order to prevent a few people from making arbitrary decisions and causing hidden problems.

One aspect of our system of combined economies that we need to take note of is that capitalism, which was eliminated a long time ago, has recovered; it has now become an indispensable part of the socialist market economy. The socialist market economy has the capability of a capitalist enterprise along with other positive factors – promoting the development of a production force and creating employment. The rapid development of the national economy over the past twenty years proves that balancing socialism with capitalism is a good choice which suits our nation's conditions.

In the agricultural sector, we have implemented the household contract responsibility system on public land. We have stipulated further that the system cannot be changed for thirty years, thus turning a debt relationship into a material right, so that farmers are able to use, own, benefit, transfer and mortgage the land for many years. Twenty years' experience shows that the operation system of combined public and private ownership is indeed welcomed by farmers. To stabilize property rights, we are now establishing a legal system to protect it. On the one hand, we need to forbid arbitrary administrative adjustment. On the other hand, we should cultivate the land market, allow for paid land transfers and maintain land transfers in the market. We did not implement land privatization under the terms of market economy conditions. It would be easy to produce a land monopoly in a country that has very limited land, and cause more instability in society.

Some say that the managerial scale of a household is too small, and will affect the changes of science and technology in traditional agriculture. This argument has merit. However, we should anticipate that the population in our country will inevitably move to cities from the countryside on a large scale. By then, the managerial scale of land will have relatively increased, but we expect that it will not surpass the level of two hectares per household. The efficiency of labor inevitably decreases because of the small size of the average land occupancy per person. We also need to innovate the system in order to reduce this negative impact. In recent years we came up with a policy of industrial development in order to extend the chain of industry to agriculture. We implemented an integrated operation of production, process and sale, established leading enterprises, and pre-production and post-production organizations, and gave farmers the advantage of the combined benefits. The innovation of new technology in modern times has been changing with each passing day. Farmers have not only bought many 'walking tractors,' but they have also started to use information and biological technology, and prospects look good. For example, the remote sensing technique can help to plan fertilization; gene reorganizing techniques can provide farmers with new, disaster-resistant seeds which can all be used by farming households. As long as the operation of family farms still accommodates the development of production power, it will not end. The modern capitalist countries have set precedents already.

The development of modern agriculture must meet the standards to protect our ecological environment and stick to the "green" reform. With the increase of the population in our country, the pressure for more food has grown. Two billion mu of cultivated land produced 500 million tons of grain, which exhausted the maximum capacity of soil and water. This is why the output of grain was stagnant in the final years of the twentieth century. We are still short of 5 per cent to 7 per cent of the amount of grain the market demands. If we try to increase the harvest through indiscriminate deforestation, over-herding, over-fishing and over-fertilizing, we will damage the environment. This is not acceptable. We anticipate that the solution will be to develop the big areas of the northwest, implement the delivery of water from the south to the north, and create more arable land. The state needs to invest hundreds of billion Renminbi in the project and it is impossible to start it in the near future due to limitations in state finances. However, delivering southern water to the northwest is a fundamental task crucial for generations to come and this amount of money should be invested sooner rather than later. The recent shortfalls in food production can only result in a dependence on imports. The import of grain is equivalent to the import of land, and land is the main factor we are much in need of. This is an opportunity to join the WTO, open the door further, use these two markets to arrange resources and ease the tension between our population and our land.

6 The democracy of constitutional government

Our citizens are demanding to participate in politics and gain the status of negotiation as economic pluralism emerges. While some become rich, others lag behind as the economy develops, and the economic gap is growing ever wider. The disparity between town and country still exists in our country. It causes several millions of people to migrate to the cities and we do not yet have a proper employment plan for them, which is one factor that produces an unstable situation. In addition to that, different classes exist in our society. They not only cooperate but also struggle against each other, which inevitably produces conflicts. Because of these factors, we must design a set of systems to solve the problems in maintaining stability in our society. We need to put the reform of the political system and strengthening the democratic structure on the agenda.

The theory of the new democracy which Chairman Mao formulated in early times was to lead the Chinese revolution to victory and establish the New China of People's Democracy. In 1956 he came up with the theory of handling contradictions among the people correctly. The main goal of the theory is to give play to democracy to solve problems. However, the unexpected Anti-Rightist Campaign was started in 1957, and the spearhead of struggle was towards those people in power who showed capitalist thinking. He also came up with the theory of the continuous revolution under the dictatorship of the proletariat. He stressed class struggle as the guiding principle and praised the philosophy of struggle in which conflict among groups is beneficial. He also called himself "Marx plus First Emperor of Qin" and to some extent the impact of his policies turned the state power of people's democracy into the rule of totalitarianism. However, looking at all this from another perspective, the problem is not only Mao Zedong's; it also has something to do with the limited experience of the people. In our generation, we cadres used to say that we were "closely following some policy," and we should add that everybody has his or her own responsibilities. Building socialism was a new cause and our pioneers had no precedent to follow, apart from the former Soviet path. It is understandable that there have been "wrong experiments."

Now we must criticize the spiritual contamination created by feudal totalitarianism in our history, replace it with the political system of democracy, and form a new kind of political culture. We must pay attention to the following values and rights, and make them the cornerstone of our social and political life. These include the values and rights of man that used to be despised, the rights of faith and thinking, the right of freedom of speech, the rights of individual security and respect, the right of freedom of association, the rights of living and moving freely, the right of property ownership and the right to legal protection. The masses can participate in national affairs, understand their rights and obligations, maintain vigilance, and have the courage to fight against any tendency towards totalitarianism and violation of people's rights. This political culture started but did not become part of our tradition within the fifty years after the establishment of the People's Republic of China. This is the cause that countless revolutionary pioneers struggled for for a hundred years, and it is the trend of the times. We expect that it is going to succeed.

The Communist Party, as the party in power, should demonstrate correct policies and hold its members to exemplary roles. It should give play to its leading role in this country. The power of the party is given by the people. We should maintain vigilance on abusing power to seek personal gain and on creating a bureaucracy that cuts us off from the masses. We should not think that as long as the socialist system is established it will naturally have a strong appeal to the masses, that they will support every activity of the party, that we can issue orders and do whatever we want without considering the will of the masses and practicing rigid discipline. This is the lesson we should learn from the collapses of the former Soviet Union and Eastern Europe. Currently, the party leads the reform but it must also reform itself. We should prevent the practice of replacing government with the party, with no boundary between the government and enterprises, and we should avoid the pitfalls of bureaucracy. We should give play to democracy within the party, inspire democracy outside the party, make close connections with the masses, and build the citizens' society. In addition to the organizations of workers, youths, women and intellectuals, we should also support farmers, organize farmers' councils, allowing them to manage themselves and protect their own interests. We should strictly regulate the party and educate party members to have the correct understanding of power, so as to prevent power from penetrating the market and being abused for personal benefit or crime. We should fit in with the trend of globalization of democratic politics, improve cooperation with various democratic parties, innovate the politics of parties, and avoid following the money-controlled path of American politics.

2 Imagining alternative modernities

Perry Anderson

Let me take Tian Yu Cao's admirable address to us as a starting point. In it, he has posed a series of questions about China's future today. At the centre of these is the issue of whether China can or should create an alternative model of modernity which is distinct from the pattern dominant in other parts of the world. There are different ways of conceiving what such an alternative might be, but at the core of all of them lies – inevitably – an institutional question. What kind of economy, state and society should be built in China? Behind this question, however, logically lies another one. What is the range of intellectual sources from which possible models of an alternative modernity might come? For institutions typically have to be imagined before they are engineered into existence. So we need to ask: What are the contemporary resources available for such imagining?

Normally, they will be of two distinct kinds. On the one hand, there will be the historical reservoir of thoughts, experiences and struggles connected to the past of the country concerned – its cultural heritage, if you like. On the other hand, there will be the range of foreign experiences that can be studied, imported or learned from, in any given period. In the first case, obviously enough, no cultural heritage is ever either homogeneous or consensual. Any use of it for imagining a national future always involves a political selection – that is, a choice among different, often quite sharply contrasting elements of the past, that rejects some, and accepts or transforms others. In the second case, foreign experiences are never just abstract institutional kits to be assembled at will somewhere else – they are always embodied in state systems that are themselves power structures within an international order. Successful attempts at building an 'alternative modernity' have nearly always rested on a creative balance between these two sets of resources – that is, selective appropriation of the national past and selective learning from the external inter-state system.

How do matters stand in this respect in China today? Historically, we can distinguish three main periods in the twentieth century so far as the issue of an alternative modernity is concerned. In the first phase, extending from the 1911 Revolution to the Second World War, but centred around the movements of May Fourth, Chinese intellectuals were confronted by imperialism on the world stage, and fissiparous regimes at home, each of them – the external menace, and the internal divisions – threatening national independence. But the collapse of the

Qing Empire had released a great intellectual ferment, in which Chinese who were anxious to build their own version of a modern civilization could adopt a very free attitude both towards the national past – in the 'new culture' movement, and associated developments – and to a wide variety of external political experiences abroad. Two of the latter were particularly important in offering alternative models of social and state construction – Japan and Russia: starkly different experiences, yet each exercising a great force of attraction on Chinese thinkers of the time. However, the range of foreign intellectual resources was by no means confined to these two countries. Chinese intellectuals of this generation were often widely travelled, and had studied or worked in many different parts of the world: France, Germany, the USA, South-East Asia, Turkey and so on.

In the second period, running from the foundation of the People's Republic in 1949 to the mid-1970s, there was much less intellectual discussion about alternative futures. But, in the Maoist period, the state itself sought very energetically to create an alternative Chinese modernity. Initially, it aimed at a synthesis of elements from the Soviet experience with indigenous conceptions and projects of its own, maintaining a certain equilibrium between the two. Yet, within less than a decade, it essentially rejected the first and radicalized the second, with the launching of the Great Leap Forward and then the unleashing of the Cultural Revolution, schemes which sought to jump swiftly into an entirely original Chinese communism.

In the third period, running from the late 1970s to the present, there was a strong reaction against what was widely perceived as the costs and failures of Maoist authoritarianism and isolationism. In the Reform Era, the state turned strongly towards the outside world with the open door policy, and greater intellectual freedom gave rise to lively debates about different futures once again. However, two features differentiated these discussions from the debates of the May Fourth period. First, the experiences of the Mao period made many intellectuals very suspicious of *any* idea of a specific Chinese path to modernity, while at the same time there were far fewer left than in the 1920s who had direct access to the culture of the classical past. Second, the external world had greatly changed. By the early 1990s the Soviet Union no longer existed, and by the late 1990s Japan – hitherto highly successful as an autochthonous modernizer – was in deep crisis. At the same time, all other advanced industrial societies, and most developing ones too, were becoming increasingly homogeneous in character under the dominance of the single world superpower, the USA. Thus, it might be said, just as China 'opened up' again intellectually, the world around it was closing down, towards just one institutional and social model dictated by the global hegemon.

Certainly, of course, enterprising Chinese minds have continued to show curiosity about other parts of the world – some looking West to the experience of post-communist Russia, Poland or the Czech Republic as possible models for China, others looking East to the developmental states of Korea or Japan. But overall, there is little doubt that one foreign country alone dominates popular social imagination in China as never before – reinforced, of course, by the huge flow of students to it. 'Joining in the mainstream', in the hallowed phrase, means essentially following its lead. So, in a sense, there is today a real risk that the resources for thinking about an alternative modernity in China may be becoming fewer, both nationally and internationally.

Of course, this does not mean that there is no variety of political hopes or projects in China today. We can, in fact, distinguish broadly speaking four contrasted models of a future for China today, both in society at large, and probably in our conference room here today. They may be enumerated as follows:

1   First, there is the market socialism of which Tian Yu Cao spoke to us at the outset, and about which David Schweickart has given us a detailed exposition here – that is, a social and institutional model that combines collective ownership of productive assets, and market exchanges between them, in a democratic political system. Such a model does not yet exist, of course, anywhere in the world.

2   Second, there is what in the former Soviet Union was called 'actually existing socialism', a term not in use in China, but whose equivalent may be taken to be 'socialism with Chinese characteristics': in other words, the current state and economic system, regarded as steadily improvable, but basically setting the path for a desirable future.

3   Third, there is what we will call 'clean-path capitalism'. That is, a social system based on private property of the means of production and market exchange, but in which ownership of assets is distributed equally and transparently, prior to such exchange, in accordance with principles of social justice. Like market socialism, such a system – advocated by thinkers such as Nozick in the West – does not exist anywhere in the world, although some believe, or hope, that there may be elements of it in Eastern Europe today.

4   Fourth, and finally, there is 'actually existing capitalism': that is, the social order based on private ownership of the means of production, marked by massive – increasing – social inequalities, whose most imposing example is the USA today. Defenders of this model do not deny the inequality or insecurity on which it rests, but regard these as the indispensable price of its dynamism. Their belief may be summed up in the observation of an American writer Alexander Stille, who recently came back from China and remarked with a kind of regretful sympathy: 'Many people there regard capitalism as a menu from which you can choose dishes *à la carte*, picking what you like and rejecting what you dislike. They have not yet realized that it is a *prix fixe*.' In this view, capitalism offers a set of dishes that is certainly nourishing, making an excellent meal, but which comes as a package. You have to swallow it whole, or not at all.

Now, obviously, if either of the last two models is realized in China, the country will indeed have changed colour, as Mao put it. Few will be shocked at that thought today. Politically, as well as aesthetically, many people prefer white to red. The question that we should consider here, however – given that differing preferences are distributed around us – is perhaps less normative than predictive. It is this. What are the most probable alternatives in China – where is the dominant trend, or trends, pointing to? To cite one famous text of Mao's: What is the 'principal contradiction' in China today – that is, what are the two leading models of modernity in conflict? Second, and crucially, what is the 'principal aspect' of the 'principal contradiction' – that is, which of these leading models today predominates over the other? The immediate future of China depends on the answer to this question.

Discussions

Du Runsheng: We in China need two things: market and democracy. If we can have both of them, then China's socialism is both market socialism and democratic socialism.

In a discussion of this issue at a meeting, a comrade suggested that we should simply take a ready-made term *social democracy*. What is good for this term? No confusion with ideal socialism, whose standard we should not lower, it is not socialism yet. Somebody asked Engels: 'What is socialism?' Engels answered that we have no right to describe its details now. If we do, it is none other than creating utopia. Thus we take socialism as a social movement; that is, socialism is still in the process of practicing. Thus somebody suggested that we call it social democracy as a transitory thing.

Socialism requires highly developed productive forces, surpassing what capitalism has. It is more important to avoid polarization, achieving prosperity together. So Comrade Deng Xiaoping defined socialism as 'highly developed productive forces, no polarization, prosper together'. He said that our present Chinese socialism is not a fully qualified socialism. But since we have put this hat on heads, it is no good removing it.

In developing productive forces we have to deal with two questions. One is the relationship between socialism and capitalism, the other is the relationship between the state and peasants. Our agriculture remains as a small peasant economy. Our industry cannot afford to give many resources to reform agriculture. Peasants have to rely on themselves to accumulate capital. This is a long process. Now we all agree Deng Xiaoping's estimation, namely that our socialism is not quite qualified. Thus somebody says that although we call it socialism, in fact it is social democracy.

As for myself, I feel that the four models mentioned in the talk are only conceptions, not reality. The problem facing China is how to construct socialism in a developing, backward country with populous peasants. We can also call it market socialism. The market cares about efficiency, but we support adding social justice to the market. We cannot care only about efficiency and ignore justice. Otherwise people would not support us. Our comrade Mao Zedong's shortcoming is that he appreciates egalitarianism too much, representing only the demands of peasants. But sine China is a big peasantry country, we cannot completely reject peasants' demands. Thus we have to add social justice to the notion of market socialism.Putting all these together, plus democracy, that is what we hoped for, namely socialism with Chinese characteristics, which is different from traditional socialism advocated by Stalin.

Zhu Houze: I answer the question from the other side: What worries me is the emergence of de facto crony capitalism.

Amin: Let me answer Professor Anderson's question directly. His speech is very interesting. Although I were not a Chinese citizen, if I am allowed to choose, I would choose market socialism: collective ownership, social democracy that is different from capitalist democracy based on private ownership, plus a regulated market. I don't care if you call this kind of Chinese socialism genuine socialism, but I take collective ownership, regulated market economy and democracy as basic values. I would also make efforts so that my own country would take on such a model. This is the realization of universal and genuine socialism under certain particlar conditions.

Second, various forces now in dominance may intend to steer China's development along the fourth direction, namely the actually existing capitalism. But this option will be resisted from within Chinese society; it will also face trouble from the United States. From what has been done by the Clinton and Bush administrations we can see that the United States will not tolerate China's development because it sees China as a potential competitor. Thus it is a completely wishful thinking to assume that globalization would allow China to successfully develop capitalism.

Wang Hui: All the above answers focus on the market economy and fairness, but the history of capitalism tells us that the political form of a state is very important. The political form of a nation state plays a dominant role. In order to talk about China's particularity or its future path, we have to discuss possible political changes in China. This is not only an issue for China. We are living in an age of globalization, there are changes in the world system, and thus what kind of political forms would emerge is of global significance.. This issue also involves the notion of tradition. Anderson's paper asserts that one of the reasons why China tends to take the US model is the loss of China's tradition. He emphatically praises the May Fourth movement, but at the same time also criticizes China for losing its tradition: China's revolution resulted in the lack of resources in resisting bad things. In terms of political form and traditional resources, what can we say about the forms of the future? This is more than an economic issue.

Part II

The historical experience of China's reform

3 Accomplishments and problems

A review of China's reform in the past twenty-three years[1]

Yu Guangyuan

1 The social economy at the beginning of reform

If we regard reform as a process, the social economic situation of China in 1978 serves as the starting point of the process. We can regard reform as the reform of "something old." This serves as the object and foundation of reform. The "old something" is precisely the situation of the social economy at the beginning of reform. In a short article, "The Three Thirty Years" published in 1993, I wrote:

> Things happened as luck would have it. It was exactly thirty years from the May Fourth Movement in 1919 to right before the establishment of the People's Republic of China. This was the thirty years in which the Chinese people conducted the national-democratic revolution (also called the 'new democratic revolution'), in which was seen ideological mobilization, three revolutionary civil wars, and finally, nationwide victory. This was the first "thirty years."
>
> It was exactly thirty years again, from the establishment of the People's Republic of China in 1949 to the Third Plenary Session of the Eleventh Central Committee of the Chinese Communist Party in the winter of 1978. This was the thirty years in which the Chinese people experienced difficulties on the road of socialist construction after taking control of power. This was the second "thirty years." In this thirty-year period, we achieved great accomplishments and also made serious mistakes which caused great setbacks. At the end of this thirty years, the Chinese people became aware that China must conduct a reform of the socialist system. Deng Xiaoping's theory of building socialism with distinct Chinese characteristics played a great guiding role in reform. This reform was another great revolution after the first thirty years in which the Chinese people had conducted the national-democratic revolution and it comprised the second thirty years in which the Chinese people conducted the socialist revolution.
>
> After these two "thirty years," I think that we may have the next, or third period of "thirty years" of Chinese history. This is the period from the beginning of the implementation of reform, from 1978 to 2008. I think that it is possible that we can basically complete the reform of our socialist system by 2008. This basic completion of reform means that we will be able to

establish an improved economic system. And under the newly stabilized economic system, we will be able to develop our economy rapidly in an orderly, continuous, and stable fashion. By then, the reforms of the political, cultural, and other social systems will have made great progress, laying a solid foundation for continuous development. Our country by then will have a new constitution in order to consolidate the achievements we will make in thirty years. This is my expectation and my hope.

Nine years have passed since this article was published. From the perspective of the past nine years, what was written concerning the first thirty-year period would not change if I were to write the article again. However, what was written about the second thirty-year period would need to be revised and more material would need to be added. What was said about the third thirty-year period would probably need to be rewritten.

Concerning the first thirty years, it would be better to add the words, "China experienced difficult times." But in general, this section on the first thirty years does not need to be revised.

Mao Zedong published *On the New Democracy* in 1940, within the first thirty years. I divide his ideology into two parts: one is his theory of the "new democratic revolution," and the other is his theory of the "new democratic society." His theory of the "new democratic society" was an original creation. He pointed out that the direct significance of the historical revolution we had conducted was not the establishment of the socialist system, but the establishment of the social system of the new democracy. In the first thirty years, the Chinese Revolution implemented this ideology, with the exception of the second revolutionary civil war. We implemented the ideology until 1948.

However, from the beginning of the second thirty years, in March 1949, at the Second Plenary Session of the Seventh Central Committee of the Chinese Communist Party, Mao Zedong started to abandon his correct ideology about the "new democratic society." In his report he adopted the theory of proletarian dictatorship put forward by Lenin after the success of the Russian Revolution, and he used it in China after the success of the Chinese Revolution. He said that after the success of the Chinese democratic revolution, the basic contradictions in Chinese society were between capitalism and socialism. However, in *The Common Guiding Principles* of the First Chinese People's Political Consultative Conference, and in the life of our country, the ideology of the "new democratic society" still exists. However, after 1951, Mao Zedong completely abandoned his theory of the "new democratic society." When Liu Shaoqi stuck to the ideology of the new democratic society in 1951, he was criticized by Mao Zedong. He put forward the theory of the "new democratic society," but completely abandoned it himself. The "General Policy in Transitional Time" that he put forward in 1953 was clearly based on the theory of the transitional period from capitalism to socialism that he adopted after abandoning the theory of the "new democratic society."

The general policy in the transitional period essentially consisted of "industrialization, and transformation of agriculture, handicraft industry, and capitalist industries and business." Beijing had been reporting good news from the Tiananmen rostrum between 1953 and 1955. Thus, China entered the stage of socialism.

The discussion at this conference of the merits and demerits of reform in twenty-three years is to figure out what system China had at the end of the second thirty years. This system started in 1956, and I have labeled it "premature socialism and monstrous." What would it be called if not "socialism"? But if we call it socialism, what kind of socialism is it? The Anti-Rightist Campaign in 1957 was called "the big revolution in the political and ideological fields." After that, in 1958, the party vigorously promoted the policy of sharing all property, and it put forward the slogans of "General Policy," "Great Leap Forward," and "Three Red Flags." The "Great Leap Forward" was actually a huge destruction of productivity. In 1963, the party launched the so-called "Socialist Educational Campaign" to criticize the people in power who followed the capitalist path. Finally, from the beginning of 1966, the ten-year, unprecedented "Cultural Revolution" pushed China into an impasse. This was the foundation of the socialist system which needed to be reformed at the beginning of the twenty three-years.

Mao Zedong maintained the theory and practice of the "Cultural Revolution" until he died. The theoretical foundation of the Cultural Revolution was summed up as "continuous revolution under proletarian dictatorship," as written in the report of the Ninth Party Congress of the Chinese Communist Party. In 1975, Mao Zedong brought Deng Xiaoping back to work, and Deng was responsible for the routine work of the central committee of the party and the State Council. When Mao suspected that Deng Xiaoping was opposing his Cultural Revolution policy, Mao launched the campaign of "criticizing Deng Xiaoping and fighting the rightist reversal of the verdict." But interestingly, in his final days, Mao Zedong met Nixon, the then President of the USA. What does it mean? It is worth studying.

The Chinese economic and cultural situation in the twenty years from 1957 to 1977 was not just stagnant – we should say that this was a time of great destruction in Chinese history. There is an ancient Chinese proverb with a dialectical meaning which says that events develop in the opposite direction when they become extreme. Thus many people starved to death during the "Great Leap Forward," and many senior revolutionaries and intellectuals who really supported the socialist revolution suffered persecution. Even Liu Shaoqi, President of the People's Republic of China, was persecuted to death. The situation in China developed to such an extreme that many cadres and people finally awoke to and understood the cause of the great destruction and the roots of the people's suffering which had obstructed the development of China, and which they had not discovered previously due to various reasons. The conclusion they arrived at was that China must conduct reform. These constituted the essential historical conditions that enabled the Chinese reform to start twenty-three years ago.

However, some people did not agree with the real and correct opinion of the Cultural Revolution. There was a famous intellectual who stressed that we should not deny the accomplishments achieved during the Cultural Revolution. He held meetings and published a series of books that included several hundred volumes. I believe he conducted an unreasoned debate. We firmly advocated the criticism of the "Cultural Revolution" because of the great destruction of the Chinese economy and culture at the time. Of course, we cannot say that China did not achieve anything during the Cultural Revolution. First, during those years people were not inactive – they achieved some accomplishments. Laborers and peasants worked in the factories and fields. Second, work was continued from the past. For example, the successful tests of the nuclear and hydrogen bombs and satellites were the result of scientific developments that began in 1956. What was the connection between some accomplishments achieved during the Cultural Revolution and our complete rejection of the Cultural Revolution?

Now, the crimes committed during the Cultural Revolution cannot be exposed and criticized. Even books discussing the lessons of the Cultural Revolution can hardly get approval for publication. The books which manage to get published are often criticized. Ba Jin used to advocate the building of a "Museum of the Cultural Revolution." This was not a unique demand; many people had the same idea. This is absolutely necessary and reasonable. Yet, even today, the museum still cannot be built. Meanwhile, articles praising the Cultural Revolution are still being published from time to time. One article notes that "in recent years, the hot topic was focused on the reversal of the verdict of the Cultural Revolution." It has been said that the theory of the Cultural Revolution included six facets. Among them, only two facets were wrong. It was said at a meeting that the arrest of people who followed the capitalist path was correct, but the arrest of principals of middle and high schools was wrong. A certain scholar has written an article entitled "The Reasonable Factors of the Cultural Revolution Should Be Used." A writer says that a friend recently recommended that he read a magazine called *Figures in Contemporary and Ancient Times* published in Shanxi Province. That magazine published an article entitled "Good Words." The article states,

> Mao Zedong pointed out many times that the focus of criticism was those people who followed the capitalist path. Are not the corrupt elements within the Party the people who follow the capitalist path within the Party? Therefore, the people who follow the capitalist path do not totally belong to the contradictions among the people – some have already become the contradiction between us and the enemy. Why shouldn't we repress, crack down, and destroy them?

2   The historical background

The above discussion concerns the impact of internal factors on Chinese reform. We must also review Chinese reform from the perspective of world history. In May 1996 I put forward a viewpoint at the Asian-Pacific Conference of China. I want to quote two paragraphs from it:

> I want to call the second half of the twentieth century the stage of the great adjustment in world history. This is my answer to the question of the characteristics of the current times. Capitalist countries are adjusting and so are the

socialist countries, and the relations among countries. These adjustments cannot be completed at one time, and the adjustments will occur many times. And, small adjustments will occur frequently and continuously. The period of adjustment will not be short. Perhaps the entire twenty-first century belongs to the period of adjustments. The period of the great adjustments that I put forward is based on observing a half-century of history. Capitalism dominated the world in the beginning of the twentieth century. But certain capitalist countries were not satisfied with their status in the capitalist world, and wanted more hegemony. Therefore, they launched WW I. The war caused revolutions, and the socialist Soviet Union emerged. After WW I, the socialist country was very young and isolated. In defeated Germany, after Hitler had seized power, he believed that he had sufficient strength and he was able to rise again to conquer the Soviet Union, England, and France, and isolate the United States.

Therefore, he united Japan and Italy, and launched WW II. In the joint attacks against China, England, France, the United States, and the Soviet Union, the fascist countries including Germany, Japan and Italy lost the war completely. In the meantime, the capitalist countries suffered heavy losses, except the United States. After WW II, the second round of socialist countries emerged in the world. The two big wars forced the capitalist countries to adjust their policies and take proper measures, in order to reduce the contradictions among the capitalist countries, and between the capitalist countries and their colonies and dependencies, and to coordinate relations among the capitalist countries. As a result of "adjustment," the capitalist countries regained their vigor, and achieved rapid development of their economies and cultures. But in the meantime, some leaders of socialist countries became intoxicated with their victories. They thought that they were guaranteed success as long as they followed the socialist path. This resulted in the backwardness of their economies and social life. These situations forced socialist countries to conduct adjustments one after another, following the adjustments of capitalist countries – this was precisely the conducting of reforms. Naturally, it was not very easy for socialism to accept reform. Each socialist country experienced a very difficult process, and eventually won support from most of the people. Because capitalist countries and socialist countries formed the main economic bodies in the world, we can say that the adjustments of the capitalist countries and socialist countries resulted in world history entering the stage of "great adjustment."

Because of China's large size, its situation also serves as important factors in this stage of history. After World War Two, China neglected the weaknesses in the socialist system, and it did not want to make adjustments. It just waited for "capitalism to become rotten day by day," as it "gets better day by day." Not only did China not focus on the construction of the country, but it also made "class struggle the guiding principle" and it advocated "vigorous promotion of class struggle at home." Class struggle was promoted in areas where "class enemies" existed. If some area did not have "class enemies," certain people would be selected from the revolutionary camp to be criticized as "class enemies." Political campaigns were launched one after another and class struggles developed in a large scale. The people's initiative for production was completely lost. The historical destruction of economic, social and cultural lives was so great that the entire Party and the Chinese people awoke and realized that China must conduct reforms.

In general, my explanations of the historical background of Chinese reform are valid. However, my explanations of the world context are not sufficient. This article was written in 1996 and, prior to that, the Soviet Union had collapsed and countries in Eastern Europe had changed their systems. The word "adjustment" does not seem to fit the Soviet situation. The conduct during Gorbachev's era may be seen as an adjustment of the socialist system. But later in the Yeltsin era, the word "adjustment" cannot describe the situation. In addition, the historical background of the Chinese reform mentioned above should include today's situation. The above discussion was about the historical background at the beginning of reform. Which classic does the word "transition" (*zhuangui*) come from? I have not read any articles that discuss it. The transformation of each socialist country was based on its historical, social, and political conditions. It is very complicated to analyze such detailed conditions. I am not able to unravel the issues pertaining to other "socialist countries," and I will not discuss them here. At first, I wanted to analyze the historical issues globally in order to help us understand the issue of Chinese reform. But now, because of the complex situation in the world, it has become more difficult to explain. Instead, I will analyze China's situation. It will be easier. One by one, I will discuss the stages of the twenty-three-year Chinese reform.

3   The first stage: The beginning

Now let us discuss how reform began. I myself attended the Third Plenary Session of the Eleventh Central Committee of the Chinese Communist Party that marked the beginning of the Chinese reform at the end of 1978. The plenary session lasted for only five days, but the work conference of the Central Committee of the Party before the Third Plenary Session lasted for thirty-seven days. The work conference of the Central Committee of the Party fully completed preparation for the Third Plenary Session of the Eleventh Central Committee of the Party. The ideology of the reform came directly from the work conference of the Central Committee of the Party. Because the status of the Third Plenary Session was higher than that of the work conference, and because the Third Plenary Session decided the general policy of the reform in principle, it is correct to say that the Third Plenary Session of the Eleventh Central Committee of the Party marked the beginning of Chinese reform. I can accept this view. The Third Plenary Session asserts that "the realization of the four modernizations requires greatly promoting the forces of production, and will inevitably require the transformation of relations of production and the transformation of the superstructure which does not adapt to the development of the forces of production, so as to transform all unsuitable modes of management, activity, and ideology. Therefore, this is a broad and profound revolution." I think we should pay attention to these words that made the reform policy assume the color of Marxist theory.

However, I should point out that the goals of the reform put forward in that plenary session were very limited, and were not as profound as claimed by certain people. We can clearly see this from the wording of the communiqué of the Third Plenary Session.

First, what I have quoted above – "the realization of the four modernizations requires . . ." – was written in the communiqué. A large part of the statement promoted reform at a fundamental level, but the brevity of the statement was too abstract. These words were included in the first section of the communiqué, and they stressed the move to focus on building the country. This section discussed how Mao Zedong focused on building the country and the major accomplishments achieved after the establishment of new China. There was also a long paragraph describing how Lin Biao and the "Gang of Four" tried to damage the construction of the country. The position of this statement in the section was not good and the paragraph was too brief. In addition, amidst these words, there was a longer paragraph mentioning class struggle. Therefore, from the perspective of wording, we can see that these statements did not illustrate the significance of the reform. In the bulletin, the statements relating to the reform of the economic system contained some detail; yet the two paragraphs contained less than 500 words. The first paragraph stated,

> Now we have achieved a political situation of stability and unity. We have recovered and retained long-term effective economic policies, taken a series of important new economic measures based on new historical conditions and practical experience, and conducted serious reform of the economic management system and methods of management. [In the communiqué the word "reform" was used only once here. It was not enough that this important word should appear a few times.] We will vigorously develop economic cooperation with other countries in the world on the basis of equality and mutual benefit, by broadly using advanced technology and equipment, and greatly strengthening scientific research and education needed for the realization of modernization.

The second paragraph stated,

> Now, the serious shortcoming of our economic management system is the high centralization of power. We should dare to decentralize it according to the direction of leadership, allowing local governments and industrial and agricultural enterprises to have more power for their own operation and management under the direction of the unified plan of the state. We should vigorously reduce economic administrative agencies at each level, and move most of their functions to enterprises or joint corporations. We should firmly follow economic laws, paying attention to the roles of the law of value, and integrating ideological and political work with economic means, thus, fully encouraging the initiatives of cadres and workers. We should carefully solve

the problem of non-differentiation of the Party, government, and enterprises, in which the Party replaces the government and the government replaces the enterprise. We should implement the system of responsibilities according to a division of labor and individuals, giving more power and responsibility to management and management institutions, reducing meetings and documents, promoting work efficiency, and carefully implementing the system of examination, reward, punishment, and promotion. We need to take these measures in order to fully encourage the initiative and creative work of the departments of the central government, local government, enterprises, and workers, and to promote the broad development of each department and each link in the socialist economy.

We can see from the above paragraphs what the drafters of the communiqué knew about reforming the economic system. They had only grasped the concept of economic management system, and they had no idea that the aspects of ownership and distribution also needed reform. I think that it is a matter of course for the communiqué to be written in such a way. This was because among the participants in the Third Plenary Session, the members of the Central Committee of the Party who attended the work conference of the Central Committee were busy introducing the conflicts and resolutions of the thirty-five-day working meeting to the member of the Central Committee who had not attended the working meeting. In addition, everyone paid close attention to the arrangement of personnel, and therefore no one had the time or energy by then to carefully revise the wording of the communiqué. Meanwhile, some economists who attended the work conference did not attend the Third Plenary Session. Some were just visiting the Session and could not put forward their opinions. Therefore, the writing of the content of the communiqué was relatively dependent on the drafters. Regardless, the communiqué was approved by the Third Plenary Session, and the drafters were not completely responsible for the communiqué.

In addition, concerning the work conference of the Central Committee, many participants, including Hu Yaobang, were not satisfied with drafts of two documents concerning agricultural issues. The president of the work conference decided to distribute the drafts to each group of the meeting, and to ask them to revise the drafts. Their revisions were given to the drafters for reference. After the revisions suggested by each group were given to the drafters who wrote the documents about agriculture, the final drafts were not given to each group to be discussed, but were rather provided to the Third Plenary Session. In the communiqué of the Third Plenary Session, there was a statement about the two documents on agriculture:

> The session discussed the issues of agriculture, and agreed to distribute to provinces and autonomous regions the following decisions to be discussed and experimentally implemented, *The Decisions of the Central Committee of the Chinese Communist Party Concerning A Number of Issues Relating to the Acceleration of the Development of Agriculture* (Draft) and *The Working Regulations of the People's Communes in Rural Areas* (Draft).

Later, in *The Working Regulations of the People's Communes in Rural Areas* (Draft) the following sentence appeared: "Contracting households for output quotas and dividing land for individual production are not allowed." This was the only document sent to the working meeting to be discussed. There were many participants in each group who were dissatisfied with the document when they discussed it. But in order to coordinate the two documents concerning agriculture, the drafters expanded *The Decisions of the Central Committee of the Chinese Communist Party Concerning A Number of Issues Relating to the Acceleration of the Development of Agriculture* (Draft). This document was passed by the Third Plenary Session and subsequently published.

In the communiqué of the Third Plenary Session, the two documents about agriculture required provinces and autonomous regions to discuss and implement the documents experimentally. If each province and autonomous region had implemented the documents, "contracting production to households," "contracting output quotas to households," and the "all-around contracting system" would not have existed, and rural reform would not have been conducted. Although the mass of peasants wanted reform, no one knew when rural reform would be achieved. This event demonstrated the limitation of development at the beginning of reform. Reform cannot be separated from the open-door practice, and the open-door practice was also reform. In the bulletin of the Third Plenary Session there was a very short sentence, "We will vigorously develop economic cooperation with other countries in the world on the basis of equality and mutual benefit, by broadly using advanced technology and equipment," which I have already quoted above.

The beginning of Chinese reform can be traced back to the meeting about issues of theories in the State Council presided over by Li Xiannian in the summer of that year. There were many discussions about economic issues at the meeting. By then, the "delegation of the Central Committee of the Party" led by Li Yimang had visited Yugoslavia to conduct field studies, and returned home. The visit changed the negative image of Yugoslavia that had been imposed on our minds by Stalin. The delegation thought that some of the Yugoslavian experience would be valuable to China. The trip opened up our narrow vision. The Central Committee of the Party had made the decision to restore the relationship between the Chinese and Yugoslavian Communist Parties. When Gu Mu, the Vice-Priemier, returned home from visiting five countries in Western Europe, he did not comment on the corruption of capitalist countries, as officials had usually done before. Instead, he said that, for China, certain experiences of the capitalist countries were worth learning. The research office of the State Council and Social Science Institute sent an article to the meeting entitled "Manage Affairs in Accordance with Objective Economic Laws."

Yao Yilin quoted Lenin's article, "On the Roles of Gold in the Current Situation and After the Complete Success of Socialism," particularly the statement, "We must learn how to howl when we are with wolves." He advocated importing grain in order to reduce the burden on peasants. The meeting about theories in the State Council demonstrated the spirit of reform, and Li Xiannian reported it to the members of the standing committee of the Central Committee of the Party, and they paid close attention to it. Later, when the work conference of the Central Committee was held, the discussion about the meeting on theories in the State Council was listed on the agenda of the working meeting. This serves as evidence demonstrating that the meeting on theories in the State Council marked the beginning of reform. This is my opinion. In contrast, people usually regard the Third Plenary Session as the starting point of reform, and I think I can accept this.

Now we will regard the work conference of the Central Committee in 1978 and the successful convening and closing of the Third Plenary Session as the first stage of Chinese reform, namely the stage of decision-making and initial implementation of reform.

4   Second stage: Developing the scope of reform

Implementation of the reform started after the Third Plenary Session, but in 1979 the systematic study of reform had not yet begun even as reform was being implemented. Four study groups were convened by experts under the financial and economic committee of the Central Committee of the Party after the Third Plenary Session. One group which was studying systems was overseen by Zhang Jingfu. A further group which was studying issues concerning the introduction of foreign technology and open-door policy was overseen by Wang Daohan. Another group which was studying structures was overseen by Xue Muqiao. The fourth group which was studying theories and methods of reform was overseen by myself. I am not clear about the situation of the other three groups. What I can report is the situation in the group that I was leading.

One aspect of the work done by the group was to call and hold many meetings to study reforms in different fields at home. These meetings influenced overall Chinese reform. However, I should say that no matter whether the influence was big or small, it was quite limited, because even when the four groups were set up in the financial and economic committee of the Central Committee of the Party, these were only "think-tanks," and not groups with actual power. In addition to the general leadership of the Central Committee of the Party and the State Council, the real power institutions that implemented reform were the departments of each province and autonomous region under the State Council. They were the main forces of reform.

At that stage, rural reform was the most successful Chinese reform. In the communiqué of the Third Plenary Session there were two restricted items that were obstructing rural reform. Fortunately, the tone was not strong. Also fortunately, after the session, some leaders of provinces did not follow the requirements stated in the communiqué. Comrade Wan Li broke the taboo in Anhui Province, and implemented the systems of "contracting production to households," "contracting output quotas to households," and even the "all-around contracting system." I can say that this constituted the real start of the reform of ownership. Anhui became the first province to promote the system, and the Inner Mongolia Autonomous Region became the second, so that the first battle of Chinese rural reform was a victory won. After Wan Li was promoted to work in the Central Committee of the Party, he issued each year the "No. 1 Document" to promote rural reform. Thus the victory became consolidated. Some tried to obstruct the broad promotion of reform, but after several years their obstruction failed. This was the situation from 1983 to 1984.

The economic management system and reform of management mentioned in the communiqué of the Third Plenary Session should be regarded as important fields of Chinese economic reform. However, it was very difficult to start the reform process, and for some time many problems could not be solved. For example, the communiqué required the implementation of the decentralization of power, but the government financial departments did not implement this policy because they were concerned about the reduction of financial income. On this issue, Suzhou, Wuxi, and Changzhou of Jiangsu Province were able to make important progress. In the beginning, they did not make any statements; they merely practiced the decentralization of power in order to protect themselves. Around 1983 or 1984, I suggested to leaders of Shijiazhuang City in Hebei Province that they attend the seminar concerning the reform of mid-sized cities that I had recommended be held in Hefei City of Anhui Province. Jia Ran, secretary of the city's committee of the Party, told me that many leaders of cities had heard that reforms were successful, and that economies were being developed rapidly in Suzhou, Wuxi, and Changzhou. They wanted the leaders of these three regions to present their experiences, but since they did not wish to talk about this the leaders simply related certain insignificant matters. The leaders of each city insisted that the leaders of Suzhou, Wuxi, and Changzhou explain their "tricks." Under heavy pressure, these leaders finally revealed their "tricks." They implemented flexible policies and did not follow the regulations that had come from the upper levels. Finally the participants were satisfied with their answers.

One aspect of the work of the "group studying theories and methods" was the study of issues concerning Chinese reform. Another aspect of our work was the study of Marxist theories of reform, and the reform experience of foreign countries, especially the Soviet Union and Eastern Europe. One of the study methods was to undertake delegation visits to foreign countries. During the period in which I oversaw the group studying theories and methods I visited several countries, especially Hungary, where I studied their theory and practice of reform, and learned about their experience of reform. After the Liaison Department of the Central Committee of the Chinese Communist Party contacted the Hungarian Communist Party, my Hungary visit was arranged. We visited Hungry as guests of the Chinese ambassador in Budapest. I believe that the Hungarian side must have known about our visits for two years beforehand, and were acquainted with the senior level of the delegation that was sent by the Chinese Communist Party.

Although the status of the leaders who met us was not as high as those of the Yugoslavian leaders, the hospitality and greeting were similar. Except for Kadar, the General Secretary of the Hungarian Communist Party, all the important figures from the Central Committee of the Hungarian Communist Party and the officials who were responsible for reform from central government met the senior Chinese scholars. I remember clearly that one of the people whom we met was Nagi, who was famous in China. Prior to the Hungarian visit in 1979, I had just come back home from visiting Holland, Germany, and Switzerland with some comrades of the Institute of Marxism and Leninism of the Chinese Academy of Social Sciences. Therefore, when I visited Hungry, I could often recall my visit to Yugoslavia with Li Yimang two years before, and I was able to compare the reforms of the two socialist countries. I was also able to compare the two socialist countries with several capitalist countries I had visited recently.

The four study groups lasted for about one year, and after that, the State Council set up the State Council Commission on Economic Structural Reform. The Prime Minister of the State Council was also the Director of the commission. It demonstrated that the state paid more attention to reform, and that it planned to promote reform. The Reform Commission was the "think-tank," and it was also the power institution. Therefore, reform was implemented faster.

By then, the four study groups under the financial and economic committee of the Central Committee of the Party had been disbanded. The products of their work were inherited by the State Council Commission on Economic Structural Reform. The jobs of three of the groups were transferred to the Commission on Economic Structural Reform. The fourth group studying theories and methods led by myself became an independent academic organization of the Chinese Economics Association, and it remained active until 1989.

We will take the seven-year period, from 1979 after the closing of theThird Plenary Session of the Eleventh Central Committee of the Party, through the Twelfth Central Committee of the Party in 1982, and up until the Third Plenary Session of the Twelfth Central Committee of the Party in 1985, as the second stage of Chinese reform. At this stage, the scope of reform was developed to encompass the aspect of ownership, and the economy was developed to include the commodity economy.

The important events which occurred at this stage included the final breaking of the taboo which forbade "contracting output quotas to households" that was contained in the documents about agriculture approved by the Third Plenary Session of the Eleventh Central Committee of the Party. The system of contracting production to households was implemented. A series of events also occurred, namely:

1   Reforms in education, science, and technology began. Reform was developed beyond the economic field and into the cultural field. The issue concerning the reform of the political system that was raised by many people, and the issue of the "reform of social ideology" which I had raised, both came later.
2   The promotion of township and village enterprises in the southern part of Jiangsu Province, and the emergence of the Southern Jiangsu model.
3   The emergence of the Wenzhou model, a local economy formed mainly by private businesses (points 2 and 3 basically refer to the reform of ownership).
4   The establishment of the four special economic zones, including Shenzhen, Zhuhai, Shantou, Xiamen, and the designation of all of Hainan province as a special zone.

5　The establishment of the development zones in twelve coastal cities, from Qinhuangdao in the northeast, to Beihai in the southwest (points 4 and 5 basically refer to the open-door practice).
6　The issue of the "Initial Stage of Socialism" was raised during the second stage of Chinese reform.
7　Debates concerning the issue of the commodity economy of socialism were contested.

Inspired by the development of reform, I wrote the article "From Many Systems in a Country to Many Models in a System and Two Systems in a Country." The article mentioned that prior to the establishment of new China in 1949, China was "a country that had many systems." There was an economic system of new democracy that included socialist economic factors in broad liberated regions. There was a colonial and semi-colonial, feudal and semi-feudal social system in the regions controlled by the Nationalists and Japanese imperialists. Tibet had a serf system. The primitive commune system existed in many minority regions in the southwest. And Hong Kong and Macao had colonial capitalist systems. This situation could be called "many systems in a country." After the establishment of new China, China established the socialist economic system, and at the same time it transformed those non-socialist systems and tried to establish a unified nationwide socialist system. In other words, it implemented a one-model system. Although this system could not dominate every field, it clearly obstructed the development of the forces of production. After reform, especially once China had established the four special economic zones in Shenzhen, Zhuhai, Shantou, and Xiamen, China actually implemented "many models in a system." Deng Xiaoping later put forward his idea of "two systems in a country." The title of my article came out of this idea.

Although the "Initial Stage of Socialism" is worth discussing, I will not explain it in this chapter because I have written a book about the issue. The scope of Chinese reform developed rapidly in the 1980s, and, I should say, in just a few years. At this stage, with the development of reform, the economic construction of our country was also developing rapidly. Of course, the achievements of reform eventually illustrated the development of economic construction. What the reform solved was the issue of the relation between production and superstructure, and the roles of advanced production relation and superstructure in promoting social development.

It was in the process of drafting the report of the Twelfth Party Congress of the Party in 1982 that I learned about the initial debates concerning the issue of the commodity economy of socialism. Prior to that, certain Chinese economists had published a number of articles about the necessity for China to develop the commodity economy, and they put forward the concept of a socialist commodity economy. But the major drafters of the documents for the convention were concerned and did not want to add the concept into the report of the Twelfth Party Congress of the Party, and they advocated sending a letter to the Central Committee of the Party showing that they did not accept a wrong idea. They had hoped that each drafter would sign his or her name on the letter. Prior to that I had been focused on discussions about the goal of socialist production, and I did not make any statements about the issue concerning the commodity economy. I was seen as a person who would perhaps sign the letter. Although I refused to sign it, the letter was sent out. The ideology of the "socialist commodity economy" was not included in the report of Hu Yaobang, who represented the Central Committee of the Party. In addition, a collection of articles that opposed the ideology of a socialist commodity economy was published after the convention.

Around the time of the Congress, the Research Office under the Secretariat of the Central Committee of the Party, which was led by Deng Liqun, prepared some material. The document divided opinions concerning the commodity economy into four groups. Among them, the view of the first group was correct, and included the view of Deng Liqun. The view of the second group was problematic, and the view of the last group was the worst. The worst articles included those by Xue Muqiao and Lin Zili. Lin Zili himself worked in the Research Office, and he firmly advocated the formulation "commodity economy." By then the situation showed that the ideology of the socialist commodity economy was opposed by certain individuals who had high status in the party, and they fought very hard against it.

In 1982, no one was able to advocate the establishment of a market economic system in China. The idea of "developing the socialist commodity economy" was a substitute for "establishing a socialist market economy." Even this vague view did not escape the sharp eyes of the opponents, but reform was continuing to develop. I was not the one who first raised the issue of developing a commodity economy in China. Zhuo Jiong of Guangdong Province raised the issue several years earlier than I, as did Lin Zili. I should be grateful to the comrade who wanted me to sign my name to the letter, which was drafted in the report of the Twelfth Party Congress in 1982. It was the request for my signature that attracted my attention to the issue of the development of a commodity economy. Therefore, when the Third Plenary Session of the Twelfth Central Committee of the Party was held in October 1984, I firmly advocated putting into practice a commodity economy. The Third Plenary Session of the Twelfth Central Committee of the Party, held in October 1984, as I said, belonged to the second stage of Chinese reform – the stage of the development of the scope of reform. Here, I want to add a few points: "The second stage of the Chinese reform was the stage at which the scope of reform was enlarging and deepening, even though it was difficult for reform to develop into a market economic system." The convening of the Third Plenary Session of the Twelfth Central Committee of the Party and the approval of "The Decision Concerning the Reform of the Economic Structure" by the Central Committee of the Chinese Communist Party were very important steps for Chinese reform in developing a market economy.

5 Third stage: China finally accepts the market economy

The Third Plenary of the Twelfth Central Committee of the Party in 1984 and the speech by Deng Xiaoping in 1992 when he visited the southern part of China may be regarded as the third stage of Chinese reform. At the beginning of this stage, for well-known reasons, reform was suspended to some extent. The entire country exhibited a warm reaction to Deng Xiaoping's speech in 1992. The ideology of the people was further liberated. Their initiatives for reform and construction were greatly promoted. Again, reform was developed, and Chinese reform entered a new stage. In 1992, after Deng Xiaoping's speech, the Fourteenth Party Congress was convened. The reports and resolutions of the Fourteenth Party Congress affirmed that the implementation of the socialist market economic system was the most important step since Chinese reform. The reforms conducted prior to 1992 could not compare in significance with the reform at this time.

In 1977, as an assistant of Li Yimang, head of the delegation of the Central Committee of the Chinese Communist Party, I visited Yugoslavia and Romania. While we were staying in the capital of Romania, I noticed that a newspaper published a talk given by a Romanian leader concerning the intention of Romania to accept a market economy. The following day, I saw the *Combat Daily*, the newspaper of the Yugoslavian Communist Party, reporting the news in the headline of the first page of the paper. The title of the report was "Bucharest Finally Accepts a Market Economy." This was because Yugoslavia had accepted a market economy earlier, but Romania had resisted. Once the Yugoslavian Communist Party saw the change in the Romanian Communist Party, it published the report immediately. At that time, China's reform had not yet started. For quite some time, no one dared to advocate a market economy in China. The term that the most radical person in the reform movement dared to use was "commodity economy," which was used as a substitute for the term "market economy."

It was later discovered that Deng Xiaoping first advocated that China practice a market economy. In 1979 he discussed this idea with Jenny, the chief editor of *Britannica*. He talked only with foreigners, and, at that time, he did not want to discuss the idea with any Chinese people (including those around him). People like myself learned about it in 1992. Prior to that discovery I had thought that I was the first one, earlier than Deng Xiaoping, to assert "the conclusion that the planned economy has a socialist nature, and the market economy has a capitalist nature is incorrect." In an article I had written in September 1986 I entitled Section 2 "Further discussing the incorrect view that 'the planned economy has a socialist nature,' and the 'market economy has a capitalist nature'." (See the article, "Concerning the Development of the Issues of the Planned Economy and Market Economy" in my collection, *The Exploration of Political Economic Socialism*, volume 4, People's Press, September 1988.) How had we gotten that far?

The resolution of the Third Plenary Session of the Twelfth Central Committee of the Party included the following statement: "We do not practice the market economy which is completely regulated by the market." Based on this sentence, those who opposed the market economy said, "the document of the Party demonstrates that China does not allow the practice of a market economy." However, those who advocated the market economy said that the market economy they were going to conduct was not the one that would be completely regulated by the market – and thus the market economy should be allowed.

I belonged to the latter group. I started to make speeches about the market economy after the convention held in June to July 1986, when I was visiting Germany and Switzerland. After returning home, I published the speeches that I had made abroad. In general, the force of resistance against the market economy in China was probably stronger than that in Romania in the winter of 1977. However, in the process of drafting the report of the Fourteenth Party Congress, the advocates who promoted the implementation of the market economic system finally prevailed. The idea was included in the report and approved by the Congress, and became the commonly held view of the Central Committee of the Chinese Communist Party and party members. The following illustrates the classic language in the report of the Fourteenth Party Congress:

> If we want to establish a socialist market economic system, we should allow the market to play the essential role of distributing resources under the macro-control and regulation of the state. We should make economic activities follow the law of value, and adapt to the change of demand and supply. We need to distribute resources to enterprises that have good economic benefit, and provide enterprises [with] pressure and motivation, in order to select the superior and eliminate the inferior. We need to take advantage of the sensitiveness of the market to various economic signals, and coordinate relations between production and demand.

China had finally accepted the market economy!

After the market economic system had been accepted, there were some detailed issues about reform policies that needed to be solved. For example, there were fierce debates concerning whether China should establish a stock-market. In the debates, some views were correct and some were incorrect. Some views had a large impact, and others did not have any impact at all. All belonged to the category of "letting a hundred schools of thought contend." They did not need to take political responsibility. But the decision-makers had to take responsibility. I believe that the early problems of the Chinese-stock market were closely related to the conduct of the decision-makers. However, the economists and politicians in socialist China really lacked an understanding and knowledge of the modern market economy. There were those who did not understand that the stock-market is an intricate machine, and it seems inevitable that China would pay a high price for learning this.

6   The current stage of the Chinese reform

Following the Fourteenth Party Congress, not only was reform developing rapidly, but also economic construction in each region was accelerating. No one was aware that in his old age Deng Xiaoping could make such important contributions to

Chinese reform and construction. However, problems caused by the overly speedy economic development emerged immediately. Adjustment after 1993 affected the process of reform.

I am not sure which year, or what event, serves as the milestone marking the current stage third stage of Chinese reform. I am also not sure how to summarize the essential characteristics of this stage. In addition, the Fourteenth Party Congress in 1992 decided to cancel the Central Advisory Commission of the Party. As a member of the Central Advisory Commission I had wanted to alter my working situation with a change of status, although I did not request retirement from my job. I wanted to study more issues concerning basic theories and I wanted to put forward various opinions. My goals for doing this were to discover the issues myself, to talk and write about my ideas, and to discuss them within the academic field, so that I could learn more and gain more confidence about my own ideas. I do not agree with the ancient idiom, "When I learn the real classics, I would not mind death." I really want to learn the "classics," but once I learn the "classics" I also want to do things by following the guide of the "classics." I do not want to "die" unless I have to. My writings are not confidential materials, and if decision-makers want to read them as references they may be found very easily.

Because my views have the nature of theory, I publish them openly. I do not send them direct to any individual or organization. I withdraw from the role of directly serving decision-making, and I actively provide ideas and plans for Chinese reform to "enthusiastic observers." It is natural for me to adapt to change: I have become older, and my status has altered. The decision-makers do not intercede due to the complexity of the issues of reform. At the same time I have endless work to do, and now I can give up the state job that previously I had not wanted to give up.

But there is an exception. In 1997 I wrote an article entitled "Yushi Concise Dictionary of the Structures of Socialist Ownership" (draft). It is a long article, and should not have been published because it was a draft. Nevertheless, since the Fifteenth Party Congress was imminent, and the work of drafting documents was almost complete, I sent the unfinished article to two old friends who were responsible for the drafting work. I was like the "leopard who never changes his spots." In the letter I sent with the article I said I believed that general public ownership is not the mark of socialism, because private and public ownership had coexisted since the latter part of primitive society up to the serf, feudalist, capitalist, and socialist societies. These five social economic formations are not differentiated by the presence or absence of private or public ownership. This is an issue that has been confusing many people for quite some time. On the contrary, they are differentiated by different types of public and private ownership. Public ownership in socialist society is "socialist public ownership." I suggested that in the report of the Fifteenth Party Congress, the words "socialist public ownership" should be used at least once. When the report used this term in other contexts, it could use "public ownership" as a short way of saying "socialist public ownership." My suggestion was accepted, but many people did not note the "real meaning" of my suggestion.

In my view, "private and public ownerships co-exist throughout socialist society – which is a society composed of diverse economic elements." As I have previously advocated, I think it is necessary to change the current view that "diverse economic structures co-exist in the initial stage of socialism." I think that we can retain this view concerning "the initial stage of socialism," but it needs redefining. Directed at this goal, I wrote two short articles entitled "The Essential Economic Characteristics in the Initial Stage of Socialism," and "Social Productivity Adapted to the Initial Stage of Socialism." Few people took note of my ideas, and I have not seen any articles responding to or questioning my ideas. We often see the phrase, "deepening reform," published in the media. What does this phrase mean? If no one is able to explain its meaning, it should be seen as empty words. However, I believe that they are not empty words. But the research work I have done is not sufficient. Now I feel that the nature of the Chinese reform will be a major conern in the future, and I have begun to think about this important issue.

Now I will talk about myself.

7   Past consideration of the nature of Chinese reform and how to understand the issues pertaining to future reform

I used to refer to Chinese reform as the reform of the Chinese socialist structure, and I paid excessive attention to the words "structure" and "system." Is there any issue concerning the completion of Chinese reform? I think there is. Of course, society is continuously making progress and it is constantly changing, but our reform should have a goal. This is why I used the term "reform." I have discovered that in Western texts discussing the reform of the Chinese system, only one word, "system," is used. The English word "system" is used to translate the Chinese words *zhidu* and *tizhi*.

I believe that the two concepts of "essential social system" and "non-essential social system" should be differentiated. I think that the term "non-essential social system" can be replaced with the word "structure" (*tizhi*). I also think that people can devise a new foreign word or use the Chinese phonetic transcription, *tizhi*. Another method is to refrain from saying "system" and use the word "model" instead. Perhaps it is easier to gain acceptance if the words "model" and "system" shared the same meaning. My idea has attracted little discussion so far. I published the idea in my articles but I have yet to write an indepth piece about it.

My basic idea was that only the "non-essential social system" (that is, the structure or model) can be affected by Chinese reform. The essential social system should not be allowed to be affected. Therefore, Chinese reform is only the "reform of the socialist economic structure." We have basically passed three stages of Chinese reform, and we are now in the current stage of reform. I feel that reality has raised the question of whether Chinese reform could, or even should, exceed the limitation of reform of the socialist economic structure.

Above, I mentioned the emergence of the word "transition" (*jiegui*). I have noticed that some have used the word very early on in certain articles published in China. An idea came to me when I noted this. In 1992, the Fourteenth Party

Congress decided to implement a market economic system. Naturally, this transformation required a period of time. However, the "transition" should not last forever. As for using the word "transition" to describe the change of a country's essential social system, to say that there are countries in transition in the world – I have noticed this in the past year or so.

I have seen the magazine *Transition* sponsored by the World Bank (including the Chinese version). I learned that the category of "transition" included China, and the collapse of the Soviet Union, and the transformation of Russia. I think that the word "transition" is being used to replace the word "reform." Many people like to use the word "transition" and they should be aware of this. At the same time, they carefully avoid relating the real meaning of the term. Although I have sensed it, I have not yet formed my own opinion about it.

8 Some issues pertaining to the reform of the political system

Scholars enjoy talking about the reform of the political system, and the authorities also do not avoid the issue. Actually, Chinese reform should include the reform of the political system, and the reform of the economic system cannot be separated from the reform of the political system. However, I believe that the "real" or "essential" reform of the political system has not yet been implemented. The situation of our political system is basically the same as the that prior to reform. Documents have mostly mentioned non-essential issues, and I do not think that the "real reform of the political system" can be put on the agenda now. Even the issue of "real reform of the political system" and the understanding of it have not yet been discussed. I regret the situation. Everyone wants reform of the political system – who would not want not to be oppressed by the political system and for their own initiatives to be fully expressed? At the same time, because reform of the political system has not yet developed, reform of the economic system has been affected.

But the reform of the political system has met larger obstacles. What needs reform is a political system lacking in democracy and a political system that has not undertaken political reform. This is a strange cycle, a vicious cycle. One thinks it is urgent, yet no sense of urgency is apparent. To avoid any idle dreams, I simply regard the real reform of the political system as a remote event. I think that the practical thing to do now is to strive for some freedom of speech. Thus, in my article "Three Thirty Years," I did not suggest that we should complete the real reform of the political system in the third thirty years.

Here, I would like to relate a story. Once, a reporter from the Hong Kong newspaper *Nanhua Zaobao* (*South China Morning Post*) visited me at my home. I told him about my thesis on the "Three Thirty Years." After the interview, I was afraid that his notes might be incorrect, so I asked someone to make a copy of my article. While the reporter waited at my home for the copy, I said to him, "After the third thirty years, there will probably be a fourth thirty years. At that time we can probably complete the reform of the political system. But if I am still alive by then, I should be 123 years old in 2038. This is impossible. So, I will not be able to see the hypothetical event. I do not need to care about the fourth thirty years." I had not expected that after the reporter returned home he would publish the joke. This really made me wonder whether to laugh or cry.

On June 19, 2004, in *Zhonghua dushubao* (*China Readers Daily*), I read an article entitled "Correctly Evaluating the Dynastic Eras of Kangxi and Qianlong." This article debated these issues with Professor Dai Yi, an expert on the Qing Dynasty. Professor Dai Yi (*China Readers Daily*, April 12, 2000) quoted Kennedy's *The Rise and Fall of Powers*: "In the eighteenth century, the Chinese industrial output was 32% of the world output, and Europe's output was only 23%." Based on this quote, Professor Dai Yi wanted to prove that "from the perspective of a horizontal view, the dynasties of Kangxi, Yongzheng, and Qianlong were very prosperous times." The article published in June of this year did not agree with this opinion. The author of the article was Zhou Siyuan, who wrote,

> The new type of industries promoted by the industrial revolution in Europe, its capitalist relations of production, and the mode of production of the great production of machine, were much more advanced than those in the dynasties of Kangxi, Yongzheng, and Qianlong . . . the temporary advantage of the total output China was producing due to its larger population size was quickly gone.

"Kangxi" refers to Emperor Kangxi whose dynasty lasted from 1662 until 1723. "Qianlong" refers to Emperor Qianlong whose dynasty lasted from 1737 until 1795. And between the dynasties of Kanxi and Qianlong there was the dynasty of Yongzheng, who ruled China for only thirteen years. Although the three emperors, Kangxi, Yongzheng, and Qianlong, had many accomplishments, their rules were extremely autocratic and they also conducted a "literary inquisition." Zhou Siyuan wrote, "This made China completely lose the vigor of its spiritual and material productions, and it increased the gap between China and the world." I think that the argument of the article should be noted. The impact of the poor political system will most likely be manifested, or mainifested clearly, for quite some time. Thus I believe think that even though the reform of the political system may be accomplished a little late, this would not matter very much and there is nothing to be done about it. However, the problem must and can be solved.

9 A summary of twenty-three years of reform

Any process of reform will be accompanied by historical struggle. The obstruction to reform comes first from the beneficiaries and conservative ideology under the old system. After the decision of the Third Plenary Session of the Twelfth Central Committee of the Party to implement reform of the political system, the Central Committee of the Party struggled with the issue of "communist" ideological education. In 1986, when the Sixth Plenary Session of the Twelfth Central

Committee drafted *The Decision of the Central Committee of the Chinese Communist Party Concerning the Guiding Policy of Spiritual Civilization*, the group of drafters were confronted by very difficult issues. Various types of ideological education had to be differentiated, such as awareness of the current reality among the masses, the "communist" ideological education of the advanced elements, criticism suggested in 1981 and 1982 of empty talk about "communist" ideological education with the theory of the initial socialist stage, and the advocacy of education fitting the spirit of reform of the masses. Following the session, at the end of 1986, in Ma'anshan city of Anhui Province, those who advocated reform held a seminar about the issue of complete reform in order to fight against ideology. This seminar immediately attracted the attention of Deng Liqun who advocated "communist" ideological education, and who accused the seminar of being a "black seminar." During the Spring Festival at the beginning of 1987 (the first day of the lunar calendar), when the Secretary of the Party Committee visited his home town in Yixing, Jiangsu Province, he got a phone call from Ma'anshan asking him to return to the city, because Beijing required him to hand in a recorded tape of the seminar concerning the issue of comprehensive reform. Although the evidence proved that the seminar had no problems, I was criticized in nine meetings, and one of my "crimes" pertained to the "Seminar on Comprehensive Reform."

This sort of thing happened many times. The above mentioned research office cooked up a document entitled "The Origin of Concessions" in order to oppose the establishment of the special economic zones. The content talked about the incompetency of each level of Qing Dynasty officialdom, and it mentioned the agreement with foreigners to establish concessions in Shanghai, and so forth. The document suggested that the decision to establish special economic zones demonstrated the incompetence of decision-makers. The debate about "the socialist or capitalist nature" was provoked by the ideological departments. They had an advantageous position. Thus the reformers needed a firm scientific ideology and to be prepared to struggle for quite a while. The twenty-three years of reform is a very good textbook case.

Now let us return to the main topic.

10 The merits and demerits of twenty-three years of reform

Let us discuss "the merits and demerits of twenty-three years of reform," which subject was assigned to me by the organizer of the symposium. I have been focusing on the topic, and writing my article, I have followed every element of the topic. However, what I have written relates only to the first ten aspects of the topic. I have only presented the facts and I have not yet commented on the "merits and demerits of the reform." Now I will begin the discussion.

The topic constitutes a unity, and my article consists of a unity as well. The introduction of the facts forms the basis of the comments that follow. Based on the facts of the twenty-three years of Chinese reform, I want to say without any exaggeration that Chinese reform has been successful and on the mark. I have only some questions about the final stage of reform, and whether certain changes belong to the issue of reform. As long as we exclude issues that do not belong to the category of reform, my conclusion about reform is that it has been successful and correct. As for particular comments on each reform, I would have to write long articles to explain them, and I do not think this is necessary. Here I want to note the most "successful element" in the reform, namely the decision to implement the economic market system. Yet at the same time, some have argued that it was a big mistake to decide to implement the market economy, resulting in unfortunate consequences. On the issue of the merits and demerits of Chinese reform, this is the most controversial issue.

As I have mentioned above, those who opposed reform tried to prove their point from the perspective of ideology. They said that [the market economy] should not be implemented. Their point was that the market economy generated many negative consequences, and the evidence was that serious corruption existed in China.

I firmly support the decision to implement the market economic system in China. Of course, I despise the serious corruption in China. I do not deny the logic that if there were no money in the world then stealing and embezzling would not occur. In other words, if the world did not have banks, bank robbery would not exist. I want to ask: Can we close the banks because we do not want bank robberies to occur, and can we abandon money because we do not want stealing and embezzling to occur? There are two kinds of people: one is the type who is confused in their thinking. I want to point out to such people that there is a difference between "events happening after something," and "events happening due to something." We should not regard events occurring after the implementation of the market system as the same as events that occur due to the implementation of the market system, and consequently, oppose the implementation of the economic system. This thinking is equal to giving up eating for fear of choking! We can help those who are confused with their thinking by reasoning with them. But we can do nothing for those who oppose reform.

11   Philosophical issues in the merits and demerits of reform

I would like to comment that scholars should have clear concepts in mind, and this requires close attention to wording. I think that "merits and demerits" is similar to "success and failure." "Merits and demerits" not only have objective foundations, but also the evaluation of "merits and demerits" may be conducted via some main body of practice. In this article, the Chinese people constitute the main body of practice within the twenty-three years of reform, and they are evaluating the activities of the reform of the socialist economic and social systems. These activities generally do not mean activities in the short term, but rather, large-scale activities within a broad scope and a long time span. For example, what we are discussing here are the activities of nationwide reform that have lasted for twenty-three years. The content of the evaluation has been designated as "merits and demerits."

Now I wish to raise the question of how to understand correctly the terms "merits and demerits." I think that "merits and demerits" refer to the evaluation of the conduct of the main body of activities. They have merits or demerits. What kinds of merits and demerits do they have?

Thus, further, the question is how to define merits and demerits. When activities have outcomes, the outcomes can be defined only through review and study. The conduct of the main body of activities should have a clear goal. The goal must be decided correctly so that the success or failure of our activities may be judged on the basis of the extent of the achievement of the goal. If the goal is decided incorrectly, then it is necessary to restudy the goal so that it may be judged. If we review the agreed-upon goal and the outcome is good, then we can say that we have merits. If it is not good, we should say that we have demerits. The ideas of "good" and "not good" are connected with the issue of criteria, even criteria in terms of quantity. Because the activities belong to the main body, so do the "merits and demerits."

When the main body starts to prepare and decide to take action, the ideology, consciousness, and will of the main body begin to function. If this were not the case, we would not be able to discuss the "merits and demerits, right and wrong." The terms "right" and "wrong" here refer to whether the ideology is related to the action, in case that action were to be taken. The mode of activity resulting in success is the right one, and vice versa.

I also want to talk about my philosophical understanding of "will." I believe that many of the movements, changes, and developments in the world are completely independent of human consciousness; that is, they are not, or not yet, influenced by human beings. There are too many phenomena of this type. It is this way with Mother Nature. However, since human beings develop from Mother Nature, there are, or were, things in the world affected by human beings. Among the things affected by human beings, there are products of the conscious, purposeful, and willed activities of human beings. The reform we are talking about here is the product of the conscious, purposeful, and willed activities of human beings. Both goal and will belong to the category of consciousness. If reform were not the conscious, purposeful, and willed activities of human beings, then the issue of "merits and demerits, right and wrong" would not exist. Nevertheless, we must classify the goals and wills. Because of the wide scope of Chinese reform that connects with so many people and complex things, the processes and outcomes of reform are unlike the product of the purposeful and willed activities of individuals. All the purposeful and willed activities of interrelated people will affect the operation, changes, and developments of reform. The process of reform is the result of the joint force of numerous matrices. To an individual, or some organization or collective, these functioning forces are not affected by one's own will. At the same time, the process of reform is also constrained by the force that connects more fields, has deeper roots, and does not belong to reform. To those individuals, collectives and organizations, this force is more objective and powerful. I believe that the study of the objective aspects of the Chinese reform has not been sufficient. Because what we have discussed at the conference are not regular issues, they are concerned with the twenty-three years of Chinese reform.

Above, we briefly recalled Chinese reform, and in this way we used the facts and materials of the merits and demerits of the main body of the reform for our discussion. But there is a problem. As mentioned above, the main body of Chinese reform is the Chinese people. This view does not seem to be persuasive and needs to be further analyzed. It seems that this issue is complicated. We should figure out what kinds of forces exist in reform, what directions these forces have worked toward, and which force is the strongest. The characteristics of the Chinese situation suggest that the strongest collective force is the power of the Central Committee of the Chinese Communist Party, and the process of the reform depends on it the most. However, it is the most important force among a matrix, and other aspects should be considered too. What kind of role can the Chinese scholar play concerning the issue of reform? I am also thinking about what small contribution I can make and what role I can play in the reform. There are also all sorts of observers outside the main body of reform; there is no issue of merits and demerits related to them. They put forward their opinions on this issue in order to help the main body. However, there are some enthusiasts who regard Chinese progress as their own concerns. Although they are not the main body of Chinese reform, they have its consciousness at heart. My view is hopefully approved by colleagues who are attending the conference.

12   Discussing China's participation in the WTO

We should add a section concerning the issue of China's participation in the World Trade Organization (WTO). This section could have been included in the section on the current stage of Chinese reform because it is one of the most important events, in the past thirteen years, in Chinese reform and open-door practice. The other important events include the return of Hong Kong and Macao to the motherland, the establishment of the special administrative region, and the implementation of "two systems, one country." The most important element in the communication between China and foreign countries is China's participation in the WTO. The reason why I am writing an independent section on this topic is because the name of the conference is "Modernization, Globalization, and the Path of Chinese Development." Thus it seems reasonable to include the section here.

We have long understood the rationale of "two systems, one country." On the issue of China's participation in the WTO, the government seemingly did not forward the theoretical logic. After World War I, China joined international organizations such as the "League of Nations," and after World War II we joined the United Nations, which was established in 1945. After that, the International Monetary Fund and World Bank were established as special international institutions. After GATT functioned for several years, the WTO was established. The issue of participation in the WTO became the practical issue that the Chinese cared about. I believe that we should pay close attention to the study of the current and long-term impacts of China's participation in the WTO. In recent years I have read many articles and listened to many speeches about the WTO. I learned quite a lot about the WTO and China's participation, and I am inspired by many ideas. The *Beijing Daily* asked me to write an article about it, and I wrote one originally entitled "WTO: What Everyone is Talking About" for the paper. The paper changed the title to "WTO and Globalization" when it published the article. I think that the revision was a good idea.

The essential aspect of my article was on *The Internationale* written by Eugene Pottier, who was a member of the Paris Commune. The last words of each section of the song are, "Then comrades, come rally/And the last fight let us face/ The *Internationale* unites the human race." In the article I said that Pottier's words are very clear. He encouraged members of the Commune to struggle bravely for the cause of the Commune. I wanted to tell comrades that we should believe in the inexorable trend of history, and a free, equal, happy, and satisfied *internationale* must come true.

The uprising of the Paris Commune failed, and many members were slaughtered. In the 1980s, I visited the "Wall of the Paris Commune" where members of the Commune were killed in Paris in the nineteenth century. Although the Paris Commune failed, we should still believe in the *internationale* about which Pottier wrote. It is an inexorable trend in world history, and must come true. However, we do not know when and in what way it may be realized.

The reality we are facing today is whether to join the WTO. Our China is a sovereign state. No one is forcing us to join the WTO. In other words, we can refuse to join it. However, we have joined it. It has become a reality. I support the decision of our government. I also believe that we are right to join it. If we do not, we will isolate ourselves, and we would be punished by history. I think that it is impossible for a country to be isolated from the world, even in 1871, not to mention that we have just entered the twenty-first century.

I have listened to many speeches and read many articles, and I get the impression that we have a right not to join the WTO. But these authors had not considered and reviewed the case that China had to join the WTO. I suggest here that we use reverse thinking. To consider the issue, we regard China's participation in the WTO as a *fait accompli* (the facts are already this way – of course we can withdraw if we want), and we must ensure that we "adapt" to it. However, this "adaptation" I am speaking of does not mean "agreement." This needs to be studied carefully, and we should strive for the current and long-term interests of China.

13 Brief final points

I did not write this chapter on the basis of printed materials; instead I relied only on my memory due to time restrictions, and quoted some material to hand. I should not use this kind of writing at the conference, but eventually I submitted my paper in a rush to the participants of the conference. Let everybody have a look and return it to me. I hoped I could eventually revise it on the basis of the inspiration I received at the conference. This is my revised material. I wanted to make a record of my own activities at the three-day conference in Hangzhou, and also because I never had the opportunity to reflect systematically on Chinese reform in which I had participated for many years. I appreciate that Tian Yu Cao's invitation has provided me with such a wonderful opportunity for reflection.

Discussion

Yu Guangyuan: The topic of my speech was decided by Tian Yu Cao. He provided the topic, and I wrote the article. In the first part of the article, I discussed history, not my opinion. But in terms of history and the market economy, I advocate reform. By then, I had retired, but I was still actively involved in reform. At the Third Plenary Session of the Twelfth Central Committee of the Party, Zhao Ziyang raised the decision to conduct the reform of the economic system. In speeches I made in Germany and Switzerland I said that, according to my understanding, China should conduct a market economy. I had made more than a dozen speeches in Switzerland, and I said, "It is not correct to say that the planned economy belongs to socialism, and the market economy belongs to capitalism." I published all the speeches in my collected essays in 1988. It was Deng Xiaoping who first put forward the idea, when he met the chief editor of *Encyclopedia Britannica*. But his talk was not published, and no one had an idea. This is the most important aspect of our reform. I think that the articles of the conference have also stressed it. I totally agree with them.

Now the issues are about merits and demerits, right and wrong. Who has merits? For example, I had some merits in the past. But later, as an observer, what merits did I have? I want to observe the reform because I enjoy it. I said, "The world is really marvelous, but I will learn it later." I want to continue to observe, and to learn the outcome. I published all my opinions, and have never made any suggestions to anybody. Nobody looks for me, and I enjoy it.

Let us change the topic. Let us talk about success and failure, instead of merits and demerits. Talking about success and failure is from the perspective of social development and progress. What we gain and what we lose. These issues have no connection with the subject. But the issues of merits and demerits, right and wrong are connected with the issue of the main body.

Because I had participated in the actual work, I can answer questions about the first part of my article, and I can demonstrate the facts of that time. As for the second part of the article, I can only put forward my opinion. My opinion is that of a scholar, and it does not count. This thing has two aspects; one is that I can make my own decisions. I call it my subjective initiative. When we make a suggestion, the suggestion is our subjective initiative. But it depends if other people want to accept it. I have talked about my views on that era, the whole world, and Chinese history. These are my own words that have theoretical significance.

Modern Chinese history has three thirty-year periods. The first thirty years are from 1919 to 1948. The second thirty years are from 1949 to 1978, and the third thirty years are from 1979 to 2008. Within the three thirty-year periods, it is impossible to implement reform of the political system, because there does not exist the proper environment and preparation. The third thirty-year period will end in 2008, and after that it will be possible to discuss reform of the political system. I think that the current reform of the political system is a touchstone of the people's situation. Can the current situation called reform be counted as reform? Can some random changes be counted as reform? Some reforms are experimental in order to examine the social reaction. The reform of the political system cannot be implemented seriously because there is no condition for serious implementation.

What institutional changes may be considered reform? They cannot be considered as constituting reform. The key is democracy. How to explain democracy? It is freedom. But how does one understand freedom? This is a crucial issue. This issue is a difficult one from the start, and we can understand it. It is not easy. However, we should formulate a public opinion now, and lay the theoretical foundation for democracy. Since the beginning when voting began with fingur-gesturing in ancient Greece, democracy has never been an easy concept to handle.

Now, I think we should talk about reform of the political system. We will not solve the issue now, but we should talk about it. We have a phrase in politics, "One ought to grasp firmly with both hands." That is, one ought to use one hand to promote the economy, and use the other hand to stabilize the political situation. This practice started with Comrade Deng Xiaoping, and this is the characteristic of Chinese politics.

I participated in work in the Policy Study Office of the State Council led by Deng Xiaoping during the early part of Deng's era. I was one of the seven people in charge in the Office. Seven people had experienced two schisms, and now I have become a loner. The first schism was four to three. The four were Wu Lengxi, Hu Sheng, Xiong Fu, and Li Xin. Recently, Wu Lengxi passed away. The other three people were Hu Qiaomu, myself, and Deng Liqun. This was the first schism. After that, our group of three had another split. Hu Qiaomu and Deng Liqun were in the same camp. I became the loner – two to one. This soured our relationship, and we do not even greet one another when we meet.

My theory is that comrades and friends should be separate. If we are friends we have the desire to communicate; otherwise we would have no contact at all with each other. This is my principle for handling personal relationships. Hu Yaobang [Chairman and Secretary-General of the Communist Party from 1980 to 1987, and a member of the politburo until his death in 1989] was not only my comrade; he was also my friend. Both Hu Qiaomu and Deng Liqun were Party members. Of course they are my comrades, but not my friends.

I want to discuss reform from a theoretical perspective. My view is that reform is only reform when it is not constantly changing. Reform should have a beginning and an end, and it should have a certain direction. Reform is not equal to change, and we cannot call any change, reform. So-called reform should advance in a certain direction. What is that direction, that goal? I talked specifically about the goal and direction of reform above. There is indeed a fundamental issue that I did not mention; namely whether socialist countries should exist. This issue is touched upon in several chapters in this volume. There are two kinds of socialism. One is socialism after capitalism, according to the order of social development. The other is current socialism that emerges according to prevailing conditions. The first kind of socialism cannot be returned to capitalism; the second can change midway between socialism and capitalism. Thus the Soviet Union could collapse, Eastern Europe could change their banners, and China could conduct reform. There are advances, pauses, retreats, and debates in the Chinese reform. There is a saying: "The world is really mysterious, only afterward can one know"; we still have to wait and see what the result is in the final analysis. That is why I want to live longer. Yesterday was my birthday. I am now 87 years old. I want to see what the result will be. What is the result I have surmised? I can be the source of my own study and enjoyment.

Qin Hui: May I ask Mr. Yu what was the main issue that caused the two schisms among the seven people?

Yu Guangyuan: I have published a book entitled *The Historical Turning Point that I Experienced*, wherein I have described the entire situation. The issue was the two "whatevers" that Hua Guofeng had advocated. "Whatever" Mao Zedong said or did was correct. I did not agree with this opinion. The two "whatevers" means that we must follow "whatever" Mao Zedong said. The goal of the two "whatevers" was to block Deng Xiaoping from controlling power. It was Mao Zedong who dumped Deng Xiaoping.

The second schism was concerned with another issue. The schism was mainly about the issue of democracy. I had put forward my view that I opposed the idea of strengthening the state apparatus. The reality was that the majority repressed the minority, and we did not need to exacerbate it anymore. I opposed the idea. Hu Qiaomu reported it to Deng Xiaoping, and Deng agreed with him, not me. We three worked for Deng Xiaoping. There was a view at that time that the working class already controlled power, so we did not need such a strong state apparatus, and it should be gradually eliminated. He opposed the view. Deng Xiaoping often talked with me before, but he stopped after that. It was January 1979.

David Schweickart: You mentioned the successes and problems reform created. I want to know what is the most serious problem China is facing today, from your perspective? What is your prediction for China's future? Are you optimistic or concerned?

Yu Guangyuan: Our current reform has not failed in principle. The implementation of the market economy is progress, although some things have negative impacts. For example, the essential driving force of reform was the extreme development of the Cultural Revolution. The Cultural Revolution developed to its end. In Chinese idiom there is the saying, "It was taken to the end, and could go no further." This is why we must conduct reform. But now we are not allowed to talk about the Cultural Revolution, or to write about it. This policy obstructs our progress.

I divide the history of the Cultural Revolution into three stages. I do not agree with the view that the Cultural Revolution was an internal turmoil. Why? The Cultural Revolution had three stages. The first stage was a coup. The second stage was an internal turmoil, and the third stage was a struggle. In the first stage, Mao Zedong overthrew Liu Shaoqi, the state President, and he did not follow either the party's constitution or the state's constitution. What could it be called if not a coup? At the beginning of the Cultural Revolution, I could have been considered a figure. After certain big figures were overthrown, I was not able to be counted as a figure at all. Therefore, it was a coup. When did the coup finish? It was completed in 1969. At the second stage, the group of Lin Biao and the group of Jiang Qing, the two anti-revolution groups, caused internal turmoil. At the third stage, Lin Biao died in a plane crash, and Zhou Enlai was given greater importance. And then Ye Jianying and Deng Xiaoping were restored to office. The three stages have three characteristics. At the beginning, I did not analyze this. But after having studied the Cultural Revolution I think that the view of the internal turmoil is incorrect. It had three stages and three characteristics. I regard these issues as a theorist. The characteristic of the theorist is his thoroughness. If a theorist does not have thoroughness, he would not have theories. Marxist theory is strong because it is a thorough theory. If a theory is not thorough, it would not have strength. Politicians should be good at making compromises, but theorists cannot do that. If a theorist makes compromises, he or she cannot be called a theorist. Theorists should have the courage of their theories.

Tian Yu Cao: Mr. Yu's division of the three stages of the Cultural Revolution provides a deep understanding of the Cultural Revolution. I wonder if Mr. Yu could divide the twenty three years of reform into several stages, and briefly talk about it. How many stages should it have, and what is the next stage? Please talk about this a bit.

Yu Guangyuan: Comrade Tian Yu Cao wants me to answer two more questions. The first is, How many stages can the twenty-three years of reform be divided into, and the second question is, What are the characteristics of each stage? I have already divided the reform into several stages. The first stage is the successful convening of the Third Plenary Session of the Eleventh Central Committee of the Party. Although the communiqué of the session established a limited goal for reform, it was able finally to put forward the issue of reform. Although the communiqué did not use the word "reform," the spirit of the bulletin had the nature of reform.

There were two important reports at the Third Plenary Session of the Eleventh Central Committee of the Party. One was the speech made by Ye Jianying, the other was the speech made by Deng Xiaoping. The speech of Ye Jianying stressed the issue of democracy. He quoted Lenin: "The socialism that achieves victory must fully implement democracy. If not, the outcome of the victory cannot be maintained." These words came from the following story. I had attended the working meeting of the session, and it was Wang Huide, the head of the Translation and Compilation Bureau of the Central Committee of the Party, who had said these words. I sent the words to Ye Jianying. He adopted them. I also asked Wang Huide if the words were correct. He said that they were authentic. I Therefore sent the words to Ye Jianying, and he used them.

When I wrote a book about this, I asked the Translation and Compilation Bureau of the Central Committee of the Party to find out from where the words came. They are in *The Complete Works of Lenin*, Volume 28. It was not at all easy for Wang Huide to remember them clearly. By then, when Ye Jianying made the speech, there was the Democratic Wall on Xidan Street. The magazine *China's Youth* had been restored. But because of the restriction of the two "whatevers," it could not be published. Therefore, they posted the magazine on the Democratic Wall, which caused a sensation. Ye Jianying said that the work conference of the Central Committee of the Party was the model for the implementation of democracy within the Party, and the Democratic Wall was the model for the implementation of democracy outside the Party. There was an argument in the articles posted on the Democratic Wall which opposed Wang Dongxing and supported Deng Xiaoping. I was very happy when I heard the news, and when Ye Jianying made that comment. When Ye Jianying's speech was printed, that comment had been deleted, but it was published within the Party in a briefing. That comment was deleted because it was related to Hu Qiaomu. Hu Qiaomu took a flashlight with him and went to see the Democratic Wall, where he found Wei Jingsheng's articles. This is why when Ye Jianying's speech was printed the words that praised Democracy Wall were deleted.

The second speech was made by Deng Xiaoping. The title of the speech was "Emancipate Thought, Seek Truth From Facts, Unite and Look Forward." Deng Xiaoping himself handed me the outline, and I drafted the speech. The final draft of the speech was made at the home of Deng Xiaoping. I and Hu Yaobang completed the final draft. Deng Xiaoping had written three pages of the outline, and handed it to me. The outline is still at my home, and it is my most valuable possession. Deng Xiaoping talked with us four times, and I also kept detailed notes of the talks. The characteristic of this stage is that many issues were put forward. One thing I need to point out is that Deng Xiaoping's talks had more fact to them than the communiqué of the session. In his talks he mentioned that we should allow some people to get rich first.

Note

1   In treating political reform, I have written about the historical facts from the beginning up until Section 8. This portion of the article consists of informal writing and may be regarded as a review of background materials. I cannot guarantee the accuracy of the article. Therefore it is used only for reference.

Section 10 on "Merits and Demerits" is directly related to the conference discussion. I want to introduce the materials and opinions that I had provided to the Central Committee of the Chinese Communist Party and the Central Government. For scholars at this conference I want to include my experience of Chinese reform, and the facts and ideological materials I had observed. The talk covers the time span of 1978 to 2002 – that is, twenty-three years. I am grateful to the conference organizers for the inclusion of my talk at the conference.

References

Yu, Guangyuan, 1988. Speeches on Market Economy delivered in Germany and Switzerland, *Explorations in the Socialist Stage of Political Economy: Part IV* (Beijing: People's Press), pp. 242–323.

Yu, Guangyuan, 1996. "Three 'thirty years'", *Explorations in the Socialist Stage of Political Economy: VI* (Beijing: People's Press), pp. 564–565.

Yu, Guangyuan, 1996. *From New Democracy to the Preliminary Stage of Socialism,* (Beijing: People's Press).

Yu, Guangyuan, 2001, "Yu's concise dictionary on the socialist ownership structure", *Explorations in the Socialist Stage of Political Economy: VII* (Beijing: Economic Science Press), pp. 34–70.

Yu, Guangyuan, 2001. The discussions about the evolution from "one country, many systems" to "one system, many versions," and "one country, two systems", *Explorations in the Socialist Stage of Political Economy: VII* (Beijing: Economic Science Press), pp. 129–148.

Yu, Guangyuan, 2001. "The civilized Asia and the Asian civilization", *Explorations in the Socialist Stage of Political Economy: VII* (Beijing: Economic Science Press), pp. 160–180.

Yu, Guangyuan, 2001. "The fundamental economic characteristics of China's socialist stage", *Explorations in the Socialist Stage of Political Economy: VII* (Beijing: Economic Science Press), pp. 272–274.

4 The relationship between China's strategic changes and its industrialization and capitalization

Wen Tiejun

It is more useful to review what China did than to discuss what China said or what comments the world made about China. In my view, what China actually did was no more than realize industrialization. This industrialization necessarily required transforming the system. The transformation took place since China had to deal with two restrictive environments: one was the domestic environment, and the other was the international environment.

1 The capital accumulation for the state's industrialization under the two restrictive conditions

We begin by discussing domestic restrictions. These restrictions fall into two categories.

The first category is resources. China is a country whose ratio of population to resources is extreme. In other words, the relation between population and resources is very strained. The Chinese population is 20 per cent of the world's population, but its cultivated land is only 7 per cent of the cultivated land in the world. Furthermore, China faces restrictions of water resources. In the southern part of China there is more available water, but land is very limited. In the northern areas there is more land, but water is limited. Under these conditions, the restriction of resources is the first and major difficulty China faces as it conducts the process of industrialization.

The second category involves restrictions relating to the system. Compared with the largest developing countries, China seems to be the only one to have completed its land revolution through nationwide war. Everyone knows that China underwent three civil wars in the first fifty years of the twentieth century, but few people stress that these three civil wars were revolutions over land distribution, and that the peasants were the main participants. The outcome of the wars was to distribute land evenly among the peasants nationwide according to household. When new China was established in 1949, one hundred million peasant households, totaling four hundred million peasants, occupied the land evenly in more than four million natural villages. This meant that when China began the process of industrialization, the cost of capital accumulation for industrialization was very high under the conditions of a small peasant economy and an even distribution of land.

Primitive accumulation of capital in its earliest stages has to handle trade between industries and agriculture, between urban and rural areas. The more scattered the small peasant economy, the higher the cost. Consequently, in the mid-1950s, the government established the collective system in rural areas in order to conduct capital accumulation for urban industries.

Although people called the centralized and unified organization system "socialism," its real function was to conduct the initial process of primitive accumulation of capital through the early stages of industrialization. The essential socialist characteristics of collectivization were mainly demonstrated in the areas that involved necessary social securities – education, medical care and retirement, and so on.

There have been numerous studies conducted abroad on the Chinese rural system, but because the beginning of the 1950s was the start of the cold war, foreign scholars had little access to Chinese materials. They tried to learn about China from ideological perspectives, and they referred to that stage of the collectivization as the stage of Chinese socialism.

After completing the capital accumulation for the state's industries through collectivization, China naturally entered a new stage of industrialization, which Marxists consider to be the "stage of industrialized large-scale production."

2 The two similar phenomena in the socialist camp

We should pay equal attention to two very similar phenomena. The first occurred in the Soviet Union. After it completed the fifth Five-Year Plan in the 1950s, the Soviet Communist Party introduced a policy of "peaceful co-existence, peaceful competition, and peaceful transition." The government participated in international division of labor abroad, and abandoned Stalin's policies at home. At this time, China was going through the stage of capital accumulation of industrialization and could not adapt to the Soviet strategic transformation. Other countries besides China which were conducting industrial capital accumulation, such as Vietnam, North Korea, Romania, and so on, also could not keep in step with the Soviets. Because of this there were debates among the socialist countries, and a distinction was made between Marxism and revisionism.

From the perspective of the economy, this demonstrates an irresistible economic law. On the one hand, the Soviet Union had completed its capital accumulation for industrialization and had met the requirements for socialized "great production" to participate in the international division of labor; on the other hand, the countries that had not completed capital accumulation for industries were not able to adapt to the Soviet strategic transformation.

The same phenomenon occurred in China after the 1970s. Around 1975, China began to implement its own fifth Five-Year Plan. It had completed the initial capital accumulation for industrialization, and needed to open up to the world. Other countries that had not yet completed their capital accumulation for industrialization (e.g., Vietnam, Laos, Albania), could not follow China's direction, and debated with China over the transformation.

On the issue of the transformation of domestic policies, China gradually abandoned the agricultural collectivization and the policies of Mao Zedong from the 1970s.

3 The strategic transformation under changing international conditions

When we analyze the historical materials, we find that, in the discussions of the Central Committee of the Chinese Communist Party as early as 1952, the party officials were already clearly aware that China should conduct the industrialization of state capitalism. Ideological propaganda reflects this as well. What was clearly proposed at that time was to enter the "transition stage" of socialism. The transition stage was defined as the new democracy (i.e. national capitalism). Later, China entered the stage of state capitalism; the essential cause of this important change was the outbreak of the Korean War in 1950. In order to support the Korean War, the Soviet Union invested in the military industry in the 1950s. Military factories and heavy industries were built in the northeast area of China in a short period of time. This would have been impossible under normal conditions.

Under normal conditions, China would have needed several decades of exchange between agriculture and light industry in order to accumulate capital for heavy industry, but because of the Korean War, it took only three years for China to build its military industry. Thus the state had to choose if it wanted heavy industry or not. If it wanted it, the state had to regard heavy industry as the foundation of its economic lifeline. If it did not, the state needed to return to the stage of the new democracy. Because of this situation, China's strategic transformation occurred after China built its heavy industry from the war, and not before.

This situation related to the restrictions stemming from the international environment and the struggle for China, as a middle ground, between the two big camps formed after World War Two. The strategic defense of the United States had not yet been set up in the Korean peninsula, but it was in place in the Japanese islands. The United States wanted to leave China as the middle ground and make China a "neutral" force. At that time, the Chinese attitude itself could be called "neutral," because China did not announce that it was a socialist country, and did not intend to join the Soviet camp.

If historical materials brought to light during the past three years are made available, people could review studies of the background of the relations between China and the Soviet Union that were declassified after the Soviet Union collapsed. Chinese scholars have obtained some of the materials and have conducted new research on this issue.

In this international situation, the Chinese strategy of the new democracy put forward in 1949 was adapted to the reality in China. The important strategic change in 1953 was the transformation of of the international environment, where China had to join the Soviet camp because of the Korean War.

China's strategic change in this special stage was mainly due to the requirements of national industrialization: the implementation of the new democracy (i.e., the choice of national capitalism under the leadership of the Communist Party, was due to the initial restriction of resources). However, because of the Korean War, China had to implement industrialization of state capitalism. After the Korean War, it was impossible for China to engage in international trade. China had to conduct mandatory trade domestically, and to gain capital accumulation from agriculture over a long period of time; therefore, the gap between prices of agricultural and industrial products emerged. When the disputes between China and the Soviet Union started up in 1957, the Soviets stopped investing in the Chinese industries and providing technological assistance. Thus, the process of gaining capital accumulation from agriculture through collectivization and the price gap between agricultural and industrial products both lasted for more than twenty years.

4 The cause of the reform in rural areas was the withdrawal of the government

After China initially completed capital accumulation for its industries in the 1970s, and started to open up to Europe, the United States, and Japan, the collective system in rural areas could not be managed. This was a very interesting change that is worth studying here.

President Nixon visited China in 1972. China opened its doors to Europe, the United States, and Japan, and won many investments from the West to change the structure of the heavy industries. The industries produced more products to support agriculture. Many products (e.g., as chemical fertilizer, tractors) were introduced into agriculture, and the cost of farming rose very quickly. At the same time, because of the price gap between industrial and agricultural products, the price of agricultural products was fixed. On the one hand, the price of agricultural products could not be raised, and on the other hand, the price of industrial products for agriculture was very high. Communes, and both large and small production teams in the countryside, fell heavily into debt. In the latter part of the 1970s, agriculture had become the industry whose input–output data showed negative value.

In this situation the system started to change, and the government, as a main body of the economy, withdrew from agriculture (in the past, people thought that it was the peasants who withdrew from the collective economy). This was the essential cause of rural reform.

In the past, the government was the only main player in the economy. Neither enterprises nor peasants withdrew from agriculture. However, the government withdrew because of the losses of agriculture. The government also abandoned its social responsibilities for peasants, including education, medical care, and social security. In fact, in the system where farming operations were based on household farms, peasants essentially returned to the mode of production of the small peasant economy. Once the government was no longer responsible for the basic security of the peasants, the socialist system which peasants depended upon could hardly be managed in rural areas.

Because of the changes in the system, a duality between urban and rural areas developed in China. From the all-round contract system to the 1990s, the dichotomy between urban and rural areas became so obvious that Mr. Du Runsheng and Mr. Qin Hui commented that peasants did not have the status of citizens at all.

5   Three important changes to the system

We will review the following to see what we have done during the process of reform and the open-door practice of the past twenty years.

The current situation is actually very clear. The Chinese economy has become the third largest in the world, according to a calculation by the World Bank, but, based on the amount per capita, China ranks number 100, or even more than 100. What people see is the remarkable change in China, and the status of its economy is greatly promoted in the world. However, based on the calculation of the amount per capita, the Chinese economy has not grown very much.

From the perspective of the study of the economic system, the important changes in China demonstrate the following three aspects.

The first is that the main economic body has become a multi-system structure. Because the state implemented reforms of investment and financial systems, such as "transforming financial allocations into loans," "taxation instead of profit delivery to the state," and "contracting according to levels," state capital was gradually transformed into the monopolistic capital of departments, while multi-interests emerged in the state economy and power was decentralized between the central and local governments.

The second aspect of note is that the Chinese resources have become capitalized. In 1978, the monetization of the Chinese economy was very low. Compared with the one trillion *yuan* of the gross value of industries and agriculture, the deposits within society were only 22.6 billion *yuan*. The state implemented the policy of "one account for finance, unified income and expenditure," took complete responsibility for the investment of expanded reproduction, and bore the long-term pressure of deficits. Therefore, the bank system had to provide loans to the state enterprises. The size of the loans was only 138 billion *yuan* in 1978, but in ten years, GDP grew to 10 trillion *yuan*, and the broad measure of money had grown to 12 trillion *yuan*. The growth rate of the former was an arithmetic progression, but the latter was a geometric progression. The ratio between M2 and GDP was up to 135 per cent (the United States was 67 per cent). The 1995 World Bank report on development pointed out that China's ratio between M2 and GDP was 105 per cent, the highest among countries that were undergoing a time of transition; by 2001, the ratio of our country between M2 and GDP was 160 per cent, the highest in the world, which demonstrated that China had become a country with surplus capital. The growth rate of currency in twenty years was much higher than the growth rate of GDP. The acceleration of the process of monetization actually means that the growth of currency economy is faster than the growth of physical economy. The monetization of economy is the external form of the capitalization of resources, and an important factor of economic growth over the past twenty years.

It should be further pointed out that the monetization of the economy itself is a main source of the government's income. The central government promoted the monetization of economy and the capitalization of resources through the continuous increase of the supply of currency. In this way it could collect seigniorage directly through the issue of currency, earn income from the economic growth caused by the issue of currency, relieve the pressure of bad assets of the financial system through inflation, and transfer losses to society. Thus, the interests among the government, finance, and financial assets, or financial capital, are the same. This economic law is the same throughout the world, and nobody can violate it.

The third aspect is the globalization of capital. As long as people respect facts, regardless of what opinions they might hold, they cannot deny that the main reason for globalization in the 1990s was the requirement of the free flow of capital. China was also included, despite its differing ideology. Especially since the mid-1990s, foreign capital has entered China on a large scale. In academic fields both at home and abroad, people believe that the interests among foreign capital and domestic capital, especially financial capital, are beginning to be connected. In other words, Chinese capital will naturally follow the regular rules of international capital to do business.

As discussed above, before the 1970s, the state was in the stage of capital accumulation; after the 1970s, however, it moved to the stage of the growth and development of the capital itself. If this point of view and the related explanations make sense, all the issues may be explained scientifically.

6 Is there a third path for China to follow?

Let us review China's prospects for the future and see if China can follow a "third path."

In the current situation, according to the requirements of Western industrialization, the path which China follows is actually the model of traditional industrialization. We have to consider that if we continue to follow this path we probably cannot go much further.

Based on published studies, the gross value of GDP for each unit of energy created in China was much lower than in Japan. Each Japanese consumed two tons of petroleum oil, on average. If the Chinese save on energy and consume one ton of petroleum oil per person, and if China's urbanization is developed by 50 per cent, in ten years 700 million people will live in urban areas. Thus, in ten years' time, the urban population alone, not including the rural population, will need at least 700 million tons of petroleum oil each year. The total output of the domestic production of petroleum oil in China is 200 million tons at the most. China will need to import at least 70 per cent of the petroleum oil it consumes in order to meet the demands of the model of its industrialization. Even if our calculations are based on half the amount of the Japanese consumption, China still needs to import petroleum on a large scale, which will inevitably cause shortages in the world oil market and raise the price of oil.

Therefore, although we hope that we can realize industrialization and urbanization, because of the shortage of domestic resources, China cannot follow the path of traditional Western industrialization. Using the same reasoning, if we hope that China accelerates the process of its urbanization, the amount of water consumption each person uses in urban areas will be more than twenty times that which each person consumes in rural areas. China is a country with very limited water resources. Right now we have more than 100 cities seriously lacking water and more than 300 cities with water shortages.

From the perspective of the limitation of the two resources, the disadvantages of the limitation of domestic resources and foreign competition which China is now facing have not yet been resolved. Even if 50 per cent of the population becomes urbanized, there will be still 700 to 800 million people living in rural areas. The widely scattered small-peasant economy will still exist, and the restrictions of the system will be unchanged.

Therefore, China must probably choose another path to follow. However, in the current situation, it does not seem that China has another choice, because the third path put forward by Europe and the United States is still a Western concept, and it would be difficult for China to follow such a path.

5 The historical origin of China's neo-liberalism

Another discussion on the ideological situation in contemporary mainland China and the issue of modernity

Wang Hui

The twentieth century seems to have ended prematurely in 1989, yet history continued. The Beijing event and the beginning of the collapse of the Soviet Union and Eastern Europe in that year marked the beginning of neo-liberalism guiding the global economy and the political structure. Society would not collapse in China, as it did in the Soviet Union and Eastern Europe, and the transformation of society maintained continuity. If we summarize the process in a simple and incomplete fashion, we can say that Chinese society, under the continued form of the state power structure, promoted the radical adoption of the market principle. Moreover, under the guidance of this state policy, China became an active participant in the global economic system. The two traits of continuity and radicalization were characteristics of Chinese neo-liberalism. Neo-liberalism depends on state and supra-state policies and economic forces, and it relies on the theoretical language of formalist economics to establish its linguistic hegemony. Its apolitical and anti-political characteristics (or its anti-historical character, or opposition to traditional socialist ideology) can never conceal the actual and firm connection between neo-liberalism and state-guided economic policies. With the prerequisite of state policy and politics, neo-liberalism cannot use the mythology of "transition" to cover up unemployment, loss of social protection, increases in poverty, and mounting social disintegration. The idea of "transition" is the key and clear prerequisite in discussions on contemporary Chinese society. It becomes the necessary linkage between the actual state of inequality and the final ideal. Therefore, it does not make sense to refuse to recognize the hegemonic status of neo-liberalism because of the existence of state intervention.

The hegemonic status of Chinese neo-liberalism was formed in the process of the state overcoming the crisis of legitimacy through economic reform. The emergence of "neo-authoritarianism," "neo-conservatism," "classical liberalism," market radicalism, and the theoretical and historical exhibition of state modernization (including the exhibition of modernization in various nationalisms) in 1989 have close connections with the formation of neo-liberalism. The replacement of these terms (even terms contrary to them) demonstrates change in the power framework of contemporary China and the world.

Neo-liberalism is a language system and an ideology. It is incapable of describing actual social and economic relations, but it is also not unrelated to actual social and economic relations. As an ideology that penetrates state policies, intellectual thinking, and media values, it uses the concepts of "transition" and "development" to deal with its internal contradictions. Therefore, the effective way to reveal the internal contradictions of neo-liberalism is to demonstrate the historical connections between its theoretical language (e.g. a free market, development, globalization, prosperity in common, private property rights) and actual social processes, and to explain the complex relation between its formulation and practice.

Obviously, in different regions of the contemporary world, such as North America, Western Europe, Russia, and China, neo-liberalism has different historical roots and social formations. The differences in historical conditions show that a convincing conclusion cannot be formulated based on a summary of the theoretical characteristics of neo-liberalism from the abstract perspective. One of the goals of this chapter is to use a historical analysis to clarify the domestic and international conditions, thus explaining the foundation of state policy, the ideological situation, and domestic/international public opinions that have enabled Chinese neo-liberalism to establish its linguistic hegemony. In addition, another goal is to analyze the different forms and internal contradictions of Chinese neo-liberalism, weighing various criticisms of the theory and practice of neo-liberalism. Finally, another goal is to analyze the main factors of various contradictions in neo-liberal theories, practices, and social movements – that is, the radical, moderate, and conservative main factors. In my opinion, progressive forces in contemporary Chinese society have the central task of avoiding these main factors in order to develop in the conservative direction, and to promote change, so that progressive forces can serve as the driving forces of broadening democracy and freedom in China and the world.

One issue that requires explanation is the economic reform which took place from 1978 to 1989, which was a process of wide-ranging transformation. Using the term "revolution" to describe the depth of these transformations is appropriate. This short chapter is not able to summarize completely the remarkable achievements of Chinese reform and its internal crisis, nor can it describe in detail the social movement of 1989. Each event mentioned here requires proof and careful review by experts. I can only restructure the historical perspective in order to understand the Chinese issues through an initial review of the causes of the social movement of 1989. I will present this first.

1 Neo-liberal anti-historical explanations and the historical conditions of the social movement

The social movement of 1989 had profound impacts not only on China but also on the world. Whether domestic or international, propaganda from the official media, and the proliferation of testimonials and analyses focused mostly on the student movement and the ideological movement of intellectuals, or the decision-making processes of top officials. Even the analyses of the so-called "civil society" focused mainly on the roles played by economic groups, such as the Sitong corporation or the "circle" of Beijing intellectuals. However, the social movement of 1989 featured a broad range of social mobilization. Its spontaneity and broadness indicate that this movement was caused by social forces which were far stronger than organizational forces.

The ideological emancipation and enlightenment movement of the 1980s indeed played an important role in dismantling the old ideology and providing a source of rebellious ideologies. However, as a group, intellectuals were neither able to provide practical social goals nor understand the real depth of social mobilization. This is because the social ideology of the 1980s – as an ideological trend critical of state socialist practices – was not able to discover and understand social contradictions. It was not able to understand the socialist tendencies of grass-roots social mobilization, nor could it think beyond Cold War ideology.

Here, it is necessary to distinguish two conceptions of socialism: one is the "socialism" of the old statist ideology that is characterized by the state's monopoly in institutional arrangements; the other is a social protection movement that develops under state monopoly and market expansion, and it has the characteristic of opposing monopoly and demanding democracy.[1] In the context of the end of the Cold War, and with the rethinking of "socialist" practice, the social protection movement that has been hidden by social contradictions (anti-monopoly, privileges, and demands for democracy) has not been fully understood. My understanding of the social movement of 1989 comes from the following issues.

First, from the mid-1980s to 1989, many student movements arose in mainland China (including the student movement at the end of 1986 that forced Hu Yaobang to step down from the government). However, they were too small to promote broad social mobilization. Why did the student movement that arose after the death of Hu Yaobang bring about such broader mobilization and participation? Why was it that the state media (such as Central TV, *People's Daily*, Xinhua News Agency, *Guangming Daily*) began to report on the movement on such a large scale beginning in May 1989, such that a "free press" emerged within the state propaganda machine, thus providing the driving force and conditions for the mobilization of the entire country and society?

Second, what is the relationship between the demands of the student movement and the demands of other social strata? I raise this question because the social movement of 1989 was not only a student movement; it was also a broad social movement. The participants included workers from private industries and businesses, state cadres, teachers, and other social groups. Even officials participated in the movement, officials from the Party Central Committee, from each department of the State Council, the People's Congress, and from each agency of the Chinese People's Political Consultative Conference (including "mouthpieces" such as *People's Daily*, *Guangming Daily*, Xinhua News Agency). We can probably say that except for the peasant class who did not participate directly, all other social strata were involved in the movement, particularly, residents of mid-sized and large cities. It is not hard to understand why the working class, intellectuals, and other social strata participated in the movement, but why did the state oppose the state, or in particular, why did the internal contradictions of state conduct emerge (the contradictions in the state apparatus, both in its entirety and partially)?

Third, why was the reform process itself criticized when the whole social strata supported reform? Who were the objects of the movement's criticisms, and what were the social conditions at that time? What factors formed the ideology of the social mobilization movement?

In order to answer the above questions clearly, we need to recall briefly the process of Chinese reform since 1978.The social reform from 1978 to 1989 may be divided into two main stages: the rural reform from 1978 to 1984, and the urban reform from 1984 to 1989. The reform from 1978 to 1984 or 1985 focused on the issue of peasants, and its essence was to partially change the dual social structure of "cities and countryside being divided" that universally elevated the social status of urban residents above that of rural residents.[2] This reform encompassed primarily two aspects. First, the people's communes were disbanded. The state redistributed land evenly among the peasants, and implemented the policy of household contract responsibility with remuneration linked to output. Second, through policy adjustments, the state raised the price of agricultural products and encouraged peasants to engage in diversified productions to develop town enterprises in order to reduce urban and rural disparity caused by the urban industrialization of Mao Zedong. Therefore, the income difference between urban and rural areas gradually declined between 1978 and 1985. In addition to the two reform achievements mentioned above, small markets in rural areas also prospered, but these were established according to the traditional Chinese distribution of land and the principle of equality. We can sum these up as "small peasant socialism," which resisted the state monopolization found in the communes. The promotion of peasant enthusiasm was achieved mainly through the flexibility of production and the reduction of the urban–rural disparity, not only by simply opening the market. The state provided protection for small community farmer markets (Broudel has discussed how transparent markets differ from the market economy) through the price adjustment of agricultural products, and it eased the tense relations between urban and rural areas. Because market reform in urban areas had not yet started, the small markets in rural areas had for the time being not been organized into an urban market economy model.

Neither bankruptcy in rural areas nor rapid social turbulence arose, even though there was an environment of low productivity, limited surplus products, an underdeveloped urban commodity economy, and low-level polarization between the rich and the poor.[3] The market was merely the main factor in rural reform of the 1980s. An economist at that time summarized the situation of rural reform as the "development of agriculture depended mainly on policies." His words were basically suitable to the situation.[4]

The process of rural reform discussed above provides a basic background for understanding the urban reform which started in 1984, and which also formed the historic conditions for urban economic development and problems. Urban reform included many fields and areas. People usually summarize the essence of reform as the introduction of the market mechanism. But from the social perspective, reform encompassed "devolving power and yielding benefits (*fangquan rangli*)." That is, reform directed by the state consisted of the reorganization of social interests through the decentralization and transfer of certain social resources previously directly controlled by the state.[5]

Some studies have suggested that in the twenty-six years from 1953 to 1978, in China, the ratio of financial income to the distribution of national income was an average of 34 per cent (37.2 per cent in 1978). After 1979 this figure began to decline gradually, to only 19.3 per cent in 1988. In the environment of the central government's finance reduction, extra-budgetary funding began to expand greatly, and local governments became more financially independent and won more authority to control their finances.[6] The process produced side-effects such as tax evasion, forced contributions, bank loans controlled by local governments, and large-scale smuggling activities.[7] Under the pressure of unemployment, the state had to increasingly implement policies which called for the merging of enterprises, or the changing of products being manufactured. Although the state closed and suspended fewer enterprises, its policy did not essentially change.

Obviously, urban reform was more complicated than rural reform. This is because, first, compared with the estimation and calculation of rural land and means of production, the estimation and calculation of industrial assets proved much more difficult. The redistribution of industrial assets involved very complex techniques and systems, and also took into account differences in industry, division of labor, and regions (and the inequality caused by such differences). More importantly, the redistribution of rural land had its basis in the system of household contract responsibility with remuneration linked to output. At the least, the state still had land ownership in name. In contrast, the process of redistributing industrial assets was a process of real privatization.

Second, rural and urban industrial reforms had totally different ownership prerequisites. In the original industrial system, the state distributed resources on the basis of planning. But the ownership of resources was totally separated from economic efficiency as well as from collective and individual incomes. (For example, large state factories had the advantage of monopolized resources, but their actual employee income almost equalled that of small collective factories.) However, when the state started to relinquish absolute authority over distribution in industry and commerce, it transformed its role from that of a decision-maker and implementer to that of a regulator. The unequal ownership of resources was immediately transformed into unequal income. In this sense, urban industrial reform involved not only the ownership of enterprises, but it also impacted upon the entire national economic system. In this complex situation, without an appropriate process of democratic supervision, without the appropriate complex techniques (for regulating the economy), and without the cultivation of a new and appropriate economic system, the process of redistributing resources and assets necessarily led to serious social inequalities.

Many of the factors discussed above explain why urban reform did not follow the principle of equity as the initial rural reform had done. In the process of urban reform, the status and interests of workers, and even those of public employees, fell into a crisis. Sociological studies have discussed the falling economic status, changes in internal social strata, violation of employee interest, and the loss of benefit guarantees for old, weak, ill, disabled, and pregnant employees.[8]

From 1985 to 1989, Chinese economists debated several reform issues, such as more radical measures in reforming property rights, the adjustment of economic structures via state intervention, whether price reform should be implemented first (i.e., the reform of the original system of planned pricing in order to create market relations), or whether the reform of enterprise ownership should be implemented first (i.e., large-scale privatization of state enterprises).[9] These debates arose due to the continuing inflation and economic chaos that began in 1985. Without appropriate price regulations to create proper market conditions, reform of ownership would cause serious social instability. The result of the debates was the opinion that the creation of market conditions through price reform while simultaneously promoting the reform of enterprises (mainly the contract system) came out on top. This reform policy was basically successful because the impact of price adjustment limited the monopoly of the traditional system, thereby stimulating the vigor of the market mechanism and restricting the process of so-called "spontaneous privatization." Comparing this with the Russian "privatization" plan, we should fully acknowledge such successes.

However, this process had the potential to bring about crisis and it caused continuous social problems. In terms of the market environment, this reform featured the "double-track price system" (namely the ço-existence of the state-planned price and the market price – the former was used primarily for the means of production, including surplus production after the completion of the plan, while the latter focused primarily on consumer goods). But the simultaneous operation of the planned price and the market price provided opportunities for corruption and government profiteering (i.e., when officials or official institutions used the pricing system to conduct speculation and profiteering). In terms of enterprise reform, the contract system was instituted and the government was separated from enterprises. But it was very hard to conduct the latter because of the untouched political system. In actuality, the slogan declaring the separation of government from enterprises did not result in the separation of politics from the economy, but rather resulted in the separation of ownership from management rights. In the confused power transition, large amounts of state assets were "legally" or illegally transformed into the economic interest of a minority.

Many economists consider 1988 a "contract year," because the contract system expanded from the contract of enterprises to the contract of foreign trade, departments, finance, and so on. Enterprises, and local governments and their departments received benefits via their special status in the old system. This worsened the contradictions caused by the "double-track price system." Local governments and interests moved the planned products to the market, and caused inflation and seriously imbalanced distribution of income.[10] In the contracting process regular forms of corruption took place, such as tax evasion, acceptance of commission, abuse of public funds, trading power for money (e.g., getting bribes for power granting contracts), and so on.

Since the reforms, the buying power of institutions has been growing continuously; bonuses have been increasing continuously, and this has caused the imbalance between supply and demand. The central government lacked sufficient financial resources to regulate and control the situation. From May to June 1988, the government announced publicly that it would implement a new price reform policy, to gradually withdraw planned prices and use market prices. This immediately resulted in panic purchases and social instability. Subsequently, the government had to return to implementing state regulation and control, and this caused conflicts between the state and local governments and local interests.[11]

The reforms during this period resulted in some achievements, but at the same time they also generated some new factors, which reflected from different angles the new inequality of social conditions. These conditions are the essential causes of the social mobilization of 1989. First, the "double-track price system" and marketization of power caused the unequal distribution of income and the phenomenon of "rent seeking," namely the exchange of power and money that resulted in the assets of the whole people entering the purses of the "rent seekers." In 1988, the price differences in the double-track pricing system rose to 356.9 billion Yuan, 30 per cent of the national income that year.[12] This served as the foundation upon which the interests of local governments and local departments formed, and it was also the main root of the corruption of the system. In the process, the conflicts between the interests of the central and local governments worsened.

Second, the income of each stratum in urban areas started to seriously polarize. The income of the working class in particular was falling. The crisis of being laid off (*xiagang*) and unemployed began to emerge, and discussions about the "iron rice bowl" could be found frequently in newspapers. Third, due to other factors such as the adjustment of the tax structure and the marketization of power, the structure of the business stratum was changing. The interest of small businesses (the so-called "self-employed small businessmen") was reduced. This was the social foundation of the student movement, and it was the stratum that supported the student movement.

Fourth, the reforms of housing, medical care, wages, and other social welfare programs had not been vigorously promoted. Inflation damaged the sense of social security. These factors not only caused dissatisfaction among salary workers, but also affected the routine life of many state employees (officials). The income differential between common state employees and other social strata as well as between those state employees involved in market activities and other state employees increased dramatically.[13] It is important to note that the social movement of 1989 was basically a social movement based in the urban areas. It had connections with the history of market expansion during the so-called "urban reforms" after 1984.

But we should not forget another background factor. The promotion of urban reform and the stagnantion of rural reform widened the gap between urban and rural areas (which mainly illustrated the problems in the pricing, residence registration, and labor protection systems, and grass-roots ecological and social organizations). From 1985 to 1989, peasant incomes started to fall, but rural society was not yet involved in the market and its crises the way it would be in the 1990s, and the urban population flow had not yet reached today's levels. This stratum was not yet directly involved in the social movement.

The political stability of the 1980s was established via the state's powerful control over society. This capacity cannot be regarded as the powerful control resulting from mere state implementation. At that time the state promoted economic reform, and the intellectual stratum participated directly in and provided ideologies for reform. Society at the grass-roots level (especially the peasant stratum) directly enjoyed the benefits of reform.

The interaction of these three factors gave legitimacy to the reforms of the 1980s. However, a new situation emerged before and after 1989. First, there existed tensions in the state, such as the conflict of interests among different departments, strata, authorities, central, and local governments. Second, the internal polarization of the state caused internal polarization among intellectuals. On the one hand, intellectuals who directly participated in the process of reform decision-making and ideological propaganda production had actually been involved in the state system, and they were highly sensitive to the internal polarization of the state.[14] On the other hand, the internal polarization of the state encompassed the transformations of state functions and the social division of labor. The employment choice and social attitude of many intellectuals had greatly changed.

Third, the urban strata directly sensed that their interests would be ignored in the reform process. Therefore, they did not simply accept the "mythology" of reform, although they basically still agreed with reform. Fourth, a new crisis began to emerge in rural society due to the development of urban reform and changes in urban and rural relations.

The factors discussed above resulted in a serious crisis of legitimacy. Not only was it a legitimacy crisis of the state that partially retained some elements of the planned economy, but it was also a legitimacy crisis of the state that was making the transition to a market economy. What people doubted was not only the result of the planned economy but also the legitimacy of the distribution of interests being promoted under the name of reform (that is, who the state is representing in promoting redistribution).[15] At issue also was the legitimacy of the procedures of income distribution; that is, the basis of the procedures, and the type of procedures to use in order to conduct administrative management and supervision, and so on.

The situations discussed above constituted the basic social conditions of the social mobilization of 1989. The basic demands from the student movement and intellectuals consisted of calls to implement political democracy, freedom of the press, freedom of speech, freedom of assembly, a legal system (against the so-called "rule by man"), a constitution, and the call to acknowledge the legitimacy of the mobilization of 1989 as a patriotic student movement. Many levels of society supported these demands and some groups added more detailed demands, such as procedures against corruption, official profiteering, the "princeling party" (the privileged class), and measures for stabilizing prices, and returning Yangpu (in Hainan Island) to China.

Furthermore, there were demands for social protection and justice – that is, supervision of the reorganization of social interests in a democratic fashion, and with the assurance of fairness. The issue that required attention was the social movement's criticism of the traditional system, but at that time the movement was not faced with the old state, but rather with a state that promoted reform, a state that was, moreover, in transition toward a market society. The distinction I am making here – that is, the old state versus the state promoting reform – does not deny the connections between the two, but rather it highlights the transformation of state functions and social conditions. In reality, the state that promoted market reform and social transformation depended on the old political heritage and ideology to rule the country.

These two incompatible factors gave rise to the state's crisis of legitimacy. On the one hand, people could use the economic policies guided by the state to challenge the legitimacy of state ideology and ruling methods. On the other hand, they could use the socialist ideology to question the legitimacy of state economic policies. Socialist countries noted well the equal distribution of income, and their ideologies took this into account. However, within different regions they protected the inequality between urban and rural areas via mandatory regulations and state planning. In the context of reform, this inequity was quickly transformed into income differences among social classes, strata, and regions, and this accelerated the polarization of society. Therefore, the essential distinction between the old state and the state promoting reform cannot conceal the historical connections linking them.

2 The complex structures of the social movement and its multiple demands

As a movement protective of society, the movement of 1989 contained the spontaneous opposition against inequitable market expansion. As a social protest movement, it also inherited the criticism of the ideological trends of the 1980s; that is, it inherited the opposition against the full-service state and its methods of governance.[16] The distinction between the two states (old state and state in the process of reform) discussed above does not mean the existence of two countries. Likewise, the social protest movement contained complex social structures.

A complex issue that requires attention concerns the fact that the levels of society which participated in the movement of 1989 included some interests that benefited greatly, in the 1980s, from the decentralization of power and the transfer of profits. Because of their dissatisfaction with the regulatory policies being implemented, these interests tried to insert their demands into the social movement in order to urge the state to conduct more radical privatization reforms. These interests were not only the product of the age of reform, but they were also the direct expressions of the exchange between power and market, so their demands unfolded between the upper reaches of the state and the social movement. They used investments, lobbied senior officials, and transferred information between the state and the movement in order to use the social movement to force the internal power of the state to be transformed for the benefit of themselves and their interests.

Here, can note the roles that the Kanghua and Sitong corporations, and other interests, played in the movement. Certain intellectuals who had close connections with the authority of the state also played similar roles. They tried to use the movement, especially the student movement, to influence the internal power structure of the state.[17] The internal division within the state in 1989 had close connections with the formation of interest groups within the state. In Chinese discourse, what is today called the ideological formation of "neo-liberalism" had already emerged. Its core content was to take the radicalization of a reform based on devolution of authority and the contract system and, under the premise of there being no protection from a democratic system, comprehensively promote a spontaneous privatization. Moreover, by going through a process of legalization, they would legitimize the class that they themselves had created and the process of dividing interests.

Therefore, "neo-liberalism" (i.e., "neo-conservatism") mainly represented the interest relations of social groups that were being formed in the course of interest groups emerging within the state. Some of its principles shaped state reform policies through the network of the administrative and economic power of the state. When the state's crisis of legitimacy emerged, this market radicalism manifested itself as "neo-authoritarianism" and "neo-conservatism" (i.e., the use of the state and elite authority to promote market expansion), and it took shape in the form of "neo-liberalism" in the multinational market movement.

There were indeed some transformations, or, in other words, changes in power and authority. Some interest groups perceived that [they could no longer rely solely] on the role of protection, restraint, and regulation that the state had played in the course of globalization and the expansion of the domestic market, so they no longer relied solely on the state to provide the motive force for market expansion, but rather came to recognize that they could use the strength of multinational capital and domestic capital to restructure China's society and market. This is the secret history of the tangled connection between "neo-authoritarianism" and "neo-liberalism."

In this sense, some contradictions between "neo-liberalism" and the state did not at all resemble the relations between liberalism and the state from the nineteenth century to the early part of the twentieth century. They were the products of the relations among new interests. The central government, local governments, and various interests were under heavy social pressure to resolve the issues of reform and relations among interested parties. These problems appeared in the non-stop debates on reform and regulation. In the context of globalization and the complex conflicts involving the state, local governments, various interests, and multinational capital, "neo-liberalism" was able to influence state reform policy by frequently using such terms as "non-governmental", "society," and "market." On the other hand, "neo-liberalism" also used terms such as opposing the "planned economy," "communist," or "autocracy" in the foreign media (especially the media in Hong Kong and the United States).

The contradictions between the Chinese version of neo-liberalism and the state apparatus with an extremely conservative ideological formation reflected at most the internal contradictions of the state's practice. Chinese neo-liberalism modeled itself as "oppositional" in every situation, but this does not prove that an antagonistic relationship existed between the market ideology and state practice. On the contrary, there existed complex and mutually dependent relations between them. Such was the ambiguous and dual nature of neo-liberal ideology – as a global and dominant ideology – in the Chinese language environment. In this sense, rejecting those things that falsely use the name "neo-liberalism" does not mean rejecting "non-governmental," "society," and "market"; on the contrary, it is a rejection of the monopoly relations that oppose the market, society, and the non-governmental. After all, the goal of neo-liberalism is to provide the theoretical possibility and foundation of the market's democratic system, social management, and the cultivation of the private sector.[18]

In the sense discussed above, the crisis of the traditional planned economy was being transformed into a new crisis of the monopolistic market. The social contradictions of 1989 should not be simplified as a situation of the state promoting reform and society resisting it. On the contrary, in the situation of the old state's decline, what people demanded was the deepening of reform.

The crux of the issue lay in the type of reform. The students, intellectuals, and other social strata who participated in the movement all supported reform (including political and economic reform) and demanded democracy. But their expectations and understanding of reform differed vastly with the reality of the relations among the interested parties. From a more comprehensive perspective, what people demanded were reforms to bring about a democratic ideal and a legal system that could assure social justice and the democratization of economic life – not a political framework and legal system used merely to legitimate the current income distribution.

These demands essentially conflicted with those put forward by the forming and growing interests, namely the demand for radical privatization, although this conflict was not fully understood at the time. The latter group dismissed the demand for social equality as a call for absolute egalitarianism and moral idealism, and it tried to eliminate the legitimacy of social protectionism via the rejection of the "Cultural Revolution" and socialism.

The complex conditions discussed above explain why some levels of society who benefited from the reforms also participated in the social movement, and why even officials of many state agencies walked through Changan Street and participated in the demonstrations and protests along with other sectors of society. Thus it is difficult to explain the characteristics of the social movement of 1989 with only the simplistic perspective of reform/anti-reform.

In general, we may conclude from the above analysis that the ideologies that mobilized society in 1989 included the value of democracy, freedom, and the concept of equality in daily life. It may be added that the traditional socialist ideology was transformed into a force for mobilization through criticism. The active participation of each social stratum has been easily forgotten, but it was a very important factor of daily life. Therefore, I believe that there were multiple significant elements to the social movement of 1989. It was a farewell to the past, a protest against the social contradictions in the new age. From the viewpoint of students and intellectuals, it was a call for democracy and freedom, and from the viewpoint of workers and other sectors of urban residents, it was a demand for social equality and justice.

These multiple significanct elements explain the movement's demand for democracy. Due to a variety of factors, the explanation of the social movement of 1989 has served the interested party that has advocated radical privatization. These factors consisted of the Cold War ideology, the state's use of violence and the crisis of legitimacy it caused, the limited historical understanding of the students and intellectuals (as discussed above), and the conspiratorial relations between the most conservative elements (i.e., the interest groups that had emerged in the course of privatization that had been brought about through the use of power) and the world order of "neo-liberalism." This interest group uses the identity of "real radical reformer" to conceal the complex relations between itself and state power and other interests, to conceal the real relations of interests in the process of reform, and to show that they were the progressive forces which promoted the global market and democracy.

On June 4, 1989, the Tiananmen event shocked the world. Later, Eastern Europe and the Soviet Union collapsed. The closing of the Cold War ended "history." The turbulence of 1989 revealed signs of the collapse of society, and in this context the state used stability as an excuse for its legitimacy. Because the state apparatus was regarded as the only force capable of maintaining stability, the issue of stability concealed the state's crisis of legitimacy that had arisen since the time of reforms.

The essential historical facts show that state economic policies had caused the social turbulence, and the stability after the turbulence became the legitimate basis for the expansion of state power. Therefore, the neo-liberal theory of "self-regulation" (and its exclusion of state intervention) was eventually transformed into a demand for control and intervention.

After the violence of 1989, the attention of the people was focused on the events of June 4, the collapse of the Soviet Union and Eastern Europe, and the end of the Cold War. They forgot the historical conditions of the social movement and its basic demands. Therefore, the movement's historic possibilities disappeared with its failure. As discussed above, the social mobilization of 1989 originated from a variety of causes, such as the protest against the inequality of the decentralization of power and the transfer of profits to enterprises, the dissatisfaction with the state's regulatory policies, the internal divisions within the state, and the interactions between each social stratum and the state apparatus.

The media in 1989 serves as an example. We may ask: How did the social mobilization of each stratum, with its democratic demands, penetrate the state-controlled media? I think that the following three conditions formed the key factors. First, the media was unable to slant its report, due to a variety of factors, such as the conflict of power among political interests, the internal contradictions between the state's economic policy and its ideology, and the shifting interests in the central and local governments.[19] Second, after the media broadly reported on the movement, society became greatly mobilized, and in turn, the state was not able to control the media as it could traditionally. Third, there were subtle and overlapping relations linking state ideology with the demands for democracy and equality. (This is the case, because otherwise it would be difficult to explain how the student movement could demand that the state admit it was a "patriotic movement.") These three factors formed relations of instability between the social movement and the state.

In other words, the essential conditions of the short-term freedom of press and open discussions in May 1989 resulted from the interactions among the state, different interests, and each level of society. The collapse of social forces led to the collapse of freedom of the press. The direct factor that caused the movement's failure was the state's violent suppression, and the indirect factor was the social movement itself, because it did not build a bridge between the demand for political democracy and the demand for equality. It was unable to form a stable social force, and to promote the fragile cooperative relationship mentioned above.

If we review the social movement of 1989 in the context of the expansion of the domestic and international markets, we can see that many of the movement's demands had connections with the protests against the WTO and IMF in Seattle from November to December 1999, and in Washington from April to May 2000, because the demands were concerned with the political arrangements of the people's daily lives, and about the establishment and development of market regulations.

Although these protests had many dimensions and included a variety of demands (even some rightist and conservative elements), we should not think that these protest movements rejected reform or free communication, because their demands for protection included their longing for fair and democratic reform and free communication. These movements illustrate that the values of democracy and freedom had close connections with the social protection moments. Without this kind of social pressure, the driving force that rebuilds the social protection system would not exist, and the concept of creating a democratic market system would not exist either.

After 1989, the popular theory of "the end of history" provided the social movement with the clearest explanation – that is, the idea that the Western social system would eventually prevail – and China was just one example of an unfinished history. The double significance of the social movement was understood as a single unit. I believe that once the idea of a singular significance had spread around the world, once it came to serve as proof of the advantages of the current system, once the protests turned into praise, then its real significance, potential for criticism, and historical importance disappeared.

Someone once commented that this was a necessity in a time of transition. But the explanation of necessity did not touch the contradictions hidden in our daily lives, and merely provided a moral reasoning to the tragedy. With the international media's reports on the Tiananmen event, the social protest movement took a new direction. People are more willing to review and understand the social movement from a new perspective. Numerous explanations of the movement by the media exhibit a strong trend. The media understands the social movement as an exception in "the end of history," and it is not aware that the great global transformation of 1989 was a criticism and protest against new historical relations, monopolies, and requirements.

3 The creation of the market society and its contradictions

If we review the debates in Chinese academia concerning the free market, state intervention, globalization and anti-globalization, private property rights, and so forth, from the perspective of historical processes, then these debates exhibit different meanings.

First, the emergence of the modern market society was not spontaneous; it was the result of state intervention. After 1989, the state continued economic regulation and reform. The dissatisfactions of society with the crisis discussed above were greatly reduced. Price reform had to end in the latter part of 1988. In September 1989, three months after the failure of the student movement, it restarted. By that time, the main adjustments were focused on prices, exchange rates, and interest rates. The following measures summarize the economic changes during the period of economic rationalization from 1988 to 1991, especially after 1989: the monetary policy became the main means of economic regulation and control; the price of foreign exchange was greatly adjusted in order to unify the exchange rates and expand exports; the mechanism of competition and responsibility for profits and losses was introduced into the arena of foreign trade; the disparities in the dual-track price system were reduced; the Pudong area (in Shanghai) comprehensively implemented a policy of opening up; and other economic development zones were established one after another. The formation of the market pricing system and the relative improvement of the market system were the achievements of a series of past reforms. But we should still ask: Why did the price reforms meet failure twice during the latter part of the 1980s, but later met with success after 1989? The reason is that the state apparatus in 1989 effectively contained the social turbulence originally caused by reforms, and the new pricing system was finally formed. In other words, the new market system and critical pricing mechanism were the results of political interventions and measures. Therefore, the linked relations between political power and the market were inevitably transferred into the new economic system. In the process, income differences among each level of society, group, and region became wider, and the population of newly impoverished grew rapidly.[20] This historical transformation made the old state ideology (i.e., the socialist ideology stressed equality) contradict state practice, and the state ideology could not function. The failure of the social movement of 1989 accompanied the failure of state ideology. The iron-fisted policies that the state implemented in actuality became the means of dictatorship (compared with the means of ideology in the past) and economic reform. It showed that the role of the old state ideology had disappeared. In this situation, "neo-liberalism" was able to become a new dominant ideology, and it provided the essential guidelines and rationale for state policies, international relations, and media control. It provided the prerequisites for the system and ideology of dual roles that were adopted by some neo-liberalist intellectuals in the domestic and international media – that is, those who served as advocates of state policies and the so-called "non-governmental intellectuals."

Therefore, the events of 1989 and the changes thereafter serve as proof of the conflicting relations between market expansionism and the state. On the one hand, it is difficult to imagine how the market system can be cultivated and developed without state regulatory policies, the legal system, and political protection. On the other hand, the market system's dependency on the state served as the prerequisite for the exchange between power and the market. From this perspective we can see the historical connections between the reforms of the 1980s and those of post-1989, such as the peculiar interactive relations between the traditional socialist system and the creation of the market, and the process of market expansion depending on "anti-market" forces (state intervention).

However, after 1989, the state overcame its crisis of legitimacy through market expansion. In this sense, using the dual market/state theories cannot explain the process of market expansion in China. The theory of withdrawal of the "neo-liberal" state can explain neither the great accomplishments achieved under active state policies (e.g., pricing, industry); nor can it explain the serious exchange of power and money and the social polarization that occurred in the course of the large-scale "privatization" of state-owned assets. Thus we should not simply deny or confirm state functions, but rather we should focus on theoretical analysis of the dual functions of the state, and thereby promote the transformation of state functions so that they benefit the interests of the great majority of society. This is the real historical issue.

Second, in terms of political arrangements, the market society did not eliminate those historical conditions that the 1989 social movement was against, but rather it legalized them. After 1989, the academic rethinking of the movement had been encompassed by the theory of the "end of the history" (and unfortunately, "history" in mainland China has not ended). Few people have carefully analyzed the historical conditions and demands of the 1989 social movement.

Even more remarkable are the roles of the old dictatorship and the old language in the process of social transformation after 1989. With the successful end of the social movement, the old system with its familiar faces lost its moral rationale. But this laid the foundation for the newly dominant social system. In the post-1989 environment, the social conditions in which the state system operated have changed so dramatically that the system itself and the relation of the social interests that the state represented had to be reorganized.

In the process of the rapid development of the Chinese economy, income differences among each social stratum, group, and region became wider, and the poor population increased rapidly. This historical transformation caused the old state ideology to contradict state practices (the socialist ideology stressed equality), and the state ideology was not able to function. It is in this sense that "neo-liberalism" had become a newly dominant ideology. Therefore, the traditional theories of socialism and capitalism cannot serve as tools for historical analysis. Only from the perspective of ideological transitions can we understand the following phenomenon: the rejection of the old ideology excluded the new ideological trend of social criticism. The modes of reform and anti-reform were used to conceal the socialist factors of the 1989 movement, its democratic demands, and so on.

It was within a complex historical environment that Deng Xiaoping visited southern China to promote market reform again in 1992. His policy was welcomed broadly by local interests, intellectuals, and overseas public opinion. This reaction was understandable after three years of weak economic performance and political repression. However, remarkably, the essential factors that had caused the 1989 movement had not really been solved. Thus the main social crisis that occurred in the 1990s had close connections with the social conditions prior to 1989. We can see these connections when surveying the impact of corruption, smuggling, unfair income distribution, public decision-making influenced by interests, over-development (i.e., Shanghai and Hainan real estate), financial crises, the social welfare system, and environmental crises.

We note also the scale of these crises widening and spreading due to the impact of "globalization." For example, the corruption of the system existed because the dual-track price system had not yet been eliminated. Foreign exchange evasion and wide-scale smuggling were related to the contract system of local and department interests, and foreign trade. The financial crisis was related to speculation, profiteering in real estate, and overdevelopment. The state enterprise system was in the worst situation ever because the market was in the worst conditions ever. The corruption of the system and the sale of official titles were similar to European phenomena in the medieval age. On the one hand, this demonstrated that business-men were still in a subordinate status in the social structure, especially in relation to the state's power. Yet, on the other hand, this demonstrated that the mechanism of state power had subtly changed with the market conditions.

The influence of the business class was growing through transitions in the power structure. A new round of financial reform measures and policies generated problems similar to those of the dual-track price system, although the details and range were completely different. Many scholars have discussed such issues as unemployment, poverty, social inequality, deflation, peasant workers, and rural resources. I am not able to discuss all these points here. I have tried to demonstrate that the main problems which mainland China was facing in the 1990s were historically related to the reform policies of the 1980s. I have tried to explain how unequal market expansion promoted social polarization, damaged the foundation of social stability, and provided reasons and conditions for heightened political control and economic monopoly.

Third, the 1989 movement was an urban social movement that exposed the contradictions of the urban economic reforms, and the new social conflicts caused by urban market expansions. People usually discuss rural and urban reforms as two independent phenomena, paying little attention to the relations between the two. The participants in the 1989 movement did not consider issues pertaining to peasants, who made up the majority of the Chinese population. Rural poverty, urban expansion, and world trade were seemingly unconnected. Yet, whether in 1989 or today, this is something we must comprehend as a prerequisite to understanding inequitable market expansion in contemporary China.

Urban reforms started in 1984, and the income difference between urban and rural areas began to grow in 1985. From 1989 to 1991, the growth in peasant income basically stopped, and the income difference between urban and rural areas returned to pre-1987 levels.[21] In the latter part of the 1980s, the speed and scale of the flow of the rural population increased greatly. The serious problems with population and land were transformed into long-term social conflicts.

But why did large-scale peasant migrations occur in the 1990s? Here I will provide several reasons. First, urban reforms promoted infrastructure development, and the open-door policy attracted a large amount of foreign investments. This led to an increase in demand for labor. Second, in the process of urban reform, rural reform did not progress. On the contrary, the basic structures of the urban and rural systems not only did *not* change but they were strengthened, which accelerated the migration of the farming population. Third, the open-door policy and special zones were mainly implemented in coastal areas, which widened the difference between inland and coastal regions. Moreover, the original mechanism used by the central government to regulate economic relations among regions had been greatly changed due to the devolution of power and granting of benefits as well as the adjustment of the tax structure.

Fourth, the relaxation of the residence registration system promoted the commercialization of rural labor, but it did not form a new system, and a proper labor protection policy was not implemented to meet the changing conditions. Thus, given the situation of deflation and economic stagnation, local urban governments vigorously restricted population migration, strengthened local protection, and re-implemented the policy of identification discrimination. Urban market expansion required a nationwide supply of salary-earning labor. This was the main driving force that resulted in the relaxation of the residence registration system. Yet simultaneously, the total relaxation of the residence registration system made unemployment among the urban population increase rapidly, causing urban governments to develop policies of local protection (demonstrated in various urban subsidies, the educational system, housing system, and so on), and to re-implement identification discrimination. In such a situation, in addition to the collapse of rural society, we find continuous inequality and the rise of the crime rate. What else could we expect? The ambiguous situation of freedom/non-freedom for the rural population guaranteed the flow of labor supply; yet, at the same time, it limited the pressure on urban society caused by population migration. This is the essential prerequisite of the phenomenon of "unequal development" in contemporary China.

The following typical examples demonstrate the systematic conditions that have formed urban–rural relations. In 1993, the state's raising of the price of grain, the growth of township and villlage enterprises, and the outward migration of rural labor resulted in increased rural income. However, from 1996 to 1999 (especially after the financial crisis) the efficiency of township and village enterprises was reduced. Surplus labor developed in urban areas, and some workers in township and village enterprises returned to rural areas. In many areas, because of migration and overdevelopment, the original structures of rural areas could hardly be recovered. This was a very serious problem. On the one hand, cultivated land was shrinking, but the rural population had increased by more than seventy-eight million (compared to the figures for 1978). On the other hand, because of the lack of labor protection and the limitation of the residence registration system, peasant workers had to migrate back and forth with the rise and fall of the urban economy.

Currently, one-tenth of the population of mainland China is migrating through the provinces. If we add the population flowing within provinces, the figure will be even larger.[22] The differences between urban and rural reforms mainly illustrate issues concerning equality. According to experts on rural issues, the key problems of the rural crisis today are the "separate governance of urban and rural areas, and the implementation of two policies in one country."[23] The inequality of the system was the prerequisite of urban market expansion and economic development. It will continue to have very important and unexpected impacts on the transformation of the social structures in urban and rural areas.

Rural problems were not the direct causes of the 1989 social crisis.[24] However, the contemporary rural crisis arose in conditions resembling 1989; that is, urban market expansionism. Unequal market expansion transformed peasants and land into partially free commodities, and damaged social organization and rural society's self-recovery capability. The growth of poverty and local tax in contemporary China results from rapid increases in the unemployed population. The development of international trade and urban expansion pushed up employment figures. International trade and urban expansion has become more unstable, and even a small change can cause the unemployed population to greatly increase.

Observing the unemployed population of rural areas, we can see the great potential of globalization and the neo-liberalist market to create poverty. Amartya Sen notes two important aspects in the theory of "free development"; that is, on the one hand, labor should be liberated from all kinds of restrictions and it should be allowed to enter the labor market. On the other hand, this process should not exclude social support, public control, or state intervention. In the age of multinational production and consumption, this idea needs to be developed and rethought. First, rural labor and the mechanism for its protection are key issues for understanding the relations between the market system and labor contract freedom. Labor contract freedom (such as immigration freedom) is one of the main standards by which to judge if the market arrangement in the contemporary world is a real free-market arrangement. Therefore, labor contract freedom should be implemented not only nationally, but also in the relations of the global economy.

Second, one of the crucial driving forces of capitalist market expansionism is the coexistence of free labor and non-free labor. The relations between free and non-free conditions and social development need to be studied. The free flow of labor is not random; rather, it should have a broad systematic arrangement that vigorously eliminates inequity as a prerequisite.

Third, market expansion means that trade activities penetrate every field of life. It destroys the original social structure (such as community and its value), and regards the living style of communities (such as those of minorities) as inferior. In this sense, focusing only on labor contract freedom, and not considering the relations between development and social condition, may result in social disintegration.

The free flow of labor, public control, and state intervention are related to the prerequisites for the market system. How to limit the destruction caused by market expansion on the environment, traditions, customs, ceremonies and alternative lifestyles and values is an important issue that needs to be studied. It is also a necessary step to attain "freedom" from certain restrictions, especially from a single economy. Therefore, we must safeguard labor contract freedom, social equity, and respect for diverse cultures. Most of all, in contemporary China, we must pay attention to the relations between rural and urban areas. From a more radical perspective, labor contract freedom (that is, exchange relations that take the form of individual labor contracts) replaced the political dependency or the coercive status system with the extortion of the surplus value that people created. This historical progress cannot replace the rethinking of the relations of the market contract (for example, note the emergence of slave labor in the form of contracts in Chinese coastal areas).

Fourth, the 1989 movement tried to promote organic interaction between society and the state in the form of mass participation, but after 1989 the market–state interactive mechanism replaced the state–society interactive process. In "neo-liberal" discussions, social concepts were gradually replaced by market concepts. The basic driving force that promoted the reform of the state mechanism and the transformation of the legal system was neither "society" nor the "masses," but rather the domestic and international markets. Thus the meaning of "politics" itself had greatly changed.

The state was the main market regulator, and it implemented the reorganization of the legal system according to WTO regulations. Certain issues need to be discussed in such a situation such as the relations among social movements, crises of reform, and the role of the state. After 1989, under the slogan of "anti-radicalism," the gradual, formalist democratic view replaced the mass-participant democratic view. This excluded the real driving force of democratic practice in theory, and the category of democracy no longer included the social protection movements of each social stratum.

When privatization becomes a trend, and private property rights becomes a crucial aspect of constitutional reform, it is necessary to differentiate two forms of privatization. One type consists of the non-governmental economy developed on the basis of civil social relations and small markets, such as the market relation formed by the link of region and blood ties in the Wenzhou area. Its market expansion was promoted by small commodity production and low-profit produc- tion. This economic model demonstrated strong vitality during the financial crisis. The other type encompasses denationalization directed by state policies, including the processing of illegal losses and transfer of large amounts of state assets. Corruption, high unemployment, social inequity, and the collapse of social welfare in contemporary China occurred while the nation was in the process of "privatization." This is reorganization in the form of "state withdrawal."

In the sense described above, we must make three basic distinctions. First, there is a distinction between the concept of a free-competition market (or self-adjusting market) and the formation and operation of the modern market economy. Second, there is a distinction between the ideology of the neo-liberal market (with frequent demands for the withdrawal of the state) and the neo-liberal market order and economic policy (often illustrating the dependency on state policy and power). Third, there is a distinction between the market category and social category.

According to the first distinction, the market society and its rules were formed and operated in the environment characterized by state intervention, creation of systems, monopolistic relations, social customs, and historical events. Free competition was only a partial condition for the formation and operation of market society. Therefore, criticisms of the current market society and its crisis should not be regarded as the rejection of the market mechanism.

According to the second distinction, neo-liberalism demanded that the state implement a "do-nothing" policy characterized by the state abandoning its responsibilities for social welfare and protection, relinquishing the means by which to regulate market activities, and thus severing the connections between politics and economics. However, the abandonment of responsibilities itself was a type of system and policy. For example, the crisis of state enterprises and agriculture was the result of the active arrangement of the state system and policy. The slogan of opposing state intervention actually became the prerequisite for state policy. Its essence was another type of "active intervention."

According to the third distinction, market rules should not be regarded as social rules, and the social democratic mechanism should not be regarded as the market operation mechanism. Therefore, state democratization should not be regarded as the transformation of the political functions of the state into the market mechanism. The 1989 crisis proved that state-directed market expansionism caused social crises, and the social crises became the opportunity for the state to completely control society (not just the market). The market mechanism was established in the process of the complete withdrawal of society from the "political" arena.

Fifth, the contemporary reform of China was a response to the transformation of the historical environment of international society, and also resulted from the active adjustment of state foreign policy. Reform and the open-door policy are two sides of one coin. Remarkably, the concept of the open-door policy might cause one to misunderstand, and to think that China had previously completely closed the country off from international exchange. Here, it is necessary to discuss briefly the relations between the Cold War arrangement and Chinese foreign policy.

First, the conflicts between China and the West, especially the United States, were closely related to the Chinese Communist Party that was in power. The Cold War after World War II and the hot war situation provided an important background for the foreign policy of mainland China. A series of events divided Asia into different worlds: the Korean War in the 1950s, the blockade of the Taiwan

Strait by the Seventh Fleet, the Indonesian military coup in the 1960s and the waves of anti-Chinese movements afterwards, the Vietnam War, Indochina War, and so on. Because of ideological and geopolitical considerations, China started to seek allies among the Soviet Union, Eastern Europe, and other Asian countries.

Second, China maintained allied relations with the Soviet Union and Eastern Europe until the emergence of the crisis between China and the Soviet Union in the latter part of the 1950s. After the split between China and the Soviet Union, China continued to implement its foreign policy formed after the Bandung Conference. It vigorously developed its political, economic and cultural relationships with Third World countries. In 1972, the government of mainland China returned to the United Nations with the support of most of the Third World countries. In the international stage, China exhibited great success in foreign policy after the Bundung Conference, and there was broad support from the masses at home. The open-door policy began during the Cultural Revolution, and China established diplomatic relations with many countries during this period. The main driving forces that opened the door to the West were the motives to change China's strategic status in terms of relations between the East and West, and in order to establish connections with the U.S.A. in resistance against the threat of a Soviet invasion. After 1978, the Chinese government gradually abandoned the diplomatic policy that had united the Third World and the non-aligned movement, and it began to focus on establishing relationships with developed capitalist countries, such as the United States and Japan. During this period, China's open-door policy was greatly developed, especially in the economic and political fields. China established interdependent trade relations with developed countries of the West.

These relations carried certain conditions. China launched a war against Vietnam in February/March 1979. This war was totally different from all other wars since 1949, such as The War to Resist U.S. Aggression and Aid Korea, The War to Resist U.S. Aggression and Aid Vietnam, the Sino–Indian War, and the Sino–Soviet War. The direct causes of the Sino–Vietnamese war were complicated. After the unification of Vietnam, Vietnam's military might was greatly strengthened. In 1978, Vietnam and the Soviet Union signed a treaty that had a military element, *The Treaty of Mutual Assistance and Alliance between Vietnam and the Soviet Union*, and Vietnam and the Soviet Union formed a strategic threat to China from the south and north. The Vietnamese military launched a blitz and invaded Cambodia on December 25, 1978. Another very important and crucial factor was the profoundly changing relations between China and the United States. The two countries became allies against the Soviet Union and its allies. Before the Chinese government declared war against Vietnam, China and the United States published a bulletin announcing the establishment of diplomatic relations between the two countries.

The war itself signaled the real start of China participating in the economic order guided by the United States. From another perspective, it demonstrated the historical connections between the market principle and violence, between the open-door policy and the structure of global power. From this moment on, the international policy of socialist countries gradually withdrew from the historical stage. China's foreign policy had changed from opening in one direction toward opening in another single direction; that is, to the West (including Japan and other developed regions). Nothing could be clearer than the international reactions after a NATO (the United States) fighter plane bombed the Chinese Embassy in Yugoslavia on May 8, 1999. In the UN meeting which discussed the bombing, Western allies had their own stand on the issue, and the Third World countries, and even the traditional allies of China, were not willing to support China.

The 1980s policy of opening up to the outside world helped to liberate many from past restrictions and impacts of the Cultural Revolution, and it received a wide welcome from society, especially from intellectuals. Many intellectuals, including myself, have positive comments to make about the reforms and the open-door policy. Any criticism of contemporary China should not be directed at the remarkable achievements of the Chinese reforms. However, for the sake of historical analysis, we have to pay attention to the profound and complex historical impacts, because this exposes the one-sidedness created by China's state ideology from the perspective of the world.

As a generation that grew up after the Cultural Revolution, China's main knowledge about the world was only about the West and the United States (i.e., a one-sided knowledge). The societies and cultures with which we had been familiar are now no longer popular, such as the cultures and societies of Asia, Africa, Latin America, and Eastern and Southern Europe. The rethinking that occurred in the 1980s, including literary works, consisted mainly of rethinking the Cultural Revolution, and not rethinking the war and international relations. The denial of the Cultural Revolution became a tool for safeguarding the dominant ideology and state policy. Henceforward, this way of thinking became popular. Criticism of the current situation was regarded as a resurgence of the Cultural Revolution, and was therefore not seen as reasonable.

Although China had experienced decades of reform and opening up, from the 1980s to the early part of the 1990s, the range of intellectual discussion was still limited to the issue of national modernization, and lacking an international perspective. Therefore, the issues of nationalism and globalization could not be broached within the arena of the issue of democracy. This ideological situation explains why intellectuals could not find any resources to criticize the driving forces and failures of the 1989 movement. It also explains why people understood global-ization and market experience only from the historical perspective of the United States, Western Europe, Japan, and the "four small dragons" of East Asia (i.e., the developed capitalist areas), without taking into account the problems and experiences of India, the Middle East, Africa, and Latin America. Finally, this situation explains why intellectuals could not understand the different social conditions and goals of those movements when the 1989 social movement had celebrated Gorbachev's new ideology, the Philippines' democratic movement, and the student movement in South Korea.

Based on the above analysis, I propose several main directions of social trans-formation. First, the economic inequity caused by market expansionism always has close connections with political, economic, cultural, and other inequities. Therefore, the struggle for freedom must also be a simultaneous struggle for social equality, including in the areas of labor contract freedom, trade freedom, political freedom, and so on. The theory that posits antagonism between demands of equality and freedom should be rejected. Second, the resistance against the monopolistic and dominant market tyranny should not be regarded simply as an "anti-market" struggle, because the social struggle itself contains factors that strive for fairness in market competition and economic democracy. Third, the resistance against economic hegemony and multinational monopoly should not be regarded as a call to close the country to international intercourse.

A degree of trade protection, to some extent, does not mean an "anti-market" approach. The social movements surrounding the World Trade Organization (WTO) and the struggles between rich and poor countries during WTO negotiations demonstrate a new mode of struggle. This struggle does not totally oppose international organizations and regulation, but rather it promotes the democratization of international institutions and regulations (including WTO), and the correlation of domestic economic justice with international economic justice.

Fourth, the maintenance of the economy always involves the political, economic, cultural, and social spheres. The struggle for fair market competition should not be regarded as the abandonment of the state's political system, social customs, and any regulatory mechanism. On the contrary, the improvement of market conditions is directed at reforming, limiting, and expanding those systems in order to create the conditions of fair trade. In this sense, the struggle for social equality and fair market competition should not be regarded as anti-state interventionism. Rather, it should be regarded as the demand for social democracy; that is, the effort of preventing the state from becoming a protector of domestic and multinational monopolies. Here, participatory democracy is still the real driving force of contemporary democracy.

The theory that posits antagonism between participatory democracy and procedural democracy must be rejected. The struggle for freedom will inevitably be shown as the struggle for democracy and equality in any category, whether in terms of nation-states or in terms of the world market. I summarize these intellectual trends as ways of thinking about a market democratic system, about social development, and not just about economic development. Only in this framework can the struggle for economic justice connect with the struggle for social justice and political democracy.

Notes

1 The socialist tendency I point out here is not the economic mode of the state with the characteristic of the planned economy. Rather, it is the social protection movement in the process of new market expansionism. It naturally tends to ask for social equality and justice, and requires social democracy to achieve its goals. In the post-socialist environment, the mobilization of the movement was also influenced by socialist value.

2 According to sociologists, the system that "separated urban residents from peasants" manifests the following four aspects. First, we see a difference in political power; that

is, peasants accepted the complete leadership of the government in the arena of politics, economics, and culture, while the government officials and staff at each level belonged to the non-agricultural population. Second, we see a difference in economic status; that is, the pricing system creates a difference between industrial and agricultural prices, thus resulting in the accumulation of capital for the development of urban industries, monopolization of economic resources and opportunities for development, and limitation of the establishment of rural industries. Third, we see a difference in income; that is, the income difference between urban and rural areas was as high as 3:1 to 6:1. Fourth, we see a difference in the welfare system; that is, the majority of urban residents (employees or cadres who worked for the state or collective units) enjoyed lifelong free medical care, retirement pensions, and stable supplies of grain, vegetable oil, and meat, but peasants were not eligible for any of these welfare benefits. Fifth, we see a difference in social status; that is, the social status of urban residents was much higher than those of peasants. See Wang Hansheng and Zhang Xinxiang, "Changes in the Chinese Social Strata Since Liberation," *Sociological Studies* 6 (1993); Li Qiang, "Report on Changes in the Social Strata of Contemporary China," in *Report on Classes and Strata in China's New Stage* (Shenyang: Liaoning People's Press, 1995), pp. 65–67; summary and commentary of Zhang Wanli, "Twenty-Year Study of Chinese Classes and Strata," *Sociological Studies* 1 (2000), p. 26.

3   Lu Xueyi divides groups of peasants into eight strata (i.e., farming labor, peasant worker, employed worker, intellectual worker, small industrial and commercial businesses and self-employed worker, private business owner, management of collective enterprise, and manager of rural society). See Lu Xueyi, "Rethinking the Peasant Issue," *Sociological Studies* 6 (1989), pp. 1–15.

4   This was the point of Liao Jili, with which Xue Muqiao agreed, in the early part of 1980. His main argument was that the development of agriculture depended mainly on planning, the promotion of peasant enthusiasm, and the development of diversified productions. It also argued that state policy did not need more energy and investment. See Guo Shuqing, *The Transition of the Economic Structure and Macro-Adjustment and Control* (Tianjin: Tianjin People's Press, 1992), p. 175.

5   Zhang Wanli summarizes it as having two aspects. First, new interests emerged from the original structure of the system. The rate at which they came to own resources increased. These were individual operators, self-employed businessmen, owners of private enterprises, senior employees of joint ventures, foreign or private enterprises, entrepreneurs of non-public business, and so on. Second, the status of interests in the structure of the original system started to change. For example, the status of peasants, cadres, professionals, workers, and so on had changed. See Zhang Wanli, " Twenty-year Study of Chinese Classes and Strata," *Sociological Studies* 1 (2000), pp. 28–29.

6   Wang Shaoguang, "The Establishment of a Powerful Democratic Country and a Discussion on the Difference Between the 'Form of Regime' and the 'State's Capability,'" *Thesis of Contemporary Chinese Study Center* 4 (1991), pp. 15–17.

7   Wang Shaoguang concluded that the reform policy of "devolving power and granting benefits" did not reduce the role of public institutions (government at various levels and branches) in the distribution of national income; rather, it reduced the role of the central government. With the increase of the financial power of local governments, their administrative capacity to intervene in economic life was not reduced, but rather strengthened. This intervention, further, was more direct than that of central government. The reform policy of "devolving power and granting benefits" did not cause the death of the traditional command economy; rather, it made the traditional system smaller. See Wang Shaoguang (1991), p. 20.

8   The income difference showed the imbalance of income between small businesspeople and employees of state enterprises. See Zhao Renwei, "Some Special Phenomena of Income Distribution during the Chinese Time of Transition," in *Studies of Income Distribution of Chinese Residents* (Beijing: Chinese Social Science Press, 1994), and

"Internal Polarization Demonstrating the Growing Gap Among Management, Technicians, and Workers," in Feng Tongqin, *The Conditions, Internal Structure, and Mutual Relations of the Chinese Employees* (Beijing: Chinese Social Science Press, 1993). The status and interests of employees, including working hours, labor protection, and labor contracts, could not be guaranteed. The people's working capacity was reduced and they could not get proper compensation. See Zhang Wanli (2000), pp. 29–30.

9 Some regard Wu Jinglian as representative of those who advocated that price reform should be coordinated with the reform of enterprises. It was well known that Li Yining advocated the stock system in the 1980s. In 1988, Wu Jinglian took the main responsibility for compiling the general report of the mid-term reform plan (*The Broad Thinking of the Chinese Reform*, Shenyang Press, 1988). Other related materials include *Collections of the General Plans of the Chinese Economic Reform* (Beijing: School of the Central Committee of the Party Press, 1987), *The Entire Design of the Chinese Economic Reform* (Beijing: China Prospect Press, 1990). See also Guo Shuqing and Liu Jirui, "Price Reform and the Guarantee of Success in the Transition of the System," *The Reform* 6 (1988), pp. 64–67.

10 Guo Shuqing (1992), p. 181.

11 Concerning the main goals of the policy of "retrenchment and consolidation of the economy," see *The Decisions of the Central Committee of the Chinese Communist Party on Further Rationalizing the Economy and Deepening Reform* (November 9, 1989), *China Financial Yearbook, 1990: The Summary of the Ten Years' Reform of the Planned System* (Beijing: China Plan Press, 1989).

12 Hu Heli, "The Estimation of the Rent Value of China in 1988," *The Comparison of Economic and Social Systems* 5 (1989), pp. 10–15.

13 Concerning changes in the cadre stratum before and after reform, see Li Qiang, *Flow and Social Strata in Contemporary China* (Beijing: China Economics Press, 1993).

14 During the time frequently called the "new period" (1978 to 1988), mid- and old-age intellectuals (including economists, scholars of political science, philosophers, historians, and literary critics) played very important roles, and most served as leaders in universities and institutes. For example, some controversial issues in the field of economics resulted from the internal debates about state policy. During the historical period, the "Leftists" and "Rightists" actually came from the internal debates and factions of the state system. Because these thinkers had important status and power, their opinions were often regarded as the differentiation between "Leftists" and "Rightists" in the academic field. Even today, some people still use the struggle of the Party to understand "Leftists" and "Rightists" in the process of Chinese social polarization. Some have even tried to use this mode to eliminate dissidents.

15 This is not because people agreed with the planned economy, but because contemporaneous problems were developing during the transformation of the system. Therefore, what people questioned was the process itself.

16 The Chinese government and the party in power always regarded the political system established in 1949 as the prerequisite for their legitimacy. Hence some were familiar with reviewing the relations between the periods of Mao and Deng from the perspective of continuity. This was one of the main reasons why some were dissatisfied with reality because of the period of Mao and the planned system. However, there were big differences in the state and main policies of the period of reform and period of Mao. Thus, when the state ideological apparatus insisted on ideological continuity, the contradictions between it and the state reform policy were completely exposed. The double legitimacy of the state ideological apparatus and the party in power (the Marxist party and the party that promoted the reform of the market economy) made the criticism against the state unclear; that is, the movement often criticized the current state policy and practice in the name of adopting an approach of "opposing the old system." As for 1989, the criticism movement, mobilized by slogans of anti-"official profiteers,"

anti-"corruption," and anti-"prince party," cannot be summarized as a criticism against the traditional socialist state; rather, it was criticism of a state that was in the process of reform, or a double criticism.

17 For example, the meeting attended by intellectuals at the *Guangming Daily*, which was later published as an announcement. Students began a hunger strike in May 1989.

18 So-called "neo-liberalism" refers to a type of ideology. Although there are many overlapping areas between the views of individual scholars and the ideology presented in this chapter, the focus of my analysis is not the views of certain individuals. The concept of ideology refers to a dominant way of thinking and it can transform the way people think. For example, after China and the United States signed a WTO agreement, every media source celebrated the news, and this caused a wide social reaction. However, common people, even intellectuals, did not understand all aspects of the agreement, yet why were they so excited and happy? Without the market and development ideologies, it is very hard for us to understand this phenomenon. After 1989, the state ideological apparatus continued to operate, but, when compared with that of the time of Mao, the modern state ideological apparatus was not able to function effectively. It was able to depend on only administrative and mandatory methods to deal with "cases of violation." We may say that, at least, state ideology had two aspects; that is, the aspect of market and development, and the aspect of traditional socialist ideology. The latter had been transformed into an invincible and extremely rigid propaganda.

19 At the same time, this shows that the criticism of the devolution of power and granting of benefits was not a fundamental criticism. Within the background of the failure of the traditional planned system, it was necessary to decentralize power. The key was to arrange and assure transparency and fairness in the redistribution of social assets through a democratic policy, ensuring that the decentralization of power did not centralize some power at another level, and achieving a balance between state regulation and the market.

20 The "Income Distribution" Study Group of the Economic Institute of the Chinese Academy of Social Sciences (Zhao Renwei *et al.*) summarized the income difference between farmers who conducted farm production and other members of the rural population. The income difference between the farmers who conducted farm production and workers employed at town enterprises was 1:1 to 2; between farmers and workers employed by business and the service industry was 1:2 to 5; between farmers and businessmen in the transportation business and construction workers in rural areas was 1:5 to 8. Peasant income per capita in 1980 was 191.33 Yuan. The ratio of peasant income in the eastern, central, and western regions of China (if the western region is 1) was 1.39: 1.11:1. In 1993, peasant income per capita grew to 921 Yuan, but the ratio of income among the eastern, central, and western regions became 2.25:1.75:1. The income for each area was, respectively, 1380 Yuan, 786 Yuan, and 604 Yuan.

The income difference between employees and employers varied according to the number of employees hired by employers, but the income difference grew rapidly. The income difference among urban residents also increased, and demonstrated the following aspects.

First, the income difference among regions had grown. For example, the income difference between residents in the western and eastern regions was 80 Yuan, between residents of the central and eastern regions it was 50 Yuan (they were, respectively, 458 Yuan, 493 Yuan, and 543 Yuan). In 1994, the incomes of the three regions grew to 2402, 2805, and 4018 Yuan, respectively. The income differences grew to 1616 and 1213 Yuan, respectively. The income differences grew 14.2 times and 32.3 times, respectively, when compared with past figures.

Second, the income difference among workers in different industries grew. For example, the income of those in the financial and insurance industries exceeded the income of those whose income was higher in the past in the power, gas, and water industries, and was 2.4 times the income of workers in farming, forestry, animal husbandry, sideline occupations, and fishery industries. The absolute value of the income difference between them was even larger.

Third, the income difference among workers employed by different ownerships grew. For example, the wage per capita of workers in joint venture, foreign, and cooperative enterprises was 1527 Yuan, or 1.14 times the wage per capita of workers nationwide. The absolute value of the income difference between the two was 200 Yuan. From January to February 1994, the income per capita of workers in joint venture, foreign, and cooperative enterprises continued to grow, and by that time the average growth rate of the nationwide income was 26.3 per cent, but the growth rate of the income of workers in joint venture, foreign, and cooperative enterprises rose to 92.2 per cent, and increased 41.7 per cent, compared with the same period the previous year. In 2000, the income per capita of workers in joint venture, foreign, cooperative, and town enterprises rose to two to three times or more of the income per capita of workers in Party and government institutions, research institutes, and so on.

Fourth, the income difference among different enterprises groups increased. This situation may be divided into two aspects. One was the income difference between employees and employers in joint venture, foreign, and cooperative enterprises, and the other was the income difference among the heads of factories, managers, and employees. The annual income per capita of Chinese managers in foreign enterprises rose to US$6600, and was around ten times the average income of the common worker. In addition, the income difference between management and workers in public ownership enterprises was quite large. It became a common phenomenon to see management getting more types of benefits in addition to their salaries.

Fifth, the poor strata emerged. They mainly included workers who had lost their jobs in the process of enterprise reform, part-time workers, employees in enterprises that had suspended production or half-suspended production, retired workers, workers who depended on government financial aid, and the non-urban resident poor population who flowed into towns and cities. At the end of 1994, the ratio of workers who lived a poor life had increased from 5 per cent to 8 per cent. There were 100 million people living in poverty, and they constituted 8 per cent of the population of mainland China.

This research comes from Zhao Renwei, *Studies on Income Distribution of Chinese Residents* (Beijing: Chinese Academy of Social Sciences Press, 1994), and Zhang Wanli (2000), p. 36.

21 Lu Mai, "Never Forget Rural Development"; see the report by Luo Yuping, *Sanlian Life Weekly* 14 (July 31, 1998, issue 68), p. 26.

22 In recent years, an increasing number of scholars have become concerned with social issues such as "urbanization" and the "abandonment of agriculture." One reason stems from the stagnant economy making surplus labor a serious social problem. Hence, discussions on the "big issue of small cities and towns" (Fei Xiaotong) was gradually replaced by discussions on urbanization. See Wang Ying, "Retrospect and Prospect of Studies of Urban Development," *Sociological Studies* 1 (2000), pp. 65–75.

23 Lu Xueyi, "Ridding the Dilemma of 'Separate Governance Between Urban and Rural Areas and the Implementation of Two Policies in A Country,'" *Reading* 5 (2000), p. 39.

24 Few economists and reform experimenters paid attention to rural reform and crisis. However, after the financial crisis of 1997, the growth of the Chinese economy slowed down, deflation emerged, and people paid more attention to peasant issues. Yet some scholars who have paid attention to peasant issues have taken the perspective of the stimulation of economic development and relief of pressure on cities. They have raised peasant issues from the perspective of economic growth, especially urban economic growth, and not from the perspective of peasant freedom, rights, and social equality. In other words, the freedom of labor contract and social equality of peasants received attention only during a stagnant economy.

6 China's economic transition, social justice and democratization at the turn of the century

Qin Hui

The Chinese version of Stolypin's Reform

The change in duration of the Chinese economy and society entered a new stage after 1989. The 1989 movement embodied the process of "purging ideology of its demons" not only for civil society but also for the party in power. It could be said that this movement had a greater impact on the party in power than it did on most common people, with the exception of the dissidents. As the ideology of the revolutionary party gradually fell to pieces, the party in power's ruling interest grew more urgent. As Geliemakin, the fundamentalist conservative in power for a short time in Imperial Russia after the revolution in 1905, was soon replaced by Stolypin and the "faction of police reform," the popularity of the Chinese fundamentalist leftists was also short-lived. Since Deng Xiaoping's "Talks During the Southern Inspection," the Chinese version of Stolypin's Reform emerged as a combination of ruling with an iron hand politically and granting increased economic freedom.

From 1992 to 1997 policies concerning foreign investment, township enterprises, and private enterprises were greatly relaxed, and the Chinese economy underwent three important breakthroughs. The first was the cancellation of the food coupon system. The end of the "coupon economy" heralded the transformation from the age of shortage of the state-controlled economy to the age of surplus of the market economy. The second breakthrough was the opening of the stock-market, which soon resulted in a fanatic "stock zealotry." Although it was not a normal capitalist market, it was surely not a self-styled gambling place. The Chinese stock-market initiated a mechanism that had two functions: transforming public property rights to private property rights, and private property rights to public property rights. It promoted the Chinese primitive accumulation from the stage of "raiding the national treasury" to the stage of "raiding the private sector through the medium of the national treasury." The third breakthrough was in the southern part of Jiangsu Province, where the developed areas of town and township enterprises, characterized by the traditional collective economy (the so-called "local state corporatism"), experienced a rapid campaign of privatization.[1] With the disappearance of this "Sunan [south Jiangsu] model," the Regulation of Town and Township Enterprises, implemented in 1997, first defined the meaning of the previously unspecified property rights within the context of "town and township enterprises." From then on, the theory that the town and township enterprises belonged to the collective economy was a thing of the past. With the promotion of the successful change of property rights in town and township enterprises, in some areas (such as Zhucheng in Shandong Province) all the local state enterprises were sold or even given away.

The Fifteenth Congress of the Chinese Communist Party in 1997 started a new stage. This conference sounded the clarion call to win the battle of "the reform of state enterprises." During the period of the Fifteenth Party Congress, the title of an article in the *Chinese Economic Times* about the reform of state enterprises, "Anything Goes," accurately reflected the atmosphere. From then on, the central cities and many provinces in China bid a final farewell to the concept of "state property rights," a rare demonstration in the history of privatization in the world.

Many provinces and cities announced one after another that they would not build state enterprises in the future. Hunan Province took the initiative that year, and other provinces, such as Shenzhen, Wuhan, Sichuan, and Chongqing, followed immediately, adding their own statements. Shenzhen City put forward that, in principle, it would not build state enterprises in the future, and that the state economy should be withdrawn from general fields of competition. The state property rights should be withdrawn from small enterprises during the period of that year and the following year. It would take five to eight years for state property rights to be withdrawn from medium to large enterprises.[2] In 1999, Wuhan City announced that it would not build new state enterprises in the future. The future model for state investment entering new fields would be to allocate some state capital as the guidance or coordination fund, encourage and introduce foreign and non-governmental capital economic involvement, and vigorously promote the combined economy.[3]

At the beginning of the new millennium, the four major municipalities directly under the Chinese central government pledged at the same time that they would withdraw state capital from general fields of competition. After New Year's Day of 2000, Chongqing City announced first that it would not build new state enterprises in the field of industry. Instead, it would vigorously develop industry composed of private enterprises as an important measure for adjustment of the structure of property rights in the city. State capital comprised more than 80 per cent of the entire industry in the city, and so the leadership took four main measures. It allowed the state enterprises with long-term losses or with no hope of going into bankruptcy or being taken over and sold, and withdrew state capital from them; it also withdrew entire or partial state capital from large and medium-sized state enterprises by introducing investments, transforming along the lines of a corporate system, sharing stocks, and so on. In the field of competition, it made more favorable policies to attract private enterprises and encourage them to take over and reorganize state enterprises; it chose some state enterprises that showed potential but faced difficult situations and provided them with favorable policies, then sold them to other businesses or to foreign enterprises that were in a superior economic situation.

One week later, Beijing City announced that it would not allow state-owned companies in industry to be built in Beijing City from that year on.[4] At the same time, Shanghai City also announced that it would not build small state enterprises in the future. Tianjin City announced in detail that it would make major adjustments in state industry. Of the thirty-three industries that involved state-owned enterprises, state enterprises were entirely withdrawn from five industries, mostly withdrawn from four, and partially withdrawn from seventeen.[5] The media thought that it was extremely unusual for the four big municipalities directly under the central government to make their announcements at the same time. To assure efficient withdrawal of state capital, Beijing City pointed out that state capital, in principle, should be mainly in the form of stock control. If the state needed to control stocks absolutely under special circumstances, the percentage of stock control should not exceed 51 per cent.[6] With the promotion of the four big municipalities, provinces such as Shandong, Jilin and Liaoning also announced in that year that they would not build state enterprises, and state capital should be withdrawn within a time limit. Some of these provinces are areas where many traditional heavy industries are located. Those announcements also included regulations about the maximum percentage of state capital (contrary to the regulations of the Eastern European countries that defined the minimum percentage of state capital). For example, Shandong Province regulated that state capital could have absolute control of stocks in public fields such as the infrastructure of transportation and municipal undertakings (stock rights of the state could exceed 50 per cent). In core enterprises of new and high-tech industries, such as electronic and biological industries, and in tourist enterprises, state capital could control stocks (the stock rights of the state could exceed 35 per cent). The state capital in other enterprises should be withdrawn more quickly (i.e., the percentage of state-owned shares should be lower than 35 per cent). The core enterprises in industries such as chemical, rubber, textile, clothing, engineering, electrification, metallurgical, shipyard, vehicle and parts belonged to this latter category. The percentage of state capital was greater in some industries, and some state assets could be changed into state stock rights. The other part could be controlled internally or leased to people within the enterprise in order to lower the percentage of state stocks. In general fields of competition, especially in small and medium-sized enterprises, state capital should be totally withdrawn, the goal being set at zero state property rights.[7]

At the beginning of 2002, Yunnan and Gansu Provinces announced in turn that they would never again build state enterprises.[8] Thus, with the exception of several autonomous regions in the country, most provinces pledged to eliminate state property rights. Privatization has become a worldwide trend, but it would be unusual for a Western government to pledge never again to build state enterprises. Although these announcements were skillfully worded, state property rights could never increase according to the pledges, and the minimum percentage of state capital was not regulated. What the announcements really meant was that if state capital does not increase, even if the absolute value of the remaining state capital does not change, its relative value will gradually decrease to zero over a long period of time. Therefore, those announcements mentioned above may be truly regarded as Chinese versions of declarations of privatization. In reality, in many areas the property rights reformers were bolder, simply instituting changes without reporting their actions. For example, currently, the central government does not allow foreign capital to control stocks in important state enterprises in industries such as energy, oil and chemical, iron and steel, and so on, but some provinces have allowed this foreign control for quite a long time. Shandong Province was prepared to change the schedule and move the timing up for foreign capital to control stocks, and to allow foreign capital to transform state stocks and buy out the entire stocks. The officials of the Bureau of Foreign Trade and Economic Cooperation of Shandong Province indicated that this action is "legal and will not have problems." Xinhua Pharmaceutical Factory and Gongzhou Coal were on the list for change of property rights and put up for sale. They were also put on the stock-market in Hong Kong. Shandong Province was not alone in its intentions and actions, even though the sale of local state enterprises might very well violate the policy of the central government.[9]

The deal of caretakers and delimitation of privatization

Under China's system, primitive accumulation, whether "socialist" or "capitalist," has been promoted with an unhesitating iron hand. While many Chinese writers were busy criticizing the "radical reform" in Eastern Europe (now given the derogatory term "shock treatment") – the leftists thought that it was too liberal, and the rightists thought that it was too populist – many major actions that would surprise the Eastern Europeans were meanwhile beginning in China, either slowly and quietly or quickly and vigorously.

The campaign to change property right in town and township enterprises demonstrates the Chinese style of "shock treatment. At the end of 1996 (December 30)" Jiangyin City of Jiangsu Province put forward the task of changing property rights for all small and medium enterprises before the end of September 1997. The detailed arrangements were:

1   During the experimental stage (December 1996 to March 1997), the city would fully implement and attempt to accomplish the property rights reform for all "small enterprises with losses," "small enterprises on the black list" and the "tiny enterprises." And it would start to experiment in three to five medium enterprises.

2   During the promotional stage (April to September 1997), the city would fully implement the change of property rights in all medium-sized enterprises. "All townships are required to follow the policy of the committee of the city." It would concentrate energy, time, and staff, coordinate from high level to low level, and basically accomplish the reform of change of property rights for small and medium enterprises.

3   During the inspection and improvement stage (October to December 1997), the city would conduct checks and approve tasks.

4   During the stage of review and promotion (1998 to 2000), the city would deal with the issues of major enterprises and groups of enterprises, and completely establish the modern system of enterprise.[10]

Jiangyin was not alone in acting with this type of boldness. In 1996, Wuxian City put forward that it would "accelerate the reform of change of property rights for town and township enterprises, from individual to overall enterprises, and promote the reform in a full scale, taking a year or a little bit longer time to accomplish the reform of change of property rights for town and township enterprises." By that time, the documents also defined the modes of property rights change: the systems of leasing and contract, the risk mortgage that was the improved model of leasing and contract, the contract of asset increase, even the stock cooperation system that "had no clear property rights" should be abandoned after the reform in order to completely clarify property rights. To achieve this goal, the county would rather abandon contracts still in force:

> Some of the leased or contracted enterprises are in conditions suitable for reform. Their villages and township need the reform. So, although their contracts have not yet expired, they can consult with their village and town authorities, end their leasing and other contracts, and begin the process of changing over property rights. They should encourage the management in enterprises to hold the majority of stocks, and encourage the legal representatives of enterprises to hold the majority of stocks among management.[11]

This complete reform of property rights, implemented in detail within a year or nine months, makes the "most radical" plan such as the "five hundred days' plans" of Central and Eastern Europe seem very humble by comparison. What Eastern Europeans with a democratic system of government did not do, the Chinese with their oligarchic system did. People found out later that the changes of property rights in town and township enterprises were simply small experiments. The reform of state enterprises in big cities would soon hold more surprises.

On November 30, 1999, the municipal Party committee and government of Changsha City put forward the policy "Several Proposals about the Issues of Acceleration and Development of the Reform of State Enterprises" (it will be called document No. 29 below). This document required enterprises to "delimit property rights" and implement "two transformations" – one was to "transform" the nature of state enterprises through the change of property rights; the other was to "transform" the identity of state employees through a one-off compensation, and allow employees to enter the market. On January 29, 2000, the general office of the municipal government printed and distributed "The Detailed Steps of Implement of the Reform of Change of Property Right of State Enterprises in Changsha City" (the short name is document No. 3), and clarified the policy according to the principles of change of property rights given above. With the promotion of the two documents, a new wave of reform of state enterprises in Changsha began immediately. During the period of April and May, Hunan Xiangjiang Paint Group Limited Company, Changsha Tongda Limited Company, and Hunan Friendship Apollo Limited Company were established one after another. They were "transformed" from "100 per cent of state capital" to a state capital that did not control stocks or relatively control stocks. The order of the percentage of state-owned stocks in the three companies was 6 per cent, 21 per cent, and 32 per cent. The remarkable thing was that this was a typical example of the saying "beauties get married first." These three companies, with good economic benefits and large-scale production, were regarded as major enterprises needing no reform. "Tongda" was a key state-owned enterprise, one of the 500 largest machine-building enterprises in the country, and one of the ten core enterprises with superior conditions supported by Changsha City. "Xiangjiang Paint" had been on the list of the 500 enterprises with the best economic gain for years. It was at the top of the list in Changsha City for several years. "Friendship Apollo" was a very large state commercial enterprise with 5,000 employees. Its total sales in 1999 were the sixth largest in the country, and its economic gains put it in seventh position in China. This change of property rights was so rapid that no one could find precedents.

"Tongda" went through all crucial steps of the "transformation" in a period of about ten days: employees bought stocks and changed their status; the first conference of shareholders was held; and employees were re-recruited. "Xiangjiang Paint" and "Friendship Apollo" also traveled down the road of stock reform with the same speed. The move caused a chain reaction: eleven enterprises, including the listed company "Jiuzhi Tang" and the municipal water company, applied to the government to implement property rights reform.

The most remarkable breakthrough in the change of property rights was thought to be the establishment of the principle of "delimitation" of property rights. According to the accounting report at the end of 1999, with the exception of land and non-operational assets, the assets of each of the three enterprises stood at over 100 million Yuan. If these were delimited as state assets, one can imagine the difficulties for the "transformation." Document No. 29 put forward the principle of "re-delimitation of property rights," and document No. 3 clarified it further: the net assets of enterprises at the end of 1983 and the assets formed by special state appropriate funds after January 1, 1984 are defined as state assets; the net assets accumulated by profits after tax and the net assets accumulated by the enterprises with losses after tax and interest deductions are defined as the collective assets of enterprises. The "collective assets of enterprises" are calculated by taking production development funds, the new product experimentation funds, the production reserve funds, and subtracting energy and transportation funds, losses from new product experimentation (part of the floating asset), the cost of employees' benefits, and other consumption costs. Through "delimitation," the percentage of state assets of "Xiangjiang Paint" was reduced from 100 per cent to 20.53 per cent. In addition, by "eliminating bad assets and cutting unnecessary budget items," the good assets that Xiangjiang Paint could introduce to the process of change of property rights were over seventy million Yuan, and among them, the state assets totalled over fifteen million Yuan. As to the remaining state assets, according to the policy that "the property rights of the state can be bought one time at the rate of 50 per cent discount," Xiangjiang Paint bought assets worth ten million Yuan for five million Yuan. The remaining assets worth five million Yuan were put into the account of the new enterprises after the change of property rights. The total of the shares of the new company was worth sixty million Yuan. Among them, the percentage of state shares were about 8 per cent, the shares of legal representatives of community were about 7 per cent, the shares of the social legal representatives were about 3 per cent, and the shares of individual employees were about 80 per cent.

Immediately after that, the "delimited" assets of the enterprise were distributed to individuals all at one time. The principle implemented in the process was "management holds the majority of the stocks." Changsha City especially emphasized that this reform should assure that management held the majority of the stocks. Both documents No. 29 and No. 3 regulated the "structure of stock rights": when setting up shares, one should pay attention to management and encourage them to hold more stocks and to control the majority of stocks. One should avoid distributing stocks evenly; one should encourage the legal representatives of the enterprise to raise funding through many channels to buy the stocks. If they do not have enough funding, one should allow them to pay within three to five years (i.e., they could pay off with their bonuses in the future). Under the condition that individual shares may be mortgaged, the short-term loans from banks could first be listed under the name of management, and the loans could become shares. In this way, one could convert the loans into shares for the management.

Thus, through reform, the managements in the three enterprises held the majority of the stocks. When economists gave interviews, they said that the majority of stock that management held was a breakthrough of the reform of the stock system in our country. The "structure of equal stock rights" was broken, and we avoided a new "mechanism of the big rice bowl system." The model of the typical guidance of management would cause a major revolution in the structure of enterprise.[12]

Obviously, what happened in Changsha was not a "sale" as reported. If one defined those enterprises worth hundreds of millions of Yuan as state assets, it may be imagined how hard it was to realize the "transformation." It was also not a "distribution" − the state assets had not been distributed to individuals. It was "delimitation!" The so-called "delimitation" was the real administrative task. Because the amount of state assets was too great to be sold, the government simply "delimited" it from "state ownership" to ownership of the internal personnel of enterprises by way of assignment, and also regulated that bosses should hold the majority of stock among the internal personnel. This type of reform may be called "delimitation" reform. This "delimitation" defined only the investments for the past seventeen years or the initial investments when the enterprises were established as state assets. Those "accumulations" based on investments were "defined" as the assets of the internal personnel of the enterprises ("collective assets"). More than 80 per cent of the assets (in the case of Xiangjiang Paint) of the enterprise was transformed from the "state" account into the hands of the internal personnel through "delimitation." Through the sale at a discounted rate, the remaining 20 per cent of state assets was consolidated to 6 per cent; with the addition of funding that was for the sale and needed to be handed into the government, the total of state assets was 12 per cent. This means that 88 per cent of state assets were "delimited off" in a period of only ten days.

I do not know if the action was "radical" in China. I do know if the countries of the former Soviet Union and Eastern Europe that implemented "shock treatment" did it in this way. Of course, I refer to legal and above-board transactions, not to sales or secret distribution of assets under the table. In the most controversial case in Russia among the three stock plans, the maximum percentage of the "delimitation" of state assets as collective assets of enterprises was 25 per cent; another plan was that 56 per cent of state assets could be bought at discount rates. For this, privatization in Russia was ridiculed as "the privatization of internal people" and regarded as the cause of failure of the reform.

It is normal in market economies for enterprises to reward those managers who have made contributions to the enterprises with property rights in addition to salaries. But this contribution itself should not overturn the original structure of property rights of the enterprise. A capable manager should not "delimit" the enterprise of shareholders as his own because of his good performance. With the exception of special contracts made for stock rights, if a manager wants a reward of property rights, it must be granted by a board of trustees (i.e., the owners).

In Changsha City, the government now granted the reward. The problem with this arrangement was that the government itself was only the caretaker of "state" assets, not the owner. Imagine if these four enterprises were non-state companies. Would their board of trustees give up 88 per cent of the property rights to other people in ten days because of their good performance as employees? If these enterprises belong to the people who conduct the "delimitation," would the owners conduct this kind of "delimitation?"

This is the paradox in the reform of property rights: the seller does not exist. It makes no difference if it is a "sale" or "distribution" in the property rights reform, it is still a form of property transfer. However, the goal of the reform of property rights is to make property rights transactional. If property rights can be transferred, is the reform needed? If property rights are not transactional, how can reform be achieved? In logic, a transaction must include the "seller" (i.e.. the owner). State assets belong to the citizens, and the government is just the caretaker of the assets. However, under the current conditions, the reform of property rights is transacted by the caretaker, whose goal is to produce the "seller." Citizens take no part in the transaction. However, since the "seller" has not been produced, how is the "transaction" to be accomplished? There are only two ways to resolve the paradox in logic. One is to distribute state assets evenly among the citizens (like the "certificate distribution method" in Eastern Europe) in order to produce the initial "seller"; they can then conduct the transaction. The second is to establish the entrusted agency through public selection and supervision (i.e., democratic mechanism), and make the "caretaker" the legal trustee. However, this would require implementing reform of the political system.

Although the Eastern European countries made many mistakes in their reform, at least they followed those two principles legally. However, in China, the "transactions of the caretaker" do not need to be authorized or supervised. Therefore, the two principles do not even exist in legal terms. This is the reason why "privatization through delimitation," rather than "distribution" and "sale," can be conducted openly and without delays.

Given this situation, it is unreasonable to conclude that the economic transformation in Eastern Europe is capitalist while China's transformation is socialist, or to say that the former is "radical" and the latter "incremental" – all this would be extremely superficial. If we were to believe what was said, then indeed Central and Eastern Europe were radical, and China was not only not incremental, but in many aspects it almost "stopped." However, if we observe various governments' actions, the conclusions we draw are very different.

The Czech government of Klaus could be termed the most radical in words. Klaus did not like the concepts of the "socialist market economy" or the "welfare market economy." He often mentioned the concept of the "market economy" without any restrictive adjectives. But in reality, he implemented the policies of high tax and high welfare, opposed annexation and bankruptcy, protected enterprises, and practiced "over-employment." Even the vice-premier of the leftist government in neighboring Poland felt that Klaus was outrageous! In recent years, none of the major enterprises went into bankruptcy. The unemployment rate did not rise but rather fell, from 4.1 per cent in 1991 to 2.9 per cent in 1995. The increase in pensions was faster than the increase in salaries during this period, and only a few European countries experienced a similar phenomenon. The percentage of average pensions in salaries rose from 43.4 per cent in 1993 to 47.8 per cent in 1996. In 1995, social welfare in Czechoslovakia was the biggest expenditure in the government's budget, being one-third of the budgeted gross incomes. Czechoslovakia was called "the biggest social democracy in Europe."[13]

Walesa in Poland called for accelerating privatization, but the union in Gadansk Shipyard where he came from vetoed several privatization plans, until the democratic leftists who were "former communists" regained power in the government. But the shipyard had to go into bankruptcy due to the delay in economic transformation and high debts. An expert from the Central Liaison Department of the Chinese Communist Party reviewed the current laws and complained on behalf of Polish entrepreneurs that "the *Labor Law* protects the interest of employees over the interests of labor and capital combined." He thought that this was one of "lessons" to draw, and that Poland did not handle its economy well. In Poland, where the "unions controlled power" for a long time, the social protection fund of enterprises increased dramatically from the ratio of 58 per cent of employees' salary at the beginning of the economic transformation to over 90 per cent in 2001. Thus, if an employee's actual salary is US$300.00, his or her employer needs to pay US$570.00. It especially surprises the Chinese farmers that farmers in Poland (free small farmers!) could enjoy very good welfare protection. In order to maintain free medical services and pension for farmers, every employee in every industry needed to pay farmers on average US$415.00.[14] Because the "unions scared investors away" and due to the financial crisis caused by the burden of state welfare, Poland's economy was experiencing difficulties at the beginning of the century.

When the Romanian authorities tried to close the coal mine that was showing losses in the Jiu Valley before the big transformation, the miners' union resisted. After this event, the union grew. It mobilized tens of thousands of workers to demonstrate many times in the streets of the capital, causing a crisis in the government and the collapse of Peter Roman's government. The group of congressmen of the Great Romanian Party spoke for the miners' interests. Through the ten years of negotiations, the demands of the miners were "reduced" to reopening the mine, and increasing their salary (by then it was already twice the average salary in the country) by 30 per cent. In addition to unemployment relief, each unemployed worker should be given US$10,000, plus two hectares of land as "compensation." Both leftist and rightist governments could see no way out of meeting these demands.[15]

So far, although China still lists the term "privatization" as a forbidden word, actually, in the name of "clarification of property rights" and "withdrawal of state capital," any method to transform state ownership into private ownership is acceptable – "Anything Goes" as the *Chinese Economy Times* put it. The Chinese workers were notified of the new policy in these terms: "When evaluating success or failure, we are proud of our life but we need to start from the beginning again." Farmers were forbidden to "visit government officials illegally." However, bosses (especially foreign merchants and merchants from Taiwan and Hong Kong) could establish their own chambers of commerce, something that workers and farmers were not allowed to do. The official union exists in name only, and there isn't even a nominal official farmer association. Where else can one find such an ideal "environment for investment"? No wonder China has attracted far more foreign investment than Eastern Europe!

The two stages of the "Chinese miracle" and minimizing the price of the transformation of the system

Even taking into account exaggerations in economic figures, the speed of growth of the Chinese economy indeed is a "miracle." Both leftist and rightist economists in the West who know only how to choose between and coordinate two systems – the democratic welfare state and the free trade state – cannot understand this miracle. In fact, neither the classic, liberal "Washington Consensus" view that emphasizes the advantage of the market mechanism, nor the Keynes–Roosevelt "Post-Washington Consensus" view that emphasizes the necessity of state control and adjustment, can explain the "miracle."

From my perspective, the formation of the "miracle" may be divided into two stages. In the 1980s, mainly due to the extreme inefficiency of the Chinese mandatory economy compared with the reasonable planned economy of Eastern Europe, the Chinese economy could be "abandoned without cost." It made no difference if China switched to the reasonable planned economy or to a market mechanism. Either way, the economy would benefit.

The majority of citizens (farmers) were in a "negative Pareto process" of being bound by the state but getting no protection from the state (which is different from the coordinated system of binding and protection in Eastern Europe), which led to "escaping from a negative Pareto process" (in which everyone benefits). By comparison, the vast majority in Central and Eastern Europe went from one non-Pareto process to another.

In the 1990s, the extreme unfairness of the commune system compared with fairness and reform, and the extreme inefficiency of the "campaign economy" compared with efficiency and reform, reached their time limits. At that time, China's advantage compared with Central and Eastern Europe's lay in the "Stolypin-type Reform" that was able to rule with an iron hand to reduce bargaining, and reduce the "transaction costs of system transformation."

Coase announced in that year that the strength of the "socialist" system was not the "fairness" of the system, but that it could use its centralized power to reduce the "transaction cost." On this issue, both the socialists and capitalists seem to have a common view. When Deng Xiaoping talked about the experience of Chinese reform, he said that "the biggest advantage of the current system is that if we want to take an action, and once we have made a decision, we can implement it immediately without any restrictions."[16] He said this in 1987, but in fact by that time under the influence of the "new enlightenment" there was already a fairly democratic atmosphere, and this "advantage" was not that powerful. The failure of price reform "storming the pass" in 1988 was due to the "restrictions."

After 1989, this "advantage" without "restrictions" recovered to the level it had been in the past. The "socialist primitive accumulation" of the past exemplifies this advantage, since the government "rushed into" the mandatory economy without hesitation or restriction at cost to the lives of tens of millions of people. So far, the power of this "advantage" of the old oligarchic primitive accumulation is once again showing strength. Public assets can be given to anyone by the authorities. Workers can be kicked out at any time "without any restriction." Did any country that had experienced the headache of the "restrictions" of unions, non-governmental media, and opposition groups have such luck?

The economist Li Yining, who has a very positive perspective on the current situation in China, said recently that the goal should not be equality. It is not possible for everyone to have equal opportunities. We should advocate the Chinese concept of fairness: we are one big family. The parents appoint the second eldest child to enroll in a university, and the eldest child to work to accommodate the second eldest child. Because they have the sense of "group identification," they do not feel there is any unfairness.[17] This kind of "Chinese fairness" does not work at all in the Eastern European countries that are unfortunately infected by the "Western pestilence" of liberalism or social democracy.

The kind of Chinese logic that insists "If a father wants his son to be poor, then he must be poor; if a king wants his subordinate to be rich, then he must be rich" enables China to conduct primitive accumulation much faster than the Eastern European countries that are experiencing democratic transformation. Scholars across the world have commented on this. For example, Shaba, the Hungarian economist, said in a teasing tone that the relatively successful operation of the planned economies in the past in Eastern Europe has made the transformation of the system more difficult. But the outrageous actions of the Cultural Revolution made the transformation in China seem like "a happy sightseeing trip, not a painful long march." China does not need to carry out social welfare, but Eastern Europe, especially those Eastern European countries that urgently want to join the European Union, had to maintain welfare systems similar to those of the other countries of the European Union. China could satisfy the International Monetary Fund more easily than Eastern Europe. "The managers who are Party members in Shanghai and Guangdong are infatuated with the spontaneous privatization achieved through partners in Hong Kong. Therefore, they will not face much hostility when they walk down the path directed by the International Monetary Fund, which is not the experience of managers in the Eastern European countries."[18] And so on.

The two stages of transformation have, without a doubt, caused great changes in Chinese society. First, the party in power itself has changed. It is well known that the "July 1 Speech" in 2001 caused a sensation. But no matter that the leftists and rightists made positive or negative comments about it, what the speech reflected was a reality that already existed.

The Report of Study of the Social Strata in Contemporary China,[19] which was the major achievement of studies of the Chinese Academy of Social Sciences, stated that the percentage of Party members who owned private enterprises had reached 19.8 per cent, which was a much higher percentage than among workers and farmers. I think that the percentage must be at least this high, based on the materials from different regions that I have read.

The organization department of the municipal Party committee of Huangshi City in Hubei Province conducted a survey in the fall of 2001. The subjects of the survey were private owners with fixed assets worth over 500,000 Yuan, annual incomes over five million Yuan, and over twenty-five employees. There were a total of 355. Among them, Party members numbered 193, or 54.4 per cent. This high percentage was not the result of "allowing capitalists to join the Party," but rather "allowing Party members to become capitalists." Among the 335 private enterprises, 110 were "enterprises that had undergone the transformation of the system." Their bosses basically were the former leaders of state enterprises (i.e., they were mostly all Party members).[20] According to statistics compiled by a department in Jiangsu Province at the end of 1999, three cities, including Lianyungang, were home to 858 private owners who were Party members. The percentage of Party members among the private owners was 42 per cent.[21] The suburb of Yangzhou City of Jiangsu Province had a total of 627 private owners and private shareholders who controlled stocks in stock companies. Among them, 148 were Party members, with a percentage of 24 per cent. Among the private owners, the percentage of Party members was 15 per cent, and among the shareholders who controlled stocks, the percentage of Party members was 94.4 per cent. Almost all were Party members. Moreover, the bigger the enterprises, the higher the percentage of the private owners who were Party members. Twenty-four per cent of Party members among the private owners controlled more than half of the assets of the private enterprises and one-third of the assets of both the public and private enterprises in the region. The total of taxes which their enterprises paid was 52.3 per cent of the total of taxes of all of enterprises paid in the region. The organization department of the Party committee in the region reported, "To some extent, the party members who are private owners have taken the responsibilities and authorities that the cadres had during the age of the planned economy."[22] In the most developed three townships in Yongkang City in Zhejiang Province, in as early as the winter of 1996, about 20 per cent of the Party branch secretaries in rural areas were private owners. Among the seventy-two Party branch secretaries in the area of Z town, twenty-three were private owners, comprising 32 per cent of all private owners in the area. Twenty-one people (i.e., 29 per cent of the seventy-two secretaries) managed both the public and private enterprises, and were developing them in the direction of purely private ownership. In other words, three out of five Party branch secretaries in the town were, or were going to be, "red capitalists." On the other hand, G town recruited sixty-one new Party members in the past three years. Among them, private owners numbered thirty-five, 57 per cent of new party members.[23]

Thus, in inland and coastal areas alike, private owners made up the largest group within the Party after the groups comprised of Party personnel, the government, and the armed forces. Although it was impossible for the percentage of Party members who were private owners to be highest in the Party as a whole, the percentage was much higher than the percentages of the Party members made up of ordinary people and workers. Five years before the "July 1 Speech," some places already allowed private owners to join the Party. It became common to see private owners in leadership positions of Party branches. The "July 1 Speech" simply acknowledged this *fait accompli*.

This perspective is practical and realistic. Setting aside any discussion about the fairness of the process of Party members becoming private bosses (about which, naturally, there is serious doubt) and about the political outcome of Party members controlling power and assets without restriction under a non-democratic system, the phenomenon of Party members becoming property owners is not really any setback at all. After all, they have property responsibilities as well as rights, compared with a situation where officials had the power to control and manage assets but did not take responsibility for the assets. However, some foreign public observers have expressed the opinion that the Chinese Communist Party may become a social democratic party. To deal with attacks from conservatives within the Party, some Party members have pretended to be serious in discussing the difference between themselves and the social democratic party. Actually, the foreign media has exaggerated the situation. In developed countries, the foundation of socialist democratic parties is the trade union (of course, not the official trade union), and the essential goals of those parties are to promote parliamentary democracy and the welfare state. So far, the Chinese Communist Party has made no progress toward the former, and has moved even further away from the latter. No matter how many private owners are Party members, the political structure has only moved from populism to oligarchy, not social democracy.

Social transformation at the end of the century: divisions of strata on top of class division

The transformation from populism to oligarchy has obviously changed the structure of the social strata in China. Ms. He Qinglian and Mr. Zhang Shuguang joined in a famous debate several years ago, which is worth mentioning here. Ms. He Qinglian quoted the large-scale survey conducted by a study group lead by Li Qiang, the famous sociologist. The survey claimed that the Gini Index of income distribution per person and per household in 1994 in China was 0.434 and 0.445: "This is more than the Gini Index of the Western countries." Mr. Zhang Shuguang did not agree with the paper at all, and called it "sentimental clamor." He thought that the survey conducted by another study group led by the economists Zhao Renwei and Li Shi was more convincing because "economists at home and abroad fully acknowledged and highly appraised it." However, if we look closely, the figures are very similar to the ones the study group led by Li Qiang came up with: the figures of the Gini Index of income distribution per Chinese person and per Chinese household, and the figure of "the average income per person and per household" were, respectively, 0.409, 0.445, and 0.444. Among them, the Gini Index based on per household by Li Qiang's group, and based on per capita by Li Shi's group, came up with the same figure (0.445).[24] The two study groups explained that their data could not count "gray income" (i.e., what the data reflected was just the prescribed minimum of the actual change of income). The different surveys conducted by the sociologists and economists confirm the same fact that, as early as 1994, the inequality of income distribution of China obviously exceeded America's.

Although there are differing estimations of the development of the disparity between the rich and the poor, everyone agrees that the disparity has grown larger since 1994. At the May 9, 2002 "China Day" seminar of the Fifteenth Annual Meeting of the Asian Development Bank, Lu Zhiqiang, the vice-director of the Development Research Center of the State Council, said that according to the international standard, China is already on the list of those countries whose national income is seriously irregular. The problem of income distribution has become the most notable among social problems in China.[25]

The polarization in China today indeed exceeds not only "the regular Gini coefficient in the Western countries," but also our country's Taiwan Province (Taiwan figure: 0.2955 in 1972; it was reduced to 0.2806 in 1979.)[26] Compared to countries that previously practiced the planned economy or countries in the process of transforming their systems, the two sets of figures mentioned above exceed not only the figures of the countries that achieved reform relatively well, such as Poland (which had the most serious "shock treatment," 0.25 in 1992)[27] and Czechoslovakia (0.25 in 1994, although others said 0.26; and 0.26 in 1996, although others said 0.27),[28] but also the figures of Russia, the country generally regarded as a model of failure in its reform, with a reputation for oligarchic upstarts and mass pauperization. According to the figures of the Russian State Statistics Committee, the Gini Index in Russia was 0.409 in 1994; it was reduced to 0.381 in 1995. But the estimates of most scholars are more serious: 0.400–0.405.[29] Because Russia had "gray income," it is conceivable that those figures represent only the prescribed minimum. Compare the figures of our prescribed minimum with Russia's, and we see that our situation is more serious.

The problem is not only the extent, but also the nature of the polarization. Our country was never an "equal and ideal society" in the past. Instead of "classes," China had a strict hierarchy almost akin to a caste system before its reform. The so-called equality in the hierarchy coexisted with a wide disparity among social strata. The Gini Index of income distribution in our country in 1978 was 0.164 in cities, and 0.227 in the countryside. But if the difference between cities and towns were to be taken into account, the Gini Index of the whole country was 0.331, quite close to the figures of the countries with a developed market economy.[30]

In general, there are two theories worldwide about the development of polarization. The first is that, from the perspective of changes in the nature of society, the polarization of social strata in traditional society will be transformed to a polarization of classes in a modern contract society. The second is that, from the perspective of the degree of development, the level of inequality will rise in the most undeveloped countries while they are developing; the level of inequality reaches its peak when those countries are well developed and then falls; and relatively equal societies are formed when those countries are very well developed. The latter theory is thought to be inevitable; the former theory is reasonable in logic. Our country was a typical traditional society characterized by social strata before reform. Among residents in the cities and farmers in the countryside, there was relative equality within each category (if one does not consider non-currency benefits), but the difference between the two was wide. The polarization between residents in cities and farmers in the countryside is probably inevitable, but if the difference between the strata can be reduced, it may be worth paying a price for social progress. China seems to have followed this trend in the early part of the 1980s.

Unfortunately, after that period, especially in the 1990s, class polarization in our country has grown more obvious, and the "traditional" difference among stratums has also become wider. The situation in China is that the polarization of strata does not translate directly into a polarization of class, but rather that both polarization of strata and classes are developed simultaneously.

The income disparity between residents of cities and rural areas was very serious by the end of the 1990s. Among residents in cities, according to the results of the joint survey done by multiple departments of the government in the third quarter of 1999, in the five categories based on the average income per person within a household in the surveyed households, the income of the 20 per cent of households with the highest income represented 42.4 per cent of the total income of the surveyed households; the income of the 20 per cent of households with the lowest income represented only 6.5 per cent of the total income of the surveyed households. From the perspective of average income per person, the average income of the 20 per cent of households with a high income was 992 Yuan; the average income of the 20 per cent of households with a low income was 124 Yuan. This is a ratio of 8:1. The difference in the average income per person between the 10 per cent of the households with the highest income and the 10 per cent of the households with the lowest income was even greater. The average income per capita was 1717 Yuan and 82 Yuan respectively – a ratio of 21:1. The degree of the polarization of income in the countryside was similar to that found in cities and towns. The income of the 20 per cent of rural households with the highest income was 40 per cent of the total income of the rural population.

Not only was the income difference in cities and rural areas very wide; the difference in total wealth, or total assets, among households was even greater. The survey done by the Bureau of State Statistics shows that, in cities, until the end of June 1999, the financial assets of the 20 per cent of households with the most financial assets was 55.4 per cent of the total of the financial assets of the total population, with a total of 146,615.00 Yuan per household. The financial assets of the 20 per cent of households with the fewest financial assets was only 1.5 per cent of the total financial assets of the total population, with 4,298 Yuan per household. The ratio comes to 34:1. The outcome of the survey of employees in cities and towns, done by six departments, including the Bureau of State Statistics, the Labor Department, and the All-China Federation of Trade Unions in 1997, showed an even bigger difference. The 8.74 per cent of the surveyed rich households owned 60 per cent of the total financial assets, while the 43 per cent of the households at low economic levels within society owned only 3 per cent of the total financial assets.

Up until the end of 1998, according to the selective survey of the Bureau of State Statistics, the bank deposits of the 20 per cent highest income households in rural areas comprised 55 per cent of the total bank deposits of the surveyed households; the bank deposits of the 14.6 per cent of households with an income below 1,000 Yuan in rural areas was only 3 per cent of the total bank deposits of the surveyed households.

However, the editor who published the survey could not help but add the following note:

> The title of the paper is "The Serious Polarization of the Income of Residents," but the author divides residents between cities and rural areas into two categories, and compares the income of residents within these two categories. Did he overlook comparing income between residents in cities and rural areas? In fact, the disparity between cities and rural areas represents the income gap, and with the economic development in recent years, this gap has become increasingly large, posing a barrier to sustainable and healthy development of the Chinese economy.[31]

This is an irrefutable fact. The increasing gap between cities and rural areas has become a common topic in recent years. It is well known that "the average per-person income of peasants" in statistics reports is incorrect. We use the statistics of market consumption of cities and towns. According to the numbers published by the Bureau of National Statistics, the percentage rate of the retail of consumer goods at and below the county level fell from 53 per cent of society as a whole in 1990 to 38 per cent in 1999. It fell 15 per cent in nine years. In recent years, the income of peasants, especially farmers and grain growers, has not decreased, but their absolute income compared with the income of other people has fallen.[32]

In fact, the increasing gap between strata in society has become so obvious in recent years that some people have even tried to use this very gap to prove that the inequality among classes in China is not as serious as people say. Mr. Li Yining strongly disapproved of recent national surveys that showed a serious polarization of the Gini Index. He thinks that people should count the Gini Index separately between cities and rural areas. The national statistics do not make sense.[33] Evidently, Mr. Li Yining believes that the polarization between the poor and the rich is not serious when cities and rural areas are considered separately. His perspective is overly optimistic. As pointed out above, when residents of cities and rural areas were separated into two categories and compared within their own category, the studies showed a serious polarization of income. More important, Mr. Li Yining seems to think that it is normal that the issue of polarization of strata is separated from the issue of polarization of classes. This does not sound like the opinion of an advocate of market economy. It was the free competition of a market economy that broke through the barriers of strata to eliminate the privilege of identity, thus enabling a class structure of civil society to replace the stratum structure of the Medieval Age. As said above, before reform in China, society was characterized by strict barriers between strata, but the polarization of classes was not obvious. Mr. Li Yining suggested that as long as residents of cities and rural areas are separated into different categories, the gap between strata within each individual category seems to be natural. This perspective would imply that China still remains in the age of Mao Zedong, and that the market economy and the reform in China have been to no avail.

Of course, the reality of the situation is different. The Chinese Stolypin-type market economy has developed much faster than in Western civil societies, and the polarization of classes in China is more obvious than in the Eastern European countries. At the same time, barriers of identity among strata have not been broken through in China. The magnificence of the big cities in China makes them look like imperial capitals. There are no "ghettoes" formed by peasants who entered cities to work, as has happened in the process of industrialization in many countries. This does not mean that the poor Chinese peasants live a better life than those who entered cities to work; it also does not mean that those Chinese who entered cities to work, and who could be expelled at any time, live better than the poor people in foreign countries who have the right to live in a house, even in a ugly house, and do not need to worry about being expelled.

The problems of peasants living a hard life of great poverty in rural areas have many aspects. Among them are "the dilemma of the market" and "the dilemma of globalization." However, even if the phenomenon of "market balance" has an aspect of identity discrimination – wages are lowered because of the labor pouring in from the countryside – it is not only a problem of "the dilemma of the market."[34] Peasants in our country still incur the traditional attributes and taxes, not just the universal income tax that every citizen pays. There are no protections for property rights, contract rights, and personal rights of peasants. Mr. Du Runsheng is still strongly advocating giving peasants the "national treatment" (not the average income of nationals! The so-called "national treatment" is the basic rights of citizens). In the past two years, some areas even launched the campaign called "administering special cases" aimed at "stopping peasants appealing illegally to the higher authority for help." Even under traditional dynasties, the peasants had the right to appeal to "an official who was a just judge" for help, but in contemporary China this right of peasants has been lost. Apart from the problem of peasants, the polarization caused by "distribution based on ruler–follower relations" is often greater than that caused by free trade – and this is a polarization of strata, not a polarization of classes.

If the polarization of classes increases and the polarization of strata disappears, even if the Gini Index goes higher, one may conclude that social transformation has been achieved at the price of unfairness. But this is not the case in China. The Chinese oligarchy depends not only on capital, but also on power and influence. Therefore, class contradictions in contemporary China have formed, and the traditional strata contradictions still exist. On the one hand, workers' demonstrations are increasing, and in extreme cases labor and capital are starting to emerge [as separate classes]. In the latter half of 2001, there were three cases in Hubei in which the leaders of state enterprises were murdered by their employees or employees' family members: "This action fully shows that the contradictions between the reform of enterprises and the interest of employees have become very serious."[35]

On the other hand, the crisis that happened in traditional dynasties is now evident. Peasants abandon land and do not grow crops due to the heavy burden of taxes and apportioned charges and labor, not because of the annexation of land, forcing peasants to become tenant farmers. According to an investigation, the phenomenon of abandonment of cultivated land has spread from the rich coastal areas where peasants left their land quite early to areas where peasants leave farmland with low rates of output for farmland with high rates of output. The phenomenon has spread from seasonal abandonment to year-long abandonment of farmland. In 1999, the abandoned farmland with high production was only 20 per cent of the total high-production farmland in Feidong County of Anhui Province; in 2000, it rose to 40 per cent, and in the first half of 2001, it rose to 50 per cent. It reached 15.6 per cent in Jinzhou City. In the same period of time, the total area of the abandoned cultivated land increased from 1.612 million mu to 1.95 million mu, an increase of 21 per cent. The year-long abandoned cultivated land increased from 386,000 mu to 510,000 mu, an increase of 32 per cent; the total of areas of abandoned cultivated land increased "only" 10 per cent, but the seasonal abandoned land increased to 5.7 per cent, and the year-long abandonment increased to 21 per cent.[36]

"Absorbing" cash in front and "withdrawing" cash behind: the "assembly line" of primitive accumulation and the functions of state assets in contemporary China

What is the net value of state assets in China after the privatization of recent years? This is an interesting question. Several years ago, somebody predicted that the net value of state assets would reach zero by the end of the twentieth century, according to the scale of "loss of state assets" at the time. Today, this does not seem to be the case, but it is an indisputable fact that the loss of state assets is serious.

Wu Jinglian, the famous economist, quoted material from research institutes when he had an interview with media in the economic group at the Chinese People's Political Consultative Conference. The total of bad loans of banks in China, the potential or actual debts of the government's investment, is estimated to be at most six to seven trillion Renminbi. The World Bank estimated at least another 1.9 trillion Renminbi. Compared with more than three trillion Renminbi of the state's net assets, the ratio of debts to assets is high, and we might even become a net debtor country.[37] So far, the rate of debt of state assets is 66 to 200, and even higher.

The optimistic opinion in academic fields is that the financial deficit is just the tip of the iceberg of the government's debts. If we count the bad assets the government is responsible for and the potential debts of social insurance, the total rate of China's debt will be at least 70 per cent. This rate is more than that of many countries in Asia and the European Union (60 per cent) and the United States' (60 per cent).[38] The pessimistic opinion, expressed by Zhong Wei, who comes from Beijing Normal University, is that, in general, state assets are smaller than state debts. The total state debt is about 12.8 trillion Yuan, equal to 140 per cent of gross domestic product. But the total of state assets is about nine trillion Yuan. In other words, the net value of state assets is already a negative number – the net debt is 3.8 trillion Yuan, and the rate of debt is 36.2 per cent.[39] The recent slump, fall, and near-collapse of the state stocks, as a result of the rumor about "reducing the holding of state stocks," demonstrated the impact of the negative number of state assets in the minds of the nationals.

On the other hand, because the mechanism of absorbing resources under the old system is covered by a "market" jacket, the state enterprises have followed a path of depending first on governmental funding, then banks, and then people. The state economy absorbed huge amounts of private capital through the stock-market in order to overcome the difficulties of the state enterprises. It is said that the total of absorbed capital is one trillion Yuan. The stock-market seems to be a site for free trade in its structure, but the "supplier" is highly monopolized. Only 3 per cent of companies on the stock-market are private enterprises. The state enterprises that comprise more than 90 per cent of the stock-market are accumulating private capital on the stock-market. According to the statistics collected in December 20, 2001, one trillion Yuan had been invested in stocks, and 80 per cent of the capital went into state enterprises.

But stockholders in China are different from shareholders in a normal market economy. Their rights in the state enterprises are equal to zero. If we say that it is a general phenomenon that small or big stockholders can hardly participate in the management of enterprises, and that this is a Chinese characteristic, then the non-distribution of dividends to stockholders should no doubt also be a Chinese characteristic. The net profit that the "Wuliang Cream Co." made per share was 1.60 Yuan in 2000, and the net asset per share was 6.60 Yuan, and the rate of yield of net assets was 24.09 per cent. The profits that were not distributed amounted 1,356,607,152.17 Yuan. The company did not pay a cash dividend to shareholders for two years; furthermore, it sold its stocks at higher prices. This is a typical example of collecting money for overcoming difficulties of the state enterprises in the Chinese stock-market. In 1999, 60 per cent of the companies in the stock-market did not distribute dividends, and 20 per cent have not distributed dividends since entering the stock-market. Since it has become the usual practice for companies on the stock-market not to distribute dividends to shareholders, shareholders can only make profits by the rise and fall of the stock price – these are the so-called "speculators."[40] In recent years, public opinion strongly criticized the strange phenomenon of the distribution of the companies on the stock-market (i.e., that the companies whose stock rights are highly dispersed do not distribute dividends). Public opinion repeatedly criticized "the chronic disease of the companies on the stock-market that do not distribute dividends" and demanded a solution. They demanded future dividends – a "looking forward to distributing dividends by the companies on the stock-market."[41]

Actually, the "strange phenomenon of distribution" is the "strange phenomenon" of the arrangement of property rights. The fact that small and medium stockholders cannot participate in the management of enterprises results in the separation between the owners and management. Since the enterprises ignore the dividend right of shareholders, shareholders lose their ownership rights. The state enterprises are like official institutions, and "shareholders" are just ordinary people. The relations between them are more like relations between officials and ordinary people, rather than relations between assets and shareholders. The high-profit enterprises such as Wuliang Cream Co. do not distribute dividends; many enterprises simply deposit the accumulated money in banks and the "internal people" enjoy the interest, and ignore anything to do with managing the money or benefiting the shareholders. Shareholders can only depend on speculation – "the first shareholder profits from the next" – in order to receive returns. In a situation where no dividends are given for investments and speculative activities fail repeatedly, the stock-market actually becomes a channel of "nationalization" of non-governmental capital.

This situation is completely contrary to that in the Eastern European countries. After "mass privatization," the shareholders in Czechoslovakia protected their rights and benefits through an investment fund. The interesting thing is that the investment fund in Czechoslovakia, a country whose stock rights were highly dispersed and which could not do much to improve the management of enterprises, took a firm stand in asking for dividends for shareholders. According to an investigation, each investment coupon after the privatization of security brought profits within several years to those citizens who held the coupons. The rate of profit averaged 6–15 per cent. In a 1994 survey, 60 per cent of respondents thought that they benefited from the reform of property rights. In the transactions of the stock-market, only 20 per cent of respondents made profits in that year, but the rate rose to 30 per cent in January 1996. This shows that the majority of citizens made profits from dividends, not from the rise and fall of stock prices. Therefore, the shareholders in Czechoslovakia seldom engaged in short-term speculation. Four years after the reform of property rights, 53 per cent of citizens had not sold any of their shares, and only 24 per cent of citizens had sold more than half of their shares. This cannot be described as "over-speculation."[42]

The Czech shareholders equally received their privatized security from their democratic country, while in China, the state enterprises take money from ordinary people. Both systems have the same problem that stock rights are very dispersed and both are unable to do much to improve the management of enterprises. But in Czechoslovakia, the practice could be called the "short-term style of privatization." In order to start out equally for everybody, the country pays the price of temporary inefficiency. In China, on the other hand, the practice is neither fair nor efficient "nationalization." The Czech media reported that some enterprises with losses that did not want to distribute bonuses were sued by the investment fund responsible for supervising them (a clear comparison with the Chinese enterprises that made big profits but refused to distribute bonuses, such as Wuliang Cream Co.). This style of focusing on bonuses rather than on improving enterprises was criticized by Keynesian economists in the West. However, our practice of ignoring improvement of enterprises and benefits to shareholders, and focusing only on getting money for the internal people in enterprises, is far worse!

In addition to collecting money from the stock-market, a second channel for collecting money is credit loss. Currently, the total of deposits from residents in our banks is seven trillion Yuan. Each year, the government distributes new loans worth around 1.5 trillion Yuan. From these, the state enterprises get 70 per cent, and the non-state enterprises get only 30 per cent.

The third channel for money is the national debt. The government has been issuing national bonds worth 0.6 trillion Yuan every year since 1998, and these national debts are turned into new state enterprises and projects. The state assets grow, but their efficiency and economic benefits are very low and very wasteful. Some reports pointed out that our country invested 3 trillion Yuan in social fixed assets at the end of 2001. Among them, wasted resources represented 30 per cent of the investment, 30 per cent of it was potentially profitable, 20 per cent was effective, and 20 per cent was stagnant.[43] Some considerable parts of the so-called "wasted" and "stagnant" investment actually entered the cycle of privatization appropriated by bigwigs.

Apart from these methods, China also has other channels for "turning private assets into public assets, then turning public assets into private assets." Here is an example.

Several years ago, many stagnant state enterprises conducted a "stock" reform and "collection of investment for employment." They forced their employees to buy stock; otherwise, the employees would be fired. But the employees who bought the stock did not have rights as shareholders. The enterprises were still managed and controlled by appointed officials, and were still in debt. The investment of the employees was eventually lost because their enterprises went into bankruptcy again. A considerable part of the investment went into the pockets of individuals in the form of "waste."

In the rural areas in the early part of the 1990s, many provinces followed the example of coastal areas, vigorously promoting town and township enterprises, and forcing peasants to invest. The "miracle of town and township enterprises" in the southern part of Jiangsu Province in the 1980s did not repeat itself in the inland areas of China in the 1990s. Most of the town and township enterprises soon collapsed after the "campaign," and a considerable part of the investment from peasants went into the pockets of the related people through the medium of "public assets."

It is generally acknowledged that the campaign of promoting town and township enterprises is one of the major sources of the current debt crisis of villages and towns. In addition, the debt crisis adds to the burden on peasants. Currently, in many areas, peasants' public debts have shifted mainly from loans for production and costs of living to debts for money and grain. On the other hand, banks have been unwilling to provide loans to villages and towns since the mid-1990s. The debts of villages and towns have changed into high interest loans provided by officials in villages and towns to "the public."[44] Thus the public financial institution chases peasants for payment of loans, and at the same time pays those officials for their loans. These are the main links in the chain of debt in rural areas. Since 2000, some rural areas launched a campaign to "chase peasants for payment of loans and solve debt problems in rural areas." In addition to confiscating peasants' land and offsetting loans, and selling public assets to pay back loans, the forced change of debts in order to release villages and towns from debts has become one of the models of the campaign. The so-called change of debt is that the loans which peasants need to pay for the public and the loans which the public needs to pay for rural officials have shifted, so that peasants pay those officials directly and "the public" can be released from the debt chain.[45] Apparently, "public" financing has become the medium for transfer of wealth from peasants to the hands of the officials.

Therefore, both the channels of "privatization" and "nationalization" in contemporary China exist and are developing. The scale of privatization in China is no smaller than that in Eastern Europe. However, this kind of "nationalization" does not exist in Eastern Europe; even back in the 1980s, the phenomenon was not in evidence in China. This explains how the impact of officials on the economy has grown to a great extent after the "bigwig privatization." However, the nature of an economy run by officials is different from the public economy in place before the reform. The state economy was the mainstream economy and the only model of the economy in the socialist age. It was an economic model that stood side by side with the non-state economy from the early part of reform to the beginning of the 1990s. But the current state economy in China is not the single mode. It has become the "medium" to conduct primitive accumulation of capital through power and monopolistic means. Currently, on the one hand, the losses of state assets are very serious. On the other hand, the "state economy" absorbed huge amounts of non-state resources. Through a policy of "collection of money in order to avoid difficulty," financial monopoly, collection of investment by threat, and absorbing of non-state resources for "public departments," those departments did not provide anything for public benefits; instead, they were active in the field of competition. Through the process of "waste" in this field, they secretly transferred the money to certain people's pockets. So China now not only has the problem of the loss of state assets, but also the problem of the loss of non-state assets. Actually, they are one and the same thing. The bigwigs' capital in China depended mainly on the national treasury for resources when the private economy was weak. Now that the national treasury no longer has many resources, the bigwigs' capital has gradually come to regard the national treasury as a medium to get resources from the private sector. On the one hand, it "turns [ordinary people's] private assets into public assets," and on the other hand, it "turns the public assets into [bigwigs'] private assets." This practice is an efficient way for bigwigs to rob ordinary people through "private capital vs. private asset." Therefore, on the one hand, the state capital is growing smaller, and on the other hand, it is expanding. Indeed, since the 1990s, the Chinese economy has moved more toward a market economy, but the process of primitive accumulation of capital – "robbing capital in order to do business" – has not ended at all.

Is fairness more important than "radical change"?

Under the current circumstances, if people do not face the issue of fairness, and address the balance of power that is the prerequisite of fairness – the issue of political democracy – both the "transfer to public ownership" and the "transfer to private ownership" will result in robbing ordinary people. So far, some people vigorously advocate promoting the state's capacity to absorb capital; some ask to accelerate the "withdrawal" of the state departments. But in the Chinese economy at the turn of the century, "absorption" in the form of robbery or cheating, and "withdrawal" in the form of sharing the loot, have gradually formed an assembly line. Some say that the practice of "collecting money in order to avoid difficulty," conducted by state enterprises, is worse than "robbing capital in order to do business." What they mean is that the practice is really "collecting money in order to drift along aimlessly, with no mention of doing business," and that "defined privatization" loots the capital in order to drift along aimlessly. Although these words are strong, they do have merit. Let us look at the facts.

Recently, many people with insight noticed that, although the companies on the stock-market were crazily accumulating money, the statistics indicated that those same companies in general did not lack capital at all. On the contrary, after collecting a lot of money, many companies put the money aside and did nothing with it. For example, according to the annual report of 2001 of the company "Initiative Stock" (*Shouqiang gufen*), by December 31, 2001, the company had currency capital of 1.91 billion Yuan in cash and bank deposits, which was 99.3 per cent of the 1.925 billion Yuan of its circulating assets. The analysis showed that the company depended mainly on subsidy and interest income to make a profit. Ninety-nine per cent of its circulating assets was in cash. Many companies experienced the same situation as that of "Initiative Stock." According to statistics, the top 100 companies on the stock-market had 148 billion Yuan in cash and bank deposits, all unused. This figure is equal to the total amount of money the security market collects every year in our country. On average, the unused money each company had was up to 1.48 billion Yuan, which is more than the normal amount of currency capital of an enterprise. People who analyzed this situation pointed out big drawbacks in the practice. First, these companies depend upon interest only for their income and are thus not motivated to do business. They just deposit the large amount of the collected money in the bank, enjoy the interest, and drift along aimlessly. Second, the large amount of the accumulated money is entrusted to agents, and returns to the secondary market, increasing risk. Third, the efficiency of use of the money is low for those companies on the stock-market. "The analysis shows that most companies on the stock-market did not pursue the goal of maximum profit. Their focus of operation and management is to pursue collecting maximum capital."[46] The mode of dependency on monopoly instead of management, and on collecting money instead of making money, not only violates reasonable behavior in the stock-market, but also inevitably depletes those companies' assets. What they do for primitive accumulation of capital is to go through the "assembly line" of "private asset–public asset–private asset."

I pointed out in the past that the biggest issue in the Stolypin type of transformed society is not whether to "divide the house," but rather how to divide it. In the early part of the 1990s the former debate sometimes emerged; at the turn of the centuries, it has basically quietened down.

At the beginning of the new millennium, the first big debate in the field of economic study was about the "black curtain of funds." Both sides of the debate (five people led by Li Yining vs. Wu Jinglian) advocated a market economy, and it is hard to tell who was the more "radical." The five scholars who criticized Wu Jinglian posed as "protectors" of the market economy. They skillfully used "main stream–side stream" methods with which we have become familiar over the years to argue for a stock-market. Wu Jinglian was well known as "Wu Market" at home and abroad. He was not an advocate of the planned economy, nor was he a Keynesian who was not enthusiastic about the market, nor did he belong to the so-called faction who advocated advancing gradually. His support for the reform of the market economy, including his support for the reform of property rights, market capital, and other main factors of the market, was no less vigorous than that of the critics he was facing at this time. However, the two sides, although both advocated a market economy, were diametrically opposed. Even Keynesians and classic liberals do not find themselves in such intense disagreement. The obvious reason for this intensity is that the issue of fairness is more sensitive than the issue of radicalization; the issue of how to "divide the house" has become more sensitive than the issue of whether to "divide the house." The interest of those economists had become more important than their doctrines.

Recently, the argument about "reduction of the state stocks" became more intense, involving common shareholders, famous scholars, and government officials. The number of people involved in the argument was greater than anyone in the field of Chinese economics had ever experienced. The "battlefield" of the argument spread from internet to media, from academic magazines to the government, from the National People's Congress to the Chinese People's Political Consultative Council. It was said that more than a thousand suggestions were put forward. People grew enraged and used political and personal attacks against each other. However, nobody thought that the state stocks should not be reduced. What they struggled with was which plan they thought was fair (or was good for their own interest).

What exactly is "reduction of the state stocks"? Does it not mean selling state property rights (i.e., so-called privatization)? The term *privatization* is still taboo in China, but all those taking part in the debate were discussing how to sell the state property rights. Nobody said they should not be sold. Among them were some so-called leftist economists who often mentioned Che Guevara; they put forward the most radical plan that asked the state to "give benefits" to shareholders – to give, rather than sell, some state stocks to shareholders! Technically, this suggestion might be feasible, but it was a shock to hear the suggestion coming from the "leftists" if one considers that "privatization" belongs to the "rightist" point of view. The people who worshipped Che Guevara advocated simply giving away the "socialist state assets" to individuals instead of selling them. It was the "rightists" who suggested considering the 1.3 billion people, the whole national population, as the owners of the state assets, instead of the 60 million people who are shareholders. The rightists did not agree with giving the state assets to "nationals" without a price. If Che Guevara were alive and heard all this, what would he think?[47]

The academic debate was a reflection of the conflict among "classes" and interest groups. The peasants' and workers' demonstrations in the later part of the 1990s became a remarkable phenomenon in China. The peasants' demonstrations were basically against the poor administration in rural areas and the peasants' heavy burden. Although some peasants complained that public security today is not as good as that in Mao's age, and that officials today are much worse than before, they were not mourning the past but rather complaining about the current situation. The peasants did not forget their restricted poor lives with no protection under the commune system (the official wording is "not enough food and clothes provided to peasants"). The majority of peasants did not want to go back to those old days, but the situation of unemployed workers was different from that of peasants. Before the reform, although they were not the masters of their own affairs and were restricted, they enjoyed their benefits in the state and collective enterprises. Compared with peasants, as "city residents" they had higher social status; compared with the intellectuals who were called "the stinking ninth" in the Cultural

Revolution, they enjoyed the vanity of being "number one" among revolutionary classes. Today, however, they still have not lost the restrictions (they still do not have the right to negotiate for their own rights). What they have lost are their benefits. They did not gain "opportunities" but paid a huge price in the reform. The situation is described thus: "to evaluate success or failure, we can do nothing for the result but start from the beginning again." For these reasons, some of the workers do mourn the old days. They harbor anti-Deng Xiaoping sentiments, and miss Mao Zedong, especially in the areas where there are many heavy industries, and in the inland provinces where there are medium- and large-sized state enterprises.

In reality, this "mourning of the old days" was caused by the unfair way of "dividing family property," not by the policy of "dividing family property" itself. Even in the area where workers demonstrated frequently, although workers did not take the initiative to "divide family property" as peasants did, they accepted and expected a fair process of "dividing family property." The C factory in Zhengzhou exhibited the most "Maoist" ideology among the inland workers' demonstrations. But it was the workers in the factory who voted in the employee committee for the agreement between the government and a Hong Kong business to transform the factory into a private company, sign "the agreement of purchase of the factory as a whole, and complete the arrangement of employees after C factory entered bankruptcy."[48] When the Hong Kong company actually took over the factory, the registered capital of four hundred million Yuan and the twenty million Yuan for "the purchase and development fund" of the company became the only three million registered capital of a "joint adventure" of the D company in Henan Province. The vice-general manager of the D company had been director of the business office of the administration that supervised the C factory, and vice-director of the bankruptcy and settlement group of the People's Court in that city. The so-called registered capital includes the capital of the purchased factory. After "catching the white wolf without paying any price" and turning public property into private property, the D company gradually broke all the promises made in the agreement. Not only did it not invest and change production, it also asked employees of the factory to "invest collectively." Soon after, it sold the equipment and the building of the factory. Finally, it revealed its intention: to sell the grounds of the factory in the city, and to fire all its employees. It was a fraud. Some government officials supported the private company to "buy" the factory in order to sell the grounds and make profits. The employees lost not only their jobs but also their settlement fund and investment.[49] No "doctrine" can tolerate this kind of "division of family property"!

Therefore, although the workers' demonstrations in places such as the C factory were in the name of "Maoism," it is hard to believe that workers were against "privatization." In recent years, the majority of workers' demonstrations were caused by the side with power and advantages which broke an agreement and refused to fill its obligations. What the Chinese model of privatization lacks is normal bargaining procedures, and the organized protection of rights and benefits between workers and other interests.[50] What the Chinese workers struggled for were those rights that workers in Czechoslovakia and Poland already have. The contradiction between labor and capital in a normal market economy is not the same thing as the problem of "how to divide family property" in China. Some of the radical leftists (*note*: they are not the same as the "new leftists" in the academic field) usually use the case of this kind of workers' demonstrations to prove the sins of reform and the working class's opposition to "capitalist restoration." Indeed, in history, the oligarchy that opposed democracy and the populism that opposed freedom usually set in motion a bad cycle between an unfair, false competition and a false fairness that opposed competition. This is the big risk China is now facing. The classic social democrats have never believed that this crisis can be solved through pitting socialism in opposition to capitalism. What they want is to use "the U.S. path" to oppose "the Prussian path" (i.e., to use democratic privatization to oppose the bigwigs' privatization).

The two prospects of the "post-commune age": "the U.S. path" and "the Prussian path"

Although both populism and classic social democracy protected the interests of the people of lower social status, classic social democracy was the product of freedom and individuality when the status community collapsed in the medieval ages. "The more we look back in history, the less independent individuals were. We see individuals who worked and belonged to a larger entity."[51] In the "community" or "entity" that oppressed individuality, individuals were "dependent on the group,"[52] and individuals themselves were the "property of the community."[53] The dependency of all individuals on community generated the dependency of members of the community on the "father of community."[54] It was not until the formation of a "citizens' society" that individuals broke the restrictions of community, ended "human dependence," and formed "human independence." Karl Marx believed that they further overcame the "alienation" brought about by private assets, and entered the ideal stage of "free individuality."

Although the social democrats yearned for the ideal of public ownership, "freedom" was more important than "public ownership" in their value system, and from this perspective it was "human independence" that got rid of the restrictions of community. Therefore, the social democrats hated the commune system and its lack of freedom as much as the liberals did. As Plekanov concluded: "Russians are divided into two classes: the exploiters' commune and the exploited individuals."[55] At that time they understood the democratic revolution as the movement of democratic privatization that liberated "individuals" from the "exploiters' commune." The complete transformation of land relations in Russia would change the conditions of purchase and distribution of land. Peasants have the right to give up their portion of land and withdraw from village communes. As Lenin said, the only demand put forward as the guiding principle was the freedom to withdraw from the commune.[56] The goal was to allow the Russian peasants to free themselves from the "medieval community," to "independently connect with the market, and to raise their status."[57]

However, this point of view was not adopted during the period of Stolypin's policies. After the process of democratization was interrupted, Stolypin promoted economic freedom under a rule of political autocracy, from the policy of protecting rural communes to forced privatization, and disrupted rural communes with autocratic measures. This reform played some role in promoting agricultural efficiency; the capitalist economy was greatly developed during this period of time. However, the robbery of rural communes by those with power aggravated unfairness in Russian society. The Russian peasants and society as a whole strongly opposed the practice and demanded that rural communes be restored. This view represented the populist view that had been severely criticized by the Russian Marxists in the past. As Lenin said, the "only demand" in our original guiding principle (i.e., peasants' free withdrawal from rural communes) "is met now through the unique Stolypin Bill."[58] On the other hand, there was a strong sentiment among peasants and society as a whole opposing Stolypin's Reform, and the "only demand" from the social democrats that was met by Stolypin. This sentiment worried many social democrats. The restoration of populism stimulated by Stolypin's Reform put the social democrats in a dilemma, and at the same time raised a question: in Stolypin's Reform, namely the nature of the contradiction between opposition factions, including the social democrats and the Tsar's authority.

The populist view had always maintained that the Tsar was guilty of introducing capitalism or the "Western plague of individualism," and damaging the great tradition of Russian collectivism. Therefore, the goal of resistance was to oppose individualism with collectivism, or, in other words, to oppose "capitalism" with "socialism." On the issue of peasants, it was to restore rural communes and withdraw private farms (including landlords and independent farmer households). This kind of perspective of the "socialist revolution" was firmly opposed by the Russian social democrats from the birth of their movement. They always thought that the struggle to resist the Tsar's authority belonged to the "capitalist democratic revolution," even though it was led by "proletarians."

When the Tsar's authority was still "the father of communes" and the social democrats called on peasants to get rid of the rural community and enter the market, this view sounded reasonable. But at the time of Stolypin's privatization, how was it possible to say that the struggle against this type of "privatization" was still the "capitalist" democratic revolution? In fact, many liberal opposition members who had thrown themselves into the democratic movement in 1905 changed from democratic liberals to oligarchic liberals and thought that it was the time to support the government in promoting capitalism (even the type of capitalism that was "policed," corrupt, and a process of "the parents robbing the family property and expelling their children"). If they maintained the opposition's position, they would become populists and walk to the dead-end of "people's autocracy."

Therefore, some social democrats (for example, Tann, a Menshevik leader) maintained their revolutionary stand, and answered with a firm "No! The capitalism Stolypin has promoted is not thoroughgoing. He has retained many feudal things. We demand complete transformation. This is still a 'capitalist democratic revolution'."

This point of view did not reflect the fact that Stolypin not only allowed peasants to withdraw from the commune but also forced them to withdraw, and destroyed communes with force. How did he do it, if not "vigorously"? Therefore, Lenin refuted Tann, saying that Stolypin's solution "was complete because he was destroying the old communes and land system in Russia."[59] "Stolypin and the landlords bravely walked on the revolutionary path, and mercilessly destroyed the old system."[60] Stolypin's Reform was "filled with the capitalist spirit"[61] (not the spirit of semi-feudalism, or semi-capitalism!). It "did not mention protecting any former economic mode of pre-capitalism" and "did not praise any type of patriarchal agriculture, etc."[62] Stolypin's land bill "used force to destroy the rotten medieval land ownership, and cleared the path for the development of Russia, and therefore, from the perspective of scientific economics, this bill has no doubt a progressive importance."[63] The populists, who opposed Stolypin, would have eliminated landlords and maintained the rural communities. They wanted to keep the old system, or at least wanted to "keep half of the old system." Their solution was not "thorough" at all.

Then the question became how to explain that supporting the peasants' movement, with its populist perspective, against such a "brave, thorough, complete, and never compromised capitalist reform," was indeed the "capitalist democratic revolution"? The explanation which Lenin put forward was that the rural community could not be saved, and populism could not restore it. The current issue was neither whether to disrupt the rural community, nor whether to disrupt it "thoroughly." The current issue was the method of disruption, or in other words, the fair way to reach the path of capitalism. Who would benefit from the path? Who would be its victims?

Lenin pointed out that the practice of Stolypin showed that when land could be transferred freely, the independent farms which performed well could quickly end the famines experienced under the medieval system, along with the various forms of exploitation and corvée.[64] Although the peasants now supported populism and opposed Stolypin, they were to promote independent farms in the future. Therefore, the debate between them was not whether to divide family property, not whether to do it thoroughly, but rather how to divide it. This was what Lenin called Russia's special time: "On the essential issue of the revolution, i.e. the issue of land, the reactionary gangs and the masses of workers and peasants were implementing revolutionary policies."[65] All of them chose the capitalist path and said goodbye to the past. But the two kinds of "revolution" had more serious conflicts than past conflicts between revolutionaries and conservatives. Lenin thought that it was much more difficult to compromise between the two opposing sides who wanted to destroy the old system than to make a compromise between the new and old system.[66]

Although the "masters" whom Stolypin represented and the masses of workers and peasants both wanted to promote independent farms, the issue was: Should the independent farms be established in the ruins of the commune economy or in the ruins of the big landed properties that transformed public property into private property? Lenin gave an example. From the point of view of aristocrats, "if independent farms are established in the land of those masters, it is 'destruction'; but if these farms are established in the land of commune peasants who went bankrupt, it is 'construction.'"[67] This was the debate over the two paths of market economy development (i.e., the debate between the path of the U.S.A. and the path of Prussia). On the peasant–land issue, it was the struggle between the implementation of "democratic privatization" in traditional rural communes and the implementation of "bigwigs' privatization."

According to Lenin, "there are only two possibilities in Russia now, either it is a Prussian type of slow and painful capitalist evolution or it is an American type of rapid and free evolution. The other types are just illusions."[68] The "American type of evolution" meant that "productivity can be developed at the maximum speed, and the best working conditions can be provided to masses of residents." . . . "Masses of workers and peasants can grow fast and freely under the general best conditions of commodity production; therefore, it creates the best conditions for working class to further accomplish the real and essential task of socialist reform."[69] Before 1917, Lenin had been using such phrases as "at the maximum speed," "the best," "the freest," and so on, and he regarded the "American path" as the direction of Russia's. In Lenin's writings during that period, almost all the positive aspects of the Russian modernization were attributed to the "American path," and all of negative aspects were attributed to the "Prussian path." The former was the best among good things, and the latter was the worst among bad things. By then, the meaning of the democratic revolution was obviously very different from the times before Stolypin and the times of Karl Marx. It was not the conflict between "feudalism" and "capitalism," between semi-feudalism, semi-capitalism, and complete capitalism, but the conflict between the two possible paths through capitalism whose degrees of fairness were very different. On the issue of land, the two possible paths were: Should independent farms be established after Stolypin robbed peasants (free peasants' farms) or after peasants robbed landlords?

As I pointed out several years ago, Lenin himself did not allow Russia to follow the "American path," or let the Russian peasants "build their independent farms on the land of those masters."[70] On the contrary, against the background of traditional Russian populism, and the populist "revolution" stimulated by the oligarchic reform of Stolypin, Lenin became the figure who promoted his social democrats (i.e., the Bolsheviks) to become populists and super-populists. He not only restored the "world of communes" in Russia in the time of Stolypin, but he also built the totalitarian system of "state socialism" plus the "people's autocracy" that the social democrats were worried about most in the time of Plekanov. On this issue it is very important to clarify "Leninism," especially when China is now facing the same paradoxical situation of Stolypin.

However, the theory of the "two paths" that Lenin used to explain the social contradictions in the times of Stolypin, from the position of classic social demoracy, was much smarter than the explanations (the theory of the "plague of Western individualism" and the theory that the "reform should depend on the strong side") offered by the populist and oligarchic factions. In fact, the transforming times of "post-communism," as in the times of the "post-commune world" in Russia in the past, face the same challenges – the transformation from the dependency of community to "human independence" (in plain words, the issue of division of family property). Therefore, it is also necessary to make the choice between the "American path" and the "Prussian path." But from the perspective of the Russian outcome and the current crisis in China, there is the third choice that Plekanov worried about most, and that Lenin thought to be impossible. However, it was Lenin himself who made this third choice: he restored and strengthened the control of community with the means of "super-populism" to such a degree that he eliminated "human independence" completely.

The process of changing tracks in China has not ended

Some people did not agree with me when I raised the issue about the "American path" and the "Prussian path." They thought that China's situation is very different from that of America and Prussia. Only the "four little dragons" model in Asia or the experiences of the "corrupted market" in Latin America and Italy could compare with China's situation. Actually, on the issue of experience, the Chinese experience belongs to China alone. Compared to any other "models" of experience the Chinese experience is special, and should not be applied to other models arbitrarily. However, the so-called "American path" and "Prussian path" were logical concepts, not concepts related to experience, at the time they were raised. The concept does not have much to do with an actual historical connection.[71] It comes from the main issue – that "dependency of community" was transformed into "human independence." This is the so-called essence of the "transformation of system." Any society in the transformative stage (such as China, Eastern Europe, and Russia that got rid of "commune world") will face this issue. But any society that is not in the transformative stage, including the so-called "Asian value" countries, Latin American countries, and Italy, who promote market economy on the basis of traditional private ownership, will not face this issue.

Yet in reality, the U.S.A. and Prussia did not experience the transformative stage. The issue raised by Russians a hundred years ago demonstrates that even the leftists (the social democrats) did not believe that freedom and democracy in the U.S.A. with a welfare system (in pre-Roosevelt times) was much better than Prussia, a country that first established the welfare system in Europe but had a relatively autocratic system.

On the issue of the "policed reform" that promoted privatization for the bigwigs under autocratic rule, the practice of Stolypin's model in Russia is more typical than that of Prussia where "disruption of communes" did not take place. Therefore, I suggested calling this type of reform "Stolypin's path." On the issue of privatization reforms under democratic conditions, the democratic constitutionalism in the Eastern European countries in contemporary times, especially in the "Vichegrad Group" (Poland, Czech, Slovakia, and Hungary), is more typical than that in the U.S.A. I therefore suggested calling this type of reform the "Vichegrad path."

The social democrats in Russia thought that, although the "masters," whom Stolypin represented, and the peasant masses wanted to build independent farms, the question was whether these farms should be established at the price of the commune peasants' interests or at the price of the bigwigs' interests. From the point of view of the bigwigs, if it was the latter, it was "destruction"; but if it was the former, it was a "construction." Is not today's society in the transforming stage facing the same kind of issue? From the point of view of some bigwigs, if state assets are divided evenly among the common people it is "destruction"; if state assets are transferred into their hands it is "construction."

Several years ago, an official who advocated "economic reform" said in a famous article that the only boundary in the reform of the state enterprises is that "equal division of the state assets among employees and residents" should never be allowed. "Except for this," any other reform of property rights should be allowed. The "conservative" officials therefore wrote articles and accused him of abandoning "socialism" and accepting "capitalism," and said he was outrageous. But the interesting point is that the "conservatives" were like some "economic reformists," and had worse feelings about common people owning state assets than the bureaucrats. They announced that the "civil capitalists, petty bourgeoisie" had become a serious threat and must be repressed. But the "bureaucratic bourgeoisie" had just "begun to burgeon"! If the "conservatives" controlled power, more civil assets might be absorbed into the national treasury. If the "economic reformers" controlled power, the assets in the national treasury would soon be withdrawn and transferred into the hands of bureaucrats who were never thought of as "bourgeois." On the surface, one side was "leftist" and the other was "rightist," one was "socialist" and the other was "capitalist." Actually, the mechanism of "absorbing" in the front and "withdrawing" in the back worked for both sides.

Before democratization in Eastern Europe, some countries (such as Poland and Hungry) implemented the policy of setting the price close to the price in the market, and started "spontaneous privatization" among officials. But the democratic movements there had the clear intention of opposing the market economy. Especially in Poland since the 1970s, almost all workers' demonstrations opposed "price reform." At the turn between the 1980s and 1990s, they opposed "spontaneous privatization" and the "transformation from political capital to economic capital."[72] These resembled the peasants' demonstrations that opposed "police privatization" in the times of Stolypin. However, nobody would have thought that the democratic movements in Eastern Europe would recall the spirit of Stalinism. Actually, as the process of the 1990s showed, opposing "spontaneous privatization" would promote democratic privatization. When prices floated freely after democratization, the people in Poland, who had always demonstrated about issues of price, showed a surprisingly reasonable attitude toward democratic privatization, and the transformation was accomplished smoothly.

The "anti-marketization" of the 1989 movement in China was not as strong as that in Poland. Although by then there was the problem of inflation, and "price reform" was not successful, opposition to price reform was not raised as it had been in Poland. Obviously, people did not want to obstruct economic reform. Students mainly asked for more democratic politics and the right of free speech. The demonstrations of city residents and some small workers' demonstrations were to show support for the students. The main demand about economy at that time was the "opposition of corruption and officials' fraudulent buying and selling." This demand ran counter to the theory that "bureaucratic capital is the first-stage rocket of economic development." It may be called the advocacy of the Vichegrad, or "the American path" against the advocacy of the Stolypin, or "the Prussian path." Yet, Mr. Wang Hui said that this movement was opposed to the market economy and nostalgic about socialism. How would he evaluate the "anti-marketization" movement in Eastern Europe that was a hundred times stronger than the movement in China in 1989? Shouldn't he think that the Solidarity Union in Poland was nostalgic about Stalin's rule and reactionary?

Actually, from the perspective of today, if only the movement in 1989 could constrain the bigwigs' privatization as effectively as the Eastern Europeans did! Today, the biggest difference between China and countries such as Poland is that the democratic movement in Poland constrained the bigwigs' privatization, and relatively speaking, public assets there were kept intact throughout the process of democratization. Privatization in Poland was conducted under the conditions of democratization. Not only did "public choice" exist, but also the bargaining and debating among interests were conducted quite thoroughly. Because the thorough bargaining and repeated debates in the process increased "the cost of the transformation of the system," economic turbulence resulted for a period of time, but the economy recovered later.

Not so in China, where the practice has been a pure Stolypin type of iron-hand rule over whatever activity, whether it was "absorbing" or "withdrawal." The masses basically have not had the capacity to bargain and debate. "The low cost of privatization" plus, prior to reform, the "unplanned mandatory economy" meant that both "could be rejected without cost." So the Chinese economy has grown continuously.

However, the final arrangement of property rights promoted by Poland's type of democratic privatization was not perfect. People's evaluation of it differed, but its fairness and legitimacy were unquestionable compared with that in China. Although the regime has switched many times from the leftists to the rightists since the "dramatic transformation," with the former communists gaining power or losing power, the arrangement of property rights was acknowledged by the public. There will never be the problem of resettlement. The normal market order and the mechanism of economic growth were achieved.

But the situation in China is different. The process of "privatization without democracy" inevitably became a process of unauthorized deals among officials. More than ten years after the fact, it is too late for workers' demonstrations to resist the bigwigs' privatization. A large part of the net public assets has been lost. The arrangement of property rights formed "without a selling party" neither went through a process of negotiation with public participation nor an established commission to handle the issue. The process therefore inevitably lacked fairness and legitimacy. The public did not have a voice in it. Once democracy is established in China, won't the public raise questions about it? By then, nobody knows how many times the "transformation cost" saved by "Stolypin's privatization" will have to be paid back. Eventually, it will be hard to say "who laughs last" between China and Eastern Europe on the issue of transformation of their systems.

We know that the period of transformation is a period of redistribution of social interests. An autocratic government can use its iron hand to present a *fait accompli*, but a democratic government can only make a social contract through bargaining. During the period of transformation in Eastern Europe, under the conditions of "democratization first, privatization second," democratic governments could use public resources to balance various interests. As did the Czech Republic, they allotted the state assets evenly among people, and everybody was responsible for his or her own choice. They established an order of transaction, similar to a "clear settlement among siblings," through the process of an "even division of family property." Some governments used state assets to increase their financial capacity in order to pay for social welfare, for other public supplies and programs, and for "historical debt." Since the transformation of their systems, even though the Eastern European countries continuously have troubles, they can still keep their societies stable because of their economic practices.

However, if public assets are lost in the process of democratization, when they face serious social contradictions, the democratic governments will have nothing to allot or sell, and they could lose the capacity to balance various interests. If the governments have to take resources from some people and give those resources to others, social stability will not endure.

Although the process of democratization differs from country to country, in general, there are two categories. The first category includes countries in Latin America, South Africa, and South East Asia that practiced traditional private ownership and market economy before democratization. They still practice private ownership and market economy after democratization, and do not have to face the issue of transformation of the economic system. What they need in the process of democratization is political reconciliation in order to avoid social disorder. In other words, when Mandela shook hands with De Klerk, the main issue was solved.

The second category includes some Eastern European countries which needed to achieve the transformation from "public assets" to private assets under democratic conditions. Their public assets were basically kept intact. Their reform of property rights could be conducted under the conditions of public participation, public authorization, and public supervision. Even though the "actual fairness" can be questioned, at least "superficial fairness" can be practiced, and legitimacy and public acknowledgment become the conditions of social stability. This is the so-called "Vichegrad path."

The practice of the Stolypin path is different from the above category. There have been no historical precedents for accomplishing democratization through this path.[73] As the experience of Stolypin's Russia demonstrated, the prosperity of the oligarchy caused the turmoil of populism, and a new, stricter autocracy emerged from the turmoil. The risk of falling into a vicious cycle was obvious. The system where "power controls assets" not only robbed citizens of their private assets, but also failed to protect public assets from being stolen by those people with power. The fair-deal market system and the system of property rights in the constitutional democracy are usually regarded as the protectors of the citizen's private assets. Actually, they are the best systems for protecting public assets.[74] The rule of populism that "five persons' decision can deprive the sixth person" can be easily changed into an oligarchic system which can deprive everybody, because "one person who claims to represent the other five can deprive anyone of anything."

Now, some people like to use the examples of "dragons" and "tigers" in Asia to prove the advantage of the path that "develops the economy first and the democracy second." But at the turn of the century, the practice in countries such as Indonesia seemed to contradict this path. I think if we assume that the model of "economic development first, democracy second" was indeed successful in the South East Asian countries, it does not mean that the model of "privatization first, democracy second" can be successful too. Those South East Asian countries did not experience the transformation of ownership, and did not have to deal the issue of privatization. The privatization of the "state assets" and the "Party's assets" in Taiwan was achieved after democratization, but in those countries that had to experience the transformation of ownership, it was very hard to promote "development" without reforming property rights. The transformation of ownership without democracy could not lay a foundation of public trust for privatization. Even though the process could reduce the so-called "cost of the deal" and was advantageous to "development," it would increase risk in the process of democratization in the future. Relatively speaking, those countries that did not need to transform ownership did not face this situation.

If China waits until its public assets are completely lost, and then conducts democratization without a clear procedure, it will have to face the big problem which the countries in the above two categories never faced when the public, once the so-called owners of "public assets," is given the right to gather information, to supervise and even to decide the fate of the government. What happens when people find out that their assets have all been stolen? How will this problem be solved? Who can assure that a "historical handshake," such as that between Mandela and De Klerk, will offer any solution? We cannot make assumptions based on history but we can make connections. The Russian peasants did not have good feelings about the "exploiter's commune" in 1905. If democratization had been successful in Russia, Russia would probably have already walked down the "path of America," as Poland does now. But the "police privatization" caused public anger in 1917. A wave of populist resettlement eliminated the Russian achievements on the path of Prussia. Russia was not able to switch to the "path of America" from the path of Prussia – the result that settled the path of Prussia was the "restoration of the Asian autocracy." Seventy years later, the Russians eventually gained the opportunity they had lost in 1905.

If the Tsar had not abandoned the "commune spirit" and agitated nationalism and joined the war, Russia might not have undergone the revolution in 1917. If Russia could have walked to the end of the path of Prussia, its fate would have been different. If the iron-hand politics could remain stable and last one hundred years after the "bigwigs' privatization," people would probably forget. But would this be possible?

If during the period of "Stolypin's prosperity," the Russian ruler could have taken the initiative and restored the process of democracy that was halted by the police factions in 1907, the outcome would have been different from the "February Democracy" in 1917 after the economy collapsed. If China can start the process of democracy without losing its chance while its economy is active and growing, many contradictions can indeed find compromises. Issues of democratization would be solved more easily. We may say that the best outcome would be this: that people who want China to be stable and democratic adopt market principles, fairness, freedom, order, and hope. This is also China's hope for relief from the "transition effect of competition."

However, if China just enjoys the "prosperity" and does not feel the need to reform its political system, once the stage of economic prosperity ends (no economy can keep growing at super speed forever) the contradictions now obscured by high-speed growth will emerge. This happened in Indonesia after Suharto's prosperity, and democracy eventually emerged only after many serious crises. Everybody saw the turmoil Indonesia experienced during the process of its democratization. However, people should know that Indonesia did not experience the transformation of ownership, and it was not a Stolypin-type "post-commune" country. If the Indonesian type of turmoil happens in a country that has accomplished the "bigwigs' privatization," what kind of situation will we experience in China?

Discussion

Amin: I want to ask Qin Hui a question. The process of the collectivization in China was easier than in the former Soviet Union and the Eastern European countries, and did not meet much resistance from peasants. Therefore, I want to know if we should pay attention to the structure of the people's communes, because from the perspective of comparison, it is impossible that all communes are the same. This is very important.

Qin Hui: The Soviets paid a high price for the collectivization. When China implemented collectivization, many Soviet experts opposed it. I think that Mr. Du Runsheng is very clear about it. One reason is that the Chinese peasants have been used to a system of small private ownership since ancient times, unlike the rural community in Russia with a tradition of collectivism. So, the implementation of collectivization in China should be more difficult than that in Russia. Because of this, they said that it was not proper to implement it. But China did, and did so successfully. There was certainly dissatisfaction in the process, but acts of resistance were few.

How do we explain this? Why were peasants who were used to a system of small private ownership easily moved to a system of big public ownership, while it was difficult for the Russian peasants, who were familiar with the commune system, to become members of the collective farms? I have a special explanation for this. The simple conclusion is that sometimes, collectivism can become a resistance force against étatism. In fact, the resistance met by the Soviet Union in the process of collectivization was an act of collective resistance by the peasants who were connected by the rural communes. But China never had this kind of tradition.

Question: why the Chinese collectivization go very smoothly?

Du Runsheng: First, the peasants in China were extremely poor. Second, the peasants were very satisfied with the land reform; it was why the Communist Party had a very good reputation. Peasants thought that it would be no problem to continue to follow the direction of the Party. We praised the Soviets' lives vigorously in that time, saying that the Soviets lived in houses with two floors, and that they used lights and telephone. People's lives in the Soviet Union were very good. The Soviet Union's today was China's tomorrow. Because Chairman Mao enjoyed such high prestige, when he called for collectivization, everybody followed.

But after the collectivization, we cannot say that there was no resistance. Peasants found some smart ways to resist. One way was called "concealment of output and secret distribution." Peasants did not report how much grain they harvested from fields, and they even deliberately left crops in fields and asked people to take them home. For example, if each mu could produce 100 *jin* of potatoes or sweet potatoes, a production team just collected 50 *jin*. Peasants could take home 50 *jin*. In some areas, peasants complained that they did not have food, and asked the production team to lend them fields. In this way peasants expanded their family plots, and transformed collective farming into the family farming. The most popular way was called "contracting output quotas to households." It first emerged in Yongjia County of Wenzhou in 1956. They found that peasants were very happy with contracting output quotas to households and worked hard on family plots. The amount of output from family plots was three or four times that of production teams. One mu could produce 1,000 *jin* of grain and other farming products. This is the origin and prototype of the system of contracting output quotas to households. The result was very good, as everybody expected. People using 7 per cent of the world's land met the needs for food of 22 per cent of the world's population.

In the 1980s, it was the Central Committee of the Party that raised the question whether the state needed to provide protection to poor areas. But the state could not afford to protect them. During that time, the state needed to give back a lot of grain to them, and give them money. The financial burden of the state became heavier and heavier. Therefore, people suggested experimenting with the system of contracting output quotas to households in poor areas. But the state would not require them to do it. They could also take other measures. This is the source of "Anything goes." Once the experiment was implemented in those poor areas, the output was increased 18 per cent. Therefore, the experiment expanded from the poor areas to non-poor areas. This was the result of interactions between masses and leaders. The masses' suggestion became the leader's, and the leader's became the masses'. This was what Mao Zedong said, "from the masses, to the masses." But Mao Zedong simply refused the system of contracting output quotas to households. We implemented the system after Mao passed away, and Deng Xiaoping supported the practice. Because Chinese peasants were too poor, people wanted to find a way to shake off poverty. After many experiments, this system was the best. Also, after land reform, we cracked down on the landlord class and feudalist force. That is why China did not have that kind of rebellion led by the rich peasants in the former Soviet Union. Basically, that is the history. The reasons come from history. I do not know if I explained the question. I am not able to say more about it.

Notes

1 Qin Hui, *The Study of the Cases of the Change of Property Right of Town and Township Enterprises in Jiangsu and Zhejiang Provinces*, (Hong Kong Chinese University, 1998).
2 http://www.gdet.gov.cn/specialtopic/gqlt/17.htm.
3 http://www.setc.gov.cn/ssdf/setc_ssdf_133.htm.
4 *Journal of Beijing's Talent Market*, January 24, 2000: "Beijing will not allow to build state enterprises industries."
5 *Wenhui Journal* (Shanghai), January 31, 2000.
6 http://zzxxaas.home.chinaren.com/xin/xin_006.htm.
7 http://www.qingdao.gov.cn/sfgwk.nsf/71b220cf3648a508482567bd0008024b/4ab72444f9fc3caa482569d70026aebd!OpenDocument.
8 http://www.ynetc.gov.cn/qygg/240.htm; Beijing Century Information Center of Economic Studies, *Daily Financial and Economic Express*, 186 (April 24, 2002).
9 http://www.stocknews.com.cn/ztyj/qt/200205290916.htm; *The Crucial Moment of Shandong 63 Companies in Stock Market.*
10 Qin Hui, *The Study of the Cases of the Change of Property Right in Town and Township Enterprises in Jiangsu and Zhejiang Provinces*, (Hong Kong Chinese University, 1998).
11 Ibid.
12 *Finance and Economy*, September 2000: "Changsha: Say Good Bye to State Enterprises."
13 Jin Yan and Qin Hui, *The Economic Transformation and Social Justice* (Henan People Press, 2002), pp. 76–93.
14 Guo Zenglin, "Some Lessons Poland Had When It Switched to Market Economy", *International Trade*, 7, 2002.
15 Bianca Guruita, *Radu Vasile's Cabinet Turns a Deaf Ear to Miron Cozma's Threats: Cozma-led Miners Threaten To Serve Up Fresh Riots In Bucharest.* http://www-old.nineoclock.ro/POL/1825pol.html.
16 Talks with Guests from Yugoslavia in June 1987. Quote from *Modern China Study*, issue 2, 2002, p. 127.
17 *Chinese Economic Journal*, June 1, 2002, "Li Yining: *Fairness and Efficiency*". Quoted from Li Yining's report to a work unit in Beijing City.
18 Laszlo Csaba, 'The Political Economy of the Reform Strategy: China and Eastern Europe Compared'. *Communist Economies & Economic Transformation*, 8:1 (1996), pp. 53–65.
19 Lu Xueyi, *The Report of the Studies of the Social Stratums In Contemporary China* (China Social Science Press, December, 2001).
20 *Study Times* (6th edn), October 15, 2001.
21 Japan, *Sun News*, March 15, 2001.
22 http://djdk.myetang.com/2001-8/2001-8-45.htm.
23 Qin Hui, *The Study of the Cases of the Change of Property Right of Town and Township Enterprises in Jiangsu and Zhejiang Provinces* (Hong Kong Chinese University, 1998).

24 Zhang Shuguang, "The Rules of Criticism, Reasonable Communication and Free Spirit", *Tian Ze Writing*, 10 (1999). *Reading*, 3 (2000).

25 Office of International Financial and Economic Studies of Zhejiang University, Hong Kong Silu Counseling Inc., Guangzhou Zhengwei Information Technology Development, Inc., *Mingde Financial and Economic Information*, 53 (May 11, 2002).

26 Jin Yaoji, "The Study of Individual Cases of Taiwan," *The Twentieth Century*, 17 (June 1993), p. 145.

27 Jiri Vecernik, *Markets and People: The Czech Reform Experience in a Comparative Perspective* (Aldershot: Avebury, 1996), pp. 61, 82.

28 Ibid., pp. 53 – 74.

29 "The Social Economic Development of Russia in 1995" (Russia), *Russian World*, 1 (1996), p. 57.

30 Yao Xianguo, *The Polarization: Good News or A Disaster?* (Xueyuan Press, 1989), pp. 38–39.

31 Beijing Tianze Economics Institutute, *Tianze Macroeconomic China*, 60 (August 4, 2000).

32 Ding Ningning, *The Chinese Agriculture, Peasants, and Rural Society*, paper presented at the international seminar of "The Transformation of the Chinese Rural Society and Modernization" in Shanghai, 2002.

33 http://www.szceo.com/news/shishi/200201071502.htm¡£. Internet note: original quote from *Guangming Journal* (January 7, 2002).

34 See Qin Hui, "The Floating of Peasants, Urbanization, Labor Rights and Interest, and Development of the West – The Market Economy in Contemporary China and the Issue of Rights of Citizens," *Zhejiang Scholars Magazine*, 2 (2002).

35 *The Chinese Youth Journal* (February 25, 2002).

36 Qin Hui, "'Preference of Setting Up'? 'Land Welfare'? – The Thinking of the Land System in Countryside," *New Finance and Economy*, 8(2001).

37 *People's Daily*, "'Powers' Forum', 'Experts Said that the Deficit Financing in China Will Lead To Add Tax", author: Kuai Lehao (March 7, 2002).

38 http://www.unirule.org.cn/symposium/c200.htm.

39 Zhong Wei, "The Plan of Amnesty," *Nan Feng Chuang* (February 28, 2002). http://finance.sina.com.cn.

40 Yang Fan, "The Black Curtain of Stock Market – Revelation of the Profound Problems", *Hexun Net – Report of Finance and Economy*, February 22, 2002.

41 *The Financial and Economic Times* (February 16, 2001): "Looking Forward to Distributing Bonus By the Companies on Stock Market," *China Management Journal* (March 16, 2001): "The Strange Phenomenon of the Distribution of the Companies on Stock Market," *China Economic Times*, February 9, 2001: "The Chronic Disease of the Companies on Stock Market that Do Not Distribute Bonus Can Hardly be Cured."

42 J. Vecernik, *Markets and People: The Czech Reform Experience in a Comparative Perspective* (Aldeshot:Avebury, 1996), pp. 158–159.

43 Xinhua Net http://big5.xinhuanet.com/gate/big5/news.xinhuanet.com/chanjing/2002-02/06/content_270325.htm, quoted from *China Tax Journal* (February 6, 2002), Zhong Dajun: "The Non-Governmental Capital of Trillion Yuan Follows Into the State Enterprises Every Year." [Author note: "Trillion Yuan Every Year" does not appear to be correct. According to the figure in the article, the accumulated money from the stock market was up to a trillion Yuan in 2001, plus the money from other channels, and the non-governmental capital (not "every year") flowing into the state enterprises totalled more than a trillion Yuan.

44 Because it was thought that it was risky to provide loans to finance villages. Villagers could not get loans at regular interest rates. The cadres in villages were mainly responsible for debts and obligatory rights of villages. For example, in village M of Jiangsu Province, there were 188 households that owed money in the village at the end of 2000. Among them, two households belonged to the cadres of the village. But the

finance of the village owed money to eighty-nine households. (not including the salaries the money from the village had not paid). Among them, thirty-six people were the village's cadres and employees, and only one person was a farmer. See Qin Hui, "The Discussion About the Crisis of the Two-Level Finance In Rural Areas" (not yet published).

45 See above. The cadres who had power and authority were not general creditors. Their eagerness to press for payment of debts was more vigorous than the government. This non-voluntary transfer of debts and its legitimacy are suspect, and are not a good sign.

46 "The Financing Fervor Rises Again In the Market, Do the Companies in Stock Market Really Lack Money?", *Security Times*, May 29, 2002.

47 This article intends not to comment about the good or bad aspects of "reduction of the state stocks," but tends to point out that these plans are for robbing "family property." We cannot see any traditional interests who "protect the family property" here.

48 *Agreement of Purchase of the Factory As A Whole After C Factory Goes to Bankruptcy by Hong Kong D Group Inc.* (December 10, 1996).

49 Former employees of the C Factory, "The Complaint To the City Party Committee and the City Government" (March 16, 2001).

50 See "The Reform of Property Right and Workers' Participation: The Study of the Case of the Reform of Kracov Steel United Enterprise In Poland". See also Jinyan and Qin Hui, *The Economic Transformation and Social Justice* (Henan People's Press), 2002, pp. 122–130.

51 *Complete Works of Karl Marx and Friedrich Engels*, vol. 46, section 1, p. 21.

52 Ibid., p. 18.

53 Ibid., p. 496.

54 Ibid., p. 473.

55 Plekanov, *Our Different Opinions* (People Press, 1955), p. 43.

56 *Complete Works of Lenin*, (2nd edn), vol. 16, pp. 256–257.

57 *Complete Works of Lenin*, vol. 1, p. 392.

58 *Complete Works of Lenin*, (2nd edn), vol. 17, p. 221.

59 Ibid., p. 23.

60 *Complete Works of Lenin*, vol. 16, p. 408.

61 Ibid., p. 209.

62 Ibid., p. 335.

63 Ibid., pp. 388, 209.

64 *Complete Works of Lenin*, vol. 22, p. 106.

65 *Complete Works of Lenin*, vol. 13, p. 420.

66 Ibid.

67 *Complete Works of Lenin*, vol. 24, p. 343.

68 *Complete Works of Lenin*, (1st edn), vol. 13, p. 307.

69 Ibid., p. 233; volume 3, p. 13.

70 Bianwu, "Leninism: The Populistization of the Russian Social Democracy," *The Twentieth Century* (October 1997), pp. 37–49.

71 In the age of Stolypin, the experiences of the "two paths" were uncertain. For example, the so-called "Prussian path" was also called the "Italian path," "British path," and so on. But the reality was that Stolypin implemented his policies.

72 J. Tarkowski, "Endowment of Nomenklatura, of Apparatchiks Turned into Entrepreneurchiks," *Innovation*, 14: 1 (1990) (Vienna).

73 As mentioned above, the practice of Prussia cannot become the typical case of autocratic privatization. Its path to constitutional government actually belongs to the first category mentioned above.

74 It is hard to imagine that the developed and democratic countries can adopt that type of privatization.

7 Theory and practice of the Chinese "market socialism" project

Is "market socialism" an alternative to liberal globalization?

Samir Amin

1

The various aspects of the experiment in economic development that has been under way in China since 1980 must be among the main points of orientation for any reflection on the future of this country-continent, and, beyond that, on the future of the global system. These aspects, characterized by some as "positive" (the acceleration of growth), and by others as "negative" (increasing inequality), include relations with the global capitalist system, the social content of the experiment (capitalist or socialist), and its political content.

This process of reflection is nevertheless handicapped by dogmatic ideological positions – I will go so far as to say positions of a fundamentalist type – which dominate as much or more so on the right as in certain parts of the left that remain attached to the values of socialism.

On the right the theses of free-market liberalism – to which unfortunately the electoral left has largely been won over in the advanced capitalist countries – are too well known to be more than briefly mentioned here: (1) that the "prices" of products and of the "factors of production" as determined by the operation of a "free" market provide the only possible efficient allocation of resources; (2) that the greatest possible opening to the exterior allows the acceleration of the rhythms of economic growth; (3) that accelerated growth in itself eventually brings social well-being for the greatest number and, in this way, brings democracy as well. Since none of these theses is grounded in theory or confirmed by the history of really existing capitalism, I will not go to any lengths to discuss the substance of these theses, even if they are widely agreed to by numerous Chinese intellectuals, especially among professional economists (recycled in Western universities). These economists are divided in China, as in other places, into "fundamentalists," apostles of maximum deregulation and opponents on principle to any intervention of the state into economic life; and "pragmatists," who defend the active intervention of the state, on condition that these interventions, on the whole and over the long term, fit in with the logic of the market economy (are "market friendly," as the World Bank has put it).

The official Chinese concept of "market socialism," although rarely stated precisely, is close to that of the pragmatists. The criterion that would separate "market socialism" from capitalism pure and simple is apparently the maintenance of an important sector dominated by public property (the state and cooperatives) – perhaps also, according to some of its proponents, forms of social redistribution attenuating the inequalities associated with the expansion of the market. Many add a concern for defending the unity of the Chinese nation, which implies public interventions intended to reduce regional inequalities and to control relations with the exterior.

Many of the leftist critics of the policies put into operation since 1980 are themselves handicapped by a dogmatism which is expressed in a not very critical – to say the least – examination of "socialist planning" in both the Soviet model and the one followed in China until Mao's death.

This planning was based on a few major principles: (1) making state property (or para-state property, i.e., property with a collective appearance) widespread; (2) the suppression of any form of autonomous decision making by the basic units, and therefore the allocation of resources by administrative measures; (3) a centralization of accounting which treats the whole of the economy as if it were a single enterprise, and therefore the establishment of prices, wages, and interest and exchange rates by this central body (the plan). None of these principles is by its nature a requirement for socialism. They are justified – in part – by the desire to "catch up" as quickly as possible from an historical delay. This form of macro- and micro-economic management has not been without a certain effectiveness when the goals were to accelerate accumulation of the extensive type by a controlled transfer of surplus labor power in the countryside into the cities, and by the establishment of industries that reproduced technological models invented by developed capitalism. Under these circumstances, there is even a quite legitimate reason for the priority given to heavy industry.

This form of central planning constitutes a reasonably broad framework that can be adapted for a spectrum of different social contents. The general equilibrium that the planner tries to bring about in this manner can indeed be grounded on the goal of the most equal redistribution possible of income among all the workers – among other things, the equalization of average income for the rural laborer and the urban worker. But the same form of planning could be equally an instrument in a strategy for maximizing, for example, the bleeding of the peasant world for the benefit of urban industrial development, of military expenditures – and indeed, of a privileged techno-bureaucracy's consumption, as was the case in Soviet history. This model's limits, whatever its social content might be, are nevertheless visible on three levels.

In the first place, we are talking about a project that at best is social but not socialist. The reproduction of advanced capitalism's technological models demands in its turn hierarchical organization of work, along with forms of social life and of consumption that, far from being "neutral," are vehicles for the culture of capitalism. It would be better to recognize that the socialism in question – if we are to call it that – is only a stage in the long transition from capitalism to communism, which brings together elements of the capitalist structure with ambitions going beyond the logic that is appropriate to those elements. This socialism is therefore contradictory and is not the expression of social relations that are at peace. The continuing class struggle manifests itself through the workers' resistance, which in turn slows down the gains in productivity which investments in modern equipment generally permit. People on the left should understand and support these popular forms of struggle, for example, by recognizing the independence of cooperative and labor organizations confronting the government (and the party), even if the government does have a certain authentic historic title to "speak in the name of the workers." This is the only means able to deepen the process of democratization, to give it its full revolutionary significance, to enlist it in the prospect for the construction of a communist society. The other option – imposing "discipline" through the hollow assertion that the state and the party are the people and that socialism is a definitive social form, at peace and completed – loses its credibility and serves as a foundation for the construction of "capitalism without capitalists," which in turn evolves toward the normal form of capitalism "with capitalists," as happened in the USSR.

The model's second limit concerns the national/global contradiction. Capitalism is constructed as a global system grounded in a particular form of the law of value which produces and deepens polarization on a global scale. The revolt against the latter, which is to a large degree the origin of modern revolutions (since the only revolutions around the demand for socialism took place in the peripheries of the global capitalist system, and not by chance), immediately poses a problem. If it is a matter of "catching up" or of "doing something different," how are we to combine these tasks, which are more contradictory than complementary? Here we cannot forget the longer perspective: that communism can be a system that is more advanced than capitalism only if it becomes global, since the positive significance of the universalism that capitalism enticed us with (but cannot bring to fulfillment) should not be erased from the strategic vision of the long transition. The socialist countries certainly did not choose the "autarky" that has always been imposed by the imperialist adversary. Communists have never been culturalists, and their ideology is one of universalist humanism, but they have always been forced to make their societies advance by isolating themselves to a degree from the dominant global system. In this sense, the decision to build socialism "in one country" is not a mistake, since the alternative (to wait for the global revolution starting from the system's centers) is completely illusory. But this decision poses a problem because what can be brought about in the framework of a "single" country, even if it is large like the USSR and China, will always remain limited. Withdrawal into oneself, even if it is compelled, has a cost, and a certain opening to the world, even if that world is still capitalist, has its advantages if you can control it. We have to deal with a contradiction of which free-market liberalism is not aware, thanks to its gratuitous affirmation, contradicted by theory and history, that enrolling in capitalist globalization is the most efficient way to "catch up."

The third limit of the model comes from the fact that central planning is in fact put together around a single goal: the acceleration of accumulation in its extensive form. The goals that may be attained by this method can be achieved in a relatively short time, say, twenty years. It should therefore have been understood that it could only be a question of the first phase in the long transition, and not of its definitive form. Once it is finished, this first phase opens up two possibilities: to pass on to intensive accumulation similar that which characterizes advanced capitalism, or to increase the dimensions of a different social structure which allows for advancing toward the communist horizon. This decision is not a "free" choice; it is obviously produced by the class struggle. But it is also burdened to a large degree by what occurred during the previous phase of extensive accumulation. If socialism has already lost its credibility, as was the case in the USSR, devolution toward capitalism, and integration into the global system that goes with it, is hard to avoid.

2

All the questions raised in these opening remarks are the object of passionate debate in China. To hear people say in Beijing that "there's a right and a left in China like anywhere else" is certainly quite refreshing for anyone acquainted with the required unanimous tone both in the speeches of the socialism of the past and in those of the capitalist liberal *pensée unique* that dominates in the West.

The discussions oppose the – numerous – partisans of a capitalism that is either totally integrated into the global system or controlled through the national and social plans, to the defenders of a perspective that claims to be socialist. They are grounded on a scrupulous attachment to the facts, and on this level Chinese statistics are of a higher quality than they are in most Third World countries. These debates are not confined to academic circles; they are just as lively in government circles and in political circles in general. It remains to be said that in my opinion the discussion is handicapped on the left by the inadequacies that characterize the examination of the Maoist phase (1949–1978). However, there is general agreement on some essential points concerning this phase. From 1952 to 1978 the annual growth rate of the gross domestic product (GDP) was 6.2 per cent (3.8 per cent per capita); the rate for agriculture was 3.4 per cent, for industry 9.4 per cent and for services 4.5 per cent. Taken together, this represented rates two times better than in India, as the World Bank itself recognized. At the same time, inequality was reduced to a minimal level, without an equivalent elsewhere in the world.

The differences in the assessment of the results are in two areas. The first concerns the inequalities between regions. Even if the average peasant income is close to that of the urban worker on the scale of China as a whole, average rural income necessarily differs not just from one province to another, but from one district or from one village to another, as a result of obvious geographic and historic factors. The second difference concerns the average gap between the city and the countryside for the Maoist period. For some, this gap – which favours the cities – was significant, but altogether explicable due to the control exercised in China over immigration from the countryside to the cities, a control that does not exist in the capitalist world. Through this control China avoided the tragedy of shanty towns replacing the tragedy of peasants without land that is a general phenomenon in the periphery of the capitalist world. The extent of the gap, in any case, depends largely on the criteria for measuring it – for example, of the relative importance given to certain services (education, health) which are undeniably better in the cities, or the extent of the countryside's consumption of its own products.

Economists are often fixated on growth rates, a sort of professional bad habit. Nevertheless, the accomplishments of Maoist China cannot in any way be reduced to the growth rates in question, although they remain quite honourable. The Chinese Revolution restored to the Chinese people their sense of dignity, mocked by imperialist aggression; it re-established its unity, put in question by the warlords and the comprador class; it rooted this unity in a sense of social solidarity produced by the egalitarian policies put into effect. William Hinton is quite right to recall in this regard the decisive positive role of the radical agrarian reform and of the collectivization that followed it, a collectivization that, in contrast to the one imposed in the USSR starting in 1930, has for the most part been supported by the peasantry. Maoism set up the basis for the Chinese rebirth. The apparently prodigious accomplishments of the past two decades would have been unthinkable in the absence of this revolution. Despite this, the Maoist phase itself was not "without errors," sometimes serious ones. Above all, it was bound to reach the limits of what could be produced by the strategies it had put in practice, and it wore itself out without having really prepared for the time when it would have to be superseded.

For the liberals of the West's *pensée unique*, Maoism, like all forms of socialism, is an aberration in itself. This a priori approach is completely ideological, reactionary, ahistorical and without scientific foundation, and it is of course taken up by the Chinese right. This right relies on invectives against the "crimes of the Cultural Revolution," to refrain from analysing the realities of the Maoist phase. Some take up the legend orchestrated by the Western media of a "famine" which occasioned tens of millions of deaths, of which no evidence (or even demographic trace) is in existence, as William Hinton rightly observes. Others, apparently more moderate and claiming to be more scientific, accentuate, with systematic exaggeration, one or two questionable or indeed erroneous aspects of the Maoist strategy, only to reject it as a whole. Among the points raised, which reappear in a repetitive way, are the distortions of the productive system, too oriented toward heavy industry and too contemptuous of the tertiary sector, or the inordinate ambitions of the communes, which is certainly true.

By refusing to discuss seriously these errors, and especially the limits of the Maoist phase, the appointed defenders of Maoism fail to help very much in advancing the construction of an alternative to the solutions advocated by the Chinese right.

Maoist China walked on two legs and did not sacrifice everything to the priority of heavy industry. A no less attentive priority was given to grain agriculture, whose average annual production went from 160 to 280 million tons between 1952 and 1978. This remarkable result was obtained by the intensification of the work of a growing rural population. The methods put in practice, including the collectivization and maintenance in the countryside of four-fifths of the nation's population, were largely justified. Thanks to these methods, China assured a security in food production beyond that of any other country in the Third World, and has avoided the transformation of its cities by shanty towns. But it remains true that this system was reaching its ceiling at the end of the 1970s, with the number of working days for each active rural adult rising from 160 in 1957 to more than 250 in 1975.

Simultaneously, Maoist China cleared away the bottle-neck that the poverty of its basic industries represented on the day after its revolution, bringing its production of electricity from 7 to 256 Mkwh in only a quarter of a century, and coal production from 66 million to 618 million tons and steel production from 1 million to 32 million tons. It was necessary in this first phase to give priority to establishing these bases, which must be taken into account for any industrialization worthy of the name. Despite this, it is useful to remember that these remarkable results did not in any way exclude errors.

The effort put into the area of basic industries undoubtedly went too far. The proof is that the consumption per unit of the GDP in China is 2.90 for energy and 127 for steel against 1.05 and 45 respectively in the United States (Yifu Lin). Simultaneously, since heavy industry offers only limited employment, this distortion hampered the reduction of the excess rural labor power and its transfer to urban industry. It remains to say that this distortion, produced by a dogmatic reference to the Soviet model, was criticized by Mao himself very early on, in theses he proposed on "the 10 major relationships" (1956) and on the rehabilitation of light industry. It is true, unfortunately, that these criticisms were not understood as they should have been by the whole of the party and state apparatus. The distortion also brought with it insufficient effort in the service sector.

The level of China's participation in global trade, still very low in 1978 ($21 billion), was not the result of a positive decision by China but was, at least in part, the result of strategies of isolation imposed by imperialism and then by the break with the USSR. It remains true that these distortions impeded the potential for light industries to take off based on the – debatable – comparative advantage of cheap labor.

The totality of the strategies put into practice between 1952 and 1978 was paid for by a modest growth in end consumption (2.2 per cent a year, according to Yifu Lin) in comparison with that of the GDP. Put another way, as in the carousel imagined by Tugan Baranovsky, the capital goods produced were allocated to the production of other capital goods, postponing their allocation to the production of consumer goods. This waste of resources indicated that the historic limits had been reached for what the choices available in the central planning model would allow.

3

In any case, toward the end of the 1970s the system of central planning and the choices that were associated with it had to be profoundly reformed. It was necessary to progress to a new development phase. It is therefore not a question of knowing whether it was necessary to "maintain the system" as it was or to abandon it, but of knowing which reforms could have been considered as a way of accelerating development and at the same time deepening – rather than weakening – its potentially socialist content.

The stages and the directions of the reforms put into practice starting in 1978 are well known. On this level China did not fall into the trap of "shock therapy," whose destructive effects on the social, political, and economic fabric are now obvious. The Chinese ruling class chose the option of "crossing the stream by jumping from one stepping stone to another," according to its own formula. Granting this, the nature of what awaits China on the other side of the stream remains subject to debate. Discussion and practice in this area concern both micro- and macroeconomic management, and the project's social and political content.

The reform rests on the principle of breaking the absolute unity of the system, which embraced the country's whole economy, managed by an exclusive owner (the state) as if it were a single enterprise. Because of this, central planning abolished market relations, but only in appearance, since the goods for end consumption remained after all subject to the constraints of demand. The fact that the labor market is regulated, with the state guaranteeing employment, does not eliminate the market character of a workforce submitting to the imperatives of the organization of production. This is the way it works as long as the producers have not become the masters of all the decisions, at all levels, concerning the organization of production. "Socialist" regulation of the labor market is only, under the circumstances, a more radical form of those put into practice in the capitalist West in the framework of the Welfare State.

In opting for breaking this system, the government indeed chose to bring the economic system still closer to that of an authentic market system. The precondition for this process is the autonomy of the basic unit – the enterprise or group of enterprises – whether that unit is the property of the state, of a collective of some sort (including those established by its own employees in the case of self-management), or of a private capitalist.

The systematic unity characteristic of central planning also had an obvious political dimension, since each individual was registered in a fixed structure (administration, urban enterprise, rural commune), which permitted planning (or control, if you wish) of allocations (place and type of work and responsibility). Under Chinese conditions, this system was in fact based on a dualism between city and countryside. Indeed, the priority given to heavy industries that were not productive of jobs imposed control and limitations on the transfer of labor power from the countryside to the city.

Such a system would prove truly efficient to the extent that there was a real priority on one side for creating a solid base for industrialization, and a real possibility on the other side for increasing agricultural production through the intensification of labor. But from the moment when the industrial system had to satisfy a considerably more voluminous and diversified end demand and when agricultural production could be increased only through the intensification of the use of facilities and inputs other than labour, releasing a surplus of labor power, the affirmation of the unity of the national labor market became necessary.

This affirmation – the abolition of the administrative controls concerning the mobility of individuals – is an affirmation of (bourgeois) freedom which suppresses the guarantee of a job and an income, which now depends only on the efficiency of the macro-economic policy and of the degree of priority that may be given to the goal of full employment. Chinese workers have understood the ambiguity of the new situation presented to them. They appreciate the gain in freedom that it brings with it, but they know that from now on they will have to struggle to have their social rights respected (first of all, their labor rights). In this regard, China is not at all in the situation of the capitalist Third World countries: the workers, who retain the memory of the revolution which they made, know how to defend themselves, as is demonstrated by the hundreds of thousands of actions and strikes which they carry out each year.

The subjugation of micro-economic management to market principles involved a whole series of rules put in effect progressively in the course of the decade of the 1990s. For the enterprises it is a question of freedom in hiring, in dismissing (although kept in check by some conditions), in negotiating wages, in fixing the prices of their products. On the other hand, the enterprises now face the financial constraint associated with borrowing capital from financial institutions instead of free transfers administered by the state budget.

The reform was launched, as we know, with the decision to make rural households responsible for themselves and with the subsequent dissolution of the communes (1978 to 1984), then by the extension of the rules of the market to the micro-economic allocation of resources – intermediary goods, capital goods, and financial resources (1984 to 1991) – and finally the reform of the macro-economic environment by the substitution of a tax on profits for direct deductions, the counterpart of the free budgetary allocations (starting in 1992). This is now quite far advanced.

The reform – understood as the affirmation of market relations substituted for the para-market relations of central planning as it was conceived and carried out up until the 1980s – was inevitable and no doubt necessary to avoid the degradation of the economic system's efficiency. But there are reforms and reforms, and the scope of possible alternative choices remains open, from the moment when we reject liberalism's dogma.

In the first place, a market system does not in any way imply the exclusivity or even the predominance of private enterprise. It remains true that micro-economic management based only on the principles of capitalist rationality by no means produces an "optimal allocation of resources," as claimed by the so-called "pure economy" theory, but instead a lot of wastage and distortions associated with the systematic social inequality which it promotes. This is how it works even if the dominant form of property is public. Thus a development strategy worthy of the name demands strong regulatory control of market relations. We need to impose coherent macro-economic policies to serve the national and social goals that define the development project in question – for example, full employment, the reduction of social and regional inequalities, and the reinforcement of the nation's autonomy in the global system. This means choosing a form of central planning that could not in any way be confused with the central planning of the Soviet model.

The simplified opposition between "central planning" (para-market of the Soviet type) and "freedom of the market" (markets "deregulated" according to the liberal dogma) from the start excludes the option that is most efficient and most progressive socially in the conditions of contemporary China. This option, characterized by the dominance of public and co-operative forms of enterprise, recourse to market relations, and a central plan that sets a frame for them could define a new stage in the long transition to socialism. Calling this "market socialism" does not seem unacceptable to me, but on the condition that the three characteristics mentioned above should be joined together firmly enough for the form of socialism not to be emptied of all social and national progressive content.

It is therefore important to see to what extent China's development in the course of the past two decades has answered these requirements.

4

During the three decades of Maoism (1950 to 1980), China had already recorded an exceptional growth rate – 6.2 per cent a year on average; that is, according to the World Bank, double the rate of India or of any large Third World region. Despite this, the performances of the past two decades of the century seem even more extraordinary: 6.8 per cent a year for the per capita GDP (Li Jingwen, Zhang Xiao). No large region in the world has ever done better in all of history.

What we have to remember, however, is that these accomplishments would not have been possible in the absence of the economic, political and social bases constructed in the course of the preceding period. Put another way, while the priority during the Maoist period was given to the construction of a solid long-term base, the new economic policy accentuated the immediate improvement of consumption made possible by the preceding effort. But on the other side, the accent placed on light industry and services starting in 1980 cannot last indefinitely, since China is again at a stage which demands further the expansion of its basic industries.

The new Chinese strategy is close to India's in its structure (priority to light industry and to services, under the pretext of drawing an advantage from cheap labor power), if not in its rates of growth, which remain considerably higher in China (Table 7.1).

China's advantage is not due to the structure of the chosen strategy, based on the same principles as India's, but is due precisely to the fact that in the preceding Maoist period a base had been constructed in China that was superior to India's.

Table 7.1 Annual growth rates 1980 to 1993

	China	India
GDP	9.6	5.2
Agriculture	5.3	3.0
Industries	11.5	6.2
Services	11.1	6.4

Source: Justin Yifu Lin, Fang Cai, and Zhou Li

If therefore China now has to follow this same strategy, its rate of growth will in its turn have to weaken to the point of approaching India's. This will happen because the strategy in question, based on the comparative advantage of cheap labor power, in no way maximizes or optimizes development as is pretended by liberal ideology in its thoughtless eulogy of the market. On the contrary, this strategy is a source of a growing wastefulness and of a deepening of social and regional inequalities, which in the long term reduces efficiency.

The strong growth of services observed for the past two decades no doubt compensates for a marked lag in this area during the Maoist period. But eventually it brings the forms of wastefulness that are specific to capitalism, forms about which liberal dogma remains completely silent.

The option in favour of the logic of the market does not automatically imply privatization, even though it does indeed encourage it. It was in this way that state property's share (in percentage of GDP) fell from 56 per cent in 1978 to 41 per cent in 1996, collective property's share from 43 per cent to 35 per cent, while private property, non-existent in the Maoist period, now has a 24 per cent share in the GDP. In 1996 the state employed 112 million urban workers, the collectives 30 million, and the private sector also 30 million (Liu Rongcang).

The most serious aspect is without any doubt the aggravation of inequality in the social distribution of income and – this is more debatable – in urban–rural relations and in the regional distribution of production and income. These negative evolutions are in part the hard-to-avoid result of the acceleration of growth and of institutional reforms in favor of the market. They would have been considerably reduced through a form of social and economic central planning that was level with the challenges – but this was not to be the case, since the government was satisfied with inadequate conjunctural macro-economic policies.

In the urban zones, where modern industries and services are concentrated along with new private capitalism, the main form of the new inequality is associated with the establishment of a new "middle class" of salaried professionals and of small business owners. There are also some "new rich" – some of them very rich – especially among businesspeople (Chinese from outside China, for the most part) associated with the state, the collectives, and foreign capital in "joint ventures." Are there also "new poor"? The suppression of the airtight administrative compartment that isolated country people from the urban labor market and the dissolution of the communes freed up an "excess" rural population which flowed toward the cities. In addition, converting the public urban sector to the principle of possible lay-offs aggravated unemployment, which was unknown in the Maoist period. Unemployment and economic insecurity now hit one-seventh of the urban workforce (Liu Wenpu). The number of laid-off workers from the public sector from the beginning of the reforms through to the end of 1997 reached 13 million, of whom only half have found new jobs, with many of them (but certainly not all) going to work in a new informal sector, or hired on through the expansion of the private sector (Zhang Zhuoyan).

The strong increase in inequality in the countryside has different causes. The opening up of a newly expanding urban demand for food products other than cereals (vegetables, fruit and meat) has obviously benefited the regions that are geographically best situated, highlighting the relative poverty of other regions. The commune system had already attracted some rural industrialization, destined to employ usefully the excess population which urban industry could not absorb. This expansion has truly exploded, starting from 1980. There are now hundreds of thousands of rural industries of various types of official status. Some are openly private, but the majority are formally "collective," with their property dependent on various local organizations. The social reality behind the juridical appearance nevertheless remains blurred, masking unacknowledged private interests of important people. This prodigious expansion of the rural enterprises has been and remains very unequally divided across the national territory, with the rich districts having the possibility to finance their establishment more easily than the others (Zhao Renwei).

In the Maoist period almost the only cause of inequality in the countryside came from historical heritage and the quality of the lands; this inequality was therefore almost synonymous with regional inequality. Within the communes – rich or poor – a very strong equality was maintained, with the "points" distributed to the team members being in practice distributed equally. Once responsibility was passed on to households, this was no longer true. Up until now the monitoring by the public authority over the granting of lands in usufruct to peasant families (and the absence of a market of agricultural lands) has managed to avoid the worst possibility – that is, the gigantic polarization that characterizes all the capitalist countries of the Third World. But a new source of inequality among rural households has appeared in the fact that access to inputs (credits, equipment, fertilizer) is subject to many conjunctural chances which strike unequally. Poverty, which is obviously always relative, and does not correspond to any possible rigorous conceptualization, has always existed in the Chinese countryside. But equality in the communes and in state policies made it possible during the Maoist era to put an end to the extreme miseries of traditional China and notably to famines. Speeches and writings about the supposed "famines" of the Maoist period depend on a dishonest propaganda in which no fact has been established, as William Hinton has correctly written. But now there are impoverished rural families, especially in relative terms. This impoverishment – which is the cause of the new rural exodus – is experienced as even worse because it takes place in a period of perceptible improvement in income for the great majority of the rural population, which is still more pronounced for a small minority. It is enough to travel through the Chinese countryside – as I have done on occasion – to see it with one's own eyes. But I should note that nowhere in China was I able to observe what is common in the rest of the Third World: an abject large-scale poverty.

A second source of inequality lies in the city–country relations. It appears from recent work that the ratio in question (which always favored the cities) evolved in favor of the countryside in the early phase of the post-Maoist period, only to reverse the trend later. This would be explained by the fact that the reform began in the countryside but that the later take-off of modernization in the cities erased the temporary advantage gained by the country people. This is quite plausible.

In any case, if growing inequality represents a problem, because of its scope and its political and social significance, the question of poverty on the other hand is posed in different terms. The situation in China on the morrow of its revolution was that of the capitalist Third World: abject poverty dominating in the cities and the countryside. Maoism reduced this poverty, which by 1978 became negligible in the urban area and was reduced to a minority of country people, concentrated primarily in the provinces of the northwest and the southwest. According to polls carried out in China by numerous researchers who are neither less competent nor less independent than their Western counterparts, rural poverty has been reduced to about 50 million people in 1997 (Liu Wenpu), while, from being negligible in 1978, poverty now afflicts 32 million city dwellers (same source). These figures are plausible, given what was said above. But they hide the new sources of impoverishment in the rural sector and of its emergence in the urban zone. Thus, contrary to the proposals for "struggle against poverty" based on "*ad hoc* projects" such as those proposed by the World Bank and which certain Chinese intellectuals take up on their own account, I have little faith for my part in the effectiveness of these methods in the absence of a macro-policy (central planning) which takes on poverty directly and gives it the priority it merits.

The question of regional inequalities is unavoidable for a country-continent such as China. But here too, conclusions that are hasty do not help identify the mechanisms responsible for these developments, and therefore the effectiveness of the corrective measures that might be proposed. According to general opinion, these inequalities have been aggravated over the past twenty years to the benefit of the coastal provinces, which throughout modern times have been integrated more systematically into global capitalism.

These facts establish that the gap between the country's eastern and western rural sectors was accentuated between 1988 and 1995 (Table 7.2).

The more rapid increase in rural income in the east of the country is not exclusively due to the increase in agricultural production, which is favored there by urban demand. On top of this is superimposed the growth in income produced by the small rural industrial businesses, a growth which is also favored for the same reasons: a good number of these rural enterprises are, in addition, subcontractors of the urban industries.

Other sources (Yifu Lin) confirm this judgment and locate the start of the aggravation of inequality in the origins of the reform in 1978. In this account the ratio of per capita income in the east to per capita income in the west went from 1.2 in 1978 to 1.7 in 1994.

Table 7.2 Rural income per capita (in 1988 constant yuans)

	1988	*1995*
East	891	3,150
West	551	1,292

Source: Zhao Renwei

The central planning of the Maoist period proved to be only relatively effective in the matter of regional inequalities – but the freeing up of market forces in the following phase accentuated the breadth of these inequalities. This tendency could be fought only by means of central planning founded on giving priority to the internal market and to the systematic development of ways for the provinces to complement each other. The option chosen, which gave priority to the external market, systematically favors the country's eastern regions, and the corrective policies put in place are too timid to slow down the dominant effects. Once again we must face the question of interior/exterior relations in the development concepts of the Maoist and post-Maoist periods.

The analysis of the inequalities proposed here concerns only the great urban and rural masses and the classes and social strata that surround them. It says nothing concerning the privileges of the ruling strata, which, if they do not represent much in macro-economic terms, do not for all of that have less important and definite political effects.

5

"Market" has been one of the catch-all terms of the past two decades. The other term is "opening." The question of opening – that is, the participation of some country or other (China, as it happens) in the international division of labor and all the other aspects of economic globalization (recourse to foreign capital, importation of technologies, membership in the management institutions of the global economy) cannot be settled in the extreme polemical terms – opening or closing! – in which the dogmatic defenders of triumphant neo-liberalism try to lock up the debate. To let oneself play this fixed game is a sure way to be put in a position which renders impossible any serious discussion on the real options which are offered to any society located geographically on Planet Earth.

The question is not even essentially a question of the "degree of opening," which one could measure quantitatively, for example, in terms of the ratio of the volume of foreign trade to the GDP. From this point of view, China's participation in global markets was almost insignificant until 1980. This is explained largely by the hostility of the external world – a compulsory blockade – but also by an internal decision which was not without some sense at the beginning. A certain withdrawal within oneself, at a time when the country is concentrating entirely on the gigantic political and social (and positive) reforms that the revolution implies is not absurd, when we understand the breadth of the supplementary difficulties with which one is confronted in relations with the global system, that has been and remains fundamentally dominated by the imperialists, and therefore hostile.

Nevertheless, it is necessary to know how to manage these relations and to be able to profit from them. To accelerate development, which implies a certain amount of "catch-up" in any case, it is necessary to borrow more advanced technologies (we are not going to reinvent the wheel!), and we have to pay through exports. What we can offer on the global market is, at this stage, products that benefit from the "comparative advantage" of their labor intensiveness. But it is necessary to know that we are being exploited in this unequal trade and that we accept this situation – temporarily – from the lack of an alternative. It is therefore a matter of planning at first the minimum needs in imports that make it possible to maximize economic growth, and then to deduce from this the type and volume of exports necessary to meet these needs. This minimum of necessary exports – and not the maximum possible – is not insignificant, and it has definitely become broadly superior to what its volume was in 1980. That the reforms would propose, in the early period, to meet this challenge and for this purpose to give a certain priority to potential export industries that are able to respond to it the fastest is not absurd.

The danger appears when the success of this choice inspires a reversal of the connections that govern the logic of a development strategy worthy of the name. Such a strategy implies the subjection of the quantitative goals of external trade to the requirements of the unfolding of a development plan that assures the strengthening of social solidarity in the interior, and therefore the ability to impose itself on the exterior with a maximum of autonomy. The liberal dogma proposes exactly the opposite; that is, the maximum enlistment in the international division of labor, which is based on the priority given to the expansion of activities through which the country "benefits" from the comparative advantage of its abundant labor power. The first option is what I have characterized as "disconnection," which means the refusal to submit to the dominant logic of the global capitalist system, not autarky; the second option is one of an adjustment that is always passive in reality (even though it is characterized as "active insertion") to the requirements of integration into the global system.

The vulgar economists have always pushed the second solution, and will continue to do so. Their arguments will always be the same, and nothing distinguishes the Chinese liberals in this regard. None of these arguments has any scientific basis, since they are all derived from a false a priori assumption (that prices determined by unregulated markets produce optimal growth). This "theory" is therefore nothing but a logical fallacy that finds in its conclusions what it put into its premises. Nothing in the history of really existing capitalism confirms the conclusions of this "theory" of an imaginary system: the history of capitalist globalization is not one of the success of "catch-up" policies based on the adjustment in question and on comparative advantages. On the contrary, it is one of polarization between the dominant imperialist centers and the compradorized peripheries, subjected and super-exploited, produced by this submission to the global capitalist system.

One more step in the drift to liberalism is proposed by the defenders of the "liberalization" of the flows of capital and of the abandonment of public management of the rates of exchange. Here too I see nothing more in the arguments of the Chinese liberals than the various standard types of liberal ahistorical dogma. Discourses of this sort produced in record time the crisis of Southeast Asia and Korea in 1997. This crisis did not force the Chinese liberals to nuance their fundamental options, since they continue to support absolute priority for "export-oriented" industries; instead they repeat the IMF line attributing the crisis to causes which, although real, are still secondary (such as the excesses of the local banking systems). The responsibility of the strategies put into practice by foreign financial capital, which made gigantic profits from this crisis and continue to do so, is completely erased. This responsibility must not be mentioned at all.

Despite all their intrinsic weaknesses, the neo-liberal propositions derive their force from two arguments.

The first is "the Korean example," the second the Taiwanese example. Here indeed are two countries, which the Chinese know well and the second of which is close to their hearts, that seem to be progressing satisfactorily along the road to a serious "catch-up," have opted for a strategy of "opening," and have nevertheless been quite capable of creeping up the rungs of the international division of labor. The particular reasons (including the geostrategic ones) of these "successes" cannot be discussed in this chapter, along with the vulnerability of the Korean economy, now subject to the full force of a strategy of recompradorization which the United States is trying to impose on it. In any case, what might indeed be possible in exceptional situations (and I doubt even that) is not the rule, much less for an immense and diverse country such as China.

Take, for example, the question of membership in the World Trade Organization (WTO), to which the Chinese government has come around. The application of the rules imposed on international trade by the founding treaty of this institution would bring disaster for Chinese agriculture, force China to renounce the autonomy in food production which it has acquired at the cost of so many efforts, dismantle its basic industries under the pretext of their "exorbitant costs," and make the country renounce any prospect of asserting itself in the technological area. It is possible that people believe they will be able to escape these rules in one way or another. I have not heard convincing evidence for this idea. For the rest, after Seattle, the WTO itself is in crisis. Why hurry to join an institution which may be stillborn? Would not a country such as Chine have a considerably broader margin for negotiation if it stayed outside the institution? These are questions that seem to me to have barely been discussed – at least in public. Unfortunately, opponents of entry to the WTO have limited themselves to defense of the pre-existing trade regime, which under the circumstances of the reform has proved to offer great opportunities for corruption.

It is this same type of situation that prevails in the debate over the choices in the management of exchange. The defenders of the past do not propose anything other than the maintenance of a fixed exchange managed administratively by the Central Bank, thus easing the task of the liberals, who can develop the habitual academic dissertations on the advantages and drawbacks of "pegging" the currency to one or several of the dominant currencies, of absolute "flexibility" (judged with good reason as unrealistic . . . the least we could say), and to propose finally an empiricism without clear perspective.

One thing is certain: the liberal opening-to-the-markets option makes Chinese society and the state vulnerable, weakens the capacity to face the real challenge which the hegemonist strategy of the United States and its junior partners in the Triad (Europe and Japan) represents, and the declared goal of which is to stop by all means – war and the dismemberment of the country included – China becoming a great power and a real competitor. The systematic campaign around Tibet and the renewed aid to the supporters of Taiwan's independence is the other side of the same coin.

6

The reform of the Chinese economic and social system, although well on its way, is far from complete, since it still leaves open the choice between a capitalist option without restrictions (other than minor or verbal ones) and the option of a "market socialism" understood as a stage in the long transition to communism.

Current initiatives to create financial institutions to manage the flood of money unleashed by the expansion of market relations, and the reform of the fiscal system to replace budgetary allocations with a tax on corporate profits, are both necessary once the market principle is admitted (even if the market is firmly regulated by a central planning system, which has not been the case up until now). The result of the state's fiscal and financial policies put into practice up until now is in any case not a bad one. China has avoided the catastrophic deficits to which shock therapy subjected the countries of the East, two-digit inflation, and massive external debt.

The question of the future of the state industrial sector has not received a clear answer, even in terms of principles. The institutional reform itself, which constitutes only the substructure, is not complete. Once these general institutional reforms are stabilized, the task of conducting reforms intended to restore to heavy industry its driving role in the orientation and acceleration of the whole, to clear up bottle-necks, to promote technological innovation – in short, the task of responding to the requirements of efficiency – remains to be addressed.

There is in general no abstract response to these problems. Universal condemnation of public property by the neo-liberal discourse is pure propaganda without scientific foundation; it rests on the idea – an a priori assumption, which is also false – that what is private is by nature more "efficient."

The state sector suffers from "widespread troubles" only when it is looked at from a great distance. And as a matter of formal accounting, it is not in deficit as a whole (Yifu Lin). It is true that the deficit in some sectors or the surplus in others are what they are only because of the current cost structure, and other factors (such as employment security or favorable rates on loans) that make the accounting comparison difficult. In many cases, if not in all, the equipment is from superseded technologies, which does not imply that the best solution is to close down these factories or to renovate them completely. To confuse efficiency and competitiveness, to reduce the first concept to the second, has no general scientific value. It would therefore be necessary to examine the problems posed in this sector concretely and case by case. Furthermore, while resolving them in this manner it is necessary to draw out from these solutions principles that are coherent with the requirements of the phase of the long transition in which the country is engaged after having passed through the phase of extensive accumulation and central planning. I do not have the presumption to think that I am in a position to say more about this here. In any case, the Chinese are right, in this case, not to hurry.

The debates about the future of the private sector, how much should be opened to it, the possible nature of the control over its expansion by macro-policies by the state and the possible cautious forms of planning, and the degree of openness to the exterior authorized to it, are barely broached. As good practical people, the authorities have only admitted that there is a place in China for an openness to private initiative – which seems to be sensible at the country's current stage of development. What is encompassed in this openness is a mixture of various factors, of no less different ideological and social imports, the bearers of more or less serious dangers over the longer term. There are local initiatives in the real sense of the term, in which the relations to local notables are blurred to say the least; there are initiatives from the capital of Chinese in the exterior (including Taiwan), whose political power is limited so far; there are foreign capital initiatives controlled to different degrees by the formulas of the "joint venture." But there is not yet any political economic philosophy considering in the longer term the relations between the government, the Chinese nation, the laboring classes, and these private interests. The debate about this area must leave the limits of a day-to-day pragmatism. The question of the organization of the political power of the state, of the autonomy of the organization of the laboring classes, of the establishment of counter-powers, cannot be separated from the questions that concern the organization of economic life.

7

The balance sheet we could draw up on the reforms is therefore a provisional one; the direction of the undertaking – which has not yet reached its end – is still open after all.

Some reforms were indispensable. Central planning did not represent in any way the completed form of socialism, but only the first phase in a long transition; a phase that was eminently positive and which cannot be ignored, but which had to be superseded once we had obtained the results that could be expected from it. This the defenders of Maoism have not understood (the Cultural Revolution itself, dealing with other areas, did not consider it useful to touch the various forms of the plan's central management model) and have in this way left the field open for the "reformers," who are at best confused, and at worst want to restore capitalism.

I am adopting a different attitude here from that of the systematic detractors of the reforms (cf. He Qinglian), who act as if the system has already come to fruition – nothing other than the restoration of capitalism. At the same time, my attitude is different from that of the system's defenders from the left (cf. Ajit Singh), who for their part imagine that the reform has already set up this famous "market socialism" which is the power structure's official slogan.

The "positive" aspects of the reforms undertaken at this point do not need to be recalled: the acceleration of growth sums up their different dimensions. In addition, this growth has been sufficiently controlled up until now (and I emphasize this limit in time) so that the negative aspects (the inequalities inside the country and the vulnerability on the international level sum them up) have been limited.

These results have been obtained by pragmatic day-by-day choices, corrected as problems arose. Thus there were years of "overheating" characterized by the accelerated expansion of the market sector, followed by moments of "cooling off" (obtained by raising interest rates and the prices of essential inputs – energy, among other things). This pragmatism cannot take the place of planning and of a serious reform of planning. In addition, it multiplies and does not reduce the occasions for hidden "negotiations" to find positions generating personal income, associated as is always the case – in China and elsewhere – with the corruption of officials (cf. Yifu Lin).

The danger that the system will evolve progressively – by means of this pragmatism without principles – toward a pure and simple capitalism is not theoretical. It already represents the main danger. Without the authentic organization of the laboring classes, who are deprived of the means to undertake the struggles necessary to all social progress, the drift in this direction is inevitable. The liberal currents in China's interior and pressures from the exterior work actively in this direction. The concept of "market socialism" would then be devoid of all real sense, and the system would be simply capitalist, even if public ownership of property is retained (and I doubt it could be under those conditions).

Even if the logic of the central planning stage was indeed based on certain systematic distortions (low interest rates, undervaluation of exchange, low nominal salaries, subsidized prices for energy, raw materials and basic food products), the adoption of the opposite market principles (positive real interest rates, flexible exchange and credit markets, integration of the labor markets and job insecurity, deregulation of markets in general, and the opening of new areas for the commodification of the land) does not correct the distortions of the preceding stage, which were necessary in their time. Instead, it creates new – and negative – distortions for the new stage. For these market rules do not by themselves produce the "optimum," as the academic talks of the liberals pretend. They bring a wastefulness that, in China's conditions, would be criminal, would destroy all hope of social progress and of national independence (the two terms being inseparable). "Competitiveness," if acquired at this cost for the islets of a modern economy submerged in a mass of regression (stagnation at best), is not synonymous with efficiency. On the contrary, it is the opposite of the requirements for the efficiency of the system as a whole.

Now these areas of waste are already visible. As Hinton shows, part of the accelerated growth of agricultural production has been obtained to the detriment of the long term, which demands a meticulous maintenance of land capital, its improvement through actions which the market – always governed by a short-term rationality – does not allow.

China had reached the point of being ranked high in the hierarchy of social and human indicators of development (by the criteria of the UN Development Program, UNDP), and it has been established that the "privatization" – or even just "market rationalization" – of social services such as health or education is the guarantee of their degradation. National solidarity requires a quality public school system, the creator of citizens. The ability to innovate is not the spontaneous product of "competition" on the markets; instead, competition devours this ability in a wasteful and deforming manner. The ability to innovate is the product of education and public support; in the United States itself it is largely dependent on military spending that has nothing to do with the criteria of the market.

I am one of those who believe that the choice for all humanity is "socialism or barbarism," that capitalism can no longer offer humanly acceptable prospects, having exhausted its progressive historic role, and that the level of productive forces potentially allows for communism on a global scale, but that it will take a long time to arrive at this. I will not try to make a prognosis on the temporal distance that separates us from this horizon, since the best (and the only) instrument for this would be a crystal ball. But no humanist political and economic strategy in any country on our planet, whether it is China, Burkina Faso, or the United States, can be thought of outside of the long perspective of the societal project for a global socialism – understanding by socialist a society where human beings, having become (relative) masters of their destiny, freed from the market alienation proper to capitalism, would be able to innovate and invent the adequate forms for a social management on every level, integrating all its social and economic dimensions. The visionary aspect of this creative utopia can substitute for the rule that capital employs – that is, exploits – alienated labor its opposite, namely that human beings – who are not reduced to the status of a labor force – shall use capital, which is conceived of as an instrument and not an end in itself. Otherwise, capitalist accumulation will more and more assert its destructive dimensions, through alienation (and the barbarism it produces), the destruction of nature, and the polarization that makes any national "catch-up" plan impossible.

I am taking this point of view to judge the possibility that a project for "market socialism" can constitute a positive phase in the long transition envisaged. The "national" project of the historical bourgeoisies has always been based on some grand principles allowing control over the labor market, the natural resources of the internal market, the flows of financing, and access to technology. Control over these elements has been possible on the basis of the relations of historical capitalism in the countries that became the centers of the global system. Because of this, such control could not be reproduced in the peripheries in the same fashion. History does not allow imitation. It forces us to combine the measures for the necessary relative "catching up" with the beginning of the development of a logic which supersedes it. Not "to do the same thing, but faster," but to "do otherwise," as Mao said in his time.

Central planning finds its place here as the expression of the strong regulation of markets required at China's stage at the dawn of the twenty-first century. This planning supersedes altogether the catalog of conventional bourgeois economic political macro-policies. It is able to distinguish social and national efficiency from simple competitiveness. It is able to put into practice measures which do not exclude social redistribution of income, regional and sectorial redistribution of the means of financing, and indeed of control of external relations. Let people call it what they want – "market socialism" if that is their wish. That is not the question.

The truly essential issue is that this central planning is effective only if it really proceeds from the aspirations of the laboring classes. Therefore it involves a real democratization, the recognition of the principle of organizational autonomy of the different sectors making up these classes (the workers' unions, the rural co-operatives), recognition of the possible divergence of certain of their interests, and the political means for collective negotiation which will permit provisional arrangements between the partners. All this goes far beyond the "low-intensity democracy" proposed by the dominant Western ideology (a multi-party political system made impotent by the dictatorship of the market) or the thoughtless praise for the freedoms enjoyed in the framework of so-called civil society, brought into fashion by the postmodernists and taken up by the populists of the Third World and China. These fundamental questions are unfortunately to a large extent conjured away in the Chinese debates with which I am familiar, but they have been raised – I know – by Maoism's best heirs (cf. Lin Chun).

References

Amin, Samir, *L'avenir du maoisme*, Edition de Minuit, 1981.

Amin, Samir, *Les défis de la mondialisation*, Harmattan, 1996, Chapter "Le projet de la Chine post maoiste."

Cai, Fang, *Options of Employment Policies in Transitional China*, CASS, 1999.

Fan, Gang, *Local Taxation Autonomy*, CASS, 1999.

Gao, Haihong, *Exchange Rate Policy: Possible Choices for China*, CASS, 1999.

Han, Deqiang, Some questions on the large scale development of China's western regions, *World Economy and China* 8(4), 2000.

He, Qinglian, *China's Pitfall*, Hong Kong, 1998.

Hinton, William, The importance of land reform in the reconstruction of China, *Monthly Review*, July–August 1998 (New York).

Howell, Jude, Sun Bing Yao, Wang Ying, Gordon White and Zhe Xiaoye, *Market Reform and Civil Society in China*, UNRISD, 1994.

Huang, I-Shu, Les minorités nationales de Chine, *Alternatives Sud*, 7, 2000 (*China Report* 32(1), 1996).

Li, Jingwen and Zhang, Xiao, *China's Environmental Policies in the 21st Century*, CASS, 1999.

Li, Peilin, *Economic Transition, Social Transformation and Social Policy*, CASS, 1999.

Li, Shi, Urban poverty research in China, *World Economy and China*, 8(4), 2000.

Lin, Chun, various articles (communiqués à S.A.).

Lin, Justin Yifu, Cai, Fang and Li, Zhou, Le miracle chinois, *Economica*, 2000.

Lin, Zhique and Ronald C. Keith, Economic crime in China's transition to rule of law economy, *China Report*, 35, 1999.

Liu, Rongcang, *The Transformation of China's Economic System and the Redefining of the Public Policy*, CASS, 1999.

Liu, Wenpu, *Poverty and the Poverty Policy in China*, CASS, 1999.

Singh, Ajit, *Plan, Market and Economic Reform in China*, UNRISD, 1993.

Xie, Ping, The convertibility of the RMB and China's exchange rate policies, *World Economy And China*, 8(4), 2000.

Zhan, Liqing, Confronting WTO, *World Economy and China*, 8(4), 2000.

Zhang, Xaiohe, The increasing income inequality in China and its causes, *China Report*, 35(2), 1999.

Zhang, Zhuoyuan, *Reform of the State-owned Enterprises*, CASS, 1999.

Zhao, Renwei, *Increasing Income Inequality and its Causes in China*, CASS, 1999.

Zhao, Xiaobin, Simon, *Spatial Disparities and Economic Development in China 1953–1992*, CASS, 1999.

Zhu, Huayou and Lin, Chenghui, *The Development of China's Non-governmental and Private Sector*, Foreign Language Press, Beijing, 1996.

Part III

Theoretical deliberations about China's reform

8 Rethinking the relationship between the state and society in the age of globalization

Zhu Houze

When I accepted Marxist ideology in my youth, the relations between the state and society had theoretical importance, and they constituted important issues. Thus, ever since the Third Plenary Session of the Eleven Central Committee of the Party gave me back my job, I have been thinking about this issue. As for the essential task that history has assigned, the twenty years of reform in China may be summarized as the process of reverting from state domination to society; that is, reverting from a situation in which the government dominated everything, to a situation of respect for civil life and the normal functions of society. Why is Chinese reform a process of reverting from the situation of state domination to a situation of normal social functioning?

This is because after we had established new China, our state devoured and swallowed up society. The state monopolized almost every resource, and put a stop to every normal social activity. Therefore, the entire processes of social productivity and life were managed by the government and officials. Each individual was only a part, a small cog, in the vast machine of the state, and each individual lost his or her independence, autonomy, vigor, and vitality. This was illustrated in social and economic life. Enterprises lost their status as independent economic entities, and the vigor of self-development, self-adjustment, and self-innovation was lost. In addition, each individual became a dependency and subordinate of his or her work unit. Several years ago, I was answering a question when I remarked that Marx stressed the "return of power over society to society." This demonstrates that the restoration of the normal functions of society is an essential task of the socialist revolution and construction. At that time, I said, "Socialists regard society as their belief, and maintain their belief in society. We should not be confused and follow others, nor regard étatism as socialism, and thus worship étatism." However, in the thirty years after the establishment of the People's Republic of China, the leadership's knowledge and practice of the leadership misunderstood this. Therefore, we are not generally and abstractly discussing the relations between state and society – rather, we are discussing it from the perspective of individuals who had become dependants of their work units for thirty years since the new China was established, when social production and life were controlled completely by the state.

This morning, Mr. Yu Guangyuan mentioned the decision-making concerning reform at the Third Plenary Session of the Eleventh Central Committee of the Chinese Communist Party. The communiqué of the Third Plenary Session of the Central Committee of the Party actually mentioned the issue of the relations between state and society, and I think it is necessary to quote it here.

The communiqué of the Third Plenary Session decided that the priority of the Party should be placed on the construction of socialist modernization, and it clearly pointed out that the realization of the four modernizations requires greatly promoting productivity, and it inevitably requires transforming production relations and the superstructure which do not suit the development of productivity, in order to transform every mode of management, activity, and ideology that do not suit productivity. Therefore, this was a profound revolution.

The communiqué also pointed out that the major weakness of the management system, as a detailed illustration of the relations of production and superstructure, was its highly centralized power. We should decentralize it under the direction of leadership, allowing local governments and industrial and agricultural enterprises to have more autonomy of operation and management. We should simplify economic and administrative institutions at each level, transferring most of the responsibilities to specialized and joint corporations. We should conduct business while firmly following the law of economics, paying attention to the functions of the law of values. We should carefully solve the problems of the confused functions among the Party, government, and enterprises, as well as the problems of the replacement of the government with the Party, and replacement of enterprises with the government. Only by doing this can we effectively fulfil the various roles of the central departments, local governments, enterprises, and labors in the aspects of initiative and creativity, and only by doing this can we also promote the development of each department and linkage of the socialist economy. I do not need to quote this further. The above will demonstrate that when reform started, the most important issue concerning how to conduct the reform of the system in social and economic life had been clearly raised.

How do we face history and reality, the system we have built in thirty years after the establishment of new China, and how do we explore and think about globalization, modernization, and the path of Chinese development? I must first point out that, in addition to the disaster of the state devouring and swallowing up society in the socialist revolution and construction, our country also has a history of centralized authority and autocratic rule. In addition, we have a political and cultural tradition that has put state interests above everything else, where authority comes above everything else – that is, the relationship between state and society is one of domination and subordination. Since Sun Yet-sen's establishment of the Republic of China, this issue has not been clarified nor completely solved. We should not underestimate history's obstructive impact on the development of the nation.

From the historical perspective of globalization and modernization, we can see that China was twice invaded by powerful outside civilizations in modern and contemporary history. The assault of two powerful civilizations on China was and is the demonstration of the process of globalization. So, what is globalization?

Globalization has many definitions. In a discussion ten years ago, I made the suggestion of connecting and differentiating between the material aspect and social-economic mode of globalization. I used the two categories "material aspect" and "social economic mode." At that time I said that globalization refers to the human activities in the world (first, economic activities, but not limited to such) which mutually communicate, integrate, connect, co-exist, benefit, explore, use, and restrict beyond political boundaries of national countries or boundaries of geographical regions in terms of economy, culture, society, politics, and so on. This process is based on the imbalanced distribution of natural, economic, historical, and world human resources. The absolute nature of the imbalanced distribution of resources determines the absolute nature of mutual communication and exploration among different regions and nations. This cannot be changed by any system. Each nation, which develops in different regions and within different natural and historical conditions, exhibits characteristics of its own civilization. In the process of human history some regions have been developed, and some have been developed slowly, some have become central regions, and some have become marginal regions. The levels of development among civilizations are different, and there are gaps among civilizations. This promotes communication, exchange, acceptance, and exploration among civilizations. These are not new phenomena in the history of the development of human civilizations. Historically, China was once the center of Eastern civilizations. Japan and other countries constantly sent people to the city of Chang'an to learn and to travel in China. Our ancestors also overcame difficulties and hardship – because they saw another civilization that was different from theirs, they traveled to India for Buddhist classics, as described in the classic novel *Journey to the West*.

In the process of communication, different national cultures have different characteristics, and when they mutually exchange, they will manifest their own national interests. Therefore, in the process of acceptance and communication there are always cultural contradictions and conflicts of interests. We should calmly analyze the cultural contradictions and conflicts of interests in the process of acceptance and communication, and we should strive for conditions acceptable to both sides in order to create a win-win situation. In this situation, if we can reduce turbulence and avoid conflict, we will bring benefit to different nations and regions.

I believe that Deng Xiaoping's ideas on the special zones and his decision-making on the opening of fourteen cities in the coastal regions were practical policy choices in the new situation of interchange among civilizations. Our special zones actually provide foreign civilizations with ports in which to anchor. They provide a garden for the seeds of foreign civilization, as well as a suitable environment in which foreign civilizations can take root and grow.

There seem to have been two characteristics in the two foreign invasions of modern and contemporary history. First, it is easy to see the material aspect. In the latter part of the Qing Dynasty it was "solid boats and big cannons," and in the 1950s it was "two types of bombs and one type of satellite." But the system and culture behind the material aspect are not easy to see and examine. Thus the slogan and policy of the Westernization Movement was, "Chinese knowledge is the essence, and Western knowledge is for practical use." Several years later, after we had been defeated by Japan, which was originally the student of China, we finally became aware of the need to reform the system. As for the development from system reform to cultural reform, the emergence of the generation of Chen Duxiu, Lu Xun, Hu Shi, and Guo Moruo belonged to the latter period. After the establishment of new China, in the international situation at that time, it was natural and necessary to promote the manufacture of the "two types of bombs and one type of satellite." But the latter practice showed that without reform and innovation of the system it would be difficult to develop a new civilization in our country.

Second, when we were faced with the invasion of a foreign civilization it was during a time of serious national crisis. Thus, in order to deal with such a situation the state would monopolize resources, and the government would send officials to control the economy and politics, and to adopt state ownership. The government did not pay enough attention to civilian forces, and it even wanted to limit, weaken, and eliminate them. Many years of practice show that without active civilian forces, social vigor, and vitality, sustainable development is impossible. The decision-making of the Third Plenary Session of the Central Committee of the Party was the result of our rethinking of these serious lessons from modern and contemporary history. Economic development should depend on societal (*minjian*) forces – this has been proven by practice in Wenzhou, in Zhejiang Province, and throughout the nation.

Now we do not have any debates on this. The current problem is this: Because of the co-existence of many types of ownership, economic sectors, and different social interests, social conflict has become serious. How can we evaluate the situation and how do we deal with it? I think that with the development of the market, privatization, and socialization, various conflicts are inevitable, and they are not scary. We should not deny, cover up, or try to block out the existence of such conflicts.

From 1988 to 1989, I was responsible for the leadership of the National Trade Union. It was the experimental period which Wang Hui mentioned [in the conference], and that was when conflicts began to emerge. My colleagues and I promoted general trade unions at the provincial and metropolitan levels in order to foster dialogue with local governments at those levels. They did not conceal the conflicts – instead, these dialogues actually revealed them to the local governments. They communicated their demands, and, at that time, they hoped that they could resolve some of the conflicts at the local level, through dialogue, consultation, negotiation, agreement, and contracts, in order to maintain a stable situation. It was Shanxi Province, in the spring of 1989, which first conducted process. I think that with the development of the market, different interests would be revealed, and we ought to allow them to address their demands in a public, legal, and normal manner, in order to develop organizations that represent different interests, and that promote the process of social consultation and dialogue. We think that it is possible to fashion a common view among different interests, because there are mutually shared common interests – that is to say, we ought to make the cake as large as possible.

However, in any historical situation, in any period, there exist certain limitations that restrict how large the cake can get. Thus how to cut the cake is an issue that requires patient discussion in order to arrive at a decision. What we want to establish are normal democratic procedures and order. I think that now we have conducted twenty-two years of reform, we ought to put democratization and democratic political order on the agenda. It will be beneficial for us to do it well so that we can consolidate the achievements of reform and develop in the future.

In the spring of 1989 I put forward the slogan, "Establish a new order of socialist democratic politics." I discussed this issue in Shaoxing, Zhejiang Province. I worried that my words would be inaccurate and that they might result in a negative impact, so I did not plan to publish my speech. But a newspaper published my speech. Across the top was the "April 26 Editorial," and below it was the content of my speech. Of course, because I was a "small potato," my speech was not that important. It was impossible for it to have had any influence on the whole situation.

In yesterday's discussions and this morning's, many scholars mentioned the issue of state and society relations, and they had some serious debates about this issue. I used to invoke such words as "big government," "small government," "big society," "small society," "strong government," and "weak government." I think that from the perspective of Marxist classical theory, the major issue is that one does not want the state to go from being a public servant to a dictator over society. Put the other way around, one wants a state that has already become a dictator over society to return to a position of being a social public servant. Insofar as a new order of socialist democratic politics has not yet been established, what I worry about most is not whether we can establish a market economy, but whether we will establish "crony capitalism."

Discussion

Wang Hui: Now our discussions focus on the issue of whether the state should withdraw and the issue of state and market relations – but we often forget the main issues. Actually, a crucial issue of democracy is society. Many issues today are concerned with the roles of the state. But how we talk about society, I think, is a crucial issue.

Zhu Houze: I noticed your speech yesterday afternoon, and you clearly mentioned that there was "society," in addition to relations between the state and market. I agree with your opinion. Therefore, when we say that the state devoured society, this meant more than having transformed the private economy, having completely confiscated or transformed it. The social migration forbidden among work units means that labor cannot freely choose jobs. The topic we have discussed concerning the state devouring society includes this issue too. The issue we are discussing now about returning to civil society also includes the issue concerning how to make labor express its demands normally among each labor group, among peasants, workers, and each social interest, and how to form legal organizations that really represent their interests, and to promote social consultation and dialogue among social interests.

Tian Yu Cao: I do not think that you answered his question. His question was concerned with the fact that in addition to the relations between state and society, the conflicts among various forces in society constitute an issue as well. The process of social negotiation that you advocated in 1989 concerns not only the issue of state and society relations – it also can be concerned with internal conflicts and contradictions in society. The more complex and diverse issues of the 1990s, according to his view, are actually the conflicts among various social interests, not just the issue of state and society relations.

Zhu Houze: There were different opinions when negotiating with the government. Some people were upset and said that your trade unions wanted the same status as that of the government. We responded right away that we had to negotiate with the government because, first, the government is the biggest boss of the country, and state ownership was everywhere – we had to deal with the state. Second, the government functioned also as the social manager, the coordinator of social interests. Many relations required state regulation. So we had to hold discussions with the state.

Just now, what Tian Yu Cao said is correct. The relations among various interests we discussed are becoming more and more complex – for example, the relations between chambers of commerce and trade unions, and between investors and management. Therefore, it is important to promote social consultation and dialogue. I think that it is difficult to avoid this issue if we want to solve the current social conflicts.

Armin: My question is, is the implementation of socialization based on democracy or based on the market? There is a conflict between the market and democracy. How do you deal with these contradictions?

Zhu Houze: When I think about issues, I always consider the actual situation in China, and I seldom study the situation in the world. In the current situation in China, there are demands for improving the market, for the promotion of the market process, for the implementation of political democracy, and for the establishment of democratic political order. We have not seen any unresolved contradictions. The reality of China is that there is no freedom of capital, nor freedom of labor under the domination of the highly centralized government which has complete authority, and which has a highly centralized mandatory economic system.

9 Liberal socialism and the future of China

A petty bourgeoisie manifesto

Cui Zhiyuan

A specter is haunting China and the world – the specter of petty bourgeoisie socialism.

Why? Both Marxism and Social Democracy has lost its political and intellectual momentum worldwide. The disillusion about neoliberalism is also growing.

Petty bourgeoisie socialism can make some sense out of the current confusion in interpreting the institutional arrangements in today's China. Moreover, since socialism should not perpetuate the proletarian status of the working class, the universal petty bourgeoisie seems to be the promise of the future.[1]

The central economic program of petty bourgeoisie socialism is to establish a "socialist market economy," especially through reforming and transforming the existing institutions of financial markets. The central political program of petty bourgeoisie socialism is to promote "economic and political democracy."

The leading thinkers in the rich tradition of petty bourgeoisie socialism are P-J. Proudhon, F. Lassalle, J.S. Mill, Silvio Gesell, Fernand Braudel, James Meade, James Joyce, Charles Sabel, Fei Xiaoton, and Roberto M. Unger.

The notion of "petty bourgeoisie" used in this chapter includes peasants. This is the main difference with the notion of "middle classes" used in the current Chinese discourses. But the concept of petty bourgeoisie socialism may be associated with the current Chinese effort to build "Xiao Kang Socialism."

Proudhon and China's landownership system

Pierre-Joseph Proudhon has challenged Locke's theory that "private property in land originated in First Occupancy" by emphasizing that population growth makes it impossible for everyone to have private property in land:

> For, since every man, from the fact of his existence, has the right of occupation, and, in order to live, must have material for cultivation on which he may labor; and since, on the other hand, the number of occupants varies continually with the births and deaths, – it follows that the quantity of material which each laborer may claim varies with the number of occupants; consequently, that occupation is always subordinate to population. Finally, that, inasmuch as possession, in right, can never remain fixed, it is impossible, in fact, that it can

ever become property. . . . All have an equal right of occupancy. The amount occupied being measured, not by the will, but by the variable conditions of space and number, property cannot exist.[2]

Proudhon's point is that, if private property in land implies indefinite control of the owner, then it is incompatible with population change. Therefore, private property in land, understood as a universal[3] right applying to everyone, cannot exist.[4] In other words, if private landownership implies indefinite control on the part of the owner, it cannot adjust to population change, therefore private land-ownership cannot be a universal right for everyone; if private landownership adjusts to population change, it cannot be private property in the sense of owners' indefinite control. It is remarkable that today's landownership in China testifies to this insight of Proudhon.

China's rural land is *not* owned by the state, or by the individuals. Rather, it is owned by the village collective. The current system is called the household contract responsibility system for rural land lease (thirty years). How much land lease a family gets is in accordance with its size, and every member of the village regardless of age and gender receives an equal share. The land was leased out to the family by the village authority[5] for five years in the early 1980s, the length of land lease was extended to fifteen years in 1984, and further to thirty years in 1993. Because the size of a family changes over time with in-and-out marriages and births and deaths, village collectives usually make a small adjustment of the land lease every three years, and a thorough adjustment every five years.

It is a mistake on the part of many Western leftists to assume that China has "restored" the "capitalist productive relations in the countryside" after abandoning the People's Communes. China's rural landownership system is a Proudhonian version of petty bourgeoisie socialism, with all of its promises and contradictions.

The Chinese government is in the process of making land contract law and trying to consolidate the household contract responsibility system while achieving economy of scale and speeding up urbanization. It is a great experiment of petty bourgeoisie socialism in that one of its core ideas is to realize socialized production without depriving peasants.

J.S. Mill and the genealogy of the "modern enterprise system"

Establishing a "modern enterprise system" is the most often used phrase in contemporary Chinese discourse of economic reform. However, few have noticed that petty bourgeoisie socialism was at the heart of the genealogy of the "modern enterprise system." In fact, a petty bourgeoisie socialist J.S. Mill was the key figure to bring one of the main features of the "modern enterprise system" – limited liability for shareholders – into existence.[6]

It was due to the concern for the development of workers' cooperatives of his time that John Stuart Mill started to study the issue of limited liability. He first analyzed the so-called "en commandites" form of partnership. This special form of partnership had many proponents in England, the Christian Socialists perhaps being the most prominent among them. In this form of organization the "active" partners were subject to unlimited liability, staying with the idea of tying liability to responsibility, while the "sleeping" partners were subjected to limited liability, since they were not responsible for running the business. John Stuart Mill advocated this form of partnership because it would have allowed workers to form associations to "carry on the business [with] which they were acquainted" and also allow the "rich to lend to the poor." Mill argued:

> No man can consistently condemn these partnerships without being prepared to maintain that it is desirable that no one should carry on business with borrowed capital. In other words, that the profits of the business should be wholly monopolized by those who have had time to accumulate, or the good fortune to inherit capital, a proposition, in the present state of commerce and industry, evidently absurd.[7]

In 1850, Mill testified before the Select Committee on Investments for the Savings of the Middle and Working Classes of the British Parliament. He proposed to establish the corporate regime with generalized limited liability for shareholders, because it would induce the wealthy to lend more freely in support of projects by the poor. The poor would also benefit by having the opportunity to invest their savings in producers' or consumers' cooperatives. As a result of the efforts of Mill and others, the British Parliament passed the 1855 Act of general limited liability for corporations.

This genealogy of limited liability has been almost forgotten by the contemporary economists. The point of retelling this forgotten chapter of economic history is to highlight that the "modern enterprise system" is not necessarily capitalist. If shareholders have only "limited liability", it implies that they are not taking the full risks as "private owners" are supposed to do; therefore they should not enjoy all the profits of the enterprises.[8] In other words, the shareholders are not the only risk-bearing group. The employee's firm-specific human capital also runs at a risk. Moreover, shareholders can diversify their shareholding through a portfolio of different firms' shares, but a single worker cannot work for several firms all at the same time. In this light, it may be argued that employees' human capital runs a higher risk due to the lack of diversification. This opened the door to our understanding of the widespread institutional innovation in China's rural industry – a "shareholding-cooperative system."

James Meade and the Chinese "shareholding-cooperative system"

James E. Meade, the 1977 Nobel Laureate in Economics, is one of the founders of modern GNP accounting. As a student of Keynes, Meade was inspired by the tradition of petty bourgeoisie socialism.[9] He always calls his program "liberal socialism." Meade's program aims to combine the best features of liberalism and socialism. It has two main components in its institutional design: "labor–capital partnerships," and "social dividend."

Labor–capital partnership

In Meade's design, outside shareholders own capital share certificates and inside workers own labor share certificates. The operational mechanism of the program is roughly as follows:

> the Labour–Capital Partnership, whereby the workers and those who provide risk capital jointly manage the concern as partners. The capitalists own Capital Shares in the business, which are comparable to Ordinary Shares in a Capitalist Company. The worker partners own Labour Shares in the partnership; these Labour Shares are entitled to the same rate of dividend as the Capital Shares, but they are attached to each individual worker partner and are cancelled when he or she leaves the partnership. If any part of the partnership's income is not distributed in dividends but is used to develop the business, new Capital Shares, equal in value to their sacrificed dividends, are issued to all existing holders of Labour as well as of Capital Shares. These partnership arrangements greatly reduce the areas of conflict of interest between workers and capitalists, since any decision which will improve the situation of one group by raising the rate of dividend on its shares will automatically raise the rate of dividend on the shares of the other group.
>
> (Meade 1993, 85–86)

In addition to this benefit of aligning interests of outside shareholders and insider workers, Meade's labor–capital partnership has an added main advantage of introducing flexibility into the labor market. The current social democracy in the Western European style suffers from a major problem: the high wage of workers on the job is maintained at the cost of rigidity of the labor market, thus implying an inefficient reduction of output and a level of employment below the potential full employment. When the labour–capital partnership uses a labor share certificate to replace a fixed wage arrangement, a degree of flexibility is introduced into the labor market which is formerly characterized by downward rigidity of wages.

It is important for the "progressive" forces in China and other post-communist countries not to imitate social-democratic policies pursued in Western Europe. There, the social-democratic parties had long lost their radical inspiration. Instead of challenging and reforming the institutions of the existing forms of market economy and representative democracy, the social-democratic program merely seeks to moderate the social consequences of structural divisions and hierarchies. We need more radical institutional innovations like the labor–capital partnership to make up for the deficiencies of conventional social-democratic policies. The flexibility in the labor market is just one case which illustrates this general point.

Social dividend

The second feature of Meade's program of "liberal socialism" is "social dividend:" every citizen is paid a tax-free Social Dividend according to the citizen's age and family status but without any other conditions. Two basic reasons for instituting social dividend are: (1) promotion of equality by providing everyone with the same basic unconditional income; (2) the reduction of risks by providing some part of income that is unaffected by variations required by flexibility in the labor market. The intuitive core of the idea of social dividend lies in the attempt to replace the demand for job tenure by an enhancement of the resources and capabilities of the individual citizen.

One of the advantages of social dividend over the conventional social-democratic policy of "conditional benefit" is that the former improves the incentives of recipients of low-earning jobs. This may appear counter-intuitive at first sight, because "unconditional social dividend" seems to reduce the incentive to accept low-paid jobs more than conditional benefit (based on unemployment or illness). However, intuition is wrong in this case. Meade argues against intuition with the following simple example:

> a recipient of a Social Dividend of 80 supplemented by a Conditional Benefit of 20 will have an incentive to take outside earnings so long as those earnings after deduction of Income Tax are greater than 20; but if he or she had relied for the whole 100 on a Conditional Benefit, there would be no incentive to accept any outside earnings less than 100.[10]

"Shareholding–cooperative system" (SCS) in China

In their effort to create a proper ownership form for rural enterprises, the Chinese "peasant-workers" and their community governments have designed an ingenious one: a "shareholding–cooperative system (SCS)."[11] It is similar to James Meade's "labor–capital partnership" in that both systems have a labor share and a capital share;[12] however, the Chinese SCS is distinct in that the capital share itself is mainly collective in the sense of belonging to the representative of the community – the township and village governments. Thus the SCS in China's rural industry may serve to harmonize the interests of inside workers and outside members of the same community. To give a sense of its working mechanism, I now describe briefly one of the earlier experiments with the SCS in rural China.

In one locality where I conducted preliminary field research in the summer of 1993, Zhoucun District of Zibo (Shangdong Province), the SCS was invented in 1982 as a response to the difficulties of dismantling the collective properties of the People's Commune. The peasants found some collective properties (other than land) to be simply physically indivisible. They decided to issue shares to each "peasant-worker" on equal terms, instead of destroying the collective property (such as trucks) to sell them in pieces (which had happened in many other regions). Soon after, they realized (or conceded) that they should not divide up all collective properties into individual shares to distribute to the current workforce, because the older generation of "peasant-workers" had left the enterprises and the local government had made prior investments. Thus they decided to keep some proportion of "collective shares" which would not go into individual labor shares. These collective shares are designed to be held by outside corporate bodies, such as local governmental agencies, other firms in and out of the locality, banks, and even universities and scientific research institutions. The following figures show the flow of profits of SCS in Zhoucun District:

10 per cent: Workers' welfare fund

After-tax profits of SCS firm – 30 per cent: Firm development fund

60 per cent: Share fund (collective and individual shares)

Clearly, the development of SCS is the joint product of two factors: (1) accumulated change of Chinese rural institutions (such as the dissolution of the commune), and (2) accidental solutions to the indivisibility of People's Commune's property. Therefore, the SCS has created an attitude of ambiguity among the Chinese practitioners and scholars on China as to how to evaluate the potential of this new form of property. As Karl Polanyi once said: "the contemporaries did not comprehend the order for which they were preparing the way."[13]

As for James Meade's "social dividend," there is so far no Chinese experiment in a similar spirit. However, it is my belief that China can benefit from considering seriously Meade's program of "social dividend" in establishing her own social welfare system.

Braudel, anti-market capitalism and real estate in China

Most commentators in the West, from the Right as well as from the Left, believe China is becoming increasingly "capitalist." But what is the meaning of the word "capitalism?" It is worth citing Fernand Braudel's struggle with this word:

> I have only used the word *capitalism* five or six times so far, and even then I could have avoided it. . . . Personally, after a long struggle, I gave up trying to get rid of this troublesome intruder. *Capitalism* . . . has been pursued relentlessly by historians and lexicologists. . . . But it was probably Louis Blanc, in his polemic with Bastiat, who gave it its new meaning when in 1850 he wrote: "What I call 'capitalism' [and he used quotation marks] that is to say the appropriation of capital by some to the exclusion of others." But the word still occurred only rarely. Proudhon occasionally uses it, correctly: "Land is still the fortress of capitalism", he writes. . . . And he defines it very well: "Economic and social regime in which capital, the source of income, does not generally belong to those who make it work through their labour." Six years later however, in 1867, the word was still unknown to Marx.[14]

Most importantly, Braudel makes a crucial distinction between "market economy" and "capitalism." According to him, "there are two types of exchange: one is down-to-earth, is based on competition, and is almost transparent; the other, a higher form, is sophisticated and domineering. Neither the same mechanisms nor the same agents govern these two types of activity, and the capitalist sphere is located in the higher form."[15] Braudel considers the market town as the typical case of the first type of exchange, and the monopoly of long-distance trade and financial speculation as the model of the second type (i.e., "capitalism," which is essentially "anti-market").

Braudel's distinction can make sense of the two types of real estate markets in China today. The first type is illustrated by He Gang City, Hei Long Jiang Province; the second type is illustrated by Bai Hai City, Guang Xi Province. In the case of He Gang city, when land speculation is prohibited by local government, the real estate market becomes the engine of local economic growth. In contrast, in Bai Hai City, real estate developers collude with the banks (borrowing money from the banks to speculate in the land market), the result being that common people cannot afford to buy houses due to the very high prices.[16] Petty bourgeoisie socialism must embrace the first type of market while rejecting the second.

China vs. Russia: petty bourgeoisie socialism vs. oligarchy capitalism

The Russian privatization program of 1992 "offered all citizen including children, for a nominal payment of 25 rubles, an opportunity to receive a voucher with a denomination of 10,000 rubles."[17] However, this happy starting point soon turned into a situation which produced oligarchy capitalism (in the sense of Braudel). The reasons are as follows:

1   Russia allowed free trading in vouchers. According to the three main advisers to the Russian government, "tradability lets people convert vouchers to cash right away, which especially helps the poor who have great immediate consumption needs . . . it vastly improves opportunities for potential large investors." Obviously, this re-concentrates wealth in the hands of the rich people, and this is the design of the program! No wonder the Russian Prime Minister Chernomyrdin said in December 1992 that the program of voucher privatization is comparable to Stalin's bloody collectivization of agriculture.

2   Each firm may choose among three options in the Russian privatization. The most widely used option is the so-called Option 2, in which workers and managers together can buy 51 percent of the voting shares at a nominal price of 1.7 times the July 1992 book value of assets, with vouchers and/or cash. Among the rest of the shares, 29 percent should be sold to the general public through voucher auctions. However, workers are prevented from holding their shares as a block. They can only own their shares individually. This is the deliberate design of Anatoly Chubais, head of the State Committee on the Management of State Property, in order to avoid any possible workers'

control.[18] As a result, the managers and big outside investors are eager to buy vouchers from the workers, and workers are not resistant to selling, even selling just one voucher for a bottle of vodka.

3   The Russian privatization did not rely on proper valuations of current state-owned firms' assets. No adjustment for inflation and "intangible assets" has been made. Anatoly Chubais "simply declared that book value of the Russian companies as of July 1992, without any adjustment, would serve as the charter capital." This decision gives tremendous benefits to the new buyers of state assets (29 percent of the firm's share as described in Option 2 above) through voucher auctions, as well as the insiders of the firm who can buy up to 51 percent of shares. Not surprisingly, the end result is the extreme low asset value of Russian industry: at the end of the voucher privatization scheme in June 1994, the aggregate value of the Russian industry was under $12 billion. Even the three main advisers to Anatoly Chubais were shocked: How could it be that "the equity of all of Russian industry, including oil, gas, some transportation and most of manufacturing, was less than that of Kellogg [one American health food company]?"[19]

James Meade's topsy-turvy state share ownership in China

There are two stock exchanges in today's China, The Shanghai Stock Exchange (opened on December 19, 1990) and the Shenzhen Stock Exchange (opened in July 1991). The corporations listed in these two Stock Exchanges usually have three types of shares: state shares, legal-person shares and individual shares:

- *State shares*. These are the shares held by the governments (both central and local) and solely government-owned enterprises.
- *Legal-person shares*. These are the shares held by other stock companies, non-bank financial institutions, and other social institutions.
- *Individual shares*. These are shares held and traded by individual citizens. They are called tradable A shares, since there are B shares offered exclusively for foreign investors.

A typical Chinese corporation listed in Shanghai or Shenzhen Stock Exchange usually has the above three types of shareholders; that is, state, legal-person, and individual. Each holds about 30 per cent of total outstanding shares.[20] By the end of July 1997 there were a total 590 companies listed in the Shanghai and Shenzhen Stock Exchanges. However, only individual shares are allowed to be traded on these two stock exchanges. State shares and legal-person shares are not permitted to be traded.

Currently, there is a heated policy debate on whether state shares should be traded on the Stock Exchanges. People who are against the trading of state shares cite mainly ideological reasons: they think trading in state shares amounts to "privatization;" those who are in favor of the trading of state shares argue that the large proportions of state shares in a corporation still cannot prevent governmental officials from arbitrarily intervening in business decisions, since the state must appoint officials to sit on the Board of Directors.

Some might think that the case of the state as shareholder is too specialized to offer any general theoretical insight. However, one of America's leading liberal thinkers, Louis Hartz, has written a definitive history on the "mixed corporation" – "mixed" in the sense that the state government is a shareholder among other private shareholders – in Pennsylvania between 1776 and 1860.[21] Upon reflection, it should not be surprising that states in the U.S.A. had to resort to shareholding as a means for their expenditure and industrial policy: it was only until February 1913 that the Sixteenth Amendment of the U.S. Constitution legalized income tax (as not being against private property[22]).

The example of "mixed corporations" in U.S. history reminds us that the state as shareholder may not be so special or exceptional. For example, the UK nationalized its steel, electricity, railways, and coal industries after World War II, yet the state in the U.K. was only a residual controller without residual claimant, since it "did not receive for its own free use the profits . . . since this was offset by the payment of interest on the national debt issued to raise the compensation cost of the nationalization schemes. Thus, the state became the owner-manager but without the benefit of an increased income."[23]

James Meade proposes to reverse the U.K. nationalization process. What he calls "topsy-turvy nationalization" is essentially giving "residual claims" rights to the state as shareholder without granting control rights. Two major benefits of this "topsy-turvy nationalization" are, according to Meade, (1) that the government can use the proceeds of its shareholding to finance "social dividend," which will provide the flexibility to the labor markets by granting a minimum income to everyone; (2) that the government can be separated from micro-managing business decisions for the companies it partly owns.

There is some resemblance between James Meade's vision and the Chinese emerging policy consensus on the state as a passive shareholder. Even the idea of "social dividend" can be partially seen in local practice: Shunda City in Guangdong Province has used the sale proceeds of government shares to finance its "social security fund." For this reason, I dub the prospect of passive state shares in China as "topsy-turvy state ownership." This raises deep theoretical questions about petty bourgeoisie socialism's vision of reforming the existing institutions of financial markets.

Silvio Gesell: petty bourgeoisie socialism's financial reformer

Keynes makes an amazing statement in his *General Theory of Employment, Interest and Money*: "the future would learn more from Gesell than from Marx."[24] Silvio Gesell (1862–1930) was a German businessman and finance minister in the government of Gustav Landauer of Ratterrepublik of Bavaria in 1919. Gesell considers himself a disciple of Proudhon. According to Gesell, Proudhon's central insight was that money held competitive advantage over labor and goods. Proudhon tried to raise goods and labor to the level of money, but failed. Since it is impossible to alter the nature of goods, Gesell proposed to alter the nature of money: "we must subject money to the loss to which goods are liable through the necessity of storage. Money is then no longer superior to goods; it makes no difference to anyone whether he possesses, or saves, money or goods. Money and goods are then perfect equivalents, Proudhon's problem is solved and the fetters that have prevented humanity from developing its full powers fall away."[25]

Concretely, Gesell proposes a "stamp scrip" or "stamp currency." Gesell's insight was that money as a medium of exchange should be considered a public service (just as public transportation) and, therefore, that a small user fee should be levied on it. In Gesell's time, stamps were the normal way to levy such a charge. Now, the generalized use of computers in payment would make this procedure much easier to implement.

To give a vivid sense of how "stamp scrip" works in reality, let us look at the Austria experiment in the 1930s. In 1932, Herr Unterguggenberger, mayor of the Austrian town of Worgl, decided to eliminate the 35 percent unemployment of his town. He issued 14,000 Austrian shillings'-worth of "stamp scrip" which was covered by exactly the same amount of ordinary shillings deposited in a local bank. A stamp is needed each month (at 1 per cent face value of "stamp scrip") in order to make this "local currency" valid. Since the cost of the stamp is a user fee for holding this currency, everyone wants to spend "stamp scrip" quickly, therefore automatically providing work for others. After two years, Worgl became the first Austrian city to achieve full employment.

Keynes specifically states his support of "stamp scrip:" "Those reformers, who look for a remedy by creating an artificial carrying cost for money through the device of requiring legal-tender currency to be periodically stamped at a prescribed cost in order to retain its quality as money, have been on the right track, and the practical value of their proposal deserves consideration."[26]

At the most general philosophical level, Gesell's "stamp scrip" may be viewed as a reform effort to separate the two traditional functions of money – money as medium of exchange and money as store of value, since "stamp scrip" eliminates money's function as store of value. This separation helps to solve one of the major economic problems of recession: when money both serves as the medium of exchange and the store of value, anybody in recession time will save more and consume less, thereby exacerbating the recession.

Gesell's "stamp scrip" proposal is a telling case of petty bourgeoisie socialism's economic vision: instead of abolishing the market economy, we can create such an economy with more freedom and equal opportunity by reforming and innovating the monetary institutions.

James Joyce and the art of petty bourgeoisie socialism

It is well known that James Joyce considers himself a "socialist artist."[27] But what kind of socialism? A clue to the answer may be found in *Ulysses*: when Bloom runs for municipal election, he declares:

"I stand for the reform of municipal morals and the plain ten commandments. New world for old. Union of all, jew, moslem and gentile. *Three acres and a cow for all children of nature. . . .* Free money, free rent, free love and a free lay church in a free lay state."[28]

Obviously, Joyce's socialism is petty bourgeoisie socialism. More tellingly, Ezra Pound, who was a great modernist poet and promoter of Joyce's works, devoted huge amount of time and energy to studying Gesell's financial reform proposal.[29] Also interestingly, the Soviet film director Sergej Eisenstein (1898–1948) met with Joyce in Paris and considered Joyce's *Ulysses* to be a great inspiration for his "dynamic montage."[30] In this context, we can understand Walter Benjamin's "The Arcades Project" – the montage of a social life of perpetual transition and juxtapositions.

The great modernist writers, such as James Joyce and Robert Musil,[31] have articulated the petty bourgeoisie socialist sensibility. Institutional innovations and personal transformations always go together!

Post-Fordism, Fei Xiaotong, Charles Sabel and Roberto M. Unger

There is a long tradition of petty bourgeoisie socialism in modern China. Hsiao-Tung Fei is especially important in this tradition. Beginning in the 1930s, Hsiao-Tung Fei has been concerned with "rural industry" and "small township." Fei realized that "to improve the produce [of rural industry], is not only a matter of technical improvement but also a matter of social reorganization."[32] Writing his dissertation in London under B. Malinowski in the late 1930s, Fei argued that "the real nature of the communist movement [in China] was a peasant revolt due to their dissatisfaction with the land system . . . it must be realized that a mere land reform in the form of reduction of rent and equalization of ownership does not promise a final solution of agrarian problems in China. Such a reform, however, is necessary and urgent because it is an indispensable step in relieving peasants."[33] More importantly, at that time (1938), Fei had already pointed out:

> Being a late comer in the modern industrial world, China is in a position to avoid those errors which have been committed by her predecessors. In the village, we have seen how an experiment has been made in developing a small-scale factory on the principle of cooperation. It is designed to prevent the concentration of ownership of means of production in contrast with the capitalist industrial development in the West. In spite of all difficulties and even failures, such an experiment is of great significance in the problem of the future development of rural industry in China.
>
> (Fei, 1939, p. 286).

It is important to note that Fei, like Proudhon, did not object to large-scale industry per se:

When the industrial revolution began, the major innovation was steam power, which caused the concentrated location of industry. Between steam engine and working machine, there must be a strap which connects them, so it was more economical to put these two machines close. . . . The use of electrical power could change the [concentrated] industrial location, [since] the distance between electrical power engine and working machine no longer needs to be short. . . . The invention of the internal combustion engine and its applications in transportation, makes concentrated industrial location even more unnecessary. . . . If the new economic opportunities opened by the new engines could not be shared by the majority of the [rural] people, it may have harmful effects on people's livelihood. The more [rural] people use these new engines and new technologies, the more likely that they will be used properly. This is the reason why I do not advocate the Western capitalism as a way to develop our new industries.[34]

Fei's concern may be connected to the theory of post-Fordism or "flexible specialization." Theoretically, China's rural industry fits the definition of flexible production. According to David Friedman, who applies the theory of flexible specialization developed by Piore and Sabel[35] (1984) to Japanese machine tool industry, "Mass production is the attempt to produce a single good at the highest possible volume to reduce costs through economies of scale. Flexible production is the effort to make an ever-changing range of goods to appeal to specialized needs and tastes with tailored designs" (David Friedman, p. 15). In comparison to state enterprises in cities, China's rural enterprises face a very unstable market for their products, subject to fluctuations due to economic and administrative shocks. Economic shocks come from the fact that their products have never been included in central planning, and central planning may be viewed as a mechanism which serves the function of "futures markets"; that is, a stabilizer of market demand. Administrative shocks come from the fact that the national tight credit policy in 1986 and 1989 had a disproportionly large impact on rural industry, because some policy coalition in the central government still favors big state enterprises in cities, especially in bad economic times. Facing highly unstable markets, China's rural enterprises have developed various technological and organizational arrangements for flexible production. Their dictum is "a small ship can change direction easily." They usually produce multiple products, and often change their product every one or two years (Fei, 1988, p. 170). If we adopt the above-mentioned David Friedman's definition of mass production as producing a single good at the highest possible volume, Chine's rural enterprises are clearly engaged in flexible production.

The conventional wisdom is that mass production is the most efficient way of modern industrial production, because it can reduce costs through economies of scale. The innovative idea put forward by Piore and Sabel is that flexible specialization is more efficient than mass production under the conditions of demand instability. The price shocks due to the oil crisis, the collapse of the Bretton Woods system which stabilized international markets from 1944 to 1973, and the saturation of consumer-goods markets in the industrial countries – all these factors make it more and more difficult to expand mass production further. The way out is "flexible specialization," which is the "second industrial divide." According to Piore and Sabel,

> flexible specialization is a strategy of permanent innovation: accommodation to ceaseless change, rather than an effort to control it. This strategy is based on flexible-multi-use-equipment; skilled workers; and the creation, through politics, of an industrial community that restricts competition to those favoring innovation. For these reasons, the spread of flexible specialization amounts to a revival of craft forms of production that were emarginated at the first industrial divide.
>
> (Piore and Sabel, p. 17)

As insightful as it is, this definition places to much emphasis on technology: multi-use, general-purpose, numerical controlled machines. Indeed, this definition may give people the impression that flexible specialization is impossible without computer-aided general-purpose machines.[36]

The Chinese rural industry highlights the importance of institutional, in contrast to technological, foundations of flexible specialization.[37] The reason for Piore and Sabel's (over)emphasis on general-purpose technology is, I suspect, that they do not distinguish between fixed costs and avoidable costs. In other words, they adopt the conventional microeconomics' distinction between fixed costs and variable costs. As they put it, "within the firm, the distinction between general and specialized resources is seen as a distinction between variable and fixed costs" (Piore and Sabel, 1984, p. 52). However, as J. Maurice Clark (1923) pointed out some time ago, fixed costs is only one of the costs under the general heading "overhead costs." William Sharkey recently picked up Clark's theme to develop his theory of "efficient production when demand is uncertain." According to him, avoidable costs, such as fixed costs, are independent of output. But

> avoidable cost, differs from the plant construction cost, or fixed costs, in that it can be avoided by taking a particular plant out of production . . . the interaction of uncertain demand with fixed plus avoidable costs requires a determination of the optimum flexible of capacity. The nature of the avoidable costs creates an incentive for smaller, more numerous plants that can be shut down when not needed in order to save on operating costs.
>
> (Sharkey, 1977, p. 370)

In other words, fixed cost is independent of both output and plant capacity; variable cost is not independent of output; and avoidable cost is independent of output, but not capacity.[38] By making the distinction between fixed cost and avoidable cost, we can open our eyes to many possible organizational innovations which reduce avoidable cost, rather than focusing only on technological innovations which reduce fixed costs. Viewed from this perspective, the scope for flexible specialization is much larger than previously perceived.

China's rural industry has often been criticized for lack of economy of scale (Zhou, 1990; Byrd and Zhu, 1990, p. 110). However, given the high demand instability caused by economic and administrative shocks mentioned above, it is not rational to pursue economy of scale single-mindedly. In fact, Sharkey proves that "in a world of uncertainty there can be no optimum scale of plant or minimum efficient scale, although the same cost functions in a world of certainty clearly do imply a single optimum size of plant" (Sharkey, 1977, p. 371). China's township and village governments seem to understand this theorem, and their decision to keep their enterprises relatively small is an institutional arrangement for reducing avoidable costs rather than a sign of ignorance about economies of scale.

Another type of avoidable costs is the fixed wage (Clark, 1923, p. 357). It follows that a flexible payment system will reduce avoidable costs and thus increase flexibility of production. China's rural enterprises have done just that. Most of these enterprises use, at least partially, piece-rate and/or a "contract responsibility system," so that wage payment is not totally independent of output. According to the survey by the State Statistical Bureau mentioned above, the closing rate of rural enterprises at the time of economic adversity (such as austerity in 1986 and 1989) is high, while the reopening rate is also high when times get better. This flexible adjustment between agriculture and the rural industrial sector is made possible by community governments' policy of "supporting agriculture from the profits of rural industry" (Yi Gong Pu Nong) which, among other things, establishes a common pool for aiding adjustment in bad economic times. All this shows that flexible specialization requires not only competition, but cooperation at the level of whole community.

Fei's concern may also be connected to Roberto M. Unger's effort to "rescue" petty commodity production in our time of post-Fordism. The "petty commodity production" refers to the economy of small-scale, relatively equal producers, operating through a mix of cooperative organization and independent activity. Both the positive social sciences and Marxism consider that "petty commodity production" is doomed to failure, because it precludes the economies of scale in production and exchange vital to technological dynamism. Unger sees "petty commodity production" differently. He neither accepts nor rejects it in its unreconstructed form. Rather, he tries to "rescue" petty commodity production by inventing new economic and political institutions. For example, we can satisfy the imperative of economies of scale by finding a "method of market organization that makes it possible to pool capital, technologies and manpower without distributing permanent and unqualified rights to their use." This solution amounts to the new regime of property rights in Unger's programmatic proposal, discussed below. We can invent new institutions rescuing from the old dream of yeoman democracy and small-scale independent property the kernel of a practical alternative, open to economic and technological dynamics as well as to democratic ideals.[39]

Unger draws out the affirmative democratizing potential in that most characteristic theme of modern legal analysis: the understanding of property as a "bundle of rights." He proposes to dismember the traditional property right and vesting its component faculties in different kinds of right-holders. Among these successors to the traditional owner will be firms, workers, national and local government, intermediate organization, and social funds. He opposes the simple reversion of conventional private ownership to state ownership and workers' cooperatives, because this reversion merely redefines the identity of the owner without changing the nature of "consolidated" property. He argues for a three-tier property structure: the central capital fund, established by the central democratic government for ultimate decisions about social control of economic accumulation; the various investment funds established by the central capital fund for capital allotment on a competitive basis; and the primary capital takers, made up of the teams of workers, engineers, and entrepreneurs.

We can appreciate Unger's ideas about "disintegrated property" from the standpoints of both the radical-leftist tradition and the liberal tradition. From the perspective of the radical leftists, Unger's program is related to Proudhon's petty bourgeois radicalism. Proudhon was a forerunner of the theory of property as a "bundle of rights," and his classic work *What is Property?* provides a thorough critique of "consolidated property." It is important to realize that, in its economic aspects, Unger's program amounts, in a sense, to a synthesis of Proudhonian, Lassallean, and Marxist thinking. From the petty bourgeois radicalism of Proudhon and Lassalle, he absorbs the importance of the idea of economic decentralization both for economic efficiency and political democracy; from the Marxist critique of petty bourgeois socialism, he comes to realize the inherent dilemmas and instability of petty commodity production. This realization stimulates Unger to reverse petit bourgeois radicalism's traditional aversion to national politics. He develops proposals for decentralized cooperation between government and business. He connects these proposals with reforms designed to accelerate democratic politics through the rapid resolution of impasse among branches of governments to heighten and sustain the level of institutionalized political mobilization, and to deepen and generalize the independent self-organization of civil society.

From the perspective of liberal tradition, Unger's program represents an effort to take both economic decentralization and individual freedom one step further. In today's organized, corporatist "capitalist" economies, economic decentralization and innovation have been sacrificed to the protection of the vested interests of capital and labor in advanced industrial sectors. Unger's program remains more true to the liberal spirit of decentralized coordination and innovation than does the current practice of neoliberalism and social democracy. Conventional institutionally conservative liberalism takes absolute, unified property right as the model for all other rights. By replacing absolute, consolidated property rights with a scheme for reallocation of the disintegrated elements of property among different types of right-holders, Unger both rejects and enriches the liberal tradition. He argues that the Left should reinterpret rather than abandon the language of rights. He goes beyond Proudhon–Lassall–Marx and the liberal tradition by reconstructing a system of rights which comprises four types: immunity rights, market rights, destabilization rights, and solidarity rights. In this sense, we can understand why Unger sometimes names his program "superliberal" rather than antiliberal. Any reader of John Stuart Mill's *Autobiography* would recognize that "superliberalism" – realizing liberal aspirations by changing liberal institutional forms – recalls Mill's new thinking after his mental crisis.

Thus, we may view Unger's programmatic alternative as a synthesis of the petty bourgeois socialist tradition and the liberal tradition. This synthesis may be called "liberal socialism." The vision of "liberal socialism" will compete with Marxist, social democratic, and neoliberal visions in China and the world.

The petty bourgeois can only liberate itself after it liberates mankind as a whole![40]

Notes

1 Marx and Engels famously predict the disappearance of petty bourgeoisie in their *Communist Manifesto*: "In countries where modern civilization has become fully developed, a new class of petty bourgeois has been formed, fluctuating between proletariat and bourgeoisie, and ever renewing itself as a supplementary part of bourgeois society. The individual members of this class, however, are being constantly hurled down into the proletariat by the action of competition, and, as Modern Industry develops, they even see the moment approaching when they will completely disappear as an independent section of modern society." However, their prediction does not come true. According to Erik Olin Wright's recent study, the petty bourgeois has been increasing in numbers. See his *Class Counts: Comparative Studies in Class Analysis*, Cambridge University Press, 1997.

2 Joseph Proudhon, "What is Property", Cambridge University Press, 1994 edition, pp. 82–83.

3 Drawing on H.L.A. Hart's distinction between "special rights" and "general rights", Jeremy Waldron makes a distinction between "general-right-based arguments for private property" and "special-right-based argument for private property." As he points out, Proudhon is successful in arguing against "general-right-based arguments for private property." See Waldron, *The Right to Private Property*, Oxford University Press, 1988, p. 324.

4 The "Proudhon strategy" may be summarized in his own words: "Every argument which has been invented in behalf of property, whatever it may be, always and of necessity leads to equality; that is to the negation of property" (Proudhon, ibid, p. 66).

5 The "village" here mostly means "natural village". In some cases, land leases are issued by the "administrative village" – a higher entity than "natural village".

6 On Mill's socialist ideals after the 1848 Revolution, see Michael Levin, *The Condition of England Question: Carlyle, Mill and Engels*, Macmillan, 1998.

7 Cited in *Collective Works of John Stuart Mill*, University of Toronto Press, 1967, vol. 5, p. 462.

8 This was exactly one of the reasons why Adam Smith was against limited liability for shareholders in his famous *Wealth of Nations*.

9 There is an interesting theoretical connection between Keynes and Proudhon via Silvio Gesell. See Dudley Dillard, "Keynes and Proudhon," *The Journal of Economic History*, May 1942, pp. 63–76.

10 James Meade, *Liberty, Equality and Efficiency*, New York: New York University Press, 1993, p. 152.

11 After three years of experiments in three areas in Shandong, Zhejiang, and Anhui Provinces, the Chinese Ministry of Agriculture issued "The Temporary Regulations for Peasants' Shareholding-Cooperative Enterprises" in February 1990. It indicates that

this ownership form will become more and more important in Chinese rural enterprises.

12 It is important to note that both systems differ significantly from the ESOP in the U.S.A. ESOP promotes "worker participation in the firm's fortunes only in so far as a part of the work's past pay has taken the form of compulsory savings rather than the receipt of freely disposable income, whereas Labor Share Certificates depend directly upon the employee's current supply of work and effort to the firm without any reference to past compulsory savings" (James Meade, "Alternative Systems of Business Organization and of Workers' Remuneration," London: Allen & Unwin, 1986, p. 117).

13 In an article I wrote in Chinese in 1994, I argued that the SCS should be considered as an institutional innovation. This article appears to have had an impact on the final decision of the top authority to allow SCS to spread in rural China. See Cui Zhiyuan, "Zhidu Chuangxin He Dierci Sixiang JiaFang", *Beijing QingnianBao*, July 24,1994.

14 Fernand Braudel, *Civilization and Capitalism 15th–18th Century, The Wheels of Commerce*, vol. 2, California: University of California Press, 1992, pp. 231, 237.

15 Fernand Braudel, *Afterthoughts on Material Civilization and Capitalism*, Baltimore, MD: Johns Hopkins University Press, 1977, p. 62.

16 For details of these two types of real estate market in China, see Wang Xiaoqiang, "Reports from He Long Jiang", *Shi Jie*, 6, 2002.

17 Maxim Boycko, Andrei Shleifer and Robert Vishny, *Privatizing Russia*, Cambridge, MA: The MIT Press, 1995, p. 83.

18 Ibid., p. 79.

19 Ibid, p. 117.

20 The governmental regulation requires that tradable A shares should account for no less than 25 per cent of a company's initial public offering.

21 Louis Hartz, *Economic Policy and Democratic Thought:Pennsylvania,1776–1860*, Cambridge, MA: Harvard University Press, 1948.

22 See Robert Stanley, *Dimensions of Law in the Service of Order: The Origins of the Federal Income Tax 1861–1913*, Oxford: Oxford University Press, 1993.

23 Meades, 1993, p. 95.

24 Keynes, *General Theory of Employment, Interest and Money*, London: Macmillan, 1936, p. 234.

25 Silvio Gesell, *The Natural Economic Order*, p. 9.

26 Keynes, *General Theory*, p. 355.

27 In his letter to his brother, Joyce said: "it is a mistake for you to imagine that my political opinions are those of a universal lover: but they are those of a socialist artist." See *Letters of James Joyce*, edited by Richard Ellmann, London: Faber and Faber, 1966, vol. 2, p. 89.

28 James Joyce, *Ulysses*, New York: Random House, 1987, p. 803.

29 See Tim Redman, *Ezra Pound and Italian Fascism*, esp. ch. 5, "The Discovery of Gesell," Cambridge: Cambridge University Press, 1991.

30 Gosta Werner, "James Joyce and Sergey Eisentein," *James Joyce Quarterly*, 1990, pp. 491–507.

31 Robert Musil also seems to be under the influence of Gesell's theory of money. Musil wrote in 1923: "During the recent period of revolution and confusion, a kind of natural economy involving every imaginable form of favoritism established itself everywhere. This point needs to be made, since many people seem to believe that abolishing money would abolish selfishness. But selfishness is as old and eternal as its opposite, social feelings" (Robert Musil, *Precision and Soul*, Chicago, IL: University of Chicago Press, 1990, p. 181.

32 Fei, Hsiao Tung, *Peasants' Life In China*, 1939, London: Macmillan, p. 283.

33 Ibid., p. 285.

34 Translated by myself from Fei's book *Xiang Tu Chung Jian (Rural Reconstruction)*, Shanghai: Guancha Publishers, 1948. The citation is from the section entitled "Electricity and internal combustion engine make it possible to decentralize modern

industrial production." However, this crucial section was missed in Margaret Park Redfield's English translation of the book (The English title is *China's Gentry*, with an introduction by Robert Redfield, Chicago, IL: University of Chicago Press, 1953).

35 Michael Piore and Charles Sabel, *Second Industrial Divide*, Basic Books, 1984.

36 Certainly, I do not deny the tremendous importance of general-purpose technology for flexible specialization. According to the data collected by the International Institute for Applied System Analysis in 1989, there are about 800 "flexible manufacturing systems" (FMS) now in operation around the world. The FMS are used to produce a variable number of product varieties: "30% produce less than ten varieties, 44% between ten and 100, 22% between 100 and 1,000, and the remaining 4 per cent used to produce more than 1,000 product varieties" (Boyer, 1991, p. 765). My intention is only to emphasize that flexible specialization is also possible in the developing countries without many general-purpose machines. This claim is consistent with Sabel (1986), who argues that flexible specialization should have implications for industrialization in the Third World.

37 In my view, only by studying institutional underpinnings can we understand why a specific flexible technology, such as the Jacquard loom, did or did not develop and spread. This is consistent with Sabel and Zeitlin's (1985) view on "historical alternatives to mass production."

38 This is my illustration, which is still imprecise. Strictly speaking, avoidable cost means that "cost function is not convex on the closed set X 0 and is convex only on the open set X 0" (see Telser, 1991, pp. 228–229).

39 Roberto M. Unger, Politics, edited by Zhiyuan Cui, New York: Verso, 1997.

40 There is a debate among historians about the political inclination of the petty bourgeois in modern history. According to Arno Mayer, the petty bourgeois was a swing sector between the conservative and the radical forces, and became increasingly conservative after 1871 (See Arno Mayer, "The Lower Middle Class as Historical Problem," *Journal of Modern History*, September 1975, pp. 409–436). George Orwell famously depicts the petty bourgeois in the following way: "The real importance of this class is that they are the shock-absorbers of the bourgeoisies" (see his *The Road to Wigan Pier*, London, 1937). However, Richard Hamilton's important study on the social basis of German fascism shows that the highest level of support for Hitler came from the grand bourgeoisie rather than the petty bourgeois (See his *Who Voted for Hilter*, Princeton, NJ: Princeton University Press, 1982). The petty bourgeois socialism program presented here may be viewed as a break away from petty bourgeois conservatism and an innovation in the tradition of petty bourgeois radicalism.

10 Pension funds and responsible accumulation

The choices facing China

Robin Blackburn

As a result of medical advances and improved social conditions, life expectancy is growing in China. This is, of course, a very good thing. However, taken in conjunction with the one-child policy, it has already raised the proportion of the elderly in the population and is set to raise it even more dramatically in future decades. As in most countries in the world today China's success brings a challenge. As it modernizes and grows, so it will need to be able to furnish pensions to its old people. With greater geographical mobility as well as longer lives, relying on the family alone – especially the smaller family produced by the one-child policy – is no longer enough. However, China is not the first state to confront these problems, or something like them. It will be able to study the lessons of pension provision in other countries.

In an ageing society, differing methods of furnishing pension provision pose a critical strategic choice, with wide implications for the health of the whole economy. In the more successful and advanced countries the ability to mobilize retirement savings has played a crucial role in fostering economic growth while the ability of the state to ensure a livelihood to its citizens in old age furnishes a key test for political leaders. The traditional pattern has been for the state to guarantee a basic state pension to all its citizens, financing this by means of a special tax or social insurance contribution. This has been true even in the United States, with its strong financial sector and famous individualism. The failure of commercial organizations to supply reliable pensions led President Roosevelt to introduce the beginnings of such a system with his Social Security Act of 1935. Subsequently US Social Security has withstood several attempts at privatization and commanded such popular support that it has become 'the third rail' of American politics. While US social and political arrangements are generally hostile to redistribution, Social Security does redistribute from richer regions, and citizens, to poorer ones. In addition, the US debate on social security has elicited outstanding contributions from such writers as Joseph Stiglitz (Columbia), Alicia Munnell (Boston College) and Peter Diamond (MIT) who defend public provision.

In the United States and Britain the basic state pension now only offers subsistence and is paid for by a social insurance contribution which works like a payroll tax. The universal pension is supplemented by occupational and private pensions which supply a secondary source of retirement income for about half of the working population. In Germany and Italy secondary pensions are furnished by corporations and financed by employees' contributions – these contributions are held as reserves by the companies and have played a crucial role in corporate finance. In postwar Japan the state used citizens' contributions to their pensions as the principal source of development funds for public infrastructure projects, with the FILP (Financial Investment and Loan Program) acting as the conduit.[1] In Singapore the Central Provident Fund has played a similar role. One way or another, using savings for retirement as a source of investment has been part of the formula of many economic 'miracles'. But of course the time comes when workers who have saved expect to draw their retirement income.

Today there are few countries where future pension provision does not furnish a challenge because the need for pensions is outgrowing existing sources of funding. Increases in longevity and the rising numbers of the elderly will certainly require more to be spent on retirement incomes. Many may be able to work past what was previously thought to be the normal retirement age. Indeed, those over age 60 or 65 have much to contribute to society, though not necessarily by remaining in their employment or profession. As we live longer we should expect second and third occupations, often preceded by a phase of education or preparation. The social contribution of the older person will be facilitated by retirement provision, rather than rendering it unnecessary. Once the older person has some security of income then they can take up retirement work or contribute to family or civil society. If they are thrown into abject poverty this contribution becomes much less likely.

In an ageing society retirement provision may well come to absorb 15 to 20 per cent of GNP, and if medical expenses are included the cost would be greater. Modern medicine does keep people fit for longer but the annual cost of furnishing health care to those over age 65 is approximately four times as great as for those under 65 years of age. In Asia families may absorb some of the costs of the ageing society but their ability to do so is increasingly limited by geographical mobility, rising medical costs and the difficulties which working families have in meeting essential outgoings. There is good reason to believe that the provision of a basic pension becomes unavoidable in a complex modern society, partly because of popular pressure and partly because it facilitates labour mobility.[2]

The Pay-As-You-Go (PAYGO) method of funding pensions through payroll taxes has proved to be administratively efficient and cost-effective. There is no better way of supplying a basic pension. Even in the UK and USA, public pensions financed largely by PAYGO are the most important source of retirement income for all except the richest 20 per cent of the population. But in a society where age cohorts are of greatly varying size, and where longevity is increasing steadily, it is problematic to expect PAYGO to supply secondary pensions, as well as basic pensions, to everyone. The revenue in a PAYGO system stems from a payroll tax whose yield will reflect the numbers in employment and their level of income. The size and productivity of the workforce thus constrain income to the scheme. The numbers in employment will be reduced by any contraction in cohort sizes, or growth in the time necessary to educate and train the workforce, and in an ageing society even a slowly growing labour force can be outpaced by a more rapidly growing elderly population. What counts in a retirement system is the ratio between the number of active employees and the numbers qualifying for a pension. Global demographic projections show an increasing proportion of the adult population living past retirement age.

The UN mid-range projection tells us that the over-sixties, who comprised 30.7 persons per 100 adults aged 15 to 59 in 1998 in the developed countries, will comprise 62.3 persons per 100 adults aged 15 to 59 in those countries in 2050. In Europe the proportion rises from 32.0 to 68.2, in North America from 26.3 to 50.9. In Asia, including China and India, the anticipated proportion of those over age 60 rises from 14.1 per 100 adults aged 15 to 59 in 1998 to 40.8 in 2050.[3]

The overall dependency ratio is likely to be improved by a declining proportion of children, but the need for longer periods of education and training will offset this to a considerable extent. Europe and Japan will soon face the challenge of a sharply rising elderly population as the postwar 'baby boom' generation reaches age 60. But North America and China will not be far behind. Life expectancy in China has already reached 68 years for men and 72 years for women, compared with 69 years for men and 77 years for women in Europe. There are 10.5 million persons over 80 years of age in China, compared to 8.6 million in the United States and 4.3 million in Japan.[4] The fall in the number of workers to dependents can be alleviated by rising productivity and by immigration, but there are inherent limits here since workers will hope to garner some benefit from rising output, and migrant populations also experience increasing longevity.

If retirement income derives only from payroll taxes and social insurance contributions from today's workers then the effect of the ageing society will be a steeply rising tax rate. In practice, older people do have other sources of income – notably from earnings or from the ownership of assets. An increase in the earnings ability of older people requires three factors: (1) efficient and comprehensive public health services; (2) some retraining, and (3) employers who make the effort to get the best from their older employees. The asset income accruing to older people can be raised if they own some small enterprise outright (a farm, restaurant or small business), though this can also be a source of risk and debt. Or it can derive from a pension fund which owns income-yielding assets, notably company shares or government bonds. In practice the asset income derived from pension funds is likely to have a crucial role to play in most parts of the world if the ageing society is not to drive up payroll taxes to counter-productive levels. As European finance ministries have long ago discovered, high payroll taxes can create unemployment, and the end result is that the tax yield does not rise as fast as anticipated. While this danger exists there remains, of course, considerable scope for taxing employment income in order to finance a variety of public services, especially education and health, and a variety of transfer payments, including a basic citizen's pension in old age. My point is that given the multitude of legitimate and necessary calls on the public purse, it would be good if they do not have to furnish all retirement incomes and if, instead, we so arrange matters that older persons have significant income from earnings and assets.

These considerations prompt many to argue that secondary pensions should be pre-funded, so that they can be paid from asset income. The question then arises as to whether these assets should be held and managed by the state, or by some not-for-profit social organization, or whether they should be handed over to the commercial financial services industry.

The neo-liberal approach to the challenge of the ageing society argues for the downgrading or scrapping of public provision in favour of commercially supplied pensions, with the large finance houses such as Fidelity, Morgan Stanley, Merrill Lynch and Barclays playing the key role. It is often argued that we will only be able to afford pensions for future generations if all citizens are legally obliged to make large and regular cash contributions to the banks and money managers. The World Bank Report *Averting the Old Age Crisis* published in 1994 remains the *locus classicus* of this approach, and the financial services industry which stands to gain new business itself constitutes a powerful lobby pressing the case for compulsory pre-funding. (The government of Hong Kong is one of the first to have adopted this model.)

Paradoxically, however, the discourse of 'pension reform', as it is often called, raises issues which are antithetical to the individualism and faith in the market which are integral to the neo-liberal view of society. The proposed pension regime will only come into being thanks to the state compulsion required to oblige citizens to contribute to a commercially supplied pension fund. The state is also likely to play a key role in selecting which finance houses qualify for receipt of this new business. Thus these particular arrangements have little to do with a free market and are more reminiscent of the 'tax farming' of Europe's *ancien régimes*, an arrangement whereby monarchs such as Louis XVI of France sold the right to collect taxes to private financiers for a lump sum. In this case the state is selling the right to collect a payroll tax in return for transferring its future obligation to pay pensions to a private finance house. A risk not confronted is that the commercial organization, after collecting these taxes for a few decades, invests them poorly and goes bankrupt. Even if this is avoided the saver could encounter heavy charges. Whatever happens, private management of pension reserves hands great power to the chosen fund managers.

In fact the pre-funding of pension entitlements could follow a logic very different from that so insistently recommended to us, namely a logic of 'responsible accumulation'. Struggles over the nature of pension provision offer extraordinary opportunities to social movements and trade unions – but only if the state empowers them by ensuring sources of finance, and principles of accountability, social responsibility and universality. And only if tax subsidies and the right to levy taxes are denied to rapacious and irresponsible money managers.

The right to adequate pensions is likely to be very precarious for all those sectors of the population who have no claim, or only a very modest claim, to asset income. So long as pension commitments are funded only on a Pay-As-You-Go basis, that is to say funded out of current taxation, they will, I believe, be inadequate and vulnerable. Social movements and trade union action will be able episodically to defend decent levels of provision, but if these movements fail to find the path to more durable institutional guarantees then there will always be the risk of weariness and distraction, or of a failure constantly to resist the erosion of popular conquests by the persistent, sapping pressure of capitalist structures and interests. In today's capitalist society only about half the population own productive assets and many of these have very modest holdings, often because the value of their pension fund or mutual fund has been eroded by high charges. This means that only about a quarter of the population will receive the lion's share of the future streams of income which privately held assets will generate. Those who do not command such productive assets when they reach their sixties will accept that their livelihood is dependent of public pension provision, with means tests that will deprive them of much of the benefit of modest savings. For the elderly this is a dismal prospect. Their chance of finding work will be much reduced and they will not wish to add to the burdens already carried by their children.

In the immediate postwar world the economic capacity of the state seemed considerable and had a tendency to grow. As Eric Hobsbawm has pointed out, the phenomenon was common to both sides in the Cold War.[5] It furnished one of the guarantees of prevailing welfare arrangements, including pension entitlements. Yet since the late 1970s and early 1980s there has been an erosion of the economic power of the state notwithstanding rear-guard battles by public sector workers. Austerity programmes were introduced, entitlements whittled down, and finally large-scale privatization programmes were successfully introduced in one country after another throughout the whole world. Commercial pension funds often purchased equity in the privatized concerns. In the early to mid-1990s some hoped that Northwestern Europe or parts of Southeast Asia might offer a model different from that of 'Anglo-Saxon' economics or stock-market capitalism, and successfully resist the advance of privatization, social cut-backs and market deregulation. But they could not. Japan became stuck in a stubborn post-bubble depression while the major European economies could not overcome 'Euroscelerosis' – high levels of unemployment and low levels of growth. Both Japan and Europe adopted elements of the stock-market formula but without overcoming the obstacles to renewed growth. The Japanese government found that one of the most crucial ingredients of its postwar growth model – the mobilization of retirement savings for public infrastructure projects – brought steadily decreasing returns.[6]

The travail of the European and Japanese economies in the 1990s combined with the soaring advance of the USA led to claims that the United States had found a miraculous formula for sustained growth.[7] But from the perspective of the twenty-first century things look very different, and it is now clear that the institutions of 'Anglo-Saxon capitalism' have their own serious problems. The dot-com bubble has burst, the large telecom companies are mired in debt, the energy traders have been found guilty of faking revenues on a vast scale, and there is widespread distrust of the accountants, bankers, lawyers and regulators who helped to devise the off-balance sheet partnerships and credit derivatives that allowed this to happen. Arthur Andersen, one of the 'big five' accounting firms and an enthusiast for privatization, has broken up. In the past four years 700 US companies have been forced to restate their accounts because of irregularities. Across the whole

US economy chief executives and their tame boards of directors have taken shareholders for a hugely expensive ride while awarding themselves ever more extravagant 'compensation'. The boards of the large companies issued stock options to senior executive and other favoured employees. They then borrowed money from the banks which they used to buy back the company's shares, thus driving up their price, supplying the shares on which options were based and making those options more valuable. Robert Brenner explains that the major US non-financial corporations borrowed $1.22 trillion in the years 1994 to 1999 but used 57 per cent of this money to buy back company shares while only 15 per cent was used for capital expenditure.[8] Such business heroes as Kenneth Lay of Enron, Bernie Ebbers of Worldcom and Dennis Kozlowski of Tyco have been forced to resign, but so far they have held on to most of their extraordinary booty. In contrast, employees who held corporate stock have seen their savings decimated.

The recent problems of Anglo-Saxon capitalism stem in large part from the failure of the pension fund managers, and other institutional investors, successfully to control the new breed of chief executive and their tame board of directors. The problem is that the fund managers of the corporate pension schemes are themselves chosen by the sponsoring corporations. Moreover, the finance houses which manage pension funds also look on the corporations for much other valuable business. Unless a business is in evident crisis the fund managers can be relied on to support the chief executive. The public sector pension funds are a little different, and have lately shown bursts of 'shareholder activism' – for example, protesting at the exorbitant extent of executive compensation. On a few occasions they have even initiated action that removed an underperforming CEO. But the norm is for the fund managers to play a passive and supine role. Characteristic of what may be called 'grey capitalism' is thus an ownership deficit, with fund managers failing robustly to represent the interests of policy holders or bringing commitment and consistency to the investment process. Large banks such as JPMorgan Chase and Citi have also found that the fund managers were willing to buy credit derivatives from them based on the loans they made to such companies as Enron and Worldcom. The pension funds are taking legal action against the banks, on the grounds that the latter knew about, or even helped to devise, their duplicitous accounting practices. While they have a good case they will have to explain why the fund managers they appointed were so lacking in vigilance.

The fund managers have an incentive structure that gives them rewards for an increase in share prices but exacts no penalty for any subsequent drop. If they do not perform as well as their peers – other fund managers – then their company might lose the mandate, but so long as they are part of the herd there is no problem. A 1993 study by Franklin Allen and Gary Gorton warned: 'The call option form of portfolio managers' compensation schemes creates the possibility of bubbles.'[9] As these authors explain, the managers have an interest in joining any share bandwagon even if they know for certain that it is heading for a tumble. Of course the bubble was not invented in the 1990s, but previous bubbles were less sustained and were fuelled by naivety alone. The rise of institutional finance was meant to reduce market volatility whereas instead it has increased.

Another pronounced feature of 1990s-style Anglo-Saxon economics has been accelerating inequality, and a declining propensity to save among the great bulk of richer consumers. The rich have seen no necessity to save, because the value of their holdings rose with the stock-exchange boom, but the generality of employees locked into pension plans continued to contribute the funds which, together with the buy-backs, drove up stock prices. The buoyancy of the consumer market also persuaded overseas investors to make acquisitions in the USA (and UK), masking the decline in domestic savings.

A major force in global capital flows has been the pension funds managed by the major banks, money managers and insurance houses. These funds are hugely important in the United States and Britain but are also significant in Japan, Australia, Canada, the Netherlands, Switzerland, Chile and Sweden. The fund managers have become notorious for 'short-termism' and the 'herd instinct' as well as for indulging corporate self-aggrandizement and malfeasance. The phenomenon of the pension funds thus represents a massive alienation of social property. Indeed, policy holders often find their own savings being used in ways which damage their own communities for the sake of speculative investment in distant and strange locales. It should also always be remembered that the private pension funds have benefited from large-scale tax relief. This buoyant world of subsided private pension funds has tended to undermine and eclipse the world of public pension provision.

So far public pension entitlements, though somewhat diluted, still remain in something like their old form in many advanced countries. The state's command of assets and ability to levy taxation has been reduced and this compounds the problem of relying only on taxation for pension provision. A public or social power which commanded more surplus-generating economic assets and larger fiscal capacities would be better placed to deliver on welfare promises. Ideally there should be an autonomous social security administration, with its own charter and its own economists, actuaries and staff, separate from the rest of the machinery of government, especially the Treasury. It would still require vigilant public opinion to make sure that there was no slippage, but at least the potential resources will be there. And states that can afford to offer decent welfare arrangements, including pensions, greatly strengthen their authority and legitimacy.

Funded pension provision could help buttress future entitlement and restore economic leverage to public authorities and social movements. This will mean both giving existing public programmes of pension provision the added clout of command of economic assets and an insistence that all tax-subsidised retirement programmes and pension funds should conform to social and ethical criteria when they make their investments. Pension funds should earn their tax breaks by demonstrating a sense of social responsibility. Likewise, concerns which are in receipt of investment from tax-subsidized pension funds should undergo a regular social audit. The perspective I am advocating would prefer the control of pension funds to be in the hands of public authorities or not-for-profit, independent and democratically accountable social bodies. But it also proposes measures to render accountable all tax-subsidized funds and to prise them loose from commercial control. Essentially it sees fully or partially democratized and socialized pension funds as (1) a way of asserting a claim to future streams of income from the productive assets concerned, and (2) pushing today's accumulation process in socially desirable directions.

But if secondary pensions are not to be financed by tax revenue where will they acquire their assets? First, employees themselves should be encouraged to make contributions according to their ability to do so. If it was possible to offer them matching funds, with the public pension authorities offering them a pound for every pound they saved, this would help to boost savings rates. Second, governments with plans to privatize assets would do better to vest them in pension funds benefiting all citizens. Third, governments could also pledge the revenue from a tax on rising commercial land values – usually themselves the consequence of public infrastructure investments – to a set of public pension funds.

But the crucial task is to find a way of restoring the employers' contribution. In traditional US and British occupational funds the employer would make a large contribution and would guarantee a 'defined benefit' on retirement. But employers are now withdrawing from such arrangements and replacing them with schemes into which they make little or no contribution, and whose benefits they do not guarantee. (These are known as 'defined contribution' schemes, since the employees know what they put in but not what they will be able to draw out.) If all citizens are to be able to receive a decent pension then ways must be found of obliging the employers to start contributing again.

The most effective way of securing further assets for the citizens' pension fund would be to require all corporations to issue shares to them equivalent to 10 per cent of their profits annually. The national and regional social funds which would be the beneficiaries of this share levy would not be able to sell the shares for a lengthy period. Unlike corporation tax the share levy would not subtract from companies' cash flow. Unlike compulsory financial contributions to each worker's pension pot it would not swell labour costs or act as a tax on jobs (something which may explain unacceptable levels of unemployment in Europe). Unlike corporation tax the share levy could not be passed on to consumers in the form of higher prices. In some cases – private firms and some types of state corporation – bonds might be issued in the place of shares. With multinational enterprises the assessment would be similar to that prevailing for corporation tax and the shares could be either in the local subsidiary or in the parent company. Employees would benefit from the fund or funds which received their employers' shares but these would be pooled on a regional and/or industrial basis so that no fund was over-reliant on any one enterprise. The matching funds used to encourage personal savings could derive from the share levy, as could contributions on behalf of carers and the unemployed.

In principle, all citizens would eventually benefit from the share levy, but in the short run the shares would be held and the dividend income generated used to buy shares and bonds; within a few years this would boost savings rates, helping to meet the savings deficit so characteristic of today's 'Anglo-Saxon' economies.

Over time the share levy would transfer control of economic assets from individual capitalists to the pension funds. It would, of course, also slightly dilute the holdings of existing pension funds but as the levy was distributed to the network of social funds most would register a net gain. This method of financing would also furnish a powerful lever to the retirement funds, enabling them to promote good corporate governance and socially responsible investment. The social funds would use their shareholding power to act against business leaders who claimed excessive compensation, or who denied good working conditions and labour rights to their employees, or who invested in ecologically dangerous processes for short-term reasons. The central power responsible for the levy could ensure an equitable regional distribution of the resulting assets and could thus help to promote national integration and social solidarity. The fund's stream of income from contributions and dividends could also be used to purchase government-guaranteed social infrastructure bonds, to build hospitals and schools, thus rendering dubious private finance initiatives unnecessary.

The share levy I advocate is very similar to that proposed by Rudolf Meidner, chief economist of the LO (the Swedish trade union federation), in the 1970s and which was partially implemented in Sweden in the 1980s. It proved to be perfectly feasible and raised large sums. The scheme was suppressed by a conservative Swedish government in 1991 and the scheme's resources devoted to a series of research institutes.[10] In many ways the share levy works in a similar way to the share options which have been so widely used by US company boards in recent years – they ran at 20 per cent of profits in 2000. While the use of this device to enrich individual businessmen arouses widespread anger it would be quite another matter if the assets were held by social funds for everyone's benefit.

The share levy can be calibrated to smooth fluctuations in the trade cycle. The Britain and the USA of autumn 2002 presents an awkward combination of a savings deficit and the risk of an ever-deepening recession. The conjunction is awkward because any immediate increase in saving would only make matters worse – yet in the medium to long run the savings rate must indeed be raised because it has sunk perilously low over the past decade. The share levy mechanism can be calibrated to meet this problem. The levy does not immediately subtract from either corporate or household expenditure. Yet, over time, it could do so as the dividend yield on the fund is re-invested and, as previously mentioned, funds could be used to encourage saving by offering matching contributions.

A new pension fund regime should also seek to ensure that existing funds earn their tax favours and keep charges under control. All funds should be expected to achieve a publicly audited social investment grade before enjoying tax breaks. Among the features of a fund which would earn it a social investment grade rating would be that: (1) it is egalitarian in its internal structuring, (2) it gives democratic representation to its members, (3) it accepts a code of practice based on social priorities, and (4) it commits to holding most of its assets for, say, five years, and (5) it limits advertising and marketing spend to 0.1 per cent of the value of the fund. Such arrangements would be an example of using social property to act as a lightning rod to earth the otherwise menacing storm-clouds of speculative capital.

In addition, the element of public subsidy would be designed to ensure that those funds shouldering the burden of social investment were not penalized by lower returns. Individuals would be expected to have rights in three different funds in order to spread risk. All members of a fund – whether beneficiaries or contributors – would have an equal voice and vote on its policy. However, the audit process would ensure that funds were kept to actuarially fair pay-out rates, so that the goal of paying future pensions was not jeopardized by excessive payments in the present. The expertise of universities could be drawn upon to strengthen fund management. While the fund managers would supply committed long-term finance, the audit process would seek to ensure that pension money was invested in deserving projects and not exposed to undue risk.[11]

The growing movement for 'ethical' and 'socially responsible' investment is given a new edge by the crisis of corporate governance and is the natural ally of 'activist' pension funds. The FTSE itself now offers FTSE4Good, a selection of the larger UK companies which has supposedly been subjected to an ethical or social screening process. Most 'ethical' and 'social' funds currently apply extremely modest criteria, and sometimes invest in concerns that are simply willing to negotiate. But these approaches can sometimes be justified. Since the pension funds together own such a large proportion of all shares, and since share-switching is expensive, they may use 'voice' rather than 'exit' in their attempts to influence company policy. Portfolio composition does play a role. 'Ethical' funds shun companies engaged in particular practices – say, arms production, the use of child labour and environmental degradation – while 'social funds' make positive decisions to reward companies they believe to be behaving well or moving in a socially desirable direction.[12] *Business Ethics* reported that the UK-based Stewardship Fund, operated by Friends Provident, had assets of around £1 billion, with companies screened out for poor quality or service, lack of equitable relations with staff or the community, or a poor environmental record. Nike had been dropped because of bad labour conditions in its East Asian suppliers' factories. The Stewardship Fund also shuns investment in arms or gambling casinos.

The adoption of modest criteria, and a negotiating approach, is not necessarily wrong so long as a coherent and cumulative direction emerges over time. Under the arrangements I am proposing, registered funds would purchase securities with net contributions but would also be in receipt of shares from the pension board which would range across the economy. While some funds might be allowed discretion – where their members had strong ethical objections to involvement in companies of a particular type – the majority would receive their entitlements by a system of more or less random allocation. However, fund members who would like to see their savings used to improve corporate behaviour should bear in mind that their fund could well have more of an impact on the conduct of a given corporation as an 'activist' shareholder than it would by refusing to purchase its shares (though, of course, the fund could, if it was unhappy with the company, be both an activist shareholder with the shares it was allocated, and refuse to build on its stake by purchasing more shares). Allocated shares could help to remedy the problem registered by Michael Calabrese, namely that 'screened funds have no ownership rights at the companies they most want to change'.[13]

The *modus operandi* of pension funds as financial institutions would also be a proper subject of regulation and differential taxation. Just as the Tobin tax proposes to discourage purely speculative cross-border financial transactions, so pension funds could be encouraged to shun speculation and demonstrate commitment. While speculative practices and 'churn' could be penalized by a small tax to be paid by all who trade shares, the pension funds might be bound by rules relating to turnover. For example, the qualifying funds might also be required to commit to holding a proportion of their assets for, say, five years and to make net sales of, say, no more than one-tenth of their holdings in any year. Alternatively transactions in excess of such norms could attract a tax. The thresholds could be set at rates which take account of the overall economic climate. Because funds have a stream of income from contributions, and may need to sell assets to meet obligations, they have considerable scope for adjusting the balance of their portfolio. They would thus still be able to threaten divestment and to contribute to the rational reallocation of capital.

In the wake of the Enron scandals in which it figured, the California Public Employees Retirement System (Calpers) announced that it was going to review all its investments in Thailand, Malaysia, Indonesia and the Philippines mainly because of concerns about social conditions in these countries. It intends to combine boycott with 'engagement'. A report explained: 'Calpers latest move follows a review of its "permissible countries criteria" which, for the first time, gives equal weight to issues such as labour standards as well as market regulation, investor protection and accounting transparency.'[14] Prior to the Enron collapse Calpers was already being pressed to clean up its act by a trade union-backed campaign. Whatever Calpers' motives may have been, the fact remains that it is one of the largest funds in the world, managing US$151 billion assets itself as well as using other fund managers. The decision itself is also not unambiguously positive. Nevertheless, it is a striking victory for the movement for social responsibility in investment and one which, if followed up, could well be refined and improved. The countries targeted in the move maintain special export zones where social protection of the workforce is particularly weak. Altogether there are believed to be some 27 million workers in 800 to 1000 special export zones worldwide.[15] The ban on labour organization in these zones has been an intense concern of the anti-sweat-shop movement, and Calpers' decision is a certain success for this campaign.

Some argue that if pension funds were democratized their pursuit of the bottom line would be all the more ruthless, but there is no evidence for this. Socially responsible businesses can be just as profitable as rapacious ones. CEOs who flout social responsibility might also be likely to cheat their shareholders. Members of a pension scheme are looking to receive income in a few decades' time and do not have the shortened horizon of a financial operator. Their fund will have a large number of investment options before it, so the financial cost of investing responsibly will be negligible or there might even be a gain.

Hard-nosed economists can demonstrate the naivety of imagining that boycotts by investors will really have much impact, but they would be wrong to dismiss socially responsible investing for this reason. SRI is here to stay and those companies which fall foul of it are likely, sooner or later, to pay a price. At the margin SRI will have an influence on the cost of the capital, and many SRI exponents, as noted above, seek to 'engage' by turning up at AGMs and raising awkward issues. Before long they will be putting up their own candidates for non-executive director and seeking to bind boards to what they see as responsible behaviour.

The pension panic, the corporate governance crisis, the financial revolution and the need to come up with new fiscal instruments are not separate issues but different aspects of an interlinked complex. To tackle them, citizens and policy-makers need to learn to factor in the future, and to do so in ways which can promote a socially responsible model of accumulation. This may sound a little like setting up a three-dimensional chess game, and to some extent it is. But it is today's confused mix of pension products and schemes which is really complicated. A unified and coherent system of decent pensions for all would soon prove itself both simpler and more reliable.

China has already set up stock-exchanges, attracted foreign capital and allowed market forces much greater scope. This means that some of the approaches I have outlined above have already become more relevant to the problem of the ageing society in China. A national network of pension funds could be financed by a share or bond levy calculated as 10 per cent of the profits of all enterprises employing more than ten people. There is no reason why foreign enterprises should not be subject to such provisions. Foreign capital will already be aware of the concerns of the SRI movement. A national network of funds would furnish extra power and initiative to provincial and local authorties, with a funding formula which ensured that the richer regions helped the poorer ones. The ordinary citizen and employee should be cnouraged to take an active and informed part in debating the policies of the pension funds. China has already outperformed the Anglo-Saxon powers in their most successful period. In this way China could avoid their mistakes, promote civic self-government and offer security to its old people.

Notes

1 Bernard Eccleston, *State and Society in Postwar Japan*, Oxford 1989, p. 97.
2 John Myles, *Old Age in the Welfare State: The Political Economy of Public Pensions*, Lawrence (KA) 1989, and Gosta Esping-Anderson, *The Three Worlds of Welfare Capitalism*, Oxford 1990.
3 *World Population Prospects: the 1998 Revision, Analytic Report*, United Nations 2000, Volume III, p. 168.
4 Ibid.
5 Eric Hobsbawm, *The Age of Extremes*, London 1994.
6 Gavan McCormack, 'Japan's Iron Triangle', *New Left Review*, new series No. 13, January to February 2002.
7 See e.g. Daniel Yergin and Joseph Stanislaw, *The Commanding Heights: The Battle Between the Government and the Market-place that is Remaking the World*, New York 1999 or Thomas Friedman, *The Lexus and the Olive Tree*, New York 2000.

8 Robert Brenner, 'The Boom and the Bubble', *New Left Review*, new series No. 6, November to December 2000. See also the expanded account in Robert Brenner, *The Boom and the Bubble*, London 2002.

9 Franklin Allen and Gary Gorton, 'Churning Bubbles', *Review of Economic Studies*, Vol. 60, 1993, pp. 813–36.

10 Rudolf Meidner, *Employee Investment Funds: An Approach to Collective Capital Formation*, London 1978. See also the contribution by Jonas Pontusson on Sweden in Perry Anderson and Patrick Camiller (eds), *Mapping the Western European Left*, London 1994.

11 The argument outlined in this and the preceding paragraphs is presented more fully in my new book, *Banking on Death, or Investing in Life: The History and Future of Pensions*, London, Verso, 2002.

12 Eric Becker and Patrick McVeigh, 'Social Funds in the United States: Their History, Financial Performance, and Social Impacts', in Archong Fong, Tessa Hebb and Joel Rogers (eds), *Working Capital: The Power of Labor's Pensions*, Ithaca and London: Cornell University Press, 2001, pp. 44–66; see also Amy Domini, *Socially Responsible Investment*, Chicago, IL: Dearton Trade 2001, and the magazine *Business Ethics: Insider's Report on Responsible Business*, published from Minneapolis, MN.

13 Michael Calabrese, 'Building on Success: Labor-Friendly Investment Vehicles and the Power of Private Equity', in Fong *et al.*, *Working Capital*, pp. 93–127, p. 120.

14 FT reporters, 'Calpers' Asian retreat is a Victory for Ethics,' *Financial Times*, 22 February 2002.

15 Noami Klein, *No Logo*, London 2000, p. 214.

11 Ten theses on Marxism and the transition to socialism

David Schweickart

Introduction

The remarks that follow are not the work of a China specialist. I am a philosopher who has spent most of his scholarly life – from my days as a graduate student in the early 1970s to the present – grappling with one of the great lacunas in Marx's work. As everyone knows, Marx thought that capitalism will eventually be replaced by a higher form of society that will resolve humanity's economic problem. He characterized this ultimate "communism" in various ways: rather whimsically as a socio-economic order that allows us to hunt in the morning, fish in the afternoon, criticize after dinner, without ever becoming hunters, fishermen or critical critics; more seriously, in accordance with the need for a compelling political slogan, as one that allows us to work according to our abilities and consume according to our needs; more philosophically, as one that reduces the realm of necessity to a minimum so as to maximize the realm of freedom. But Marx was no utopian dreamer. He knew that we would have to pass through a transitional stage to get from capitalism to this truly human society. This would be a stage marked by its origins, hence imperfect, even in theory, and yet capable of surmounting the fundamental contradictions of capitalism.

Well and good – but Marx never told us what this transitional society would look like. He made suggestive remarks here and there, but he offered no blueprint, not even a rough sketch. I do not criticize him for that. Marx was too much the scientist to spend long hours speculating about things he could not possibly prove. There were no data. No great experiments had yet been undertaken.

This is no longer true. The twentieth century has witnessed a plethora of large-scale socio-economic experiments – experiments with various forms of capitalism, experiments with various forms of socialism. Economic theorizing has also developed considerably since Marx's time. (There have been regressions as well, but that is another story which need not concern us here.) Techniques of data collection have advanced enormously. My work over the past thirty years has involved sifting through the evidence, constructing a theoretical framework to make sense of it, and attempting to answer the question that Marx did not: What would a transitional economy from capitalism to communism look like? What would be its institutional structure?

I would like to take this occasion to summarize the results of this research, and to use them to reflect on the future of China. I beg your indulgence here. China is a vast and complicated society of 1.2 billion people. I am one person, not Chinese, not knowledgeable of the language, not a scholar of China. I have long been interested in the world-historic experiment that has been going on in this country for half a century, but this is my first visit. The theses that I will discuss here are general in nature, but they would seem to have implications for China. I will have occasion to suggest some. I offer these deductions as suggestions only, since I am in no position to make dogmatic pronouncements about the exceedingly complex developments now underway here.

Thesis 1: The basic principles of historical materialism are correct

I think it important to assert this basic claim. It has become an unquestioned axiom, at least in the West, that three factors – the collapse of the Soviet Union, the conscious attempt on the part of Eastern European countries to restore capitalism, and the widespread introduction of market reforms in the countries still calling themselves socialist – taken together constitute definitive proof that the basic tenets of Marx's theory of history are false. But if we actually examine these tenets, we see that recent historical events constitute nothing of the sort. Let me simply enumerate what I take to be the salient principles. The truth of these principles – or at least their enduring plausibility – should be obvious:

1   We are a pragmatic, problem-solving species, capable of inventing new solutions to pressing problems. We are a creative species. We learn from our mistakes.
2   We have over time, by means of technical and organizational innovation, increased both our power over nature and our capacity for species solidarity. Hence it is meaningful to speak of "progress" in human history.
3   This progress is not steady, but dialectical. Proposed solutions do not always work. Sometimes they fail dramatically. Even when successful, solutions to one set of problems often give rise to new problems, which intensify over time, and hence call forth new solutions, "negations of negations" that do not return to the original position, but represent a genuine advance.
4   Economic structures profoundly condition a society's political institutions, ethical values and cultural life.
5   Class struggle is endemic to class-based societies and has often been a decisive force for historical change. Individuals who stand in similar relations with respect to the means of production tend to have common interests, which they usually perceive to be universal interests. They try whenever possible to advance those interests. (Class contradictions, however, need not always be antagonistic; fruitful alliances are possible.)

I will not defend these principles here. Surely the burden of proof must lie with anyone who seriously disputes them. But if these principles form the constituent core of historical materialism, it should be obvious that the failure of the first great attempt to move beyond capitalism in no way refutes the theory. What is surprising is not the failure of the Soviet experiment but the fact that it was able to endure as long as it did in the face of such powerful and aggressive hostility. It should not surprise us, either, that the Western powers worked mightily to ensure that the Soviet system did not reform itself into a more viable form of socialism.[1] (The West wanted a viable capitalism to replace Soviet socialism, but an economy in ruins was deemed preferable to a reformed socialism.)

Thesis 2: Marx's basic insights into the nature and dynamic of capitalism are correct

Let me list what I take these insights to be. These are more controversial than the basic principles of historical materialism, but they are, in my view, equally valid.

6   Capitalism is a distinct form of human society, with a specific historical origin, that may be characterized by three dominant institutions: private ownership of means of production, the market, and wage labor. Wage labor – labor power as a commodity – was the last to develop, and is the most important in determining the distinctive nature of the system.
7   Unlike earlier economic systems, capitalism is inherently dynamic rather than conservative, in that it provides maximal incentives, both positive and negative, for continuous technological and organizational innovation.
8   Capitalism is based on class exploitation. (I will elaborate on this point below.)
9   Capitalism is fraught with internal contradictions that intensify as the system matures.

Let me highlight four contradictions that I take to be central to our current global predicament:

* *Intractable unemployment*: Capitalism, although creating employment possibilities undreamed of by earlier societies, renders increasingly large masses of humanity "superfluous," i.e., unemployed. Capitalism's "invisible hand" cannot ensure that sufficient employment opportunities will be created to absorb those "set free" from production by technological change. Moreover – and this is the system's dirty little secret – a healthy capitalism *requires* unemployment, since the threat of unemployment is the fundamental disciplinary mechanism of the system.
* *Economic instability*: Capitalism is haunted by the prospect of "over-production," and hence is prone to recessionary instability. Competitive pressure to keep costs low tends to hold down wages – the ultimate source of effective demand – while at the same time this pressure forces the introduction of ever more productive technologies. (From a systems-historical perspective, this sort of instability is most peculiar, since it arises not from externally induced scarcity – war, drought, etc. – but from internally generated surplus.)

- *Poverty in the midst of plenty*: Capitalism's need for ever-expanding markets, coupled with the ever-increasing mobility of capital itself, give rise to desperate poverty in the midst of dazzling wealth, both in its core countries and in the world at large. Capitalism, despite its enormous productivity, cannot resolve the problem of global poverty. On the contrary, the problem intensifies as capitalism globalizes. The destruction of local agriculture and local enterprise frees up more labor than the system can absorb. Lacking sufficient effective demand to stimulate the local economy, and plagued by ever-more intense social pathologies, large regions of world – and significant sections of core-country populations – are abandoned to their own misery. The income gap between rich and poor countries is estimated to have been 3:1 in 1820, 11:1 in 1913, 60:1 in 1990, and 74:1 in 1997.[2] The number of poor, living on less than one constant U.S. dollar a day, rose 25 per cent between 1987 and 1999 – a figure that would have been even higher had not China succeeded in reducing dramatically the numbers living in poverty during this period.[3]
- *Irrational development*: Capitalism's "grow or die" imperative inhibits the shift to an economy of more rational consumption, more leisure and more meaningful work, and puts increasing strain on the fragile ecology of the planet.

These specific contradictions form the basis of the system's ultimate contradiction:

10 Capitalism develops the technological and human preconditions for a truly free society, but such a society cannot come into being so long as the basic structures of capitalism remain intact.
(It does not follow that each and every society must pass through a capitalist stage. Marx's insight is that capitalism, as a world system, makes possible for the first time in human history a world of peace and abundance, but that the very institutions that have created this possibility block its actualization. Each and every society need not pass through a capitalist stage, but post-capitalist societies must learn from the accomplishments as well as the failures of capitalist societies.)

A final Marxian insight, already mentioned in my introduction:

11 To get from capitalism to this free and fully human economic order, societies must pass through an interim stage, a stage marked by its origins, but capable of surmounting the central contradictions of capitalism. (As is usually done in the Marxian tradition, we will call this stage "socialism.")

Up until this point I have done little more than state what every Marxist knows. Let me now advance to the more controversial theses, which, in my view, are fully consistent with the basic tenets of Marxism.

Thesis 3: We can now discern, more clearly than Marx possibly could, the institutional shape of the socialist "successor system" to capitalism, at least as an ideal type. It is appropriate to call it "Economic Democracy"

We can see, more clearly than Marx could, the institutional shape of a viable successor system to capitalism, because the century that has just come to an end has witnessed an extraordinary number of large-scale economic experiments. It has also witnessed considerable scientific analysis of these experiments. We are far better situated than Marx or Lenin or Stalin, or Mao, to say what will likely work and what will not. As a pragmatic species, we learn from the successes – and the failures – of our predecessors.

For example, we can see now that a blanket rejection of "the market" is wrong. There are various Left theorists today who insist that "market socialism" is a contradiction in terms, but their numbers are dwindling. For good reason. The evidence, empirical and theoretical, is compelling that:

12 Some form of market is necessary to coordinate, and correctly motivate, the vast number of economic decisions that must be made in a technologically advanced economy.
13 There exists, at least in theory, an economically viable form of market socialism capable of overcoming the fundamental contradictions of capitalism.

Needless to say, it is the second of these claims that is most controversial today. Demonstrating its truth has been the central preoccupation of my academic career.[4] Rather than rehearse the full arguments here, allow me to offer at least an outline.

If it is not the market that is the most objectionable feature of capitalism, what exactly is most objectionable? To answer this question, we can do worse than turn to Marx himself. Let us recall Marx's critique, as presented in Chapter 7 of *Capital*: "The Labour-Process and the Process of Producing Surplus-Value." In this theoretically central chapter Marx assumes that the market is in equilibrium, and hence that prices are "right." He looks closely at a paradigmatic firm. He looks at a typical worker.

This worker, supplied with machinery and raw materials by a capitalist, works six hours. Marx calls these six hours "necessary labor," since the worker is in effect replenishing by his labor the labor that others have expended on him to provide him with food, clothing, shelter, and other necessities of life. (The value created by this labor is precisely the value of his wage, which he will use to purchase these items.) Were he to stop working at this point, he would have given back to society the exact equivalent of what society has given him.

But the worker does not stop working at this point. He has been hired – as a wage laborer – for a day, and the working day has been set at twelve hours. Of course, the length of the working day is not a natural phenomenon, but the result of class struggle, as Marx makes abundantly clear. Be that as it may, the worker must abide by the terms of his contract and work an additional six hours. This six hours of "surplus labor" creates six hours' worth of "surplus value," the source of the capitalist's profit. Marx designates the ratio of surplus labor to necessary labor, "the rate of exploitation."

The question to ask here is this: Why does Marx call the ratio of surplus labor to necessary labor a rate of *exploitation*? No economist, in his day or in our own, would deny that the "value added" by workers in production must exceed the wages paid if a profit is to be made. But no non-Marxist economist, in his day or in our own, would call this discrepancy "exploitation." Why does Marx introduce a normative category here? What is wrong, ethically, with the process described above – which Marx sees (correctly) as the defining moment of capitalist production?

One thing is certain: Marx does not hold that the worker should be paid the *full value* of his labor. Marx does not think that the worker, under socialism, would in fact stop working after six hours. This he makes clear in his scathing critique of the Lasalleans in his *Critique of the Gotha Program*. If workers were paid the full value of what they added to the raw materials with which they worked, there would be no surplus available to provide citizens with "public goods" – education, health care, and other free or subsidized cultural amenities. There would be no surplus available to maintain the people who cannot work. There would be no surplus available to devote to the scientific research necessary to enhancing our technologies and improving the quality of our lives. Indeed, it is precisely the magnitude of this "surplus value" that defines the degree of material freedom in a society – the real possibilities that are open to it.

What then is the substance of Marx's critique? I submit that Marx's critique is, at bottom, a *democratic* critique. Although labor is the source of value, those who create that value have little or no control over:

14 The conditions under which this value is produced, i.e., no control over their conditions of work.
15 The disposition of the surplus value created by their surplus labor.

Instead, this decisive control is exercised by the class that owns the means of production. It is the prerogative of the owners of means of production to determine the conditions of work and to determine what is to be done with the surplus.

If this is the substance of Marx's critique, how might it be addressed? How might a society be structured to avoid this twofold *democratic deficit*?

The simplest solution, conceptually, is to institute a planned economy, where the planners are charged with acting in the interests of the working class. Both conditions of work and disposition of the surplus are to be determined by a party whose duty it is to advance those interests.

This solution has been tried, and, although not without significant accomplishments to its credit, it has shown itself to be inappropriate for an economy that has reached a certain level of material and cultural development. This is the great lesson to be drawn from the failure of the Soviet experiment.

The correct solution, one fully compatible with a society of advanced technological and human capabilities, addresses the two elements of the Marxian critique separately:

16   To give workers meaningful control over their conditions of work, *enterprises should be run democratically*. Workers should have full authority to select their managers.

17   To give workers collective control over the disposition of the social surplus, *investment should be socially controlled*, and not left to market forces.

If these two imperatives are institutionalized, the economy can continue to function as a *market economy*. Enterprises compete with one another to satisfy consumers. Workers in a given enterprise receive, not contractual wages, but contractual shares (not necessarily equal) of their enterprise's profits. (Thus their incomes are determined by how successfully their enterprise performs in a market environment.) To be sure, the market will have to be regulated, for reasons well recognized by all reputable economists: to block monopolistic tendencies and to compensate for externalities and various other market failures. (Economists differ as to the seriousness of various forms of market failures and the efficacy of proposed solutions, but none pretend that an unregulated market will produce an optimal allocation of resources in the real world.)

It is my contention that this model of socialism, a market socialism with worker control of enterprises and social control of investment, is the logical successor system to capitalism. Of course, the model is stylized and highly simplified, as are all economic models, but it highlights the essential structural features of an economic order that is qualitatively different from both centrally planned and capitalist economies. Let us call this "ideal type" *economic democracy*.

Economic democracy is not only economically viable, but it is capable of overcoming the central contradictions of capitalism. It is a worthy successor to capitalism, an economic order that has outlived its world-historic progressive moment. I will not defend this claim here. As indicated above, I have done so at length elsewhere. Let me take a moment, though, to elaborate a little more on the defining institutions.

Workplace democracy is straightforward enough. Ultimate authority for the management of an enterprise should rest with those who work there, one person, one vote. Needless to say, in enterprises exceeding a certain size, some form of worker representation will have to be established, some sort of worker council – the functional equivalent of a board of directors in a capitalist corporation – which will appoint the upper management and ratify major decisions. Among these decisions are those pertaining to inequalities of income within a firm. Since managers and skilled workers are free to seek work elsewhere if they feel themselves under-compensated, and since everyone's income is tied directly to the firm's performance, worker representatives are motivated to make optimal trade-offs. The consequences of bad decisions will be swiftly felt.

Social control of investment is a general requirement that can be institutionalized in a variety of ways, depending on specific circumstances. Whatever the specifics, however, there must be two conceptually distinct institutional components to this feature, answering to two distinct questions: How are investment funds generated? How are investment funds allocated?

As to the generation of investment funds, it is essential – at least as an ideal to which a socialist society should aspire – to replace reliance on private savings as the source of investment funds with public savings, i.e., taxation. The national investment fund should be generated publicly, not privately. For economic reasons, the optimal tax is a flat-rate tax on the capital assets of each enterprise. The capital assets of enterprises should be regarded as public property, to be leased to worker collectives. The tax is the leasing fee. (There is a strong affinity here with the Chinese household responsibility system in agriculture. The land remains the collective property of society, but families have long-term control over its use.)

For historical reasons, capitalism has relied on private savings to finance investment – these private savings being concentrated in the hands of the capitalist class. However, as governments everywhere know, it is exceedingly difficult to control the quantity of such savings. Savers must be induced to save more or spend more, depending on economic conditions. This is not so easy to do – as Japan, for example, has recently learned. When an economy slumps, many people feel the need to save more, so as to protect themselves from an uncertain future, whereas increased savings is exactly the opposite to what an economic recovery requires. (By some accounts, China is also encountering this problem today. People are saving rather than spending; hence aggregate demand is suffering.)

If an economic system is to rely on public, not private, savings, it is imperative that it institute social programs which eliminate – or at least sharply mitigate – the *need* for individuals to save. That is to say, the society must provide free health care, free education, and decent retirement benefits for its citizens – traditional benefits associated with socialist and social democratic societies. If people must save so as to protect themselves from such life contingencies, it will be far more difficult to regulate macro-economic variables than if private saving is largely incidental.

If investment funds are generated by taxation, the state has far more control over their allocation than if it must rely on indirect means. Private investors – especially the large, powerful ones – strongly resist allocational controls, since they feel that the money they wish to invest is theirs (which by law it is), and hence they should be free to invest it wherever and in whatever they choose, or not invest at all if prospects do not seem conducive to a maximal return. Governments under capitalism must therefore devise intricate systems of interest rates and tax incentives to "encourage" private investors to behave in ways that enhance the common good – systems that sometimes succeed but often fail. It is far better to generate investment funds publicly, so that they may be allocated directly.

Tax-generated funds should be allocated though a *public* banking system, according to criteria that will promote the common good. Needless to say, such criteria are not easy to devise, but there are good reasons for thinking (as I have argued elsewhere) that such a system can outperform a market allocation. (Market considerations will not be absent from the allocation procedure, but they should not trump all others.)

As an aside, let me note that there is little to be gained – and much potential for mischief – in setting up some sort of "socialist stock-market" as an instrument for investment allocation. As Nobel Laureate Joseph Stiglitz has demonstrated, stock-markets are useless as a mechanism for rationally allocating investment funds. Bank allocation – although by no means trouble-free – is more likely to be effective.[5]

An exceedingly important function of this socially controlled allocation is to provide for harmonious regional development. If capital is allocated by market criteria alone, it will inevitably flow disproportionately to regions already relatively plentiful in capital, at the expense of regions that are less so. (Neoclassical economic theory asserts the contrary, but the empirical evidence overwhelmingly confirms this pattern.) If regional stability is to be maintained and large-scale population migrations averted, capital must go to where the people are, and not vice versa. Regions should not have to compete for capital. It should be allocated to them by a visible – and publicly accountable – hand.

What I have outlined so far is an ideal type; but anyone can draw up "recipes for cookshops of the future" – to quote Marx's sardonic phrase.[6] If one takes the basic tenets of historical materialism seriously, one must make the case that this particular "ideal type" is on the historical agenda.

Thesis 4: There are objective forces in the world pressing for reforms that move in the direction of economic democracy. There are no forces pressing for the wholesale elimination of the market

This thesis consists of three distinct claims:

18   There are forces pressing in the direction of workplace democracy.
19   There are forces pressing for social control of investment.
20   There are none agitating for wholesale elimination of the market.

The last claim is the most obvious. The market caters to consumers, and since everyone is a consumer, a pro-market constituency is enormous in almost every country. There exist no political movements of significance anywhere that are calling for the wholesale abolition of the market. In retrospect we can see that the early socialist experiments blundered mightily in eliminating markets altogether. The lack of consumer goods – which a market economy certainly would have supplied – was doubtless a key catalyst in cutting short the socialist experiments of the Soviet Union and Eastern Europe. The fact that every remaining socialist society has introduced market reforms should be regarded neither as a betrayal of principle nor as proof that capitalism is inevitable, but as evidence that a viable successor system to capitalism must be a market socialism.

Is workplace democracy on the historical agenda? There can be little doubt that "democracy" as a normative concept has shown itself over a long historical period to have energizing power. Western countries that began their experiments with political democracy more than two centuries ago have seen the steady expansion of formal rights to all the citizenry – to non-property holders, to women, and to ethnic minorities. These struggles have been mostly peaceful, but often intense. In other parts of the world we have observed a steady decline in personal and military dictatorships, since these have proved almost everywhere to be corrupt and inept. Where they persist, they lack legitimation, and must rely on the police and often torture to maintain their hold on power. (Let me note here that the category "personal or military dictatorship" is not meant to include one-party rule. It is by no means obvious that democracy requires multiple political parties. It may well be that the institutions of genuine political democracy can be developed within the framework of a single party.)

It is difficult to predict when a strongly articulated demand for workplace democracy will make itself felt in developed capitalist countries, but it is hard to imagine the demand being forestalled indefinitely. "If we are competent enough to elect our political representatives, why can't we elect our bosses?" This question is bound to be asked sooner or later.

In fact, the two central components of workplace democracy – profit-sharing and worker participation – are already being promoted by Western management consultants and industrial relations researchers, since these elements, particularly when combined, produce a better motivated and more efficient workforce. As the evidence mounts that workplace democracy works in limited and extended forms, we can expect the demands for workplace democracy to become more insistent.

In socialist countries such as China, large numbers of experiments are underway with various forms of enterprise organization, many of which involve significant degrees of worker participation and worker self-governance. Even more so than in "democratic" capitalist countries the dominant ideology in socialist countries supports ever-increasing worker involvement in enterprise governance. It is hard to see how this trend can be reversed, apart from a regression from socialism to capitalism.

As to social control of investment, the series of financial shocks that have rocked the world over the past decade, from the Mexican "tequila crisis" to the East Asia débâcle to the current crisis in Argentina, have increased calls for at least some serious regulation of capital flows. The widespread protests against the WEF, the WTO, the IMF and the World Bank have given clear expression to the deepening sense that the great promise of free trade and free capital mobility was a false promise. Free capital mobility is making the world economy less stable and poor countries poorer. Although "reputable" voices are not calling for replacing private savings with public savings, or private investment with public investment, the appeal of deregulation is clearly losing ground. The great neo-liberal experiment – although still strongly supported in policy-making circles – is running out of excuses. The invisible hand will *not* solve the world's economic problems. A more visible hand is needed. When economists of the stature of Joseph Stiglitz and Amartya Sen dissent from the dominant view, others can be expected to follow.[7] (This not to say that Western economists – other than a small minority – will any time soon call for an end to capitalism. Historical materialism is surely correct that the academic superstructure of a country is ultimately subservient to the economic base.)

There would seem to be a clear recognition in China that the state must play a major role in the allocation of capital if regional inequities are to be addressed and some sort of balance restored to economic development. The recent decision to invest massively in the infrastructure of the poorer regions evidences an understanding that the freeing up of market forces will not, in and of themselves, advance the common good. Tax-generated public funds are being allocated here according to non-market criteria. What the theory of economic democracy suggests is that publicly funded investments should not be confined to infrastructure, and that reliance on private investment should be kept to a minimum.

Thesis 5: There are two serious challenges that a society which has moved beyond capitalism to economic democracy will have to confront: (1) providing full employment, and (2) motivating adequate "entrepreneurial" activity

The theory underpinning economic democracy as a successor system to capitalism makes it clear that even the form of socialism best suited to humanity's current level of development will not eliminate all economic problems. One will be particularly acute in the immediate aftermath of the transition (if the transition should occur abruptly), and will require considerable creative energy to resolve.

Unemployment is endemic to capitalism. It constitutes the fundamental disciplinary mechanism of the system. Capitalism must have unemployment, and, moreover, the condition of being unemployed must be sufficiently degrading that workers will submit to the rules imposed upon them at work. Of course, these rules vary from enterprise to enterprise, but all are shaped by the fundamental contradiction that lies at the heart of each and every capitalist firm: so long as labor power is a commodity, it is in the immediate interest of capital to extract as much labor from the workforce as possible for as little pay, and it is in the immediate interest of labor to secure as high an income as possible for as little work.

Economic democracy dissolves this basic contradiction. By tying the incomes of workers wholly and completely to the profitability of the firm, a positive incentive replaces a negative one. It is in the interest of each and every worker to work efficiently, and to monitor his or her fellow workers. The threat of job loss, although still present, loses its predominant importance. Sustainable full employment, impossible under capitalism, becomes possible.

Full employment has long been a socialist objective, and not without reason. Work is fundamental to a human being's sense of self-worth. Since every living being is a consumer, every human being benefits from the labor of others. Self-respect demands that this labor be reciprocated. Moreover, it is through labor, as Marx clearly saw, that human beings exercise their faculties and develop their powers. (Not only through labor, but labor is a major medium.) Capitalism is incapable of satisfying this basic, universal, human need – the need for good work.

It does not follow that transcending capitalism guarantees a full-employment economy. One of the undeniably positive accomplishments of centrally planned socialism was its ability to do just that – although at the cost of considerable "disguised unemployment" and inefficiency. Full employment is more problematic under economic democracy. Democratic firms do not automatically take on new entries into the workforce, or those displaced from shrinking sectors of the economy. If anything, they are even more resistant to taking on new workers than are capitalist firms, since both income and control must be shared with these new workers.[8] Economic democracy does not require unemployment, as does capitalism, but it must still face the problem of creating jobs for all.

In my view, this problem is the paramount economic problem confronting contemporary China. There are no magic solutions. Theoretically, it is always possible to reduce the length of the working day until all surplus labor is absorbed, but in practice this solution is enormously difficult to implement.

One thing, however, should be clear. Transforming China from a socialist to a capitalist society will *not* solve the problem. On the contrary, such a transformation would guarantee that the problem will never be solved. (This is not to say that there is no place in China for capitalists. As my explication of Thesis 6 will demonstrate, having capitalists in a socialist economy and transforming socialism into capitalism are two quite distinct matters.)

Although economic democracy does not automatically tend toward full employment, it is better positioned to solve the unemployment problem than is capitalism, for two basic reasons. The first has already been noted. Economic democracy does not require unemployment to keep its workforce in line. The second is social control of investment. Investment funds may be allocated so as to enhance employment creation, even if this comes at the expense of optimal efficiency. Needless to say, there is potential for abuse here, but this potential must be set against the terrible social costs of unemployment, particularly when it becomes endemic. Solving this problem may well be the fundamental task of socialism in the twenty-first century.

It should be noted that neoclassical economics – and experts blinded by the mathematical brilliance of the theory – will be of little use here. For example, many "experts" hold that if China is to continue to develop, it must reduce the size of its agriculturally based peasant class as rapidly as possible. It is argued that the low productivity of agriculture, as measured by either technical comparisons with Western agriculture or the value of output per worker in comparison with other sectors of the Chinese economy, is a fundamental obstacle to growth. Neoclassical theory is often invoked to demonstrate that, if growth takes place, a Pareto-optimal increase in well-being is possible; that is to say, that some people can be made better off without anyone being made worse off.

There are two problems with this argument. First of all, if raising the productivity of agriculture entails a massive increase in unemployment and large-scale labor migrations, it is by no means assured that the net effect on economic growth will be positive. Neoclassical theory assumes that workers will automatically find employment elsewhere. But as Joseph Stiglitz points out, "New jobs are not created automatically. Moving workers from a low-productivity sector to unemployment does not – let me repeat – does not – increase output."[9]

Second, even if growth should be positive, it is by no means assured that the general well-being of society will be enhanced. The neoclassical theorem shows that Pareto-optimality is *possible*, but it does not show that the fruits of increased growth will in fact be so distributed. It is equally possible – more likely in fact – that the benefits will accrue to those already better off, at the expense of those currently worse off. It might well be preferable for China to devise policies aimed at promoting the quality of rural life, so as to keep a large fraction of its population engaged in agriculture, rather than embracing the dogma that progress demands an urban/rural population distribution comparable to what is found in the West.

The second problem confronting a society that has made the transition to economic democracy should be less serious than the problem of unemployment, but is not one to be ignored. It is the problem that took a heavy toll on centrally planned socialist societies: the lack of entrepreneurial innovation. To be sure these societies, particularly the Soviet Union, made some impressive contributions to basic science, and to certain targeted projects – space exploration, for example. But the gap between socialist and capitalist countries in the development and distribution of new and better consumer products was glaring. Clearly, the early socialist experiments failed to find satisfactory substitutes for the innovative energy with which Marx himself credited capitalism.

This is not to say that alternative institutional substitutes cannot be found. Perhaps they can. The entrepreneurial activities associated with the Mondragon complex of cooperatives in the Basque region of Spain have been impressive.[10] So too have been the accomplishments of Cuba's biotechnological industry, which is the most advanced in Latin America and leads the region in the production of pharmaceuticals and vaccines that are sold worldwide.[11] Moreover, it should not be forgotten that many of the most sophisticated technological innovations produced under capitalism have come from publicly funded research centers.

It should also be noted the peculiar entrepreneurial activity associated with capitalism – focusing as it does on the creation, production and distribution of new consumer products – may be less important than the other kinds of creativity required by a post-capitalist society: new and better ways of providing public goods, or meaningful work, or a better balance between work and leisure, or more ecologically sustainable ways of living.

With these caveats in mind, we must still insist that a post-capitalist society should not be complacent about the level of entrepreneurial energy it generates, certainly not in a world still dominated by capitalist countries.

Thesis 6: Entrepreneurial capitalists may play a role in resolving these employment and entrepreneurial difficulties. Allowing capitalists to play such a role does not necessarily compromise the socialist character of a society

In thinking about the role of capitalists under socialism, it is important to be clear as to the function of capitalists in a capitalist society. What exactly do capitalists do? Historically, capitalists have served three functions:

21 Capitalists have invented new production processes, new products and new ways of marketing. They have set up new enterprises. This is the *entrepreneurial function* of the capitalist class.

22 Capitalists have been the managers of enterprises. They have made the key decisions as to the operation of their firms, and supervised the implementation of their orders. This is the *managerial function* of the capitalist class.

23 Capitalists have provided investment funds to individuals wanting to start up new businesses, and to existing enterprises wanting to introduce new technologies or to expand production. This the *financial function* of the capitalist class.

As capitalism has matured, these functions, combined initially in the person of "the capitalist," have become increasingly distinct. Of course, in many small businesses these functions remain united in the owner, but at the opposite end of the spectrum, the modern corporation, the capitalist as an active agent has been almost eclipsed. Entrepreneurial activity in a large corporation is undertaken at the instigation of management, often employing ideas from the firm's research and development department. The owners – the stockholders – play no part in this. Stockholders play no role in managing the corporation either. Managers, from top to bottom, are employees of the firm. Major stockholders are sometimes able to replace senior managers who are held to be underperforming, but such actions are rare, and in any event they have nothing to do with the ongoing management of the firm. As for financing, funds for expansion come overwhelmingly from retained earnings, supplemented by bank loans and bond sales.[12] (Firms acquire cash from owners only when new stock is issued, which is not often. In recent years U.S. corporations have bought back far more stock than they have issued, so that net equity financing has been negative.)

Let us ask another basic question: "What exactly is meant by 'a capitalist'?" Definitions here are important, particularly in a country such as China, where until recently, to be a "capitalist" or a "capitalist roader" was to be an enemy of the people, whereas now capitalists are being welcomed into the Communist Party and awarded May 1st Labor Medals.

But what is "a capitalist"? Three different definitions are commonly employed:

- A classical Marxist might define a capitalist as a person who hires wage laborers, supplying them with means of production and raw materials, to produce goods or services that will be sold on the market.
- Alternatively, a Marxist might focus on sources of income, and define a capitalist as a person who derives enough income from his capital that he can live comfortably on that income without working.
- A neoclassical economist will define a capitalist as the person who supplies capital to an entrepreneur, who will use these funds to rent space, hire workers, and purchase the necessary equipment to produce marketable goods or services.

In considering the problems and possibilities of capitalists under socialism, the second definition is the most fruitful. The classical Marxist definition, although analytically central to our understanding of the basic structure of capitalism, does not pay sufficient attention to the functional distinctions noted above. These distinctions, as we shall see, have important policy implications.

The neoclassical definition makes the important distinction between capitalist and entrepreneur, but the distinction is too sharply drawn to be useful in practice, since real-world entrepreneurs must have at least some capital of their own before they can get additional funding from the capital markets. Real-world entrepreneurs are at least "petty capitalists."

If we are going to consider "actually existing capitalists," the second definition is the most promising. It picks out the class of individuals that most closely corresponds to the "ruling class" of a capitalist society. If capitalists are to play a role in a socialist society, we must concern ourselves with the danger that this class might come to constitute the ruling class, in which case the socialist society would be socialist no longer, but capitalist. Neither the classical Marxist nor the neoclassical definition is of much help in assessing this danger.

Before considering this danger, let us discuss some of the benefits that follow from allowing some capitalism under socialism.

Not surprisingly, all significant benefits flow from the *entrepreneurial* function of the capitalist. Clearly we do not need capitalists to manage enterprises or to provide them with capital. (Non-capitalists have long managed enterprises in capitalist as well as socialist countries. Public savings can readily replace private savings as the primary source of investment funds.) It is the entrepreneurial function that is crucial; so let us analyze this function more closely. We begin by observing that there are in fact two kinds of "entrepreneurs" in capitalist societies, both of which are economically important.

First of all, there is the class of people that may be designated "petty entrepreneurs," the individuals who start up small businesses. Although it is relatively large and quite active, very little technical innovation comes from this class. The vast majority of new small businesses are patterned on existing businesses: retail stores, repair shops, restaurants, and small-scale production or service enterprises. Setting up such businesses takes energy and skill, but little or no technical innovation.

Second, there is the class of "grand entrepreneurs," the great innovators, the founders of new industries, the economic "revolutionaries." These entrepreneurs gain access to large amounts of capital, and often take large financial risks. There are spectacular successes and spectacular failures. The spectacular successes often result in spectacular fortunes: we think of John D. Rockefeller, Andrew Carnegie, and Henry Ford, and of Ray Kroc (of McDonald's), Sam Walton (of Wal-Marts), and of course Bill Gates (of Microsoft). Although such figures are rare, they embody, in the public mind, the image of "the capitalist."

In fact, such figures are not representative of the capitalist class, certainly not in an advanced capitalist society. These figures are grand entrepreneurs. Most capitalists are not. If we employ our preferred definition of a capitalist (i.e., someone who can live comfortably solely on the income from his investments), we find that this category includes the "grand entrepreneurs," but also many other individuals as well, few of whom are entrepreneurial in any significant sense.

It is not hard to see why. In a capitalist society, money breeds money. Two million dollars in the bank, earning a mere 5 per cent interest, yields $100,000 per year (two-and-a-half times the median family income in the United States) – more than enough to "live comfortably." This $100,000 keeps coming in, each and every year, without any entrepreneurial ingenuity on the part of the depositor; indeed, without any effort at all.

In the United States there are one million or so households with assets in excess of two million dollars. These households constitute a small class (our capitalist class) – 1 percent of the population – but vastly larger than the class of grand entrepreneurs.

Since it is the entrepreneurial function that is necessary to socialism, it is important to distinguish the entrepreneur from the capitalist. On the one hand, most "petty entrepreneurs" are not true capitalists. They are employers of wage labor, but they have to work themselves – often long hours. They are not nearly rich enough to live off their holdings. On the other hand, most capitalists, at least in capitalist countries, are not entrepreneurs, petty or grand. They may well work. Most of them do, at least the working-age men, and for high salaries. But the work they do is not particularly innovative or entrepreneurial. It is the kind of work many non-capitalist managers or professionals do.

Let us apply these distinctions to the question: What should be the role, if any, of capitalists in a socialist society?

If we think of economic democracy as the logical successor system to capitalism, it should be clear that there should remain a place for petty entrepreneurs under socialism. These individuals serve a useful function, and they constitute no great danger to the socialist character of the economy. Individually owned and managed, small businesses can provide jobs for many people. As we have observed, the problem of providing jobs for all will not disappear under economic democracy. Ultimately, the government must function as an employer of last resort, but to keep this obligation manageable it is useful to have a private sector of small businesses that can also provide people with employment.

The government can and should help small groups of workers set up cooperatives, but the fact of the matter is that it is more difficult to set up a cooperative than it is a "petty capitalist" business. The kind of initiative and skill required to set up a successful small business is in short supply in every society today. (Witness the large numbers of small businesses that fail every year.) Those setting up a cooperative must possess the business skills of a petty capitalist, and the additional skills necessary for recruiting a congenial workforce with whom they will share control. Perhaps a time will come when these skills are so abundant that worker cooperatives will displace the petty capitalist small businesses altogether, but until that time comes, a petty capitalist sector should be permitted, even encouraged, in an economic democracy.

To be sure, the interests of the class of petty entrepreneurs will not coincide with the interests of their workers, and it will be a relatively large class. But this sector should be easy to control. Such businesses can be licensed and taxed. Workers can be encouraged to organize and bargain collectively. If necessary, limits can be imposed on the number of employees a petty entrepreneur can hire. Moreover, with most enterprises in the economy democratically run, petty entrepreneurs will be under constant pressure to expand the participation and profit-sharing rights of their employees, which will more closely align the interests of the two classes.

What about grand entrepreneurs – real capitalists? The primary rationale for permitting a class of petty entrepreneurs to exist is employment creation, and the provision of services the need for which might otherwise go unmet. The primary rationale for permitting a class of grand entrepreneurs is technical and organizational innovation. It may be that the lure of great wealth is necessary, at least at a certain level of cultural development, to motivate the sort of technological innovation that is capitalism's pride and glory. I am not altogether persuaded of this, but it may be true. If so, it may be desirable to give scope to this motivation by allowing for some private ownership of large enterprises.

We should be clear here about the rationale, and about the danger. The rationale is not employment creation. Large capitalist firms employ many people, but they also lay them off in large numbers. The technical and organizational innovation that is the hallmark of these firms is often oriented toward decreasing labor costs. This is not, in and of itself, a bad thing. In the long run, we want our society to produce its goods and services with less labor, so as to make more leisure available to all. But in the short run, the labor displaced by technological change places a burden on the state, particularly if the state is a socialist state, committed to full employment. We should not expect our large capitalist firms to absorb the labor that their technologies set free. Labor absorption will be the responsibility of the democratic sector (with capital for expansion supplied by the public banks), the petty capitalist sector, and ultimately the state – as employer of last resort.

What we want our large capitalist firms to do is to produce efficiently, and to innovate. Our large worker-run enterprises will have to compete with these firms, and so will be under pressure to innovate as well, or at least to be quick to copy the innovative strategies of their capitalist rivals. This is healthy competition, beneficial to the common good.

To what extent would the existence of large capitalist firms – and a class of capitalists who own them – present a danger to the socialist character of economic democracy? Perhaps none. So long as most enterprises are democratically run, this class may pose no threat. Rarely if ever do people relinquish their democratic rights without a struggle. It is hard to imagine wage labor being re-established on a grand scale, once it has been largely eliminated.

Still, some controls might be in order to check the potential ascendancy of the capitalist class. But what sorts of controls?

The distinctions developed above are suggestive. What is wanted is a set of rules that will allow an entrepreneurial individual to employ his talents and resources in an active fashion, such as an entrepreneurial capitalist under capitalism, but will block his ability to translate the wealth he acquires into assets that will reward him (and his heirs) indefinitely. That is to say, we want to confine our capitalists, so far as this is practical, to their entrepreneurial function.

Since in practice the entrepreneurial function requires managerial control, this control can be granted so long as workers are allowed to form unions to protect their own rights. The financial function of the capitalist is another matter altogether. An economic democracy generates its investment fund from a capital assets tax. Capitalists are not needed to "provide capital." Public banks can provide financing for all enterprises, capitalist as well as democratic.

These considerations point to a fairly straightforward set of rules. The owner of a capitalist enterprise may at any time sell his enterprise – but only to the state. If he remains with his firm until the mandatory retirement age, he *must* sell it. The state can then either turn the enterprise over to the workforce, to be run democratically, or it can look for another entrepreneur to buy it. What a grand entrepreneur cannot do is maintain a claim – via stock ownership or any other mechanism – on the firm's profit stream, once he has ceased his active involvement with the firm.

These rules would prevent the class of grand entrepreneurs from evolving into a permanently entrenched capitalist class – a class of people whose wealth and position derive, not from ongoing entrepreneurial activity, but from their passive ownership of means of production. These rules allow individuals to become rich, but they cannot translate their riches into a permanent claim to a portion of society's surplus value.

It should be noted that since economic democracy's investment fund is tax generated, the savings of the grand entrepreneurs are not needed for investment. Hence their incomes can be made subject to a significantly graduated income tax. The rates should not be so high as to discourage people from trying to become rich (after all, it is precisely this motivation that we want to exploit), but they can help to keep the inequalities in check, and at the same time generate additional revenue for the investment fund.

I should emphasize that the specific policies discussed here are suggestions only, deriving from a consideration of a simplified model. The general conclusions I have tried to established are these: A viable, democratic socialism should permit a petty capitalist sector to exist, and may even want to avail itself of the innovative potential of a full-blown capitalist sector. Both these sectors may require regulation to prevent the interests of these sectors from becoming dominant and hence undermining the socialist character of society. Such regulation appears feasible.

Let me conclude this section by broaching another topic. You may have noticed that my discussion of capitalists under socialism has made no mention of stock-markets. Let me mention them now – in a negative tone. The theory of economic democracy – and the empirical record of actually existing stock markets – suggests that these mechanisms have little to offer a socialist society. Stock-markets were much in vogue among "transition theorists" a decade ago, who saw them as a way of addressing what many took to be the central problem of transition: clarifying property rights. Perhaps these theorists had a point – if the transition in question is a transition to capitalism. But if the transition in question is a transition to a more efficient and dynamic socialism, that is another matter altogether.

I do not mean to be dogmatic here. I am not an expert on stock-markets, certainly not on Chinese stock-markets. But the evidence is pretty clear that at least in an advanced capitalist economy, stock-markets do little to enhance the overall performance of an economy. Let me quote Stiglitz again:

> Much of the activity in the stock market cannot really be explained by any rational behavior. It is what I have referred to elsewhere as the "rich man's horse track," or the middle class gambling casino. Since trading on the stock market is essentially a zero-sum game, it increases risk without on average increasing mean returns.[13]

Although in theory a stock-market reveals information about an enterprise that might enhance rational capital allocation, in practice this information is of limited value, since stockholders have little access to the sorts of information that a rational allocation would require, and little motivation to seek it out. Moreover, stockholder fixation on profit reports motivates managers to concentrate on short-term results, and to manipulate the numbers when these results are not good – activities of which investors in the United States have suddenly become acutely aware, as scandal after scandal unfolds.

Stock-markets arose in capitalist societies, under specific historical circumstances, to make it easier for private savings to be mobilized for investment. But economic democracy does not rely on private savings for investment, and therefore has no need for what is in fact an anachronistic mechanism – one that might play a role in a regression from socialism to capitalism, or perhaps even a transition from capitalism to socialism, but unnecessary to socialism itself.[14]

Thesis 7: There are additional problems which must be faced by a society that is trying to bypass the stage of capitalism so as to reach economic democracy, among the most serious being (1) raising the cultural/educational level of the population so that worker self-management and democratic control investment is viable, and (2) developing the productive forces of society so that the basic needs of everyone for health care, education, and old-age security may be met

My discussion here will be brief. The problems of unemployment and (perhaps) an insufficiency of economic innovation are problems a society would have to face, even if it reached the state of economic democracy. But there are preconditions that a society would have to attain before the structures of economic democracy, if put in place, could be expected to yield optimal results. Let me discuss two such preconditions.

The first has to do with democracy. The economic structure of economic democracy has workplace democracy as its centerpiece. In most enterprises ultimate authority over the management of the enterprise rests with the workers who work there. Management is not appointed by the state, nor by stockholders, nor is it exercised directly by a private owner. Management is selected by the workforce, either directly or by a representative worker council. The question of course arises: Are workers competent to select good managers?

The general answer to this question is "yes." There have been many experiments with, and many studies of, worker-run enterprises, at least in the West, and the results have been overwhelmingly positive. However, in a poor country, particularly one in which workers are uneducated and/or have little experience with democratic procedures or a market economy, worker competence may be more problematic. The transition might best be phased in gradually, with education provided that focuses on developing the skills and values necessary to functioning effectively as a worker-self-managed collective. This period of tutelage need not be long. We should remember that the question of competence has always arisen whenever the democratic franchise has been extended to people previously disenfranchised. Rarely, if ever, have the doubts proven to be well founded. In general, one becomes competent at the practice of democracy by practicing it.

The second precondition has a less obvious connection to the internal structure of economic democracy. That everyone should have free access to health care, education, and decent retirement benefits has long been a demand of socialism – a demand that has come close to fulfillment not only in centrally planned socialist societies, but also in social-democratic ones. (Not, however, in the world's dominant capitalist country – to our shame.) There has also been regression in countries that have moved away from central planning – terrible regression in the countries of the former Soviet Union and most of Eastern Europe, but regression as well (I am given to understand) in China. This should be a matter of serious concern in its own right, but also for a structural economic reason that was mentioned briefly in the discussion of Thesis 3: economic insecurity makes it difficult to move away from private savings as a significant macro-economic variable.

As Keynes has made clear, a capitalist economy always runs the risk that savings will outstrip investment. Since savings are, in and of themselves, a subtraction from aggregate demand, and since it is aggregate demand that drives the economy, these savings are always dangerous – although also necessary, since these savings constitute a capitalist society's investment fund. Economic democracy does not rely on private savings to fund investment, and so private savings are unnecessary to the overall health of the economy. They remain, however, a danger. In small enough quantities they pose no threat, and indeed can be useful in funding an expansion of consumer credit.[15] In large amounts they can be detrimental.

But if people face fundamental uncertainty as to their economic security, they will tend to save a disproportionate amount of their incomes. Thus it is advantageous, economically, to reduce that fundamental uncertainty as much as possible.

Therefore, it should be a fundamental aim of any society making a transition to socialism to maintain and even enhance people's access to decent health care, education, and retirement benefits – as socialist values in their own right and as a means to keep down the level of private savings. (This is not to say that the overall savings rate of society should be low. Tax-generated investment funds constitute *public* savings. This quantity may be as high or as low as is deemed necessary.)

Basic health care, education, and pensions should be funded from general tax revenues. They should not be the responsibility of individual enterprises, for that would put those firms that are generous at a competitive disadvantage *vis-à-vis* those that are not, and, moreover, it would makes a firm's failure a far more serious event, in human terms, than it would otherwise be. (In a genuinely competitive economy, some firms will fail. In a socialist society that has assumed the responsibility of ensuring jobs for all its citizens, the temptation will be ever-present to loosen the hard-budget constraint and bail out such firms. In general this temptation should be resisted – but this is particularly hard to do when workers' health care and retirement benefits are also at stake.)

Thesis 8: Foreign capital may play a positive role in the transition to economic democracy

If an economy were structured as a pure model of economic democracy, there would be little room for foreign capital in the economy. Foreigners could not buy domestic firms. These firms belong to the society as a whole, and are not for sale. They could not buy shares of firms, since there exist no ownership shares. They could not loan money to firms. Firms obtain their financing from public banks. The only entity authorized to borrow on the international capital markets is the government itself. Presumably it would be cautious in doing so.

It should be recognized that borrowing always carries with it a danger. Common sense is not always a good guide to economic rationality. (Common sense does not suggest deficit spending in times of recession. It took a Keynesian revolution to drive home that maxim.) But common sense is correct in this instance. If borrowed funds are invested domestically so as to enhance future productivity, and if the productivity gains are sufficient to repay the loan with interest, well and good. Borrower and lender both benefit. But it is not easy to ensure that borrowed funds will be properly invested. It is easy to spend money. It is not so easy to spend it wisely.

In general it is not hard for governments to borrow money. The risk to the lender is relatively slight. Although not the iron-clad maxim it was once thought to be, governments (almost) never go bankrupt. If the funds are invested badly, they will still be repaid with interest. The populace will simply have to be squeezed – something governments generally have the power to do – and will be pressured to do so by the international agencies and creditor nations involved.

The least problematic reason to seek foreign capital is technology transfer. To this end joint ventures should be the preferred option. If foreign companies will agree to implement technologies that are unavailable locally and difficult to acquire otherwise, and to train local people in their use, it is reasonable to grant them a share of the profits to be obtained from the business. There is minimal risk in doing so.

Borrowing so as to be able to import technically advanced equipment is also reasonable, although the dangers are more serious. It is one thing to pay for such imports with export revenues. Borrowing is riskier. As indebtedness mounts, so too do the interest payments, which begin to compound if the investments have not been as productive as they were expected to be.

The most problematic influx of foreign capital is finance capital – investments in real estate and in local stock-markets. International financial markets are notoriously unstable. A fundamentally irrational "herd mentality" prevails, which has been well documented.[16] This irrationality can be destructive – but tempting as well, since in the beginning the consequences are benign, even thrilling. Asset prices soar – for no good reason, apart from the fact that outside investors want them. Fortunes are made. Business is buoyant. Enterprises and individuals borrow excessively, spend excessively, invest excessively. Then the bubble bursts, as all financial bubbles do, dragging down healthy companies as well as weak ones.

Thesis 9: Trade can and should continue under economic democracy, but such trade should not be "free" trade

How should a socialist society interact economically with the rest of the world, assuming that a large part of that world is capitalist? Let us consider certain basic principles derived from the theory of economic democracy.

Economic democracy in its pure form differs internally from a capitalist economy in that it replaces wage labor with worker self-management and capitalist financial markets with social control of investment. In effect, a capitalist economy employs three markets – a commodities market, a labor market and a capital market, whereas economic democracy employs only one – the commodities market. Implicit in the judgement that the labor and capital markets should be curtailed under socialism is the assumption that not all forms of competition are good. More specifically, it is assumed that:

24 Competition among commodity-producing enterprises is generally a good thing.
25 Competition among regions to attract capital is generally not a good thing.
26 Competition among workers to offer the most work for the lowest wage is generally not a good thing.

The structures of economic democracy are designed to embody these principles. In an ideal socialist world, these principles would apply globally as well as at the national level. Some alternative mechanism would be employed to allocate capital globally. International wage competition would be blocked. But we are assuming here that our economic democracy is embedded in a largely capitalist world. How would the basic principles apply in this instance?

The first principle implies that the country would trade with these capitalist countries, rather than cut itself off and attempt an autarchic developmental strategy.

The second principle is consistent with the analysis of the preceding thesis. Economic democracy should not try too hard to attract foreign capital, although such capital need not be excluded altogether. Foreign capital may be permitted a role in the economy, but a restricted one, with the emphasis being on technology transfer.

As for the third principle, if a socialist country is poor, its primary comparative advantage may well be the low incomes of its workers. It may be worthwhile to exploit this advantage, but only as a temporary strategy. Since the world contains a near-infinite supply of cheap labor, socialist values rule out competing with this cheap labor as a long-term strategy. Such a "beggar-thy-neighbor" strategy harms all poor countries in the long run – and requires keeping the incomes of one's own export-sector workers low.

Although socialist principles do not preclude trade with capitalist countries, they do make one wary of wholly free trade. Western economists are incredibly proud of Ricardian trade theory, the famous theory of comparative advantage, since it is, as Nobel Laureate Paul Samuelson once quipped, one of the few principles of modern economics that is both true and non-obvious. Free trade, the theory purports to demonstrate, is always mutually beneficial, even if one country is more productive than the other in every area.

Unfortunately, as Samir Amin and others have repeatedly shown, the theory is *not* true.[17] Among other things, it is based on the assumption that workers can shift smoothly to sectors in which they have comparative advantage from sectors where comparative advantage is lacking. Marx's observation is vastly more realistic. He quotes from the Governor General's Report of 1834 to 1835 on the effects of imported British textiles into their colony: "The misery hardly finds parallel in the history of commerce. The bones of the cotton weavers are bleaching the plains of India."[18]

I sometimes think that this quote should open *every* academic and political discussion of free trade. It certainly points to the greatest danger that free trade poses to a poor country – which is what makes China's entry into the WTO particularly worrisome. Poor countries must be exceedingly careful about opening their markets to rich countries, particularly when the sectors likely to be most vulnerable employ large numbers of people. There is *nothing* in the nature of the free market's "invisible hand" that guarantees a balance between jobs lost in these sectors and jobs created in the export sectors.

Thesis 10: The transition to economic democracy, from either capitalism or a current form of socialism, will be a peaceful transition. The age of "socialist revolution" is over – but the age of socialism is just beginning

This thesis is, of course, highly speculative. There is no "science of history" that permits apodictic certainty. Nevertheless, there are good reasons for thinking that the future of socialism is brighter than most people (even on the Left) currently imagine.

One reason for Left pessimism is the tendency to conflate the advent of socialism with "revolution," where the latter term conjures up images of workers storming

Winter Palaces and peasant armies sweeping all before them. The conflation is not unreasonable, given the history of the past century. Marx and Engels might have envisaged a peaceful, democratic transition to socialism, at least under certain circumstances, but no such transition has ever occurred. The only transitions to socialism in the twentieth century have come about through the force of arms. But socialist revolutions of the violent, insurrectionary sort that marked the twentieth century are now anachronistic. Therefore, if we conflate the advent of socialism with socialist revolution, we (on the Left) are bound to be pessimistic.

Why do I say that socialist revolution is no longer on the historical agenda? Because I am an historical materialist. As all historical materialists know, technology matters. I am convinced that technological developments have rendered socialist revolutions of the classical form obsolete. I doubt that we will ever see another. If one such should occur, it will be in a poor, war-ravaged country on the periphery of the world economy, and will be of little historical significance. Unless much else in the world has changed by then, it will have little chance of realizing its goals or of even surviving.

Let me develop this argument further. As is always the case, technological causation is mediated by other factors.

In the final analysis, the socialist revolutions of the twentieth century all have their roots in the devastation of internecine great power warfare – warfare among powerful capitalist nations that spilled over into other parts of the world. (The Cuban Revolution stands as an exception to this rule, for reasons we need not pursue here.)

There will be no more such wars. Our technologies are now too powerful. A full-scale war between major powers would be suicidally destructive, and the ruling classes of all the major powers know that. There is no longer any plausible economic gain to be had from such warfare. It is also the case that the political and ideological superstructures of advanced capitalism no longer support such warfare. Ruling classes can garner support for short wars against weak opponents, but they are no longer able to mobilize popular sentiment for a large-scale war that would involve large-scale casualties on the part of their own forces. (Humanity owes a great debt to the Vietnamese people – and to the anti-war movement that their heroic struggle inspired – for this permanent restraint.)

It remains true that conditions in many poor countries breed insurrectionary sentiments and armed opposition, but there no longer exists a superpower willing to aid such insurrectionary movements in coming to power, and, if they succeed, to supply them with material and technical assistance, and protect them from counter-revolution. Without such assistance, the technologies of counter-revolution – which will be made available to groups that want them – will prevail.

We should not lament the fact that socialism can no longer come to power through force of arms. It cannot be denied that violence has sometimes been liberating – but it cannot be denied either that such violence has often taken a toll on the victors, hardening them, making them too ready to impose force on domestic critics who have raised legitimate objections to ill-conceived policies. It should be clear now that the educational and institutional infrastructure necessary to sustain a viable contemporary socialism must be constructed painstakingly over time, and under conditions of peace and trust, not war and suspicion. (I do not mean to suggest that these ideal conditions will ever be fully attained, but they do need to be approximated.)

If socialist revolution (in the classical sense) is no longer on the historical agenda, it does not follow that all is well with capitalism. Quite the contrary. Capitalism, as a creative force, has almost exhausted itself. There have been numerous "experiments" in the twentieth century with forms of capitalism that deviated from the *laissez-faire* model that was dominant until the Great Depression. None has proved capable of resolving the basic problems identified so long ago by Marx. All exhibited some initial success, but all developed internal contradictions that have proven insuperable. The twentieth century has witnessed experiments with fascist capitalism, semi-fascist military-rule capitalism, social-democratic capitalism, and variations on Japanese authoritarian-communitarian capitalism. None of these models looks promising today. The first two have been wholly discredited, and the latter two are in crisis. Today the gospel of neoliberalism is preached to all nations as the path to salvation, but that model, where it has gained political ascendency, has delivered little of substance, and has usually made bad situations worse. (That this should be so is not surprising, since neoliberalism differs little from *laissez-faire* capitalism, the failure of which set off the search for alternative forms of capitalism in the first place.)

Capitalism's exhaustion has been little remarked in intellectual circles, yet it is hard not to notice the dearth of bold, new ideas for social or economic reform coming from the advanced capitalist parts of the world these days. Our best social-democratic economists and political theorists are good at debunking the neoliberal theology, but they have no energizing alternative vision to put forth. Our economies continue to produce new toys, some of them quite impressive, but these have not made us happier or more secure. (I am speaking now as a citizen of an advanced capitalist country.) In spite of our astonishing wealth, we are not embarking on new crusades to end poverty, not even at home, much less in the world at large. We are not dancing in the streets, exultant about our victory in the Cold War, or even (we Americans) about our overwhelming military pre-eminence. Instead we are hunkered down and fretting about "terrorism."

If the human species is indeed the creative species posited by historical material-ism, this situation will not endure. The forces specified in Thesis 4 will grow stronger. Demands for more workplace democracy and more social control of investment will begin to make themselves felt. In capitalist countries these demands, coupled with demands for a reform of the political process itself, will be raised by progressive forces operating within the constraints of liberal democ-racy. The transition to economic democracy from advanced capitalism, if it takes place, will be marked by reforms aimed at advancing this agenda. (The transition to full economic democracy – to a true socialism – may well require a major economic crisis as its spur. Such a crisis is quite imaginable, perhaps even likely, given the fragility of the current global financial architecture. To what extent progressive forces are prepared to act creatively in such an event remains to be seen, but the more reforms in place prior to the crisis, the better the chances for a positive outcome.)

The theory of economic democracy suggests that the transition to economic democracy would be easier if the country in question were already a socialist state, and did not have to contend with the deeply entrenched power of a long-standing capitalist class.

Concluding remarks

If the twentieth century was America's century, the twenty-first may well be China's. But not for the same reasons. Even if China's GDP should overtake that of the United States – which is certainly possible – its *per capita* income will never approach what Americans currently enjoy. The ecology of our planet is not capable of supporting that level of consumption. This fact need not be regarded as a bitter fact. Human flourishing does not require the extravagant consumption to which the advanced capitalist countries have become addicted.

China will never surpass the United States in military might either. The gap is too large, and besides, it would be pointless to compete with the United States in this domain. As the Soviet Union learned, an arms race can be draining, and, as America is learning, military supremacy counts for little in the modern world. The United States may be more arrogant now than ever before, but the quality of life for U.S. citizens is certainly no higher than it was prior to the events of 1989 to 1991, nor are we happier.

The twenty-first century will be China's if its audacious experiment in "market socialism with Chinese characteristics" is successful. If China is able to perfect the mechanisms required for a genuinely democratic, worker self-managed socialism, the example will be even more inspiring than was the example of the Soviet Union, which, for all its flaws, remained potent for half a century. The wretched of the Earth are desperate for a viable developmental strategy. Workers in advanced capitalist counties, everywhere on the defensive, might well be energized to press for a rational and democratic economic order of their own – a market socialism with, say, German or French or Italian or Swedish or British or Japanese or American characteristics.

Such a future is possible, but it may not come to pass. A very different future is also imaginable. "Market socialism with Chinese characteristics" may evolve into "capitalism with Chinese characteristics." Many observes think this has already happened. The theory of economic democracy inclines one to think otherwise – although it by no means precludes the possibility.

What would it mean for China to become a capitalist country? What criteria should we use to determine whether or not it had? Marxism suggests criteria of two types, both of which are plausible. The first focuses on the dominant class's relation to the means of production. According to this criterion, China will be a capitalist society if its dominant political class succeeds in reorganizing the economy so that their positions are secure in virtue of their private ownership of the means of production.

The most effective means for making such a transition would likely involve privatizing state and township enterprises by transferring ownership shares to managers and workers, and then allowing these shares to be sold. Most workers will, in due course, sell their shares, thus allowing them to concentrate in the hands of a small class that has access to finance (i.e., to well-placed members of the politically dominant class or to successful entrepreneurs).

The second type of criteria focuses on the interests of the dominant class. According to this criterion, China will be a capitalist society if the politically dominant class sees the general interests of society as congruent with the objective interests of the capitalist class, specifically, those interests that are at variance with the interests of workers and peasants.

If the Chinese ruling class should decide that wages need to be kept low so as to ensure international competitiveness, that widespread unemployment must be "tolerated" so as to keep the workforce disciplined, and that entrepreneurs should be given maximum freedom to invest wherever opportunities for profit are most promising, then China would be well on its way to becoming a capitalist society – whatever the technical relationship of its ruling class to the means of production might be. If these decisions become institutionalized, the transition to capitalism will be complete.

What would be the results of a capitalist restoration in China? Given our theoretical understanding of the laws of capitalism, as confirmed by historical experience, we can safely predict:

- Widening regional disparities – and heightened regional tensions.
- Massive population migrations – and attendant social dislocation.
- Significant sections of the population living in conditions of permanent destitution and despair.
- Ever-increasing consumption as the dominant goal of development.
- Ever-increasing ecological devastation.
- A depoliticized citizenry, at once cynical, apathetic, and easy prey to ethnic demogoguery.

Needless to say, such a development would be tragic for China. It would be tragic for humanity. It need not come to pass. There is class struggle going on in China right now – as there always is and always will be, at least until the stage of full communism is reached. At this historical juncture it would appear to be a muted, covert struggle, mediated by a state – and a party – that has significant room for maneuver.

Since I am a philosopher, not a soothsayer, I will not attempt to predict the outcome of this struggle. I can only join you in hoping that the true, long-term interests of the working class – and of humanity – will prevail.

Notes

1 See Peter Gowen, "Western Economic Diplomacy and the New Eastern Europe," *New Left Review* (July to August 1990): 63–84.

2 *United Nations Development Programme*, 1999 (Oxford University Press, 1999), p. 3.

3 *World Development Report* (World Bank, 1999), p. 25.

4 *Against Capitalism* (Cambridge University Press, 1993) has just been translated into Chinese, and will be published by Renmin University Press shortly. See also my book, *After Capitalism* (Rowman and Littlefield, 2002).

5 Joseph Stiglitz, *Whither Socialism?* (MIT Press, 1994), p. 92ff.

6 Karl Marx, *Capital*, Vol. 1 (International Publishers, 1967), p. 17.

7 For a particularly scathing attack on "market fundamentalism," see Joseph Stiglitz's most recent book, *Globalization and Its Discontents* (W.W. Norton, 2002). Stiglitz's critique has unique weight, since he is not only a Nobel Laureate in Economics, but also former Chief Economist of the World Bank and, prior to that position, Chairman of President Clinton's Council of Economic Advisors. Sen, also a Nobel Laureate, has been a long-time critic of unbridled faith in free markets. For a recent statement, see his *Development as Freedom* (Alfred A. Knopf, 1999), ch. 5.

8 This feature was highlighted in the first formal model of worker self-management, Benjamin Ward's "Market Sydicalism," *American Economic Review* 48 (1958): 566–89. A large literature developed in response. For a contemporary technical discussion, see Bruno Jossa and Gaetano Cuomo, *The Economic Theory of Socialism and the Labour-managed Firm* (Edward Elgar, 1997), p. 164ff. For a less technical discussion, see *Against Capitalism*, pp. 88–98.

9 Joseph Stiglitz, "Two Principles for the Next Round, Or, How to Bring Developing Countries in from the Cold." Address given in Geneva, September 21, 1999. Text at www.worldbank.org/knowledge/chiefecon/articles/geneva.htm.

10 Roy Morrison emphasized this dimension of the Mondragon experiment in his *We Build the Road as We Travel* (New Society Publishers, 1991). For more recent information on this remarkable "cooperative corporation," now employing about 47,000 workers, with joint ventures in some twenty countries (including China), see George Cheney, *Values at Work: Employee Participation Meets Market Pressure at Mondragon* (Cornell University Press, 1999) or visit their website at www.mondragon.mcc.es.

11 See Michael Kranish, "In Cuba a Biotech Revolution," *Boston Globe*, May 17, 2002 for an overview. For more details, see Ernesto Mario Bravo, *Development within Underdevelopment? New Trends in Cuban Medicine* (Havana, 1998).

12 Stiglitz notes that "there is by now quite strong evidence that equity markets account for a relatively small fraction of new capital raised in almost all countries." *Whither Socialism?*, p. 95.

13 Ibid.

14 For a discussion of the role of stock-markets in the movement from capitalism to socialism, see Robin Blackburn, "The New Collectivism: Pension Reform, Grey Capitalism and Complex Socialism," *New Left Review* (January/February, 1999). See also David Schweickart, *After Capitalism* (Rowman & Littlefield, 2002), ch. 6.

15 I discuss the matter of "Socialist Savings and Loan Associations" in *After Capitalism*, ch. 3.

16 See Robert Shiller, *Irrational Exuberance* (Princeton University Press, 2000).

17 See Samir Amin, *Unequal Development: An Essay on the Social Formations of Peripheral Capitalism* (Monthly Review Press, 1976), p. 133ff.

18 Karl Marx, *Capital*, Vol.1 (International Publishers, 1967), p. 432.

Part IV
Globalization and China's modernization

12 China's governance and political development under the impact of globalization

Yu Keping

People are now increasingly aware that globalization is first of all the integration of the global marketplace, signaling a high degree of interdependence of the global economy. However, globalization does not mean only economic globalization. In view of the political and cultural transformations caused by the integration of the global economy, it may be said that globalization is taking mankind toward a new age, that is, the age of globalization. We ought not simply define globalization as the integration of politics, economies, and cultures, but rather, we ought to recognize that the trend of globalization consists of an integration that is filled with essential contradictions, containing trends toward integration and fragmentation, and containing not only uniformity but also diversity, centralization and also decentralization, internationalization and also localization. Hence, for such reasons, it should be noted that globalization is not only a process of economic transformation, but also a process of cultural and political transformation.

The impact of globalization on political life speaks for itself. From the perspective of international politics, the political impact is transforming the traditional concept of state sovereignty and leading toward a new global governing order. Economic globalization has greatly changed the main bodies, structures, modes, processes, and importance of government and governance, thus seriously challenging the traditional assumptions about nation states, state sovereignty, governmental systems and political processes, and profoundly affecting and vigorously promoting political life.

Nation states have served as the core of human political life since modern times. Nation states are established on the foundation of three main, well-known factors: territories, sovereignties, and citizens. When any independent political entity wants to become a country it must have a certain expanse of territory that is independent and inviolable. This independent and fixed territory must have a sovereign organ that represents the will of the state. State sovereignty cannot be divided, nor be imposed by way of intervention by any other country. Within a certain territory there must be a sufficient number of citizens, whose responsibilities and rights are protected only by the laws and government of this territory. Such citizens can only express their wills and use their rights when they belong to a territorial country. Therefore, citizens (*gongmin*) are usually identical to nationals (*guomin*). Up until now, this type of nation state has been the center of the political life. Therefore, it has served as the essential basis of the people's political imagination. However, the inevitable processes of economic globalization have seriously challenged the three main factors of territory, sovereignty, and citizens, and therefore, globalization is unsettling the image of the nation state in people's minds. The famous German scholar, Baker Wooldridge, has noted:

> People can either deny and attack globalization or applaud it. But no matter how people evaluate globalization, a [certain] popular theory will be involved, which is to say, that the use of territories to characterize and define social realms, which has attracted and inspired political, social, and scientific imagination in every way for [the past] two centuries, is now disintegrating. Global capitalism is accompanied by processes of cultural and political globalization that cause the collapse of the self-images with which people have been familiar and the [collapse of the] picture of the world based on territorial socialization and cultural and intellectual systems.[1]

Economic globalization is mainly seen in the globalization of capital, products, and communication. These modern economic factors have increasingly required breaking through barriers of nation states, and have also demanded to flow as freely as possible throughout the world. Without the free flow of capital, products, and communication there is no globalization to speak of. The flow of global capital, products, and communication not only raises objective demands but also subjective demands. In other words, they require an appropriate space for global flow in the world market. They also require global organizations that administer and coordinate the worldwide flow of capital, products, and communication. The organs of global governance and coordination consist of various international organizations, especially multinational corporations. Therefore, in a certain sense, economic globalization means the formation of the global market and signifies the increased role of multinational organizations.

The global market and multinational organizations have an essential conflict with the concept of state territory. The global flow of capital and the activities of multinational corporations objectively require breaking through the constraints of territory. When state territories and boundaries contradict the global requirements of capital, multinational corporations and organizations will manage to make the requirements of the state territories meet the necessities of capital expansion. In other words, when economic globalization conflicts with state territory, the traditional concept of territory gradually gives way before the demands of economic globalization. When economic globalization breaks through the constraints of nation state territories, we are able to see clearly the political results, as Ralph Dahrendorf has noted:

> Globalization points out a direction, and only a direction. The space of economic activities is expanding and it goes beyond the boundaries of nation states. And the important thing is that the space for political adjustment and control is also expanding.[2]

The main factors of nation state territory are closely connected with the main factors of sovereignty. Insofar as economic globalization has challenged the main factors of nation state territory, it has also challenged the main factors of sovereignty even more obviously and seriously. As Smith and Naim, in *The Altered States*, have noted:

> In this aspect, globalization has a powerful and complex impact: the regulations of globalization concerning human rights and democratic governance are penetrating national boundaries and reshaping the traditional concepts of sovereignty and autonomy . . . these regulations have been formed, are developing, and are making legitimate international intervention which prevents serious violations of human rights and collective security.[3]

The challenges that economic globalization has made on state sovereignty may be understood according to the three following aspects. First, global economic activities such as multinational investment inevitably require that participating nation states have appropriate political environments. There are many differences among the political and economic systems of various nation states, and it is very difficult for them to meet the requirements of foreign capital. When global economic activities conflict with the original systems of nation states, the latter usually have to make compromises. Under such conditions, the original processes of political and economic decision-making of nation states undergo greater or lesser degrees of change. Such systemic changes, directly or indirectly, challenge sovereignty. Second, economic globalization has resulted in the generalization of certain political values, particularly those concerning freedom, democracy, human rights, and peace. When a nation state's political values are totally destroyed in such situations as seen in the violence of ethnic genocide, international intervention in that state receives increasing moral support. Finally, economic globalization has made domestic problems more internationalized, as may be seen in such cases concerning the ecological environment, shortage of resources, poverty, crime, drug problems, over-population, and so forth. Such problems can hardly be solved by the sovereign governments of nation states alone, and thus multinational and international cooperation is needed. This kind of international cooperation often weakens traditional state sovereignty.

Economic globalization also challenges the fixed territories of nation states and traditional concepts of citizenship and race. One of the inevitable outcomes of the globalization of capital is the globalization of the labor market. The heads of multinational corporations, their senior managers, technicians, and even their general laborers, travel frequently to various multinational corporations and allied branches established in different countries. They are usually more loyal to their multinational corporations than their own countries or nations. In addition, the number of immigrants is also increasing at an unprecedented rate. According to statistics published by international immigration organizations, the number of new immigrants who moved abroad totaled over 100 million in the beginning of the 1990s. Most of them were legal immigrants, although a small number were illegal. These immigrants have basically lost their sense of national identity. Even for general citizens who live at home, traditional notions of political identity are experiencing a serious test. Economic globalization, the internet, and the internationalization of ecological and environmental concerns have made the sense of national identity among citizens less important than global awareness. So-called new identity politics have appeared, and some among the pioneering parties, such as those who see themselves protecting the international environment, have even called themselves "global citizens."

Because economic globalization challenges the territoriality of nation states and sovereignties, and it undermines the identities of citizens, some scholars have defined the globalization process as "de-statification." Such scholars believe that globalization is eliminating the unity between economic and political space. The elimination of this unity makes the rule of nation states invalid, and moreover, as some have noted, "at least, it is impossible for the Western World to go back to the age of the nation state." This trend of "de-statification" has become characteristic of our age. As Dittgen has noted, "The trend of de-statification in various societies means that the connections and roles of the economic, ecological, cultural, and military behavior are quickly developing, so the creation of a multinational political administrative organ is of critical practical importance but develops only very slowly."[4] Some scholars have even noted that globalization has damaged national autonomy, and a "social world" is replacing the "national world." The end of East and West conflicts has reduced the value of nation states. Therefore, as Dittgen has noted, "the nation state has become obsolete," and "the nation state is perishing."[5]

To conclude from the impact of economic globalization on nation states that "the nation state has become obsolete" and that "the nation state is perishing" is a biased and exaggerated view. Nation states and sovereign governments will play their essential roles in the political life of mankind for a long time in the future. Nevertheless, there is no doubt that the nature of the nation state and sovereign government, and their roles in the political life of mankind, will be greatly transformed because of the impact of economic globalization. In terms of the mainstay of politics, the [role of the] state as the sole governing entity is being gradually reduced, and governance formed by citizens and civilian organizations is gradually increasing. The ideal of "governing without government" or "stateless governance" dreamed of by mankind is becoming a reality in many realms of political life. In terms of political systems, it should be noted that democracy, human rights, and the legal system have gradually become universal values of the world, while autocracy is losing the final foundation of its existence. This transition process of rules and governance that accompanies economic globalization will occur simultaneously at home and abroad.

From an international perspective, global governance has become one of the most notable issues in the global realm in the post-Cold War era. In 1992, the United Nations established the "Commission on Global Governance" under the initiative of Willy Brant, the former German Prime Minister. Carlsson, the former Swiss Prime Minister, served as the first leader of the Commission. In 1995, the Commission published the study entitled *Our Global Partnership*, which has had a profound impact on international relations even until to today. In the same year, the Commission also created the magazine *Global Governance*.

Politicians and scholars pay attention to each issue of *Global Governance* for the following reasons. First, the end of the Cold War does not mean the end of conflicts among regions and countries – on the contrary, conflicts are widespread in the world. In certain regions, these conflicts are very fierce. Such conflicts are the main source of threat to human existence, peace, and human rights. The international community cannot ignore the violence and conflict among various regions and countries, and it should take active measures to mediate and eliminate them in order to maintain the peace of mankind. Second, political, economic, cultural, scientific, and technological cooperation among countries, while located in the background of economic globalization, have increased in an unprecedented way. Such cooperation and communication have gone beyond differences in political systems and ideologies – particularly in situations requiring the establishment of a common regulatory system to which each country adheres in order to respect and preserve the universal value of mankind and increase the common interest of mankind. Third, every country is needed to make efforts to protect the environment, eliminate poverty, contain international terrorism, and eliminate multinational crimes, so that the normal order of the international community is maintained.

Seeking the promotion of the maximum common interest, global governance consists of democratic consultation and cooperation among all governments, international organizations, and the citizens of each country. Its essential components should encompass the improvement and development of a whole set of new worldwide political and economic orders for the maintenance of the security, peace, development, welfare, equality, and human rights of mankind, and also for the handling of international political and economic problems, and global regimes and systems. In some sense, global governance is the extension of the domestic governance into an international scope. As Pierre de Sanerkellens has noted,

In the field of international relations, global governance is first of all the product of agreements and practices among countries, particularly, among powers. The regulations and systems cover not only governments, but also the non-governmental mechanism that depends on its own means to realize its will and achieve its goals. Governance is regarded as a regulatory system formed by major agreements. It can implement certain collective projects without the authorization and approval of governments. The informal process promoted by various organizations of governments, non-governmental organizations, and multinational corporations, is also included in governance. Therefore, it is not only the product of international negotiations in which each country participates, but also, it is the result of combinations of individuals, collectives, organizations of governments, and non-governmental organizations.[6]

In the post-Cold War age of economic globalization, there is a need to re-establish and maintain the new global political and economic orders on the one hand, and the current existing international organizations, governmental organizations on the other, and nation states are not able to depend on their own strengths to govern the world. Under such conditions, some people wish for the role of the United Nations to be increased, that sufficient authority be granted to the United Nations so that it can take on the functions of a domestic government, so that on this basis, the United Nations will be developed and will become a "world government," a global authoritative organ. Obviously this is not a feasible vision; in the foreseeable future it is not possible that a world government similar to a domestic government will emerge.

In its history of over fifty years, the United Nations has played a very important role in maintaining the security of the international community and promoting the common interest of mankind. It will continue to play this essential role for a long time into the future. Nonetheless, it is impossible for the United Nations to become the sole responsible party in global governance; it is also impossible for the governments of all countries to be the sole authority for global governance. The responsibilities for global governance should be held by the governments of each country, the international organizations of governments, and the worldwide civil society. As the Commission on Global Governance has stated, "At the global level, governance basically refers to the relations among governments. However, we must understand now that it also includes non-governmental organizations, civil movements, multilateral cooperation, and the global capital market."[7]

Worldwide civil society consists of international non-governmental organizations, global civil networks, civil movements, and so forth. In the age of economic globalization, the important role of the worldwide civil society in global governance should be especially stressed. With the development of economic globalization, the number and roles of international non-governmental organizations in international affairs are increasing every day, and are having a greater impact on global governance. According to statistics published in the latest edition of *The Yearbook of International Organizations*, of the existing 48,350 international organizations, non-governmental international civil organizations constitute 95 per cent, that is, numbering at least 46,000. For another example, note that in 1972 there were less than 300 non-governmental organizations participating in the United Nations' Environmental Conference, whereas, by 1992, the number of registered non-governmental organizations in the Environmental Conference rose to 1,400. Meanwhile, in the same year, the number of non-governmental organizations participating in the Forum of Non-Governmental Organizations rose to 18,000. Again, in 1968 at the Tehran International Human Rights Conference, non-governmental organizations that gained the status of observers numbered fifty-three, and there were four non-governmental organizations attending the preliminary meetings of that conference. In contrast, at the 1993 Vienna International Human Rights Conference there were 248 non-governmental organizations that had gained the status of observers, and there were 593 non-governmental organizations that were attending the conference. Once more, at the 1976 Non-

Governmental Forum of the World Women Conference in Mexico there were only 6,000 attendees, and 114 non-governmental organizations attending the formal meetings. However, by the 1995 Non-Governmental Forum of the World Women Conference in Beijing, there were 300,000 attendees, with three thousand non-governmental organizations attending the formal meetings.[8]

In addition to international non-governmental organizations, another major sector of worldwide civil society that has developed may be seen in the global civil networks established on the basis of the internet and other high-tech means. It is impossible to calculate accurately the number of global civil networks in existence, though it is certain that various global civil networks are being generated at every moment of every day all over the world. The number of global civil networks is much higher than that of global civil and social organizations. Up until today, certain governments and multinational organizations (such as the United Nations) have played the major roles in global governance, but their roles are being increasingly shared by global civil society.

It should be noted that there is a very dangerous trend in Western theories of global governance. This trend lies in the possibility that theories of global governance can serve as the theoretical basis which allows certain multinational corporations and countries to intervene in the internal affairs of other countries in the hope of establishing international hegemony. Certain Western theories of global governance have been established on the premise of downplaying governmental roles, national sovereignty, and the ambiguity of national boundaries, while emphasizing the multinational and global nature of governance. The danger lies in the weakening of the important roles played by national sovereignty in domestic and international administrations, which in turn provide the theoretical support for certain powers and multinational corporations to intervene in the internal affairs of other countries in order to implement policies of international hegemony. Therefore, we must be highly vigilant in observing this dangerous trend in Western theories of global governance.

The impact of economic globalization on domestic politics proves to be as strong as that on international politics. In addition to the challenges with which sovereignties, territories and people of nation states have to face – challenges that can be summarized as "anti-nation state" – economic globalization is also having a profound impact on domestic politics and culture, as well as the expanse, processes, and systems of politics. In terms of politics and culture, with the development of economic globalization we see that modern political values such as democracy, freedom, equality, human rights, and so forth, have increasingly become the universal political values and standards of political evaluation in the whole world. In terms of political expanse, with the rise of satellite television, the internet, and electronic publications, we see that the monopoly and privileges which domestic political information has heretofore exercised are losing their existing foundations. Moreover, in terms of political processes, since economic globalization consists mainly of bilateral or multilateral communication and interaction, we see that domestic political processes are gradually changing from the traditional form of vertical interaction (top to bottom) to a form of horizontal interaction. That is to say, mandatory governmental action lessens as consultative and cooperative action increases. In terms of political systems, we see that economic globalization directly or indirectly promotes countries that, in participating in international economic life, establish a set of more democratic and effective political mechanisms to ensure a stable and peaceful environment for economic development. People not only enjoy participating in their increasing economic interests, but also increasing political interests.

Briefly, in terms of domestic politics, globalization is transforming the traditional operational mechanisms of power, the way in which politics are conveyed, the organizational structure of politics, and political culture. Globalization is transforming governments from traditional good government (*shanzheng*), to modern good governance (*shanzhi*). The impact of globalization on political life occurs not only in the developed countries, but also in the developing countries. The recent wide-scale transformations in Chinese political life fully demonstrate this.

China's process of reform and opening to the outside world is indeed a process of breaking out of self-isolation and going into the world, while also signaling a process of participating actively in globalization. As the chief architect of China's reforms and its opening to the outside world, Deng Xiaoping had organically integrated domestic reform with the policy of opening up. This shows that Deng Xiaoping had a good understanding of the characteristics of our age: that is, against the background of economic globalization, domestic affairs have indispensable connections with international affairs. Domestic development cannot be separated from opening up to the world, and opening up to the world definitely affects domestic development. Hence, against the background of economic globalization, domestic reform and opening up constitute two sides of a coin. In the more than twenty years of reform and opening up, Chinese society has experienced great changes and has achieved remarkable accomplishments. Academic circles, especially overseas scholars, have long held this view. However, such accomplishments have been basically limited to the economic sector, and there have been no fundamental changes in the political realm. Some scholars have even theoretically concluded that the successes of the Chinese reforms stemmed from the Chinese government implementing a policy of economic reform before political reform. The failure of reform in the former Soviet Union stemmed from leaders of the former Soviet Union implementing policies that conducted political reform before economic reform.

It is a fact that Chinese political reform has lagged behind economic reform. However, to think that China has experienced only economic transformation without any political changes is not accurate. The logic of historical development stipulates that opening up to the world and participating in the processes of economic globalization, sooner or later, will change domestic politics accordingly. This logic cannot be changed by the will of the people, nor by the will of the state, and China is no exception.

Since the beginning of reform and opening up to the world, the Chinese government has signed a series of international human rights treaties, particularly *The Treaty of International Human and Civil Rights*. It is also reviewing and preparing to participate in a series of important international treaties, such as *The International Treaty of Economic, Cultural, and Social Rights*. Generally speaking, such measures will greatly promote the systematic and international safeguarding and protection of civil rights. Therefore, the Chinese people and their international friends are very happy about this. In fact, the measures that the Chinese government has adopted have a more profound importance. It shows that the traditional political culture or political ideology that has ruled Chinese society for quite some time has been greatly changed by the impact of globalization. China's political ideology has never possessed nor acknowledged universal political values that transcended national borders, political systems, and political ideologies. Hence, the Chinese government signed economic and trade treaties with international organizations, or with other countries, while abstaining from civil rights treaties that had universal binding force. China's participation in *The Treaty of International Human and Civil Rights* and *The International Treaty of Economic, Cultural, and Social Rights* shows that, to a certain extent, the Chinese government has begun to acknowledge the existence of universal political values that transcend national borders, political systems, and political ideologies. The realization of universal political values requires the integrated efforts of the international community, including the cooperation of countries that have different political systems and ideologies.

In terms of civil political culture, the existence of universal political values that transcend national borders has become a generally acknowledged truth and has been accepted by more and more Chinese people. Ever since the beginning of reform and opening up, the Chinese people have enjoyed not only the sweet fruits of economic development, but also the great accomplishments of political progress. The terrible era of so-called speech crimes, the period of brutal oppression and struggles that the Chinese people have had to endure, have all passed. And yet we can still hear fierce criticism of the government and of the current political system forwarded by Chinese citizens, particularly by Chinese intellectuals. Such criticism has proven so fierce that the sharpness of the rhetoric appears unprecedented since the rise to power of the Chinese Communist Party. How do we understand and evaluate such a contradictory phenomenon?

On the one hand, this is due to the current situation of political reform lagging behind economic development. Some negative political reality may be seen, such as serious political corruption, social inequity, violation of democratic rights, and so forth. On the other hand, this is also due to the transformation of the standards of evaluating politics. During the Cultural Revolution, which was a politically disastrous period completely devoid of law and democracy, the majority of the people who did not criticize the political system and instead worshiped it did so because of the dogmatism of the extreme Left which had decided the standards for evaluating politics. Ever since the beginning of reform, politics has gradually opened up, and people now often express their dissatisfactions with the political situation, sometimes even making sharp criticisms. This is due to the fact that a newly modernized and democratic value has gradually become the standard by which people evaluate politics. The new standard of democracy incorporates current democratic ideologies of each country, and encompasses a universal political standard that transcends national boundaries. As a result, the people's evaluation of politics has changed from a vertical to a horizontal perspective. Among young intellectuals we hardly hear comments concerning how well China is doing compared to the past – instead, we hear more often how China is backward compared to other countries.

Such transformations constitute changes in political values, which are the essential components of political culture and the standards for evaluating politics. In other dimensions of political culture, such as political attitude and political ideology, we see obvious changes as well. An increasing number of China's citizens, especially among the younger generations, no longer submit to government oppression, or merely mimic the views of others. They have begun to hold relatively independent attitudes and responses to government policies and actions. We seldom hear loud slogans from the past such as, "We will fight wherever the Party directs us!" or "We will follow the Superior's directions whether or not we understand them!" On the contrary, the awareness of civil rights and self-protection has increased greatly. The general trends in civil politics and culture are gradually deviating from the traditional form of Chinese political culture, and are moving closer to the universal political values that are being widely acknowledged in the world. There can be no doubt that without opening up to the world, and without impacts from the outside world, it would have been impossible to see profound political and cultural transformations within a situation of complete isolation. Economic globalization has accelerated processes of political and cultural transformations. Without the wave of globalization in the 1980s, it would have been difficult for the Chinese political culture to have undergone such a great change in such a short time.

Civil political values, ideology, and attitudes determine the nature and mode of civil political conduct. The transformation of the Chinese civil political culture has inevitably resulted in changes in social and political life, which in turn reflect the transformation of the Chinese political culture. Since the 1980s, changes in Chinese politics have directly and indirectly reflected the change in political culture caused by the impact of globalization.

The beginning separation of Party and state

The integration of the Party and the state, and the Party and government, has characterized traditional politics. Mao Zedong called such a political system "the absolute and centralized leadership of the Party." This is a typical mode of centralized leadership. In such a political mode, the Communist Party, as the sole party in power, controls power over all aspects of administration, legislation, and judiciary, even economic and ideological management. The Party is the state and the government.

At the start of reform, the leaders of the Chinese Communist Party had considered "the separation of the Party and the administration" an important aspect of reform, and it once regarded this as a breakthrough in the reform of the political system. After twenty years of effort, the Party has not achieved this ideal and goal

– because in reality it is impossible to completely separate the Party from the government under one party rule – although the Party has nevertheless made some important progress and has broken out of the mode of "absolute and centralized leadership of the Party."

Of the types of progress that the Party has made, there are two that are most important. First, the Chinese Communist Party itself has formally announced that it should not place itself above the laws, and that it must act within the scope of the laws. The new Party constitution's stipulation that "the Party must act within the scope of the constitution and laws" expresses a very important principle. From the Central Committee to the grass-roots level, all of the actions of the Party's organizations and members should not conflict with the state's constitution and laws. They are obligated to follow the constitutions and laws, and they do not have the privilege of standing above the constitution and laws.[9]

Second, the Party does not replace the government's role as the direct administrator. The political report of the Thirteenth Central Committee of the Party particularly expounded on the issue of the separation of Party and government, stipulating that the Party may not replace the government as the administrative organ. The key to reforming the political system is to first separate Party and government, that is to say, to stipulate that the functions of the Party remain distinct from those of the government: "The Party leads the people and establishes national authority, the organization of the people, and various economic and cultural organizations. The Party should ensure that authorized organizations play their roles to the fullest, and it should respect the work of enterprises and institutions rather than seek to replace their roles." The report also reiterated that the Party's authority over the state shall not constitute a simple administrative leadership, but rather it shall constitute "political leadership, that is to say, leadership in political principles, direction, critical decision-making, and recommending important cadres to positions in the government organs."[10]

The emergence of civil society

During the time of Mao Zedong, not only was there high integration between the Party and the state, but there was also high integration between state and society. There was virtually no independent civil society. However, ever since reform and opening up to the world, a relatively independent civil society has gradually developed, and has the following four characteristics (1) a sharp increase in the number of civil organizations, (2) a sharp increase in the types of civil organizations, (3) strengthening of the independence of civil organizations, and (4) strengthening of the legitimacy of civil organizations. Before the period of reform and opening up, even though there existed some organizations of the people and the masses, such as trade unions, the Communist Youth League, and the Women's Federation, strictly speaking, they were all subordinate to the Party and government; they were integrated with the organs of the Party and government, and they had no independence. The emergence of civil society has been the product of reform and opening up.

Since the 1980s, civil and social organizations have begun to dramatically develop. Before reform, from the 1950s to the 1970s, the number of various communities and organizations of the masses was very small. During the 1950s there were only forty-four nation-wide communities and during the 1960s there were less than one hundred national organizations, and only about six thousand local communities. In contrast, in 1989, nation-wide communities had dramatically increased to 1,600 and local communities had increased to 200,000. In 1997, communities and organizations above the county level numbered 180,000 and those at the provincial level numbered 21,404, while nation-wide communities and organizations numbered 1,848.[11] Although we do not have any formal statistics for the number of various civil organizations, a conservative estimate would be at least three million.[12] Among these we find some 730,950 village committees, and 510,000 union organizations at the grass-roots level.[13] In addition to community organizations, since reform and opening up, China has developed another type of special civil organization, the so-called civil non-enterprise unit.[14] Civil non-enterprise units are civil service units. Based on initial estimates, in 1998, this type of organization numbered over 700,000.[15] These civil organizations currently play important roles in Chinese democracy and administration.[16]

The goal of political development is to establish a country that has a legal system

One of the reasons the political tragedy of the Cultural Revolution occurred was because the Chinese legal system was neither complete nor consistent. Political governance depended on human governance, rather than on the legal system. Because of such serious lessons, since the beginning of reform, Chinese leaders and intellectuals have particularly emphasized the construction of a legal system, and the establishment of a long-term goal of setting up a country with a legal system. In September 1997, the Fifteenth Central Committee of the Chinese Communist Party formally announced that its political goal was "administering this country according to law and establishing a socialist country that has a legal system." This goal was included in the report from the meeting. In March 1999, the Second Meeting of the People's Congress revised the existing constitution and formally included the stipulation of "administering this country according to laws and establishing a socialist country that has a legal system" into the constitution. It also promoted the stipulation "administering this country according to laws" as a principle in the state constitution. From 1979 to 1999, the People's Congress and its standing committee passed 351 laws and related resolutions, while the State Council established more than 800 administrative legal regulations. The local People's Congress and their standing committees established over 6,000 local legal regulations.[17] From 1994 to 1996, the national People's Congress and its standing committee established a law almost every thirteen days. The State Council established one administrative law every six days. The goal of the Chinese government is to establish a good legal system before 2010.[18]

Enlarging the scope of direct election and local autonomy

Ever since reform and opening up, Chinese leaders have paid attention to implementing democracy at the grass-roots level and they have stressed grass-roots democracy. Accordingly, *The Election Law of the National and Local People's Congresses of the People's Republic of China* stipulates that the people's representative at the county level and below should be directly elected by voters. Even though the leaders of the Party and government who hold power at various levels have not been directly elected by citizen voters: one administrative village (*xiang*) head and one town (*zhen*) head were directly elected by voters in Sichuan Province in 1989, and in Shenzhen Special Economic Zone in 1999. This indicates that the scope of direct election may gradually be enlarged. In terms of grass-roots democracy, the most remarkable development may be seen in the broad implementation of village autonomy. *The Organization Law of Village Committees of the People's Republic of China* passed by the Standing Committee of the People's Congress in December 1989 stipulates that the autonomous system for villages will be gradually implemented in China's rural areas, that the authoritative organs of the state will no longer administer village affairs, and that the village head and cadres will be freely elected by villagers. At the end of 1997 about 60 per cent of China's rural areas had begun to implement village self-governance and had elected more than 900,000 village committees. The rate of participation of villagers in elections rose to 90 per cent. Village self-governance consists of four main systems:

1   *The System of Village Election*
    The village head and members of the village committee are elected by villagers through a direct, free, and secret vote.

2   *The System of Village Discussions Concerning Village Affairs*
    Any large village event, including plans for economic and social development, public welfare issues, and "hot" topics, with which the majority of the village is concerned, must be discussed during a consultation of village representatives and the village meeting, according to related regulations.

3   *The System of Openness in Village Affairs*
    Any issues of interest to the entire village should regularly be made public and should be supervised by members of the village.

4   *The System of Village Regulations and Agreements*
    The routine affairs of a village are administered through making autonomous rules and agreements for the village.

Of China's population of 1.2 billion people, more than 800 million are peasants. The initial implementation of village self-government in rural areas has played a very important role in developing Chinese democratic politics.

The separation of government and enterprises

Government ownership and direct management of enterprises constitute one of the characteristics of traditional socialism. Under such a system, the state holds a monopoly and operates each important enterprise. The leaders of the enterprises are appointed by the Party and the government. These leaders enjoyed the attention of administrative officials. These enterprises featured a strict hierarchy identical to those of the organs of government. The most important enterprises enjoyed political and economic attention from the ministries. At the ministerial level officials served as the main leaders. The integration of the government and enterprises formed the basis of the traditional command economy and was the inevitable result of the planned economy. The implementation of a market economy requires the establishment of the system of modern enterprises. The prerequisite of the system of modern enterprises stipulates that an enterprise must be an independent legal entity. The new generation of China's leaders has regarded the separation of government and enterprises as a major task of reform. The twenty-year reform, in a certain sense, has been a process of separating government and enterprises. The Fourth Plenary Session of the Fifteenth Central Committee of the Chinese Communist Party that was held not long ago centered on the main topic of reforming state enterprises. The plenary session passed a resolution that formally decided to establish the system of modern enterprises adapted to a market economy.

The separation of government and enterprises is a very difficult process, and it is far from finished. Nevertheless, there have been remarkable accomplishments. All enterprises, including those heretofore under state management, have been completely separated from the administrative system. The government no longer directly manages enterprises. The majority of state-owned enterprises have transformed, or are in the process of transforming, their form of ownership and mode of management. Leaders of enterprises will no longer enjoy the attention of Party and government officials.

The integration of the administration and enterprises serves as the crucial foundation of absolute, centralized politics – and since this foundation no longer exists, traditional, absolute, and centralized politics has been fundamentally shaken.

Local government innovations

With recent changes in political ideology and the political environment, local governments, particularly government at the grass-roots level, have proven to be a powerful force for system innovation. Innovation has become a conscious act for many organs of the Party and administration. Reviewing the available materials, we can see that in recent years local government innovation has featured the following characteristics:

1   Political transparency

- Openness in administrative affairs
  Before making important policy decisions, leading organs of the Party and
  the administration broadly accept advice and suggestions from the people

and experts, and, where possible, involved persons are able to participate in the decision-making process to avoid "operating in a black box." Policy is made public before it is issued and implemented.

- Openness in police affairs
  On issues of interest to citizens, such as public security, registration of residence, detainment, and so forth, the authorities inform involved people of police affairs and allow them input into police affairs.

- Openness in judicial affairs
  Open trials are conducted, and citizens are allowed to attend and listen to trials.

- Openness in procuratorial affairs
  In terms of maintaining public openness in procuratorial affairs, lawyers are allowed to participate ahead of time in lawsuits against a criminal suspect.

- Openness in making appointments
  The authorities publish a candidate list before appointing leaders of the departments of the Party and administration, while listening to the opinions of the public within a period of time.

- Government on the internet ("e-government")
  The government issues administrative messages, conducts government business, and directly handles public affairs and accepts citizen visits on the internet.

2   *Administrative services*

- Mayor's hotline
  A twenty-four-hour Mayor's Hotline is set up. Citizens can make direct phone calls and contribute criticism, opinions, and suggestions concerning government policies and actions. The government maintains responsibility for handling such calls.

- Leader visits
  The main leaders such as mayors, county heads, town heads, and Party secretaries make regular visits at the grass-roots level, accompanied by leaders of the organs of the Party and leaders at each level of the administration, to solve problems "on the spot," and to listen to citizen complaints, requests, and suggestions. When an issue can be solved "on the spot," each organ makes an effort to solve it. If a resolution is not forthcoming, such problems are solved within a determined period of time; otherwise a response and explanation is issued to the party concerned.

- "Government affairs supermarket"
  Grass-roots governments concentrate their administrative organs on doing business in order to provide convenience to residents who live in that administrative area.

- Assistance to the poor
  The government makes concrete plans and policies to help the poor or disadvantaged groups in society to rid them of poverty within a certain time frame.

- Public security and joint defense
  A patrol system is established within communities, including the 110 Emergency Phone Call System, and increases in criminal activities are prevented.

- Universal education
  The government sets up various types of compulsory schools in rural areas and urban communities in order to provide free education to residents.

3   *Cadre selection and power restriction*

- Appointing cadre through competition
  Authorities publish information concerning official position openings, as well as encouraging qualified citizens to apply and participate in fair competition. Candidates are selected and employed according to scoring and performance. Currently, open competition for the highest official position depends on the level of the department head under the provincial government.

- The direct election of town heads
  In recent years, some provinces and towns have implemented direct elections that have developed from elections of directors of village committees and town heads. For example, direct election of township heads has occurred in Buyun Town in Sichuan Province, and Dapeng Township in Shenzhen.

- Public recommendation and selection, or the "two votes system"
  Some grass-roots action has integrated the election within the Party with the recommendations outside the Party for selection of candidates of a Party branch secretary.

- Administrative lawsuit ("citizens sue officials")
  Citizens may forward suits against the illegal conduct of the government in court. If the court decides that the government had conducted illegal activity, citizens have the right to ask for remuneration of damages due to illegal actions.

- Financial audit at the time of leaving post
  Before cadres of the Party and the administration leave their posts they are required to accept the financial audit of the government, in order to determine if they had violated state and Party rules during their time of service.

- Supervision of public opinion
  Some local governments have made special legal regulations to ensure that the media can supervise government actions, and to allow the media to expose and criticize illegal actions of government officials.

4   *Administrative efficiency and honesty*

- Simplification of administrative approval processes
  Many local governments provide "a package" of administrative services in order to reduce the time of approval and the administrative costs.

- Focus on administrative responsibilities
  The government implements various types of duty systems in order to prevent bureaucracy and a "ball game" situation.

- Handling emergencies
  The government should break regular administrative processes in order to handle public service emergencies.

The political developments in China discussed above have different characteristics. Some of these characteristics are universal, some local; some have developed from the elite level to the grass-roots level, and some have developed from the grass-roots level to the elite level; some pertain to systems and some pertain to policy, and some are merely formal in nature and some have had a real impact. Yet there exist common elements underlying these various political developments and government innovations.

First, all these developments and innovations result from reform and opening up to the outside world. They are related to domestic political reform. However, domestic political reforms have had close connections with the policy of opening up to the outside world. Without this policy it is difficult to imagine internal reform in China. In this sense, political reforms have been the products of economic globalization. Without the active participation of the Chinese government in economic globalization, it would have been very difficult to achieve such political developments.

Second, all these political developments and government innovations have emerged out of Chinese territories, and they are the creation of the Chinese people and the result of being integrated with China's national characteristics. At the same time they manifest the universal political values of human society. The universal values that support these political changes are basically freedom, democracy, equality, and human rights.

Third, the basic goals of these political developments and government innovations have been to establish a modern, democratic administrative system, and to ensure that people are able to enjoy democratic rights such as freedom, equality, dignity, and so forth.

As many scholars have clearly noted, China's participation in globalization as a developing country is not a matter of whether it is willing to participate, but rather of how to seize the opportunity, and of choosing a way to participate while avoiding as much as possible the negative impacts on domestic politics and domestic economy brought about by economic globalization. The Chinese government has actively implemented the policy of opening up to the world, as well as developing economic and trade cooperation with every country in the world, and it made a great effort to join the WTO. This shows that China is actively participating in economic globalization in a certain sense and at a certain pace. As noted above, in a certain sense, China's reform and policy of opening up constitute active participation in economic globalization.

Economic globalization has both positive and negative impacts on Chinese social life. China ought to bravely face the challenges of globalization while actively participating in it, implementing effective measure and policies, as well as avoiding and reducing as much as possible the negative impacts in order to increase positive impacts. This is the correct attitude with which to face economic globalization.

In brief, economic globalization will inevitably have an important impact not only on China's economic life but also on the entire social life, including the political life, of our country. In terms of political life, economic globalization will inevitably impact upon global and domestic governance. In terms of global governance, China has actively undertaken important responsibilities in international peace and security, and it has played important roles in the United Nations and other international organizations. It has been dedicated to establishing a set of new international political and economic order, and to seeking the peace and development of mankind. In terms of domestic governance, China has gradually established political values such as democracy and a legal system, and it has actively followed the standards of democracy, a legal system, efficiency, honesty, responsibility, cooperation, participation and fairness in order to improve its governance. Such are the political requirements of economic globalization. They demonstrate the direction in which Chinese politics is developing against the background of economic globalization.

Notes

1   Ulrich Beck, "How Feasible is Democracy in the Age of Globalization?," *Globalization and Politics* (Central Compilation and Translation Press, 2000), p. 14.
2   Ralph Dahrendorf, "On Globalization," *Globalization and Politics* (Central Compilation and Translation Press, 2000), p. 212.
3   Gordon Smith and Mois Naim, *Altered States Globalization, Sovereignty, and Governance* (IDRC, 1999), p. 27.
4   Mitchell Zen, "The Reactive Mode of Black, Green, and Brown Concerning the Trend of Anti-Nation State," in Ulrich Beck and Jürgen Habermas, *Globalization and Politics* (Central Compilation and Translation Press, 2000) pp. 162 and 171.
5   Herbert Dittgen, "World Without Borders? Reflections on the Future of the Nation-state," *Government and Opposition* 34.2 (1999), pp. 161–179.
6   Pierre De Sanerkellens, "The Crisis of Administration and the Mechanism of International Regulation," *International Social Science* (Chinese edn) (February 1999).
7   "The Commission on Global Governance," in *Our Global Partnership*, ch. 1 (Oxford University Press, 1995), p. 3.

8 Ann Marie Clark, E.J. Friedman and K. Hochsterler, "The Sovereign Limits of Global Civil Society," *World Politics* (October 1998).

9 The Central Committee of the Chinese Communist Party, "The Announcement of the Central Committee Concerning the Firm Safeguarding of the Socialist Legal System" (July 10, 1986). See *Selected Documents of the People's Congress by* the Research Office of the Standing Committee of the People's Congress (China Democratic and Legal System Press, 1992), p. 166.

10 See "Advancing Along the Socialist Road which Features Chinese Characteristics," and "The Political Report of the Central Committee of the Chinese Communist Party," in *Selected Documents of the People's Congress by* the Research Office of the Standing Committee of the People's Congress (China Democratic and Legal System Press, October 25, 1987, p. 185.

11 *Yearbook of China's Civil Work: 1998* (China Society Press).

12 Since the 1990s, many civil organizations have been developed in villages and towns. China has a total of 2,135 counties, 44,689 towns, and approximately 740,000 villages. According to a conservative estimate, registered and unregistered civil organizations number up to at least three million or over.

13 *Yearbook of China's Statistics: 1998* (China Society Press, 1999).

14 Concerning the definition of civil non-enterprise units, see *The Temporary Regulation of the Registration of Civil Non-Enterprise Units* ("Instruction of the State Council of the People's Republic of China, No. 251" passed by the Eighth Standing Committee of the State Council on September 25, 1998).

15 *Yearbook of China's Statistics: 1998* (China Society Press, 1999).

16 About the rise of Chinese civil society and its impacts on political life, see Yu Keping, "The Rise of Chinese Civil Society and Its Impacts on Governance," *China Social Science Quarterly*, Hong Kong (fall 1999).

17 See *People's Daily*, April 14, 1999, p. 3.

18 Jiang Zemin, "Holding High the Great Flag of Deng Xiaoping's Theory and Promoting the Socialist that has the Chinese Characteristics Into the 21st Century," *The Collected Documents of the Fifteenth Central Committee of the Chinese Communist Party* (People's Press, 1997), p. 33.

13 Globalization and economic development

Ch'u Wan-wen

1 Introduction

China joined the WTO at the end of 2001. How does this impact upon economic development in China? This will prove an important issue. In addition to the impact of specific issues such as WTO regulations and the conditions for joining GATT, the central issue remains the impact of globalization on economic development. That is, if underdeveloped countries such as China participate in the process of globalization, will it be advantageous to their economic development? Thus, before addressing the impact of China joining the WTO, we must discuss the impact of globalization.

The term *globalization* has become a mainstream everyday word, but what is its real meaning? Is it an irresistible trend? With participation in globalization, will underdeveloped countries lose their independence and fall into the margins of the global capitalist economic system?

Among the theories about the impact of globalization, mainstream economics as represented by neo-liberalism are in the dominant position in the world. Neo-liberalism is the neo-conservative ideology that has been popular in Europe and the United States for the past thirty years. The scholars of neo-liberalism believe that the free market is the best mechanism for solving economic problems and promoting growth. Based on the theory of interest comparison they think that any country can find a position which suits its conditions for joining the division of labor in the international market. Since the division of labor must promote efficiency, free trade is the best mechanism that can benefit all the participants. As for capital flow, these scholars think that direct foreign investment (the actual investment in industries) will inevitably bring advanced technology and will be advantageous to the local economy. However, if free trade is supposed to bring about the free flow of financial capital and the complete opening up of capital accounts, resulting in a win-win outcome, then this scenario is controversial even among neo-liberals.

Neo-liberals explain that globalization has emerged because the development of transportation and communication technology greatly lowers the cost of circulation, thus easing trade and investment flow among countries, or they cite GATT/WTO[1] trade negotiations and the liberal policies guided by the United States in recent years. In the eyes of neo-liberals, since free trade is the best strategy, it is justifiable to press underdeveloped countries to open their markets and implement liberalization, both of which have been advocated in the past twenty years by the American government and organizations such as the IMF.

The neo-liberal point of view is currently still in the dominant position in the world. Neo-liberalism is being challenged by the so-called revisionist school, whose criticism is a revision, not a complete rejection. In recent years the debate mainly encompasses issues concerning developing countries in East Asia, the role of industrial policy, how to conduct economic reform in former socialist countries, the World Bank and IMF forcing underdeveloped countries to implement free-market policies, and global financial liberalization causing the financial crisis and instability of international finance (these theoretical debates will be discussed in Section 3 below).

The revisionist school neither totally opposes globalization nor does it advocate that underdeveloped countries refrain from joining the international market and the WTO. It mainly challenges the free-market theory, and offers different opinions about systems and policies.

Dependency theory, which used to be very popular, advocated that underdeveloped countries refrain from joining the international market, but the influence of this theory is very insignificant now, even in the anti-imperialist camps of the Third World. However, in advanced countries, such as the United States, unions that have been advocating protectionism, and their allies who oppose globalization, sometimes use this theory to justify protectionism, and to claim that protectionism will not harm Third World labor.[2]

Many underdeveloped countries have made extensive progress along the globalization path. Among them, East Asian countries have gained benefits in the process of globalization. Although other underdeveloped countries have not gained many benefits, they can yet hope to achieve good conditions when they join the international market in the current situation. Only an economic body such as China – which was late in opening its doors and which has a vast inland territory – had the room to weigh the gains and losses when it considered joining the WTO.

This chapter is a concise review of the phenomenon of globalization and systemic transformation. It mainly discusses the revisionist school's point of view on the impact of globalization on underdeveloped countries.

2 The globalization trend

The transformation of the global system

The continuous increase of the integration of the international market is not a new phenomenon. This phenomenon emerged in the fifty years before World War One. However, during the period between the two world wars protectionism and control became very popular. Moreover, there were hostilities between the world powers over the control of global regions. With the end of World War Two, when the United States re-established its hegemony, advanced countries such as the European countries and the United States restarted the process of integration in the post-war era.

After World War Two the blueprint of the world economic order was based mainly on the design of Keynesianism. The plan was made at a meeting in Bretton Woods, in the United States. Compared with the bad experience before World War Two, the newly established system focused on the stability of order and control. Advanced countries used financial and currency policies to adjust domestic economies, maintain fixed exchange rates and capital control, and at the same time established the World Bank and the International Monetary Fund in order to maintain order in the system. Having experienced the failure of pre-war protectionism, the advanced countries established GATT in 1947, and decided to open their markets to each other and gradually lower tariffs.

There were only twenty-three members when GATT was established. The order and system of GATT were naturally decided by the European countries, while the United States and the opening of markets concerned only advanced countries. When many colonies achieved independence after World War Two, the United States was in no hurry to force underdeveloped countries to open their markets as it does now, perhaps because the strength of the underdeveloped countries was very insignificant. Moreover, the U.S.A. was quite relaxed toward imports from underdeveloped countries. Thus, before the 1980s, underdeveloped countries could not only protect their domestic markets but they could also export goods easily because the markets of advanced countries were quite open.

The opinion that "the level of market opening increases with successful GATT trade negotiations" is actually true from the perspective of Europe and the United States. For example, trade negotiations among advanced countries in the early stage of GATT discussed how to adjust and lower tariffs in the principle of interest exchange, but the level of protection among the advanced countries was not high. For example, between 1973 and 1979, Tokyo Round Trade Negotiation[3] lowered tariffs among advanced countries from 7 per cent to 4.7 per cent (average). Comparatively, the tariffs of underdeveloped countries were much higher than those of advanced countries. Therefore, under pressure, underdeveloped countries had to greatly lower their tariffs.[4]

The most important changes occurred when Europe and the United States became completely conservative in politics and ideology. After 1970 it became difficult to maintain the post-World War Two world order. Keynesian economic policy, social democracy and social welfare met a bottle-neck. Earlier policies could no longer solve problems such as unemployment, stagnant productivity, financial deficits, and inflation. In this situation, neo-liberalism re-emerged. In politics, Margaret Thatcher was elected as the British Prime Minister and Ronald Reagan was elected as President of the U.S.A. Neo-classical economic theory which advocated the free market became the dominant ideology.

In the 1980s neo-liberal economic policy became popular. Under the leadership and advocacy of Thatcher and Reagan, privatization (it was deregulation in the U.S.A.), liberalism, and globalization became highly justified goals. Among advanced countries, the system of fixed exchange rates collapsed in the early part of the 1970s. After that, the advanced countries adopted the floating exchange rate, gradually relaxed capital controls, and began to develop the integration of the financial market. On the other hand, in the early part of the 1980s, underdeveloped countries were trapped in the crisis of international debts. Under the advocacy of the United States, the World Bank and IMF switched completely to neo-liberal policies. New measures formulated austerity programs for underdeveloped countries that had financial difficulties. These measures required underdeveloped countries to open their markets, implement privatization, reduce financial deficits, and social subsidies. Such reforms served as prerequisites for receiving assistance. This was the neo-liberal plan known as the "Washington Consensus."[5] However, in recent years, the "Consensus" has met with many challenges. Especially after the Asian Financial Crisis, the IMF and the World Bank faced vast problems, and they had different opinions about related policies.[6] Meanwhile, neo-liberal scholars who agreed with free trade did not necessarily agree with completely and quickly opening capital accounts.[7] Therefore, some scholars thought that the "consensus" was dying.[8]

Meanwhile, since the early part of the 1970s, productivity growth in America became stagnant. Its annual growth rate fell from 2.6 per cent on average to about 1 per cent, and the American economy experienced many problems. Even its position of economic hegemony was being challenged by Japan in the 1980s. People were surprised, and some even started to think that America might follow the footsteps of the British Empire and begin to crumble. The more important fact was that American trade deficits became larger and larger starting in the 1980s. In only a few years the United States had changed from the biggest creditor country in the world to the biggest debtor country.

Some older American industries, such as textiles, autos, and steel, felt threatened by imports and began to ask the government for assistance.[9] The U.S. government started to take measures to provide assistance. For example, it asked countries such as Japan to "automatically limit exports." America itself imposed anti-dumping duties and so forth. The most important change for America was the promotion of liberalization. It vigorously forced Japan and other new East Asian industrial countries to adjust and raise their exchange rates, as well as open their markets. The advanced countries formulated the Plaza Accord in 1985. First, the United States forced Japan to raise the value of the Japanese Yen, then forced South Korea and Taiwan to raise the values of their currencies. At the same time, the U.S. Congress passed the so-called Super 301 Act. Thus the U.S.A. started to use the trade sanctions as a weapon to make threats. It asked some countries to open specific markets, and allowed American capital to invest.[10]

During that time GATT members held the eighth round of negotiations from 1986 to 1994. Under the influence of neo-liberal ideology, Europe and the United States promoted further liberalization, and began to regulate the service industry and intellectual rights, in addition to industrial and agricultural products. The most important resolution was the decision to establish a permanent organization – the World Trade Organization (WTO) – and a mechanism that coordinates and arbitrates trade disputes. The WTO was established in 1995 and at the beginning of 2002 it had 144 members.

Although superficially the average current tariff has been reduced significantly, and non-trade barriers have been gradually reduced, this framework still has a long way to go before realizing real non-barrier free trade. For example, research and development subsidized by governments are still allowed. Because it is impossible for America to give up its subsidy of the defense industry, the European countries therefore maintain their right to subsidize their developing areas. The European countries and the United States themselves, of course, are the leaders who decide the relevant regulations. Meanwhile, each country can use anti-dumping measures to resist imports; and it is the United States and the European Union that have used the anti-dumping measures most frequently.[11]

Changes in the globalization trend

The above was a brief introduction to the transformation of the current global trade system. Under this system what level of global integration has been reached? Does the globalization trend really exist?

Generally speaking, globalization is studied from three perspectives: trade, capital outflow, and labor flow. In terms of trade, the ratio between gross value of export (or trade) and GDP is used as an index to measure the level at which each economic body participates in the world market. The global ratio between gross export and GDP has indeed increased from 7 per cent in 1950 to 19 per cent today. The amount of trade has increased by sixteenfold, but GDP has increased by only a factor of 5.5. Although the trade ratio certainly grew after World War Two, Western European countries had the ratio before 1913.[12] If we review the change in trade ratios in different historical periods, we find that the most significant changes occurred in the nineteenth century. Relatively, the growth rate of the trade ratio after World War Two was not very high.[13]

Thus, although the ratio of trade has indeed grown after World War Two, the rate of growth is not rapid. The growth rate exceeded the highest rate of the nineteenth century only recently. Meanwhile, economic boundaries between countries are still obvious. Even among neighboring countries, the level of market integration at home is much higher than the level of across-border market integration. The product prices of every country have not equalized. Nevertheless, international trade has seen significant changes. Since the ways in which underdeveloped countries have integrated into the system are different, the impact of integration is different compared with that of the past. For example, the ratio of export industrial products has risen from 42 per cent in 1983 to 66 per cent in 1997,[14] while dependency on trade (the ratio of the gross amount of trade to GNP) of underdeveloped countries has increased significantly in the recent decade, from 35 per cent in 1987 to 48 per cent in 1997.[15]

Capital flow may be divided into two types: direct foreign investment and financial capital flow. Direct foreign investment comprises 6 per cent of global investment. The capital stock of direct foreign investment now comprises 10 per cent of the gross value of global production. In 1913 this ratio was 9 per cent. In fact, during the colonial period of the nineteenth century, the amount of overseas investments of England, France, and Holland was sometimes larger than the amount that those countries invested domestically, and the ratio was larger than that of today.[16] Direct foreign investments to underdeveloped countries have increased in recent years. However, in 1997, 70 per cent of capital stock still consisted of investments among advanced countries. Investment flow to underdeveloped countries was only 30 per cent.[17]

Direct foreign investment has been closely related to the role of transnational corporations. Although direct foreign investment has focused on advanced countries, the impact on underdeveloped countries has been profound. Insofar as transnational corporations have been the owners of advanced technology, they have long served as the main leaders of global industries. Even today, this status has not been challenged by underdeveloped countries. The ratio of output value of foreign subsidiary companies of transnational corporations to the global gross product rose from 5.3 per cent in 1982 to 6.9 per cent in 1997, and the exports of those subsidiary companies have comprised 32 per cent of total global exports.[18]

In recent decades, mainly under U.S. pressure, each nation has indeed significantly relaxed limits on capital flow. Therefore, the flow of global financial capital has significantly increased. The trade of financial goods between countries has grown almost 30 per cent annually. The ratio of U.S. securities and stock trade between countries to GDP has risen from 9 per cent in 1980 to 135.5 per cent.[19]

The great increase of financial capital flow constituted the major cause of the financial crises of recent years,[20] such as the Mexican crisis in 1994 and the East Asian financial crisis in 1997. Although domestic financial problems in specific countries contributed the essential conditions that caused the crises, the frequent flow of short-term financial capital served as the primary cause of the crisis. Neo-liberal scholars who support the opening of financial markets theorized that so long as financial markets remained healthy, their opening would not become a problem. However, one of the characteristics of market systems of underdeveloped countries was that they were not fully established, and they had their own problems and did not need more risks and burdens.[21]

Although circulating financial capital has increased the instability of the entire international financial system, the international system has not formed into an integrated market. The level of domestic integration was higher than the level of international integration. The source of domestic investment came mainly from domestic deposits. Even interest rates among advanced countries did not show a trend toward equalization.[22]

In terms of labor flow, there has been no integration trend. From the seventeenth to the eighteenth centuries many Africans were sold as slaves to America. Over ten million Asian coolies were sold globally. Moreover, about sixty million Western Europeans migrated to new colonies. Immigration control in the imperial period was not popular. However, after World War Two, immigration control became routine, but in the early part of the post-war period, advanced countries imported labor from underdeveloped countries due to their lack of labor. Since the slowdown in economic growth in 1970 to today, immigration control has been strengthening. The phenomenon of labor globalization has been limited to specialists, managers, and technical personnel of transnational corporations, or the "brain flow" of underdeveloped countries to advanced countries. Although underdeveloped countries have requested in trade negotiations that advanced countries relax labor flow limits, such a possibility obviously does not exist.

Will the globalization trend go in the opposite direction?

We can see from the above discussion that trends in the globalization of trade, capital, and labor have different characteristics. But will globalization continue into the future? Answers to that question even today are different. Optimists believe that the development of globalization is inevitable. The promoters of globalization have been Europe and the United States, particularly the latter. However, because U.S. domestic politics have changed, it is a question of whether the American government will still vigorously promote globalization.

For example, the 1999 Seattle WTO Conference and the World Bank and IMF meetings attracted many demonstrators, with remarkably large demonstrations in recent years. Although the demands of the demonstrators varied, they reflected European and American concerns over the impact of globalization. Moreover, the demonstrations have affected American politics,[23] and U.S. protectionism has obviously increased.

There has been an example of this trend in history. From the end of 1913 to the dawn of World War Two, every advanced country changed the trend of nineteenth-century globalization, and started to implement protectionist policies. Some scholars claim that this might have been a reaction to globalization causing domestic inequality.[24] Are similar problems now accumulating in advanced countries, with contradictions worsening, thus fomenting future reaction to globalization? Might the United States change its political position and stop promoting globalization?

Income distribution in the U.S.A. has been worsening over the past thirty years. The income gap between skilled and unskilled workers has increased (i.e., the so-called skill premium has risen). Has this resulted from trade with underdeveloped countries? That is, do imports from underdeveloped countries cause the salaries of unskilled U.S. workers to decline?[25] American Leftist scholars, the U.S. government, and pro-union scholars, indeed advocate protectionism and demand that the WTO implement labor and environmental protection regulations. Many studies on the impact of international factors on U.S. salary differences conclude that there are certain impacts on salaries but these are not significant.[26] However, this remains a controversial issue.

Some scholars believe that the impact of globalization centers only on the skill premium. Globalization has enlarged the gap between those who have capital and skills and who are able to benefit from globalization, and those who cannot benefit from globalization. Simultaneously, under the influence of neo-liberalism, a social welfare system that could help the latter has been weakened in the past twenty to thirty years, thus making the problem more serious. Even if the reaction to globalization does not eventually happen, serious confrontation between classes will cause social problems, and the winners in the globalization process will pay the price.[27]

In general, domestic situations in advanced countries, especially in the U.S.A., will determine whether the U.S. government will promote globalization. These developments will have decisive impacts on the continuity of globalization. If the global trade system is out of order, the development of underdeveloped countries will face negative impacts.

3 The impact of globalization on the growth of underdeveloped countries

Changes in economic theories

We can see from the above discussion the changes in the international capitalist system. The leaders in the system are mainly European countries and the U.S.A. Does this mean that underdeveloped countries do not have independence in the system, and are they thus doomed to be exploited? Does this mean that it will be a good decision for underdeveloped countries to not join the system?

In the early period after World War Two, mainstream economic theories had an optimistic perspective on the economic development of underdeveloped countries. Among them, modernization scholars believed that if underdeveloped countries were given enough time they would be able to follow the steps of the advanced countries and develop. But structural theorists claimed that underdeveloped countries had structural weaknesses, and these countries would need to encourage and support private investment, as well as adopt the policy of import substitution. Around the 1970s, due to the lack of success in economic development of many underdeveloped countries, dependency theory emerged as a criticism to the modernization theory. Dependency theory was based mainly on the unsuccessful experiences of Latin American countries. The theory claimed that key problems were rooted in the relations between underdeveloped countries and advanced countries. The closer the trade and economic relations between underdeveloped countries and advanced countries, the more the underdeveloped countries were harmed in their growth and development. Whether it was trade relations or investment relations, advanced countries always benefited and underdeveloped countries always lost.

Meanwhile, neo-liberalism became very popular. Neo-liberals criticized structural theory from another perspective. They claimed that the reason why the "four little dragons" of East Asia were successful and Latin America was not was because East Asia adopted export-oriented and open-door policies, while Latin America went in the opposite direction. This, according to neo-liberals, proved that the free-market theory was correct.

The revisionist school had a different explanation for the East Asian experience. Revisionist scholars claimed that the East Asian success was due to those countries having developmental governments. In the process of economic development the government used administrative policies to intervene and support new industries, and also implemented export-oriented and import substitution policies. The international market provided not only the opportunity to engage at the economic level, but it also provided the tools by which those countries could regulate capital.[28]

Dependency theory found it difficult to explain the success of the "four little dragons" of East Asia, because those East Asian economic entities were highly dependent on exports. "Dependency" relations did not obstruct growth, but rather helped development. More importantly, in theory, it was difficult to define "dependency." Why did trade and investment have different results in different situations? How did trade and investment become the mechanisms by which the center exploited the margins? These theoretical questions are very controversial. Even among Marxist economists we find different opinions. In *Imperialism: Pioneer of Capitalism* (1980), Warren criticized dependency theory as a nationalist mythology of underdeveloped countries. In fact, in the past twenty years, dependency theory has lost popularity.

The East Asian experience proved again that underdeveloped countries must acquire the technology and experience of advanced countries. Small countries found that policies of self-sufficiency and self-reliance were not practical choices. Gerschenkron (1962) has suggested an explanation of the term "underdeveloped." Gerschenkron says that being "underdeveloped" is not only a burden, but it can also be a motivational force. The more underdeveloped a country is, the more opportunity it has to make progress, the more advanced technology it can learn. It can use the most advanced technology to industrialize by way of leap-frogging. However, this seems too optimistic when the gap between underdeveloped and advanced countries has become wider and wider in the twenty-first century.[29] Regardless, closing the door to the outside world is not a reasonable way to develop the economy.

Neo-liberalism has guided global economic development for almost twenty years. Recent debates criticize its theories and policies, and many scholars have evaluated and criticized global economic reforms in recent years. For example, on the issue of the economic transition in Eastern European countries, the revisionist school criticized the "shock therapy" plan put forward by neo-liberalism. Revisionists claim that these economies could not recover to pre-reform levels because those economic bodies depended too heavily on the free-market theory, and they neglected the fact that the market must depend on the support of many non-market systems to operate.[30] For example, international financial crises in recent years aroused many questions concerning financial opening, and instigated much criticism of the IMF.[31] Meanwhile, in the past twenty years criticism and debate have been centered on Third World economic reforms promoted by the World Bank and IMF, particularl, the impact of deflation policy on Third World growth.[32] Therefore, today, dependency theory has lost its popularity, although it emerged again when American union protectionists opposed globalization and used dependency theory to oppose the export-orientated policies of underdeveloped countries.

Today, globalization has become a noteworthy issue. Controversy surrounds world trade negotiations, particularly the demands of advanced countries (especially the U.S.A.) for implementing labor and environmental protection standards in trade regulations. Above I have shown that neo-liberalism has a positive and affirmative attitude toward globalization. In the next section I will discuss the different views of the revisionist school.

The views of the revisionist school

What is the path of growth for underdeveloped countries? Can underdeveloped countries benefit from globalization? These questions are not new, and theories addressing them are also not new, but the environment has since changed.

From the perspective of the development of advanced countries, the growth of productivity brought by the division of labor is undeniable. Adam Smith's *The Wealth of Nations* claimed that the degree of the division of labor depends on the size of the market. The bigger the market, the finer the division of labor and the more advanced the forces of production. However, Karl Marx argued that the driving force of the continuous development of the forces of production comes from capital pursuing profit and market competition. But Marx's view concerning the relation between the division of labor and the forces of production is basically the same as that of Smith.[33]

As for underdeveloped countries, whether participation in the international division of labor can develop the forces of production is still an unanswered question. Neo-liberalists believe that the answer is clear and affirmative. Dependency theorists reply in the negative. The revisionist school thinks that the answer has two sides, positive and negative aspects, under certain conditions.

Neo-liberalism claims that according to the comparative advantage, under the conditions of free trade, any underdeveloped country can find products suitable to its production and trade in the international division of labor. But the problem is that underdeveloped countries have ill-suited conditions and what underdeveloped countries find are low-value products that "fit" their production. More importantly, the theory of comparative advantage does not explain how underdeveloped countries can climb the ladder of comparative advantage under the conditions of free trade. For example, the comparative advantage of African countries may consist only of the export of mineral products or primarily agricultural products. There does not seem to be a way to board the locomotive of globalization.

The revisionist school has noted that, up until now, any country that has successfully developed a capitalist economy (perhaps except England, the pioneer of the Industrial Revolution) has experienced a stage in which the state intervened and protected young industries, and industrialization was based on domestic markets. The United States, Japan, and Germany did likewise, as did the underdeveloped countries in East Asia. There has never existed development in the context of free trade.[34]

In fact, after World War Two, the growth of underdeveloped countries has not been effective. East Asia is the only region that has been able to reduce the gap with advanced countries.[35] According to a report by the World Bank (2000: 14), over the past thirty years the per capita income of one-third of the mid-level countries fell from 12.5 per cent of the income per capita of the advanced countries to 11.4 per cent, and the ratio of one-third of the countries that are poorest fell from 3.1 per cent to 1.9 per cent. Some studies have noted that from 1870 to 1990 the difference in income per capita between the poorest and the richest countries has increased sixfold.[36] Advanced countries have basically maintained a stable growth of per capita income, and the amount of their income per capita has gradually become balanced, but the income gap between the majority of the underdeveloped countries and the advanced countries has become greater and greater.

Importantly, after World War Two, the differences in economic development among underdeveloped countries were very great. The most successful region, East Asia, used state power to intervene and support economic development. In contrast, the development trend in Latin America was not stable. This region was developed at a rate quite close to that of the advanced countries at the beginning of the twentieth century, but it has been surpassed by East Asian countries. Portions of the African continent south of the Sahara suffer in miserable conditions. From World War Two up until today, the growth rate of income per capita has been almost zero. The "four little dragons" of East Asia have been able to maintain growth. The growth rate of income per capita has been more than 5 per cent since World War Two.[37] Other so-called "second success" countries have quite a high growth rate, but the trend of growth was short-lived and unstable prior to the Asian Financial Crisis.[38]

East Asian countries have indeed adopted export-oriented policies, and with the rapid development of export they have quickly acquired production technology. But more importantly, East Asian governments have also implemented the policy of import substitution to support heavy industries and the high-tech industry. That is, East Asian states guided the strategy for industrial development, and took the initiative to promote the status of their economic bodies in the international division of labor. As Amsden (1989) has noted, the phenomenon of the state subsidizing capital exists everywhere in the world. The difference of East Asia from other regions is that its governments managed to regulate capital by the standard of international competition.

As Amsden, a revisionist, has noted, the past developmental strategy of East Asia was for local enterprises to undertake production and learning, not foreign or transnational enterprises. It was those local enterprises that had acquired advanced technology and laid the foundation for further development. In contrast, in Latin America, the main industries that implemented import-substitution policies – not export-oriented policies – continue to be controlled by transnational corporations, and governments are not able to manage the fate of the development of capitalism. This result is contrary to what supporters of the dependency theory would expect. It is not necessarily the case that trade dependency must conflict with the growth of local capital. More importantly, there must exist those industries which get the opportunity to grow and learn, and these must be local enterprises.

Of course, the lessons of the East Asian experience must be carefully explained. East Asian countries constitute the minority of underdeveloped countries, and they are comparatively small. It is impossible for them to depend on domestic markets to develop. The East Asian experience means that the cases of large countries such as mainland China, India, Indonesia, and Brazil need to be re-examined. Although East Asian countries have successfully developed capitalism or have depended on capitalism to develop productivity, they are only followers. The gap between them and the advanced countries remains wide and will not be easily reduced.

But the East Asian experience remains important for underdeveloped countries. If we can properly explain this experience, underdeveloped countries can benefit. The main lessons of the East Asian experience teach us why this region has been successful in development: States successfully guided industrial development, using export and the international competition capacity as the standard of rewards and punishments to regulate and support industries, while they protected markets and implemented export-oriented and local capital-supporting policies.

The governmental implementation of these policies was successful because East Asia had a balanced distribution of social wealth at the beginning stages, and the fruits of development could be shared as development progressed. In 1995, Campos and Root argued that the key to the East Asian success was in "making shared growth credible." That is, in industrial policy the state should grant subsidies, and allot rewards and punishments. Campos and Root (1995) argued that East Asian countries convinced people that they could share the fruits of future growth. Thus those countries were able to implement industrial policy smoothly to promote complete growth. In addition, Amsden and Wade, both revisionist scholars, also stress the benefits of even distribution of income in this economic mode. There exist many papers on the issue of the formation of developmental governments and their relations to political democracy. Because this chapter focuses on economic globalization, we cannot delve deeply into this research.[39]

The fact that East Asia was able to adopt this strategy prior to 1980 when it developed export substitution was due to Europe, and especially to the U.S.A. – which constituted the main East Asian market – being fairly open. At that time the U.S.A. was not feeling threatened by underdeveloped countries. Thus East Asia could not only protect domestic markets, but it also entered the American market. However, Europe and the U.S.A. are not as open today, and when the U.S.A. feels threatened by Japan and other East Asian countries it uses the "big stick" of super 301 to force underdeveloped countries to open their markets.[40]

Thus the international market which underdeveloped countries are now faced with differs from the one which East Asia faced then, and which is now more difficult for underdeveloped countries to join. If an underdeveloped country is forced to open its market too early by the conditions of free trade, it is not good for industrialization. In addition, it is not easy for that underdeveloped country to enter the markets of advanced countries. It will not be able to implement export-oriented policies to study foreign technology and experiences. If the WTO under the advocacy of Europe and the United States passes labor and environmental protection standards, it will be a big blow to the industrialization of underdeveloped countries.

The WTO has been established and membership is continuously increasing. Small countries feel compelled to join.[41] East Asian countries had a leeway and came prepared to join.[42] They have learned how to deal with U.S. demands and bypass WTO rules. They also hope to use the framework of the organization to resist the U.S.A.'s threat of super 301. Those underdeveloped countries that are weaker than the East Asian countries can only hope that the organization will help them to open the markets of advanced countries, and avoid the U.S.A.'s autocratic rule. The WTO was created as a system for opening markets, and, though it was designed by advanced countries, underdeveloped countries find that the WTO is better than a U.S. dictatorship. Perhaps large countries such as China and India may feel likewise.

Globalization and international competition widen the gaps between underdeveloped countries and advanced countries, and the gaps may increase further in the future. But East Asian countries with better conditions are able to use their political strength and industrial policies to guide economic growth, seize the opportunity to participate in international markets, and catch up with advanced countries. But some African countries do not have these beneficial conditions, and they cannot bear the pressures of the international markets. They have difficulty in developing their economies, and they also have to deal with famines, civil wars, and natural disasters.

In the environment of fierce competition the roles of the state do not disappear in globalization. Because of the change in the environment, the measures of the state must change. The state faces greater challenges and requirements. Therefore, if underdeveloped countries want to improve their conditions for survival, they must develop their economies on the basis of their nation states. They have no other choice.

Europe and the United States depended on capitalism and developed highly their forces of production. But the process of development over the past 200 years has never been a beautiful history. East Asian developments in recent years have illustrated the uglier aspects. Exploitation of labor, social inequity, and environmental destruction have occurred in East Asia.

But some progressive people in advanced countries have advocated anti-developmentalism because economic development destroys the environment. This is really a wrong approach. Asking underdeveloped countries to study the successes and failures of environmental protection in advanced countries, in order to use this knowledge for economic development, is very reasonable and helpful. "Not caring about anything besides development" does not accord with the long-term interests of the peoples of underdeveloped countries. However, some believe that non-development is the best way to protect the environment, and they ask underdeveloped countries not to develop in order to protect the environment. This thinking ignores unemployment and poverty in underdeveloped countries, and ignores the demand of the people who want to improve their lives, and it is really a view one finds in Europe and the United States. The various existing international treaties and negotiations handle issues such as environmental protection and global weather change quite well. Hence, why does the U.S.A. suggest adding environmental protection standards? Naturally, people suspect its intention is protectionism.[43]

4 The impact of China joining the World Trade Organization

What is the impact of China joining the WTO? How do we evaluate this event?

The impact is uncertain. First, there is no certainty about the impact of China joining the WTO. In this chapter I cannot discuss in detail the impact on the production, agricultural, and service industries. Nevertheless, I must point out that although WTO regulations have been established, how to use those regulations to protect the interests of a country have not been set out. Still, there are some actual opportunities. But how to seize these opportunities depends on the underdeveloped country's ability and will-power. For example, in the past, mainly advanced countries have used the anti-dumping policy to resist imports. However, in recent years, the number of cases that underdeveloped countries have filed is close to that which advanced countries have used (the ratio of the number of cases underdeveloped countries have filed to the number of global anti-dumping cases has increased from 20 per cent in 1987 to 50 per cent in 1997). This also means that the ability and will-power of an underdeveloped country are directly correlated with its status and interest in the international organization.

Taking the initiative to participate in making regulations

Second, besides the immediate impact, the more important issue is concerned with long-term future WTO trade negotiations and how to influence the regulation of competition. The emergence and transformation of the WTO has no doubt been guided by the advanced countries. The agenda of the next round of trade negotiations, such as negotiations on intellectual property rights and investment agreements, is clearly geared toward maintaining the interests of the transnational corporations of Europe, the U.S.A., and Japan in the markets of underdeveloped countries. The advanced countries use their large and rich markets as leverage to force underdeveloped countries to accept their demands. Individually, underdeveloped countries are neither strong nor large. It is better for each to join the WTO than to face the heavy pressure of powerful countries such as the U.S.A. Hence, WTO membership is continuously increasing. Today, more than 90 per cent of global trade is conducted under WTO regulations. Uniting the strengths of other underdeveloped countries to resist the advanced countries, and protecting individual interests, are important international responsibilities of China.

The impact of September 11, 2001

After the events of September 11, to some extent the negotiation strength of the underdeveloped countries has increased somewhat. These events made the advanced countries realize the importance of the stability of the international order, and that poverty in underdeveloped countries is a main factor of instability. If China uses its influence in the world to unite important underdeveloped countries such as India and Brazil, and strives for the interests of the underdeveloped countries in the WTO, this will benefit China, the underdeveloped countries, and the global economic order. Insofar as the WTO is guided by the interests of the advanced countries, it must be harmful to the economic development of underdeveloped countries, and it is neither advantageous to the balanced development of the world nor to world peace.

The conflict between fair competition and development

The publicly acknowledged goal is to maintain the smooth operation of the global economic system. Disorder in the economic system would certainly cause the world, especially underdeveloped areas, serious harm. To maintain the operation of the system, regulating fair competition is a reasonable and necessary measure.

Yet there exist contradictions and conflicts between short-term fair competition and long-term need for economic development in underdeveloped countries. As discussed above, due to status and situational variations between advanced countries and underdeveloped countries, fair competition is difficult to define. If underdeveloped countries want to change their unequal status and catch up with the advanced countries, they must have opportunities to implement interventionist economic policies. The goal of participation in international trade and the smooth operation of the global commercial system should be to help underdeveloped countries develop their economies. The fairness of international trade should be a means, not the goal. When underdeveloped countries strive for opportunities to implement industrial policies in the WTO, they should have perfect assurance.

The protected policy leeway

There is indeed some special treatment for developing countries in the WTO. Such regulations mainly state that underdeveloped countries can impose higher tariffs and have longer extensions. In fact, they serve merely as defensive measures for underdeveloped countries. Actually, what underdeveloped countries really need is the opportunity to implement industrial policies and the initiative to promote development in order to support local industries. East Asian countries successfully began the mechanism of economic growth after World War Two, but many policies and the opportunity to implement these policies have become forbidden by WTO regulations.

As discussed above, although new WTO regulations have limited underdeveloped countries, and most of the industrial policies that East Asian countries have used have become forbidden, this does not mean that there is no opportunity to implement industrial policies. Some leeway for policy implementation still exists, such as subsidies for development and research, or subsidies for underdeveloped areas in some countries. Advanced industries in the United States, such as the defense and pharmaceutical industries, are heavily dependent on government subsidies for their research and development. To maintain balance among the regions, the European Union also implements subsidies.

The difficulty of defining fair competition

On the one hand, the so-called regulation of fair competition of the WTO cannot cover all aspects of competition. On the other hand, these regulations have different goals based on the needs of certain powerful member countries. Thus so-called fair competition regulations are actually "fair" in limited areas. Subsidies for research and development, and subsidies for balance among regions (mentioned above) are not included in the limited areas. Hence, it is impossible to have complete fairness. However, for underdeveloped countries in disadvantaged positions it is important to understand the reality of the situation and strive for their own interests. This means that major underdeveloped countries such as China should consider the needs of underdeveloped countries as much as possible when they participate in making and revising WTO regulations.

In recent years, with changes in the rules of the game, East Asian countries have altered their policies. Policies that previously supported new industries have been revised, and have turned into subsidies for development and research, and preferential duty. With the progressive stages in economic development, policies have changed accordingly. Underdeveloped countries do not have the power of advanced countries to revise the rules of competition. Yet, insofar as these rules can never cover all contingencies, as long as underdeveloped countries strive to look for room under the current framework they can find their paths for survival and development.

The case of East Asia: foreign trade and investment policies

What foreign trade and investment policies are advantageous for the growth of underdeveloped countries? This chapter tries to use the East Asian experience as a case study to evaluate the lessons that may be learned.[44]

In the process of East Asian development, the export industries indeed became the locomotive of growth, but in fact export industries create local value and thus increased the opportunities for Taiwan's industries. That exports were subsidized goes without saying; policies also encouraged local enterprises to produce materials and parts for export. Government policies included investment in capital-intensive industries, subsidies for the development of key sectors, and use of import certificates (which has now been forbidden as a non-tariff barrier) to require export enterprises to use local products. When export enterprises imported parts that local enterprises were already producing they were required to provide reasons and proof for not using local products (when the value of imports exceeded 15 per cent or were incompatible with the quality of the product).

For example, early development in post-war Taiwan saw a rapid increase in the export of labor-intensive products such as clothes and plastic shoes. The state therefore supported petroleum and chemical industries to provide the fabric and plastic materials for the export industry, and also used the import certificate as another means of support. When notebook computers became popular, the state formulated plans to develop and produce liquid crystal displays in order to replace expensive imports, and the new industry is currently prospering. Now, under the so-called rule of "national treatment" (i.e., no discrimination against imports), such policies and measures that the East Asian countries have skillfully employed can no longer be used to benefit underdeveloped countries.

The East Asian strategy was clearly geared toward supporting local enterprises. In contrast, Latin America has generally depended on transnational or joint-venture enterprises. It is clear now which strategy is better. The benefit of supporting local enterprises does not reside in meeting nationalist sentiments in underdeveloped countries, but rather in supporting local enterprises in learning.

Is the impact of foreign enterprises on the local economy good or bad? Based on past experiences, the answer has to depend on specific situations and on how an underdeveloped country uses foreign capital. If underdeveloped countries have clear strategies for developing industry, and if foreign investment were introduced under the guidelines of these strategies, and if foreign investment were required to provide technology transfer and assist in the development of local enterprises, then foreign investment would result in beneficial impacts in the local economy. If these conditions do not exist, then the impact of foreign investment will not be beneficial.

The Taiwanese foreign investment policy has been the former. Although Taiwan welcomes foreign investment, foreign investment must submit to a process of evaluation that is not open to the public. Foreign investment has to have a high ratio of export, and it must gradually purchase more local products and provide technology transfer. These measures have had a good impact on many Taiwanese industries. The best result may be seen in the fact that when local industries prosper, foreign investment becomes unimportant.

For example, Taiwan's early electronic industry focused on assembling parts for European and American investments. It was labor-intensive and involved simple processes. Under the state's industrial policy, the local electronic industry gradually developed. Foreign electronic companies provided employment opportunities, and trained and skilled workers, and they promoted the development of related industries. After the development of the local electronic industry most of the foreign investment in cheaper labor moved out and the industry was not upgraded. This proves that upgrading an industry necessarily relies on local enterprises. For example, the Xinzhu Scientific and Industrial Zone is the cradle of Taiwan's high-tech industry. When it was established, foreign investment comprised 30 per cent of the total investment, but after the development of local industries, foreign investment fell to 3 per cent.

Most of the measures and policies that Taiwan has used to handle foreign investment have now become forbidden by new WTO regulations. A small portion of the investment regulations related to trade have not been passed by the WTO. Yet the WTO forbids measures that stipulate local shares, export ratios, and balanced foreign exchange. The U.S.A. and Europe plan to discuss the issue further in the next round of trade negotiations, and they hope to restrict underdeveloped countries from making certain requirements on the investment of transnational corporations. Transnational corporations of advanced countries have established powerful positions in the world, and underdeveloped countries can barely compete with them. It is very reasonable for underdeveloped countries to require that transnational companies provide technology transfer, increase local shares of production, and help local industries. Underdeveloped countries should resist as far as possible such restrictive agreements drafted by advanced countries.

Neo-liberal scholars find pleasure in listing cases of underdeveloped countries failing to develop their economies due to interventionist policies. Such scholars believe that intervention results in political disorder, inaccurate bureaucratic judgments, opportunities for corruption, competitive leasing conduct, and laziness caused by protectionism. Indeed, successful intervention requires high-skilled operation, and a variety of suitable conditions. Although intervention exists in East Asia, Latin America, and Africa, cases of failure outnumber cases of success. Nevertheless, it is impossible for underdeveloped countries to develop their economies without implementing interventionist policies. Yet, in order to follow the principles of free economy and the so-called regulations of fair competition, underdeveloped countries have to abandon their industrial policies. This will result in the loss of the possibility of promoting the economies of underdeveloped countries, the world becoming more unequal, and international order becoming more unstable.

In recent years many scholars have begun to study the conditions that make industrial policy successful, and they have arrived at certain insights. In general, industrial development strategy should have clear designs and goals. Subsidies must have clear standards of rewards and punishments (based on economic performance). The system should have transparency and should establish a mechanism for supervision. The state should have autonomy. Implementation of policies should have the public trust, and people should be convinced that they can share the fruits of economic development. Different countries have different situations. Underdeveloped countries must review the experiences of other countries, evaluate their own conditions, and design the system and policies that are suitable to their situations.

5 Conclusion

This chapter has reviewed current trends in globalization. It has discovered that in terms of trade and investment, global integration has indeed been progressing since the end of World War Two, but that the rate of development has been quite uneven. The boundaries of nation states are now still very clear, and the real integrated global market has not yet emerged. Even though financial capital has flowed quickly among countries in recent years, the global market has not yet taken shape.

Yet globalization is not a new phenomenon. The integration trend that existed before World War I was interrupted by wars and protectionism. After World War II, this integration trend re-emerged as the international capitalist system under the leadership of certain advanced countries, including Europe and the United States.

Indeed, the motivating force of globalization comes from the needs of capital expansion. Under the pressures of market competition, enterprises have to continuously expand and strive for more markets. New technology that can lower the costs of transportation and communication are developed due to the needs of capital expansion. The international market is further developed and market competition becomes more intensified. The systems and regulations of the global capitalist mechanism are still decided by the negotiations and struggles among nation states. National domestic policies also play decisive roles in economies, and many factors may influence or interrupt the so-called trend of globalization.

In terms of trade, the global trading volume has continuously increased since the end of World War Two, and the growth rate has been exceeding the growth rate of GNP. Therefore, dependency on trade has increased in the world. The dependency on trade of underdeveloped countries has increased greatly in the past ten years, and it has exceeded that of advanced countries. The ratio of industrial products to exports of underdeveloped countries has also increased continuously.

The relation between dependency on trade and economic growth is different from country to country. The economic development of underdeveloped countries as a whole after World War Two has not been good. The annual growth rate of income per capita in Africa is zero. In Latin America it is lower than 2 per cent. In East Europe, after the era of opening up, there has been negative growth, and this growth rate cannot recover to its original level. Only the growth rate of East Asia is close to 6 per cent, and this exceeds the growth rate of advanced countries. East Asia is the only region that has reduced the gap with advanced countries. In sum, the rich have become richer, and the poor have become poorer. Meanwhile, East Asia is a region that is highly dependent on trade.

After World War Two, when the international market order became stable, Europe and the U.S.A. started to negotiate for opening markets among themselves, and they established GATT. By then, their markets were quite open to underdeveloped countries, and there was no demand for underdeveloped countries to open their markets. Hence, East Asian countries took the opportunity to implement export-oriented policies.

In terms of capital flow, direct foreign investment has been fluctuating, and most of the investments have been flowing to advanced countries. Although capital flow to underdeveloped countries has increased in recent years, the distribution of capital has been uneven. Dependency on foreign investment was very limited during the economic development of East Asia.

In the past ten years the flow of financial capital has increased rapidly, and its growth rate has exceeded the growth rate of trade and direct investment. In the early 1970s, after the system formulated at Bretton Woods, the flow of financial capital started to cross the national borders of advanced countries. As for underdeveloped countries, after the 1980s, the U.S.A. along with the World Bank and IMF pressed underdeveloped countries continuously to lift capital control, and the underdeveloped countries started to feel the impact of this trend. International financial crises have occurred one after another in recent years because the development of the financial systems of underdeveloped countries has not been thorough and effective

During the 1970s free-market advocating neo-liberalism arose in Europe and the U.S.A., and it promoted the policies of liberalization and privatization.

Meanwhile, U.S. productivity growth became stagnant, trade deficits increased, and some traditional industries asked for protection because they felt threatened by imports from East Asia and other underdeveloped countries. The strategy of the American government was to use its superpower status to take protectionist measures at home, while making threats of overseas trade sanctions, asking other countries to implement liberalization, and requesting the opening of product and financial markets. The U.S.A., along with the World Bank and IMF, also required underdeveloped countries to promote liberalization and to implement the "Washington Consensus" policy. Simultaneously, during the eighth round of trade negotiations, the advanced countries promoted further liberalization policies, including regulations protecting U.S. and European intellectual rights. It was the resolution of the Uruguay Round that established the World Trade Organization. The organization was established in 1995.

Although underdeveloped countries do not trust the fairness of WTO trade regulations, the WTO has already been established. Underdeveloped countries need to join it with the hope that they can use WTO regulations to resist U.S. demands. The dependency on trade of underdeveloped countries has also increased in recent years.

While the U.S.A. has benefited the most from globalization, it supports adding labor and environmental protection standards to trade regulations because of the anti-globalization movement at home and because the U.S. government wants to win union votes. Some studies have noted that protectionism emerged during the interval between the World Wars because interest in globalization was not distributed evenly at home. Under the influence of neo-liberalism, social welfare was reduced, and this did not relieve social tension. Whether the American government pursues liberalization vigorously in the future will have a decisive impact on trends in globalization.

Revisionist scholars believe that from either the perspective of theory or of historical experience, a purely free market cannot bring economic development. They basically believe that the market can never be perfect. The operation of the market needs many non-market systems for support. In addition to infrastructure and hardware, market operation also requires non-market factors, such as the regulation of property rights, legal systems, social welfare, and educational systems, and so forth. The establishment of these systems requires state promotion and coordination.

If an underdeveloped country wants to catch up with advanced countries, it must use industrial policies and formulate industrial development strategies. It must support and cultivate new industries and local enterprises by means of subsidy, and it must establish a mechanism of rewards and punishments. It must acquire advanced technology as soon as possible in order to progress in the international market, thus gradually upgrading its status in the international division of labor. It must develop its economy and productivity continuously within the context of intensified competition and an increasing gap between underdeveloped and advanced countries.

If underdeveloped countries refrain from joining the international market, it will become very difficult to acquire advanced technology and difficult to cultivate production capacity, because advanced countries and their transnational corporations currently control advanced technology. It is reasonable for underdeveloped countries to participate in the international division of labor in order to acquire advanced technology and develop the production scale.

The question is: How can underdeveloped countries develop their own productivity and continue to promote their own interests while participating in the international division of labor? To achieve such goals, underdeveloped countries not only need to fulfill the role of developmental states, but they also need to join the international market. In the environment of intensified competition, it becomes more difficult, but not impossible, for underdeveloped countries to achieve such goals. The extent and way in which a country joins the international market should depend on each country's situation. In any case, there is no theoretical foundation and no practical way to refuse to join the international market.

Post-war East Asian growth serves as the model. Sensing crisis, the states in developing East Asia actively guided industrial development. On the one hand, they encouraged enterprises to join the international market in order to develop productivity and acquire technology. On the other hand, they promoted upgrading industry by means of industrial policy. Compared to the unsuccessful economic development in other underdeveloped countries, the economic growth in East Asia after World War Two has been an exception. This experience of success proves that development can occur in this way and this also supports the revisionist theories discussed above.

The post-war economic growth of both advanced and underdeveloped countries suggests to underdeveloped countries that the international capitalist system is a serious test. Many countries have failed or have come close to failure. Neither the essential assistance of advanced countries, nor neo-liberal theory and practice, was successful. Sometimes they were even harmful. In the current international situation, only underdeveloped countries can save themselves. This is the essential point this chapter aims to present.

As long as underdeveloped countries have not caught up with advanced countries, they will have needs and will require theories and policies different from those of advanced countries. Underdeveloped countries need the markets of advanced countries and the opportunity to implement policies which cultivate and support export industries and domestic enterprises. When the U.S.A. and Germany were catching up with England in the nineteenth century they benefited from this opportunity, as did the East Asian countries after World War II. But in the past twenty years, advanced countries have started to pay attention to new markets, and they have begun to reduce the opportunities of underdeveloped countries.

The original goal of establishing the WTO was to coordinate the rules and mechanisms of competition among advanced countries. However, due to the dominance of neo-liberalism and the intensification of competition among advanced countries in recent years, advanced countries have become eager to enter new markets in underdeveloped countries. Hence, advanced countries have heavily pressed underdeveloped countries to open their markets, and have forced underdeveloped countries to join the WTO. The agendas that the advanced countries want to put forward in the next round of negotiations encompass intellectual rights related to trade, policies on investment, and so forth. Obviously, these agendas do not promote the interests of underdeveloped countries; rather, they limit the opportunities for underdeveloped countries to implement their own policies.

In view of the post-September 11 situation, underdeveloped countries should unite to strive for their own interests in the WTO. They should resist negotiations on intellectual rights and investment policy that the advanced countries have promoted and they should strive to implement their own industrial policies. It is advantageous to China's interest to unite underdeveloped countries to strive for the interest of underdeveloped countries. Moreover, as a member of the international community, this has become China's responsibility.

Discussion

Amin: I want to add a point to Ms. Ch'u's speech – that is, the significance of the global movement that is now starting. I do not call it the anti-globalization movement, because they want to seek another type of globalization. Now, some different forces are joining the movement. In the West, the movement in Europe, particularly in continental Europe, is different from the one in North America. In terms of an alternate concept of globalization and the relations among social and political forces, the situations vary in Western, Central, and Southern Europe. Movements are starting to appear in developing regions such as Latin America, Central and Eastern Africa, India and South East Asian countries. They are holding meetings to discuss the issue and their differences. Unfortunately, up to now China has yet to join this movement. I think that we need to face globalization, neo-liberal globalization. We need to unite the forces that oppose neo-liberal globalization in different regions, in order to protect the different interests of these countries and regions. This is very important.

Tian Yu Cao: I think that Ch'u Wan-wen's article is extremely important. Its significance is that it enlightens us on how to redefine nationalism within the context of globalization. Because an array of nation states participates in globalization, the new theoretical issue of redefining nationalism should be addressed. This is also related to another type of globalization, as Amin has noted. It relates to many issues that can be discussed.

Notes

1 GATT (General Agreement on Tariffs and Trade), WTO (World Trade Organization).
2 Anti-globalization organizations have emerged in recent years, as may be seen in the opposition to the 1999 Seattle WTO meeting, and the large demonstrations against the annual meetings of the World Bank and IMF in Washington. These clearly illustrate social forces in the U.S.A. Some leftist scholars in the U.S.A. have also written papers against globalization (see Baker, *et al.*, 1998). The American government advocates adding labor and environmental protection standards to trade agreements to get union support. Such standards would subject certain products to trade sanction and prevent

them from entering the U.S.A. Labor standards that have been recommended by the U.S.A. require establishing and/or raising the minimum wage, limiting work hours, and forbidding child labor as well as the right to organize unions. As may be expected, underdeveloped countries have opposed these standards. See Amsden, 1999.

3 There have been eight rounds of trade negotiations up until now. The participants in the early period were few, the areas of negation limited, and the duration of negotiation short. The seventh round of negotiations was held in Tokyo. Ninety-nine countries participated. The eighth round was held in Uruguay from 1986 to 1993.

4 In the case of Taiwan, the average tariff fell from 30.8 per cent in 1984 to 9.8 per cent in 1997. The actual tariff incidence (i.e., actual tariff income divided by amount of imports) fell from 8 per cent in 1980 to 3.4 per cent in 1997. See Chen Tianzhi (1999, Figures 1 and 4).

5 Williamson (1994: 26–28) lists the Consensus.

6 See Stiglitz (1998b, 1999).

7 Those who agree with this believe that when capital pursues maximum profit without restraint it can promote the efficient use of resources, but opponents argue that the flow of short-term financial capital can bring only financial instability and harm. If a country lacks capital, it should introduce foreign long-term investment in production, not financial capital. J. Bhagwati, who vigorously advocates free trade, displays anger toward those who improperly take advantage of free trade theory to promote the free flow of capital. Bhagwati contends that there exists an elite group on Wall Street, and in the Treasury, World Bank, and IMF, who have resorted to liberalization, to promote the free flow of financial capital in order to benefit themselves. See Bhagwati (1998) and Rodrik (1998). As the World Bank has shown (2000: 37), the fluctuation of foreign investment is lower than that of financial capital.

8 Following Krugman (1995b) and Gore (2000).

9 Cline (1984) has noted that when industry imports exceed a certain market limit, domestic demand for protection will emerge.

10 Stiglitz has criticized the American government for forcing other countries to open up their markets with the excuse of reducing the bilateral trade deficit (1999: 10–11). This excuse was not only wrong, but it also caused underdeveloped countries to become suspicious of America's intentions, the benefits of liberalization, and even the fairness of the entire trade system. On the one hand, the bilateral trade deficit may not indicate the existence of trade barriers. Trade deficits mainly show the difference between deposits and investments in a country. On the other hand, liberalization should benefit underdeveloped countries, not become a form of punishment.

11 Some newly arisen countries have learned this from advanced countries. They have started to use this tool frequently. Therefore, anti-dumping cases of such countries have gradually exceeded those of advanced countries. See World Bank (2000: 60).

12 See *The Economist* (October 18, 1997); World Bank (2000).

13 See Baker *et al.* (1998, Table 2, p. 6).

14 World Bank (2000: 269).

15 World Bank (2000: 5).

16 See *The Economist* (October 18, 1997); Baker *et al.* (1998, Table 5, p. 9).

17 See UNCTAD (1998, Table 1.3, p. 5). The ratio has changed dramatically in recent years. For example, the ratio of direct foreign investment in advanced countries was 72.3 per cent in 1985, and 79.3 per cent in 1990.

18 See UNCTAD (1998, Table 1.5, p. 6).

19 See Baker *et al.* (1998, Table 6B, p. 10).

20 There are numerous papers discussing the causes of the financial crises in East Asia. See Adams *et al.* (1998), Stiglitz (1998a, 1998b), Radelet and Sachs (1999), and Nouriel Roubini's homepage on *Asian and Global Crisis*.

21 See Stiglitz (1998a, 1998b).

22 To maintain the stability of European currency, E.U. member countries have adjusted their currency policies, but the effect is as yet unknown. This was the result of political decisions, not market trends.

23 See *The Economist* (April 15, 2000): 29–30. The survey indicates that 61 per cent of Americans agree with globalization. Yet meanwhile, more people believed that the U.S. trade policy neglects the interests of American labor. They agree to adding labor and environmental protection standards to trade regulations.

24 See Williamson (1996).

25 Perhaps through the strength of unions, the wages of unskilled workers in Western European countries have not fallen as sharply as in the U.S.A. However, some believe that a high unemployment rate is the cost.

26 Cline's estimate (1997) is 20 per cent. That is to say, international factors have widened the differences among U.S. wages. This estimate is one of the higher ones. Krugman (1995a) has claimed that the amount of trade in manufactured products was very small, comprising only 2 per cent of the GDP of advanced countries. Hence it did not have a big impact.

27 See Rodrik (1997) and James (2001).

28 See Amsden's studies on South Korea (1989), and Wade's studies on Taiwan (1990).

29 Amsden (1989) has claimed that in the latter part of the twentieth century it was impossible for East Asian countries to have leap-frogged because of the wide technological gap with transnational corporations. It was only by acquiring advanced technology that East Asian countries were able to lessen the gap with advanced countries.

30 See Chang and Nolan (1995).

31 See note 18 (above).

32 See Stiglitz (1998a, 1998b).

33 Here it is impossible to discuss in detail the division of labor, and to show how technological innovation is advantageous to capital domination.

34 See Shapiro and Taylor (1990), and Singh (1994).

35 Even so, today, the income per capita in Taiwan is only 40 per cent of that in the United States.

36 Following Pritchett (1997, Table 2). The ratio of income per capita between the richest and poorest countries was 8.7 in 1870, and 45.2 in 1990. The ratio of income per capita between advanced countries and all other countries rose from 2.4 in 1870, to 4.5 in 1990.

37 See World Bank (1993: 2). From 1965 to 1990 the growth rate of income per capita in Latin America was 1.8 per cent.

38 Following Pritchett (1997: 13–14). Among 108 countries from 1960 to 1990, the growth rate of income per capita was 4 per cent for 10 per cent of those countries (most of which were from East Asia), 1 per cent for 37 per cent of the countries, less than 0.5 per cent for 26 per cent of the countries, and negative growth for 15 per cent of the countries. Clearly, the differences are quite significant.

39 As Evans (1995) has noted, states in development cooperate closely with society while maintaining their autonomy. Robinson and White (1998) have discussed the issue of the establishment of democratic states in development. They were responding to those who believe that states in development are necessarily in non-democratic countries.

40 According to Yoffie (1983), newly industrialized East Asian countries have successfully used long-term strategy to deal with short-term policy limitations imposed on their markets by European and American governments. They used short-term compromises and gained long-term benefits, thus successfully maintaining stability of the trade system and increasing trade income.

41 According to the World Bank's report (2000: 53). In 1982, 23 per cent of global exports was not within the regulations of either GATT or WTO. This number fell to 10 per cent in 1997.

42 Even underdeveloped countries such as South Korea, which had been quite strong, have suffered heavy losses during the financial crises, because their financial systems were not set up properly.
43 See Stiglitz (1999).
44 See Ch'u Wan-wen (2001).

References

Adams, C., D.J. Mathieson, G. Schinasi and B. Chadha, 1998. *International Capital Markets: Developments, Prospects, and Key Policy Issues* (Washington, D.C.: International Monetary Fund).

Amsden, A.H., 1989. *Asia's Next Giant: South Korea and Late Industrialization* (Oxford: Oxford University Press).

Amsden, A.H., 1999. "The Left and Globalization", *Dissent* (spring): 7–9.

Amsden, A.H., 2001. *The Rise of the Rest* (New York: Oxford University Press).

Amsden, A.H. and Ch'u Wan-wen, forthcoming. *Second Mover Advantage: Latecomer Upgrading in Taiwan* (Cambridge, MA: MIT Press).

Baker, D., G. Epstein and R. Pollin (eds), 1998. *Globalization and Progressive Economic Policy* (Cambridge: Cambridge University Press).

Bhagwati, J., 1998. "The Capital Myth: The Difference between Trade in Widgets and Dollars," *Foreign Affairs* 77.3 (May–June): 7–12.

Campos, J.E. and H.L. Root, 1995. *The Key to the Asian Miracle: Making Shared Growth Credible* (Washington, D.C.: Brookings Institution).

Chang, H-J., and P. Nolan (eds), 1995. *The Transformation of the Communist Economies* (London: St Martin's Press).

Chen Tianzhi, 1999. "Taiwan's Trade Liberalization since the 1980s," *Taiwan's Experience of Economic Development Since the 1980s*, March 1999 (Taipei: Institute of China's Economy).

Ch'u Wan-wen, 2001. "The Initial Evaluation of the Effects of Taiwan's Industrial Policies," *Taiwan Social Studies Quarterly* 42 (June 2001): 67–117.

Ch'u Wan-wen, 2002. *The Mechanism of Economic Growth – Cases of Taiwan's Petroleum and Chemical Industries and Bicycle Industry*, Taiwan Social Studies (October 2002).

Cline, W.R., 1984. *Exports of Manufactures from Developing Countries* (Washington, D.C.: Brookings Institution).

Cline, W.R., 1997. *Trade and Wage Inequality* (Washington, D.C.: Institute for International Economics).

Evans, P., 1995. *Embedded Autonomy: States and Industrial Transformation* (Princeton, NJ: Princeton University Press).

Gerschenkron, A., 1962. *Economic Undevelopedness in Historical Perspective* (Cambridge, MA: Harvard University Press).

Gore, C., 2000. "The Rise and Fall of the Washington Consensus as a Paradigm for Developing Countries," *World Development* 28.5 (2000): 789–804.

James, H., 2001. *The End of Globalization: Lessons from the Great Depression* (Cambridge, MA: Harvard University Press).

Krugman, P., 1995a. *Technology, Trade and Factor Prices* (NBER Working Paper No. 5355, Cambridge, MA: NBER).

Krugman, P., 1995b. "Dutch Tulips and Emerging Markets," *Foreign Affairs* 74.4 (1995): 28–44.

Maddison, A., 1995. *Monitoring the World Economy, 1820–1992* (Paris: OECD).

Pritchett, L., 1997. "Divergence, Big Time," *Journal of Economic Perspectives* 11.3 (summer): 3–17.

Radelet, S. and J. Sachs, 1999. "What Have We Learned So Far from the Asian Financial Crisis?", Paper presented at the ASSA meeting in New York.

Robinson, M. and G. White (eds), 1998. *The Democratic Developmental State: Politics and Institutional Design* (London: Oxford University Press).

Rodrik, D., 1997. *Has Globalization Gone Too Far?* (Washington, D.C.: Institute for International Economics).

Rodrik, D., 1998. "Who Needs Capital-Account Convertibility?," *Essays in International Finance 207* (International Finance Section, Department of Economics, Princeton University, May): 55–65.

Shapiro, H. and L. Taylor, 1990. "The State and Industrial Strategy," *World Development* 18.6 (1990): 861–878.

Singh, A., 1994. "Openness and the Market Friendly Approach to Development: Learning the Right Lessons from Development Experience," *World Development* 22.12 (1994): 1811–1823.

Stiglitz, J.E., 1998a. "Must Financial Crises Be This Frequent and This Painful?," McKay Lecture, Pittsburgh, Pennsylvania, September 23.

Stiglitz, J.E., 1998b. "More Instruments and Broader Goals: Moving Toward the Post-Washington Consensus," The WIDER Annual Lecture, Helsinki, Finland, January 7.

Stiglitz, J.E., 1999. "Two Principles for the Next Round; Or, How to Bring Developing Countries in from the Cold," Speech delivered at the World Bank event, Geneva, September 21.

UNCTAD, 1998. *World Investment Report 1998: Trends and Determinants* (New York and Geneva: United Nations).

UNCTAD, 2002. *Trade and Development Report 2002* (New York and Geneva: United Nations).

Wade, R., 1990. *Governing the Market: Economic Theory and the Role of Government in East Asian Industrialization* (Princeton, NJ: Princeton University Press).

Warren, B., 1980. *Imperialism: Pioneer of Capitalism* (London: Verso).

Williamson, J., 1994. "In Search of a Manual for Technopols," in J. Williamson (ed.), *The Political Economy of Policy Reform* (Washington, D.C.: Institute for International Economics).

Williamson, J., 1996. *Globalization and Inequality Then and Now: The Late 19th and Late 20th Centuries Compared*, NBER Working Paper No. 5491 (Cambridge, MA: NBER).

Wood, A. 1995. "How Trade Hurt Unskilled Workers," *Journal of Economic Perspectives* 9.3 (summer): 57–80.

World Bank, 1993. *The East Asian Miracle* (New York: Oxford University Press for the World Bank).

World Bank, 2000. *World Development Report 1999/2000* (New York: Oxford University Press for the World Bank).

Yoffie, D.B., 1983. *Power and Protectionism: Strategies of the Newly Industrializing Countries* (New York: Columbia University Press).

14   What is China's comparative advantage?

Lin Chun

This chapter seeks to identify China's comparative advantages for national development in the contested processes of economic globalization. Through a critique of the widely assumed correlation between cheap labour and desirable foreign trade, and further between export and growth, growth and development, development and social benefits, it questions a prevailing neoliberal doctrine. The discussion shows how in our times certain classical insight has been turned into not only a flawed dogma that obscures strategic options for the developing countries, but also a political weapon against their workers, and indeed workers everywhere. Moreover, in China as elsewhere, the (potential) comparative advantage of cheap labour in trade may endure only at the cost of persistent low labour productivity and an ever weak national economy. As such the concepts of cheap labour and of development are essentially in contradiction. The argument is thus a rejection of current strategic thinking based on cheap labour, drawing attention instead to state capacity and social power for rational and democratic control of resources.

The notion of 'comparative advantage' in development economics originated in David Ricardo's work along with his idea of 'competitive equilibrium' in international trade. These notions upon their immediate implication are technical, accounting for the obvious positive correlations between production cost and prices in exportation in a world of free trade regimes. Because of such correlations, those industries that have a relatively high productivity enjoy a comparative advantage. Consequently, it is believed in classical economics that productivity differentials determine the international division of labour for specialization. That is, countries tend to export wherever they are relatively capital (labour) abundant by producing relatively capital (labour)-intensive commodities: there is a well-defined relationship among trade flows, factor intensities and physical–human endowments (Heckscher–Ohlin hypothesis). Behind this hypothesis is the more fundamental Ricardian theory of value adapted from Adam Smith. This depicts, among influential propositions such as prices being regulated by labour time and a falling rate of profit, that wages 'naturally' remain at subsistence levels due to the logic of capital seeking a faster rise in productivity than in wages to increase return on itself, unless demands in the labour market drive wages up (Ricardo, 1817). Without the concept of abstract surplus value, he is unable to explain or calculate exploitation inherent in the processes of capital accumulation. But he is empirically accurate to describe conflicts of interest between labour and capital; and his trade for national wealth of all nations is a world apart from unequal exchange characteristic of the age of globalization.

Ricardo's 'comparative advantage', having lost its original historical and intellectual context, is transmuted into a short-sighted and one-sided doctrine of 'cheap labour' in today's popular reading of development economics. First of all, the precondition of free trade that has long passed is uncritically confirmed, as though the real conditions of trade barriers, export subsidies, monetary disparities and volatile exchange rates, and protectionist policies do not exist. Second, total factor productivity is reduced to labour productivity and, partial still, to the opportunity cost taken as determined mainly by the cost of labour input – the cheaper the labour, the more competitive the exports and hence the stronger the growth. Cheap labour then becomes a foremost advantage for low income countries. Third, much else in the classical insight on the formation of trade patterns is ignored, from environment essentials of nature and geography to economic fundamentals of rent, taxation, technology, currency and exchange rate. Management, R&D and information among more recent concerns could be easily added to the list. One of the Ricardian theses is precisely that labour is not the lone primary contributor to domestic resources cost. Only an optimal fit of all the factors involved may foster perfect competition and ideal comparative advantage.

In other words, even not counting whatever the social meaning of cheap labour, low labour cost plays a rather limited part in any potential national advantage in international trade. As far as production cost is concerned, it also depends on the purchase of additional inputs including all kinds of transaction and the composition of total factor productivity. Commenting on 'the spectre of China', for example, the *South China Morning Post* asks why many other countries with a similar advantage of cheap labour have failed to become manufacturing powerhouses. 'The answer is that the competitiveness of Chinese-made goods relies on many factors other than wage rates. Only about 13 per cent of the final cost of manufactured exports is attributable to labour' (19 April 2004). Researchers came up with slightly different figures here, yet it is commonly agreed that even in the relatively labour-intensive industries, labour cost is not the same as production costs. Whether and how might income and redistributive mechanisms impact on the relationship between productivity differentials and foreign trade is not settled in empirical research (Feenstra, 2000). In fact it happens that a country possessing certain productive advantages (e.g. in raw material or technology or skilled labour) in a particular industry may still import the goods that its own companies could produce for artificial reasons – the perceived costs and benefits are then evaluated outside the labour market. It also happens that when the relative price of a particular product upsurges in the world market, international competition could cause the wages in affected industries to rise (Stelper–Samuelson theorem). In truth, labour cost and export scale may somehow influence each other, but no stable correlation has been found between wage ratios and export shares (Balassa, 1989). It is a mere myth that connection can be simply assumed between a low paid workforce and a favourable foreign trade structure.

Before going further, it should be noted that this discussion is not concerned with how labour (and labour power) is defined, differentiated, measured and priced or why the labour theory of value continues to be debated. The signification of 'labour' apparently varies, meaning one thing as the opposite to reaping without sowing, another to leisure, and yet another in our appreciation of how human self-consciousness has been enhanced through labour or work. The terminology – 'labour', 'work', 'job', '(un)employment' – across languages, occupations and activities in scholarly discourse and social recognition is also laid aside.

Suffice it here to emphasize social norms and economic policies, which, more than spontaneous market forces, are crucial in determining the price of labour in a modern economy (Nichols, 1983). The market alone can decide on neither wages nor many other forms of earned and unearned income due to the working of powerful non-economic variables. Apart from the subsistence cost of labour reproduction, government intervention by means of monetary, industrial, incomes and employment policies, and governmental and non-governmental public welfare heavily adjust the 'market price' of labour, including deliberate pay disparities for incentives and other public reasons among different sectors and trades. These policies are also directly or indirectly responsible for the curves of national income. No less important are collective bargaining and class struggle, demanding eight-hour working days and legislation on minimal wages being best-known examples in the history of capitalism. The world economy, having experienced booms and downturns and polarization between centres and peripheries, is no longer a virgin space in which labour is priced by 'nature' as a given 'fact'. Labour cost, whether relatively cheap or expensive, must be the result of locally and globally specific socioeconomic and political movements.

In China, a current example is that salaries (supplemented by research grants and other subsidies) of university teachers have been raised sharply in recent years, at a rate far greater than any other professional groups on the state payroll. This has little to do with market demand but much to do with a public policy shift. In comparison, China's vast countryside has seen stagnation or decline in household income in the past decade or so, including the earnings of many of those who worked in the township and village enterprises or who had a temporary, low-paid job in the cities. Again nothing else is more blamable than policy biases manifested in price scissors, agricultural taxation and service fees, and residence control in discrimination against rural migrants. Even confined to the relationship between the international market and the national industries participating in that market, it is plain that the competitive pressure on the domestic labour cost is limited. Also at work are local constraints, moral as well as pragmatic.

Is there, then, really a comparative advantage of cheap labour? Obviously, other things being equal, the smaller the unit cost of labour input in a given product, the greater a chance of the production cost being reduced, hence a selling advantage in the product's market price. But there could be productive advantages (and for that matter disadvantages) other than labour from raw materials and infrastructure to technology and management. Although cheap labour and a competitive advantage in low production costs are logically consistent, in the real world of trade, the importance of labour cost may range from predominant to trivial. In the labour-intensive, so-called 'sunset' industries, such as mining, textiles, garments, toys and household durables, the cost of labour could be decisive. Yet even there, electronic machinery and automation are gradually replacing hands in assembly lines, reducing the proportion of labour cost in total production costs. Industrial and technological progresses inevitably tear down the traditional labour market, 'deindustrializing' the workforce and forcing any cheap labour-based advantage to shrink or marginalize.

No doubt China's labour cost is generally many times lower than the advanced economies due to the country's low GDP per capita and oversupply of workers. Yet looking at Chinese agriculture as an example, where labour cost is arguably the lowest of all sectors, are China's staple products in the world market really competitive? Even with the protection of double tariffs which limited extra importation, the country's domestic market was immediately hit by its entry into the WTO (as seen in the case of soybeans from the USA, which compelled the Chinese government to set up new requirements on genetically modified imports). China is losing around $2.3 billion a year in agriculture-related income as a result of the current 'trade-distorting measures' imposed by the industrialized world (Diaz-Bonilla, 2003). That is, in reality both in China's domestic and foreign trade, low labour cost in agriculture has no advantage to speak of; it cannot even level off the sector's existing competitive disadvantage. The situation only worsens in the absence of free competition seen in the huge subsidies to farmers and farm exports in the developed countries on the one hand and the absurd continuation of China's own developmental strategy that sacrifices rural society on the other. In theory, China could expand its international market share in high value-added goods, but the prospect is not immediately feasible due to obvious obstacles. Austerity and deflation since the mid-1990s until 2003, echoing global over-production, also suppressed the price indexes of state purchase as well as market retailing of agricultural products. Farmers suffered – their fruits of hard labour were frequently sold below cost or simply wasted from overstocking. According to the economist Hu Angang, between 1997 and 2000, falling prices alone cost rural Chinese 300 billion yuan or $37 billion. Here any supposed advantage of cheap labour simply vanished.

Furthermore, as the potential advantage of cheap labour is preconditioned on a given market, it is subject to the preference and coercion of that market operation. It is true that post-Second World War industrialization in parts of East Asia successfully took the opportunity of adopting an export-oriented strategy. However, it must be stressed that most countries/regions involved had previously built up national productive capacities and accumulated human capital through manufacturing for internal consumption during a period of import substitution. Without a largely educated, well-trained labour force, and without a 'developmental state' committed to the flagship national industries while disciplining capital as much as labour and pursuing a degree of equity in redistribution, their successes would not have been possible. Also vital were the specific conditions of cold war geopolitics – huge American aid and a market open only to the US allies in the region. The terms of trade for the 'tiger economies' in the making were in sharp contrast with war threat and economic blockade against the former socialist countries in the foreign policies of the USA and the NATO members. That is, China did not have a chance to industrialize by taking a path similar to that of its anti-communist neighbours, even if it had so intended. Indeed China's autarchic position of self-reliance was not so much a free choice as forced by the perilous international circumstances at the time.

Even if the advantage of cheap labour could be actualized, it is at best transitional, and the game may still not be worth a candle. In the history of capitalist globalization, because of the tendency of falling profits, earlier industrializing countries all explored overseas markets for what is today called 'outsourcing', and exploited cheap materials and goods in the colonies. The contemporary developed countries continue to advocate free trade and free movement of capital while jealously guarding their own domestic markets. As such, those nations dependent on cheap labour face a dilemma. Either they allow the price of labour to rise naturally along with rising labour productivity and Smithian specialization, and consequently achieve higher general living standards, therefore pushing capital to move out wherever labour is even cheaper; or else they must keep the income and hence consumption level of their population low enough to retain a particular 'advantage', simultaneously repressing demand and the entire economy. They either seek to be competitive while bidding down wages as well as the level of public provision, or if they tax capital and multinationals they would be 'punished' by uncompetitiveness and inefficiency. In other words, the comparative advantage of cheap labour may endure only when labour productivity stays relatively low and the national economy remains ultimately weak. The very notion of 'advantage' thus becomes ironic or incomprehensible in a lose–lose situation in which trading competitiveness and economic strength, low labour costs and the goal of national development are incompatible.

By the same token, once a developing country, especially a major one, benefits in certain aspects or certain senses from participating in the world market by depressing its labour costs, it would hurt corresponding labour groups in the advanced countries, especially in job losses. Union protests in the West against Third World workers are not always unjustifiable. To protect American factory workers, AFL-CIO filed a document in March 2004, 'The condition of the working class in China', with the US Congress, and sought sanction against China for its violation of labour rights. 'This petition is not targeted against 'free trade' or against China's 'comparative advantage' in global markets. Rather, this petition challenges the *artificial* and *severe* reduction of China's labour costs below the baseline of comparative advantage defined by standard trade theory' (AFL-CIO, 2004: 12). More devastatingly, of course, trying to maintain an advantage of cheap labour intensifies competition, racing to the bottom within the less developed world (e.g. Mexico is reported to have lost about 230,000 jobs since 2001, most of them to China), even creating a zero-sum game between the poor and poorer countries. The fashionable promise of a 'win–win' situation is often wishful if not an outright lie.

Surely the destination of capital movement is not limited to the places where labour is cheap. As argued above, any advantage in production costs may not entirely, even mainly, rely on labour cost. Many Japanese garment and textile companies operating in China, for example, have recently reallocated their production back to Japan for higher productivity in spite of a much higher wage level. In the past twenty years, China came to be the biggest recipient of foreign direct investment but the attraction has not principally been the country's low-paid labour, since labour is even cheaper in the subcontinent and in parts of Southeast Asia. Rather, there are other things considered favourable in political stability, growth record, market potential, human capital and infrastructural fundamentals. Devoted support from wealthy overseas Chinese is an exceptional contribution. In addition, but controversial, is a 'good environment' for foreign direct investment (FDI) that implies low corporate taxes and preferential treatment of foreign investors along with a politically unorganized domestic workforce without much bargaining power. Addressing this last factor of the competition for FDI, Henry Liu points out that 'Profiting from the lowest wages through cross-border wage arbitrage has been the driving force behind trade globalization, reducing trade from a process of gaining comparative advantage between economies to one of reinforcing absolute advantage for capital at the expense of labour for the benefit of the rich economies'. Ricardo's iron law of wages cannot therefore be a guide today. By adopting policies that structurally and systematically keep 'wages at their lowest levels, a nation condemns itself to the lowest possible level of national wealth' (Liu, 2004).

The argument so far is to repudiate the doctrine of cheap labour being the dominant competitive advantage for developing countries. Many endogenous and exogenous factors may be responsible for a nation's competitive advantage and disadvantage. Most obvious in the negative category are monopoly, corruption and legal defects in terms of domestic deficiencies. But there could also be price shocks, financial turmoil and debt crisis, which are caused or significantly contributed to by external forces. Some of the structural barriers identified earlier in the unequal trade and dependency theories remain pertinent. Each of these barriers can stand in the way of the standard expectation of a comparative advantage in cheap labour. Variations in exchange rate (especially against dollars in an international financial regime dominated by the dollar) affect prices and hence trade constantly and powerfully. High institutional transaction costs easily cancel out low labour costs, making the supposed trend of equilibrium among primary production factors across regions unrealistic (cf. Franzese, 2001). Great developmental gaps between China's coastal and inland regions, or between rich and poor countries on the global stage, are all too evident.

In the end, 'cheap labour' cannot be an innocent concept anywhere. It unmistakably signifies the subordination of labour to capital and exploitation, and consequently labour's disadvantageous position. Worse still, once cheap labour is claimed as an advantage in attracting foreign capital and in foreign trade, labour income could be 'rationally' repressed under the banner of national development in which the power and greed of capital wins. In the case of China, workers, women (and even children) in particular in sweatshops, unregulated mines and part of the service industry are not minimally protected in terms of hours, pay and safe working conditions. Since the government has not made the minimal wage compulsory and failed to universally increase income to keep pace with economic growth through policy tools, a growing reserve army of surplus labour only further restrains wages. The US National Labour Committee and China Labour Watch reports that 'workers received an average 16.5 cents an hour when the legal minimum in China was 31 cents an hour. The working week was seven days when five days was legal and people toiled for up to 20½ hours per shift' (*Washington Post*, 10 February 2004). Extra-economic exploitation becomes possible wherever the Labour Law, the Law for Security in Production and the Trade Union Law (and legally bound stipulations on environmental protection, which are often linked to labour conditions) are merely recorded on paper without being rigorously enforced. If, as it should be, firms and factories throughout the country all implemented the forty-hour working week by law, how many jobs could have been created? If workers in public as well as private sectors exercised their legal rights and contracted entitlements to salaries and fringe benefits from sick pay to unemployment compensation, why did their labour become cheaper and cheaper, even to the extent of 'cheap life'? The poet Shao Yanxiang mourns the loss of young miners in workplace accidents – 4,150 in the first eight months of 2003 alone: 'cheap labour! cheap lives!' The official statistics show that China's work-related deaths and injuries in the mining industry are twelve times higher than the world's average. The political economist Wang Xiaoqiang and his team among many researchers surveyed Guangdong where the monthly salaries of migrant workers were shown to have been virtually frozen for twenty years despite waves of inflation. The *China Daily* admits that migrant workers in the Pearl River Delta, earning as little as 510 yuan ($61.4) among the worst off, have witnessed an average increase of only 68 yuan (US$8) a month over the past twelve years. 'When measured next to inflation, it means the true level of their incomes has either stayed the same or even fallen' (17 September 2004). In fact the artificial low wage level led to a surprising 'labour shortage' in the affected areas in an overtly labour-surplus economy.

Of course the price of labour power in the marketplace is no indicator of workers' individual human worth or class dignity. In addition, low wages do not necessarily entail low social status. There was a time in the People's Republic when 'low wage, full employment' was an adopted policy in the cities (the countryside was a different story), supplemented by protective measures in labour conditions and heavy public provision in housing, transportation, education and medical care for urban workers. These provisions raised real wages, enabling Chinese workers, especially in the state sector, to enjoy an actual living standard that was much higher than what their money salaries could buy. In particular, their respected political status was recognized at least in the official ideology and social consciousness. By comparison, the current conception of cheap labour has become widespread in society, affecting not only blue-collar, migrant, laid-off and agricultural workers and poor farmers, but also China's labour force as a collective identity. The leaning of state power towards capital – public as well as private and foreign – is only causal to the downgrading of labour.

This is by no means to suggest that China should retreat from reforming its economic and political structures. Beginning with the open policy, the reform project has been far-reaching, since externally it has broken down the imperialist encirclement and, internally, it has opened up a closed and profoundly flawed system. In order to achieve the needed technological transfers and to transplant some advanced managerial methods for renovation and modernization of its own economy, China should join the global economy and permit no turning back. This could then empower the country to break the foreign exchange and other bottle-necks by mobilizing, expanding and upgrading its existing capacities and to allocate resources optimally according to its comparative advantages beyond cheap labour. This would also enable useful importation for China to overcome its shortage of certain resources, such as land. What is to be clarified here is that using foreign markets is not the same as an 'export-oriented' strategy, although the two are practically connected. Putting aside the unsolved issue of assessing the records of export-oriented developments in Asia and Latin America, as far as China is concerned, manufacturing for export is only one of several ways or aspects of its strategic opening up to the outside world. That aspect alone is too partial to epitomize or replace many other parallel moves in the general picture. The re-alignment of state enterprises and the restructuring of financial institutions as major tasks on the reform agenda, for instance, are in principle independent of the business of foreign trade. It is common but entirely misguided to reduce China's open policy to promoting exportation, to attribute the reform's achievements to trade growth, and to count a favourable balance of trade on low labour costs. Such assumptions distort the reality with the effect of concealing China's real comparative advantage.

What then are the secrets of the specific and limited successes of China's economic reform? Relatively low labour cost is certainly a factor, as is the rapid growth of export and related industries. In 2004, China became the world's third biggest trading economy with its exports making up over a quarter of the national GDP and its total volume of imports and exports reaching $1 trillion. However, let us remember that this accomplishment in foreign trade depended initially on decades of heroic struggle and arduous work by the Chinese people on self-reliance prior to the reforms, during which China was able to build the foundation of its modern industry and basic socioeconomic strength. Second, the economy grew spectacularly during the reform period, which further strengthened China's productive capabilities. Third, tax and policy incentives granted to the Special Economic Zones, and government subsidies in exports and attention to technological progress constituted powerful backing for foreign trade. Finally, the USA, by virtue of the dollar hegemony, could use its capital account surplus (subsidized by Asian buyers of its treasury bonds) to make up for its trade deficit (cf. Wade, 2002). This allowed China's present trading pattern to persist, which it does so while paying for the runaway US debt, so to speak. (Incidentally, since China still relies heavily on the US market for export and China's foreign reserve is mainly in dollars while holding a huge amount of the US bonds next only to Japan, at the cost of $10 billion as a result of over 20 per cent devaluation of the US currency in 2004, the risks are all too visible.) These, rather than the single and multifaceted factor of 'cheap labour', have so far enabled China to survive and benefit from the global market.

Aside from being a gradually integrated political economy, Chinese growth since the reform is also due to the following developments: a massive 'consuming revolution' based on a broad increase in household income in the 1980s; the invention of the household contract system in rural China followed by the flourishing of township and village enterprises up until the mid-1990s; a systematic redefinition and reform movement around the role of the party; and the function of central and local governments, especially a measured degree of decentralization and managerial autonomy. It should be noted however that all these developments had been lost or distorted by the early years of the twenty-first century; decentralization in particular has increasingly degenerated into outright privatization.

Facing the current reality, what is daily alarming are rather the negative effects of labour price being too low. According to the World Bank, 120 million Chinese still live in poverty. By China's own criteria, by 2002 there were still 30 million rural residents under the poverty line and about 20 million households requiring minimal security in the county towns and cities. The Gini coefficient of household income increased from 0.33 in 1980 to 0.45–0.47 in 2002, surpassing not only the advanced countries but also most transitional economies including Russia (cf. Li, 2002; Qin, 2002; Riskin and Khan, 2000). The government reported to the Asian Development Bank Conference in May 2002 that China had one of the world's greatest wealth gaps. This inevitably undermines demand, not to mention social cohesion and stability. While inequalities along class, sectoral, regional, gender and other lines are on the rise, hitherto free or inexpensive public services are falling apart, badly affecting future expectations and hence current consumption. Prior to the policy adjustment in 2004, the government's annual spending on export tax rebates (fixed at 15 per cent in 1999) was far greater than that on public welfare facilities. The cost was between one-fifth to one-third of the central government's total expenditure between 1991 and 1997, 'crowding out other expenditures on education and social security' (Cui, 2003). These trends, putting political legitimacy at stake, also prolonged austerity and weakened general demand and purchasing power. As such, the standard 'middle-class' thesis is utterly inadequate for China, where a tiny minority of the new rich and a small middle layer of less than 10 per cent of the total population are far from sufficient for stimulating internal market demands. If labour is so cheap that it harms both the national economy and people's livelihood, is it really an advantage or rather a disadvantage?

This is a tight corner where we ought to begin to pursue an alternative answer to the question about China's developmental advantages. The following list is tentative and meant to invite discussion:

- National independence and security. China is safeguarded against being dependent on any particular foreign markets or controlled by any international banking and lending institutions. It is therefore self-protected from the possibility of sudden regional/global financial meltdown or crisis of balance of payment. Resisting the pressure on 'freeing' its capital account and currency values, the government is capable of monitoring inflow and outflow of capital movement and retaining its capital and currency controls. A high savings rate (around 40 per cent) helps investment rely more on domestic than foreign capital, which protects infant and vanguard national industries, whether or not in the public sector.

- Public control over the mainstay of the national economy through the slow but persistent construction of economic democracy. Side by side with mushrooming small non-state (*minying*) firms, the nation's economic lifelines and commanding height industries are retained in the public hands in various and yet-to-be-created forms of social accountability and legal liability. Democratic management is set as a goal and develops through initiatives from above and below to involve workers and their union representatives in the decision-making processes.

- The great potential of a vast domestic market. This is an advantage of large countries which could basically rely on their own needs to be cultivated and met by their own consumption scales and productive abilities. Along the way, and ideally also aided by the right amount of international competition, the products and services in countries such as China could be improved through compressed industrial and technological revolutions.

- Rich in human capital and organizational resources. China's greatest asset is its workforce which has gained in the past fifty years from the country's earlier massive sanitation and antiepidemic works, prioritized health care (especially for women and children), public education and training programmes, commitment to equal pay for equal work and, more recently, compulsory nine-year schooling which is yet to be implemented. To retain and develop human capital, an effective organizational system embracing an integrated network of self-governing societies would be indispensable. The institutional infrastructure of such a system is in need of thorough reforms, but it has also been proven to be the nerve centre of China's dynamic central–local and vertical–horizontal relations on 'one chessboard'. The social function of the governments at all levels to invest in human development is characteristic of the protective and redistributive capacity of a socialist developmental state.

- A cultural tradition in defiance of market logic and money fetishism. From *xiaokang* (moderately well-off) to *datong* (great harmony), from individual freedom to collective liberation, from community welfare to national prosperity, the dreams of the Chinese people over generations may come true in our own century. Different from a profit-driven primitive capitalism, China's advantages may only be found and enhanced in the magnificent creativity of its ordinary citizens working in the factories, the fields and offices; its young volunteers, 'socialist entrepreneurs', and a population crying out for social justice; its poverty alleviation efforts, legal aid and other solidarity-inspired undertakings; and its growing social movements for labour rights, gender equality, a clean environment and broader democratic change.

These perceivable advantages are a marvel for most developing countries. In China, they are yet to be fully institutionalized, if not lost to the misconceptions of 'free market' or 'cheap labour'. Letting things go in their supposed 'natural order' as promoted in the seductive Hayekian paradigm, China would find itself, in the steps of the troubled Latin American economies, potentially the biggest victim of globalization. After all, globalization is a process that could destroy a national economy as much as revitalize it, depending largely on local political will and manoeuvre.

The rational choice for the Chinese is thus a serious rethinking in public debate of the nation's advantages and disadvantages, and to adjust and act accordingly. An obviously plausible policy intervention would be to raise the price for labour to a more adequate (in received social norms) yet affordable level as universally and equitably as possible. Such a move would require corresponding fiscal and taxation measures to compensate for any loss caused by higher labour costs, so that the major economic operation in production, circulation and foreign trade would not be adversely affected. Moving in this direction is not only a moral but also a socioeconomic imperative, given the headaches of deficient domestic demand, unemployment, polarization and mass discontent. To do so, the first steps may include a re-evaluation of current minimal wages and the regime of their enforcement while halting the privatization of public enterprises which hurt a large number of workers. As soon as the central and local governments side with labour, as they are politically bound to do in a 'socialist market', labour disputes and protests could be turned into an integrative social reform movement. State imposition may be called on to ensure workers' rights, equal among urban, rural and migrant residents, to decent pay, to safety at work, to lawful working hours, vacation leave, health insurance, a pension scheme, retraining and re-employment opportunities, and union organization. Meanwhile, increasing household incomes for the farmers requires adjustments in price manipulation in the industrial, agricultural and service sectors; a radical reduction, even elimination, of most surcharges and taxes; and a basic-needs maintenance network in the countryside to be rebuilt. The state has to invest far more in rural productive and social development, while also encouraging community-generated activities and provision. Moving in such a direction, a strong incomes policy based on the principle of sharing profits between labour and capital would be the key.

It is also important to strengthen social security, so that by repairing China's public welfare institutions cheap labour would be transformed into cheap service. A better security arrangement and higher quality of life for the greatest possible majority of the population would be positively related to work incentives and to stimulating consumption and production. The two sides are mutually supportive. Take an example in education. It has been recommended by some policy-makers in China that each university student be charged an annual tuition fee of 1,000 yuan (about $120), hence generating a rapid increase of internal demand of 12 billion yuan from the four million students currently on campus. Yet, as the State System Reform Commission official Ding Ningning argues, if a quarter of current junior high school and three-quarters of senior high school students are prepared to enter university, and if each of these 24 million families would have to begin to save 1,000 yuan per year for this future purpose, 24 billion yuan would be blocked from immediate consumption. As a result, domestic demand would not increase but sharply decrease (2002). If we further consider the impoverished groups, how much purchasing power do they have? The point, in line with economic rationality, is that if, without artificial curbing, labour cost normally rises along with productivity, then a healthy labour market needs to be not only mobile for employment flexibility but also strong for the development of human and social capital.

Is not all this, one may wonder, empty talk? Where to find the money? Nothing should be obscure here, since ample funds are available. If the channels of stealing state assets could be obstructed, corruption cracked down upon, the super rich taxed proportionally, and waste in mismanagement and bureaucracy controlled, a large amount of funds could be returned to the public's disposal. Since economic development itself is the ultimate source for public financing, we must recognize a basic fact that China's economy has grown much faster than its population and the country is now much wealthier than before the reform, at least a sevenfold increase in GDP by comparable currency value (from 362.4 billion yuan in 1978 to 10,000 billion in 2002). Given this overwhelming fact, if more people turned out to be unable to afford schools and medical care, if county and township governments fell into impossible debt, and if the State Treasury found a larger loophole in minimal social security, how could we blame any shortage of money? Is it not a problem of allocation and management of national wealth? Without confronting such questions and having them clarified, any statistical figure attached to the notion of 'per capita' is meaningless. That is, China at its present developmental stage is already capable of supporting a population in the middle range of human development in general (cf. UNDP reports including HDI Indexes 1995 to 2001) and a well-nurtured, relatively highly priced workforce in particular. The comparative advantage of cheap labour as a conditional, local truth is coming to an end for the PRC (as in Singapore or Taiwan). The stained label 'Made in China' will be cleared and rectified in consequence: it cannot indicate sweatshops any longer but only the honour, pride, wisdom and accomplishment of Chinese workers.

Speaking of comparative advantage, the so-called 'privilege of historical backwardness' as seen by the Russian populists and Eastern Marxists also comes to mind. However, actual historical experiences have revealed disadvantages more than advantages for the 'backward' nations in the term's usual usage in the development discourse. It was precisely the desire and need to overcome their country's disadvantages that the Chinese people endured enormous hardship and sacrifice of an epic revolution and post-revolutionary striving. Indeed, the Chinese revolution with its popular base and modern ambition has been China's greatest privilege. Only because of that privilege can the comparative advantages suggested above become possible. And only with all these privileges and advantages secured and developed might China 'leap over' some perceived historical or technological developmental stages, and its market socialist project survive capitalist global integration.

In an age of national interdependence, the ideal arrangement would be a rational international division of labour in accordance with each country's comparative advantage, so that the well-being of the entire humanity in democratically managed economic units and their eco-environment may be most rationally and efficiently served. Such advantages may travel or shift between and among industries and economic regions for local and global benefits. The reality and the ideal, however, are too far apart. The concept and practice of cheap labour is typical of the classical contradiction of capitalism between the forward march of productive forces and the tendency to decline in mass consumption. Only by grasping and constructing its genuine advantages other than cheap labour can China, in alliance with Asia and the Third World, change the rules of the game and break free from its still evolving predicament.

References

AFL-CIO (2004) 'The condition of the working class in China', *Dissent*, summer.

Balassa, Bela (1989) *Comparative Advantage, Trade Policy and Economic Development* (New York: Harvester Wheatsheaf).

Cui, Zhiyuan (2003) 'China's export tax rebate policy', *China: An International Journal*, September.

Diaz-Bonilla, Eugenio (2003) 'Report' by the International Food Policy Research Institute, *South China Morning Post*, 30 August.

Ding, Ningning (2002) 'We cannot introduce the market mechanism in the sphere of education', *Economics Weekly*, 6 August.

Feenstra, Robert (2000) *The Impact of International Trade on Wages* (Chicago, IL: University of Chicago Press).

Franzese, Robert J. Jr. (2001) 'Institutional and sectoral interactions in monetary policy and wage/price-bargaining', in Peter Hall and David Soskice (eds) *Varieties of Capitalism: The Institutional Foundations of Comparative Advantage* (Oxford: Oxford University Press).

Li, Qiang (2002) 'The new changes in China's social stratification', in CASS, *2002 Blue Book of Chinese Society* (Beijing: Social Sciences Documentation Publishing House).

Liu, Henry C.K. (2004) 'The wealth of nations', unpublished manuscript.

Nichols, Donald (1983) 'Wage measurement questions raised by an incomes policy', in Jack Triplett (ed.) *The Measurement of Labour Cost* (Chicago, IL: University of Chicago Press).

Qin, Hui (2002) 'On the question of Gini coefficient and social polarization', in Jin Yan and Qin Hui, *Economic Transition and Social Justice* (Kaifeng: Henan People's Publishing House).

Ricardo, David (1817) *Principles of Political Economy and Taxation* (Kitchener, Ont: Batoche, 2001).

Riskin, Carl and Khan, Azizur (2000) *Inequality and Poverty in China in the Age of Globalization* (New York: Oxford University Press).

UNDP Beijing Office (1995–2001) *Human Development Reports* (New York: Oxford University Press).

Wade, Robert (2002) 'Special drawing rights as the *dues ex machina* of the world economy', 7 March.

15 Globalization and vulnerability

India at the dawn of the twenty-first century

Amiya Kumar Bagchi

1 Globalization as process and as policy

The word 'globalization' has been tortured and made to assume many different meanings since the time it was invented. At the risk of adding to the fragmentation in its connotation we can distinguish between two different generic classes of meaning attributed to it. One is the spread of human civilization, artefacts, institutions, patterns of living, information and knowledge to span the planet earth (and the stratosphere surrounding it). The other is a policy aimed deliberately at spreading certain institutions, modes of doing business, producing and trading commodities, services and information across all the states of the world. An analyst can trace the process of globalization in the various senses of the first generic class without accepting the agenda implicit in the second.

Following the usage of other analysts, we can distinguish the subclasses included in 'globalization' in its analytical sense. First, there is a spread of international trade in goods and 'commodities' in the Marxian sense (the latter are distinguished by the fact that they are produced with the help of inputs traded in the market and are destined primarily for sale). Second, people migrate from one country or region to another, either temporarily or permanently. Third, money or means of payment are exchanged on an increasing scale between different countries or regions (when different regions within the same country have different media of exchange, as happened in India under British rule until the eve of World War I). Fourth, capital flows from one country to another to help produce goods and services. Fifth, finance – not necessarily linked to the production of goods and services – flows between different countries. Sixth, transnational companies arise which engage increasingly in the activities listed thus far. Seventh, technology is traded between different countries. Increasingly, with the spread of the patent regimes governed by the Paris Convention as modified by the provisions of the World Trade Organization, frontier technologies take an increasingly proprietary form. The eighth aspect of globalization is the spread of print and electronic media. The ninth aspect is the growth in international trade and production of services of all kinds – shipping, insurance, banking, health care and, of course, finance. As is clear from this list, the categories sometimes overlap, but if we do not list them separately we are likely to miss out on the multifaceted nature of globalization as a process.

As in the case of other aspects of capitalist development, globalization also displays many features of combined and unequal development. The growth of international trade may be said to be the earliest feature of the process of commercial internationalization. It has, however, often been associated with an exchange of money at a fast pace, and also with migration of people. For example, in the three centuries after the Europeans' discovery of navigable routes from Europe to the Western Hemisphere and around Africa to Asia, commodities travelled mainly from Asia to Europe, silver from the Americas to Europe and thence to Asia, and enslaved Africans were subjected to forced migration from Africa to the Americas. Within Europe itself, before the Netherlands became industrialized enough to attain the status of a leading commodity-producing nation, it financed the European wars and the economic progress of competing nations, especially of England, and thereby helped hasten its own economic and political decline. We can produce a chronology of stages of globalization, from increasing commercialization of a basically self-sufficient economy through its increasing involvement in international trade flows and attendant specialization in particular branches of production, to its involvement in flows of portfolio and direct investment, to its integration in international production structures through an increasing tempo of exchange of inputs between firms (often affiliates of the same firms), to the increasing domination of its production, exchange and banking structure by transnational non-financial corporations and transnational banks, and finally to its entanglement in seemingly uncontrollable flows of finance across its borders (Bagchi, 1994). But this evolutionary sequence is neither linear nor inevitable nor irreversible. In the case of India and the international economy as a whole the flow of international trade had accelerated from the 1870s to 1913 and had decelerated from the middle of the 1920s (Bagchi, 1993). In India's case, however, the ratio of foreign trade to national income tended also to decline over the period from the 1950s to the early 1970s, but it increased slowly again from the late 1970s.

The ebbs and flows in the components of different aspects of involvement of a national economy in international trade, production and finance are influenced strongly by broad developments in the international economy as well as by domestic policies. For example, foreign trade was used from the beginning of British rule as the chief conveyor belt for the remittance of the tribute extracted from the Indian Empire to Britain. However, its importance as the transmission mechanism for the extracted tribute grew in the period of the spread of the gold standard to the major industrializing economies of the North Atlantic and the acceleration in the rates of growth of their national income and resulting demand for industrial inputs and primary commodities. Contrariwise, the worldwide depression in trade in agricultural products which set in from 1926 (i.e. some years before the Great Depression starting in 1929) badly affected Indian exports. Again, the rise in the ratio of Indian foreign trade to national income in the late 1970s was much less induced by policy than by developments in the world economy, and especially by the growth of demand for Indian exports in West Asia and some other oil-exporting regions. However, global recession in the early 1980s brought down the share again. In 1985 to 1986, the share of India's exports to India's GDP was 4.7 per cent. The corresponding figure rose to 6.8 per cent on the eve of the spate of liberalization measures adopted in June to July 1991. The share of exports to GDP rose to 10.3 per cent in 1996 to 1997, but has stagnated at around that level over the past two years, with a slowdown in the growth of both exports and national income.

What then are the policies which have promoted the globalization of the Indian economy in its various aspects in recent years? Virtually all the elements of the policy of economic liberalization which started in an attenuated form in 1985 but were adopted as an official policy stance from 1991 have promoted capitalist globalization of the Indian economy. We devote the next section to a brief outline of these policy measures.

2 A brief outline of the so-called economic reforms in India since the 1980s and some of its results

In India, partly as a legacy from the days of World War II and partly as the outcome of moves to ration scarce resources and direct them to planned uses and to curb the power and the socially damaging behaviour of foreign capital and monopoly houses, a number of regulations sought to delimit the fields of operation of the private and public sectors, allocate investment and finance, and control the inflow and outflow of foreign funds.

The retention of most of the restrictions on foreign trade and foreign exchange was partly motivated by the compulsion of the policy-makers to contain balance of payments crises. However, the introduction of restrictions on the sectoral deployment of large-scale private investment and retention of controls on capital issues were motivated by the desire to give a socially beneficial direction to both public and private investment . Private investment was stimulated not only by the restricted access of foreign goods into the domestic market but also by a system of cheap loans provided by new term-lending institutions set up by the government after independence. In order to see why, despite all this effort, the Indian economic performance or human development standards did not match the East Asian achievements, especially from the latter half of the 1960s, it is useful to introduce the concept of the developmental state.

I have argued elsewhere (Bagchi, 2000) that virtually all economically advanced countries constructed developmental states in their drive towards industrialization but that there were some which, in spite of an initial effort, fell by the wayside. The most dramatic case of such failure is that of Russia under the Soviet leadership in its later years, but there were others, such as India and Brazil, which proclaimed economic development as their public policy but did not implement some of the basic measures needed to advance development on a sustained basis. I would put forward four basic conditions for the rise and sustenance of a developmental state . First, private non-market power must not be allowed to shackle the freedom and energy of ordinary people or to waste national resources in the maintenance of such private power. This means that the state must get rid of feudalism or landlord power. Neither India nor Brazil fulfilled this condition.

Second, the ruling class must be guided by a vibrant nationalism, so that even if there are conflicts of interest within the ruling group, such conflicts do not prevent all measures from being directed towards the benefit of domestic producers rather than foreign firms. Even though the early Indian leaders were overtly nationalist, they continued to harbour foreign interests in various forms in domestic investment and policy-making. Third, the leadership must try to raise the standards of education of ordinary people up to the best international standards. Otherwise, the country will lose out in competition with foreign producers in the arena of international trade. From the nineteenth century on, the best international standard in this respect has included the universalization of elementary education and a sustained diffusion of higher levels of education among the people. Again, Indian leaders failed to pursue the policies needed to attain this goal even over a period of fifty-five years. Finally, the leadership must cultivate a culture of learning, and diffuse it among the people, from their own experience and from the experience of other countries. This cannot really be achieved in a hierarchical society with a huge mass of illiterate people. (This is where the Soviet rulers from the time of Brezhnev's leadership failed badly, and that failure contributed disastrously to and brought about the downfall of the Soviet regime.)

The increasingly faltering progress of the half-way developmental state in India bred multiple contradictions. Industrial growth occurred at a much faster rate after independence than before, and the so-called Green Revolution obviated the need to import food grains. But pressure built up among a class of businessmen and technocrats and economists of a neoliberal persuasion to ease government regulations on foreign trade, foreign investment and domestic investment as a means of stimulating private investment further and thus accelerating the rate of economic growth. From the late 1970s, however, some of these regulations were relaxed and the foreign exchange value of the rupee was allowed to drift downward on a crawling-peg basis. In 1981 India obtained an Extended Funding Facility credit of SDR 5 billion from the IMF, but did not draw the last instalment of the loan, and no major changes took place in the array of policies pursued by the government. However, in 1985 a series of moves began which essentially amounted to an expansive, debt-dependent fiscal policy directed at stimulating the growth of the economy (for a description of the policy changes see Datta, 1992; Bagchi, 1995, Section 5; Nayyar, 1996, chs 2 and 3). The changes effected in 1985 covered all the major fields of regulation except the capital market. The rigour of the Monopolies and Restrictive Trade Practices Act (1969) was considerably reduced, making it virtually irrelevant as far as the expansion of monopoly houses was concerned. The government encouraged foreign investment into many areas which had earlier been barred to such investment. It considerably liberalized the import of capital goods and materials, especially those needed for large projects in electricity generation, and in industries using natural gas and oil. Along with these moves, the burden of taxation on high-income and propertied groups was considerably lessened. India raised fewer resources as a percentage of its GDP and especially through the instrumentality of direct taxes than not only the developed market economies but also most of the major developing economies. The situation has deteriorated rather than improved since 1985 (Dasgupta and Mookherjee, 1998). Since 1985, the government has resorted to higher and higher doses of deficit financing to defray its expenditure, and this has led to a rapid accumulation of internal, and even more ominously, external, debt. By the beginning of 1991, India was faced with the prospect of defaulting on her debt obligations and accordingly being unable to secure even short-term loans except on very onerous terms. In June and July 1991, in order to restore confidence among India's debtors and in the rupee, the government entered into an agreement with the IMF for a standby first-tranche credit of SDR 551.93 million (about US$754 million) and drawings under the compensatory and contingency financing facility totalling the equivalent of SDR 1,352 million (about US$1,847 million). Later in the year, the IMF granted another standby credit authorizing drawings up to the equivalent of SDR 1,656 million (about US$2,262 million) (International Monetary Fund, Press Release No.91/64, 31 October 1991). In accordance with the memorandum of understanding reached with the IMF, the government of India carried out a series of policy reforms. The rupee was devalued by about 24 per cent. Initially a dual exchange rate was introduced, a lower rate being obtainable by exporters for their requirements. By the beginning of 1993, the currency was made convertible for current account transactions and the two rates were unified. Quantitative restrictions on imports were moderated or removed altogether, and import tariffs were reduced across the board. Earlier restrictions on foreign investment were done away with and a Foreign Investment Promotion Board was set up in order to attract foreign capital.

Internal deregulation accompanied these changes in the foreign trade and payments regime. Many of the industrial sectors which had been earlier reserved for public enterprises were now thrown open to the private sector as well. The government sold off large proportions of shares in public enterprises to private purchasers, including mutual funds and foreign financial institutions. The system under which firms had to seek permission from the government to establish new enterprises above a certain size or investment above a certain limit was abolished, except for a specified group of industries. The provision under the Monopolies and Restrictive Practices Act imposing restrictions on investment and production on firms of groups with assets above SDR 1 billion was abolished.

A degree of financial liberalization seeking to unify capital and money markets was also effected. Control over new capital issues was abolished. Banks were allowed to deal in shares by setting up mutual funds. Foreign financial institutions were allowed to enter the stock-market and buy up shares of Indian companies, subject to some mild restrictions. Banks were permitted to set their own rates for accepting deposits and lending money, but the central bank, of course, still has control over minimum cash reserves or rediscounting facilities, and thus can influence the supply of base money and terms of lending. Lending to 'priority sectors' at preferential rates has been continued but de-emphasized in actual transactions by banks. The government has also tried, though not very successfully so far, to bring down subsidies to agriculture, by raising water rates for public irrigation facilities, electricity tariffs and fertilizer prices. Subsidization of phosphatic fertilizers has been discontinued with a strongly negative effect on their use. The NPK combination at the core of the Green Revolution belt has become unbalanced and has resulted, in combination with other factors, in a slowdown in productivity growth, if not in an actual fall in productivity. The government has been trying continually to cut down import tariff rates, subsidies and other marks of Cain identified by the gods in Geneva and Washington, even as the children of the greater gods in Washington or Brussels think up new ways of pampering their farmers and shutting out imports from poorer countries. In recent years, the central government has also accelerated the privatization of public sector enterprises (PSEs), including those which have been profitable by any standards. This has been done with the excuse of bridging the ever-widening deficit in the central budget, but the contribution of the returns from privatization has been quite meagre. Their main function has been threefold: to keep the vociferous and powerful international claque for privatization happy by throwing mouth-watering morsels their way; to strengthen the patronage network of big business in India by allowing them to grab large chunks of business without having to go through the arduous process of building them up; to shore up a continually sagging stock-market and thus keep speculators and brokers happy. Many of the latter have been found guilty of fraud in judicial trials; in addition, virtually all the top ministers of the central government have been accused of corruption, and some have even been indicted, but practically none have been cashiered, and the liberalization process has generated a climate of complaisant corruption at the top of the decision-making process. Such a 'capture of the state' by corrupt politicians and businessmen in the wake of liberalization and privatization is, of course, not confined to India but is to be found in virtually all the transition economies of the defunct Soviet bloc and in most countries of Latin America.

One major claim of the advocates of economic reform was that it would significantly raise the rate of economic growth of the economy. In Table 15.1 we have reproduced the figures of GDP in India at factor cost at constant 1993 to 1994 prices for selected years. To give the reformers the best case possible, we have taken 1991 to 1992, which was the year neo-liberal reforms were fully unleashed and at once produced a severe recession in the industrial sector, as the base year for reforms, so that the procedure would exaggerate rather than minimize the post-reform rates of growth. We have compared the rates of growth over the nine years after reform with the nine years between 1981 and 1982 to 1989 and 1990, because, according to reformers, the US–Iraq War of 1990 distorted the Indian external balances and was a major factor behind the crisis, so that the year 1990 to 1991 should be omitted in any reckoning of the effects of reforms. At first sight, the reformers would appear to be right: the growth of GDP from 1991 to 2000 was faster at around 64 per cent than over the period 1981 to 1990 when it was 55 per cent. However, practically all that difference was due to the growth of income from services: the pre-reform nine-year growth rate was 66 per cent whereas the post-reform growth rate was around 83 per cent .The rate of growth of manufacturing was distinctly lower for the post-reform period (77 as against 82 per cent for the earlier period). The growth of manufacturing has slipped further during 2000 to

2001 and 2001 to 2002: the rate of growth of industry, which includes electricity, gas and mining and quarrying, was 5.2 per cent in 1999 to 2000, 5.0 per cent in 2000 to 2001 and 2.7 per cent in 2001 to 2002. If we take changes in the index of industrial production (or IIP, with 1981 to 1982 as the base year) as the criterion of industrial growth rates, it turns out that three of the lowest rates of growth of the IIP were recorded in the post-reform period: 0.6 per cent in 1991 to 1992, 2.3 per cent in 1992 to 1993 and 2.7 per cent in 2001 to 2002 (The Hindu Business Line, 11 May 2002). The higher rate of agricultural growth recorded for the post-reform nine-year period up until 1999 to 2000 is partly a fluke of the base year chosen, since the year 1991 to 1992 had witnessed a decline. There were three years during the 1990s in which agriculture had witnessed an actual decline, namely 1991 to 1992, 1995 to 1996 and 1997 to 1998. Moreover, the rate of growth of the production of food grains was lower than that of the non-food grains during the post-reform period, and lower than that of the food grains output in the pre-reform period. The rate of growth of GDP at factor cost in 2000 to 2001 has been a meagre 4 per cent. Thus the claim of the reformers regarding the effect of the adoption of neo-liberal measures on output growth has been disproved by the available evidence.

Even official reports, such as the *Report on Currency and Finance* published by the central bank, namely the Reserve Bank of India, and the *Economic Survey* published by the Ministry of Finance, Government of India at the time of the presentation of the central government budget, have identified the demand constraint and, more particularly, the depressed state of the domestic market as the major factor keeping down the rate of economic growth in India. However, instead of adopting policies that address the lack of access of peasants to land on equitable terms or channelling resources through fiscal and monetary devices, the Government of India has reversed or whittled down some earlier policies that might have benefited the poorer sections of the population. One of the tragic consequences of this policy is that while, through price support policies that have mainly benefited the richer farmers of regions favoured with better infrastructural facilities, the government has stockpiled huge quantities of grain, it is unwilling to distribute that

Table 15.1 India: Gross domestic product at factor cost 1981 to 2000 (figures in Rs 10 million at constant, 1993 to 1994 prices)

Year	Agriculture	Manufacturing	Services	Total, including other sectors
1981–82	151477	59881	180434	425073
1986–87	168707	83290	242894	536267
1989–90	195756	108703	301151	656331
1990–91	204421	115282	319374	692871
1991–92	200634	111075	333648	701863
1995–96	230469	161424	440808	899563
1999–2000	266848	196763	610223	1151991

Source: RBI (2001)

grain to the poorer sections through a public distribution system (Swaminathan, 2000). The stock of food grains lodged with the Food Corporation of India reached a level of 58 million tonnes in January 2002 (GOI, 2002, ch. 5), but the amount distributed through the public distribution system (PDS) was only 11.72 million tonnes in 2001 to 2002, when it is admitted that even for the very stringently defined below-poverty-line families the minimum requirement to be distributed through the PDS would be 18.52 million tonnes (ibid., par. 5.33); the total amount issued through ration shops also includes that bought by above-poverty-line families. This is occurring in a situation in which India accounts for the largest number of malnourished people in the world. It was estimated that in 1991 to 1992 for India as a whole, 56.2 per cent of all children between the ages of 1 and 5 were severely or moderately malnourished (Swaminathan, 2000, ch. 3). Although the situation may have improved a little in some regions, it is unlikely that the burden of malnutrition has declined since then.

Yet another argument advanced in favour of liberalization was that, by releasing the private sector from the shackles of government regulation, it would stimulate the growth of output in the public sector and raise the growth of employment. The only sector to offer decent employment, to use a phrase favoured by the ILO, is the formal sector, or what is termed as the organized sector in Indian official parlance. Between 1991 and 1992 and 1999 and 2000, the growth of employment in the organized public sector has been zero: it was 19.28 million in 1991 to 1992 and 19.28 million in 1999 to 2000; it has shrunk from 19.56 million in 1996 to 1997 to 19.28 million in 1999 to 2000. This complete stagnation or worse has by no means been compensated by the growth in the organized public sector. Employment in that segment rose from 7.85 million in 1991 to 1992 to 8.75 million in 1997 to 1998 and has more or less stagnated at that figure since then (RBI, *Handbook of Statistics on Indian Economy*, 2001, Table 10). What happened to the 60 million-plus addition to the labour force that occurred in the 1990s? Officially, the rate of unemployment in India remains low, no more than, say, 3 to 4 per cent per year. However, most of that employment occurs in the informal sector, at wages that may not even cover subsistence, and under poor working conditions (Bagchi, 1995).

3   Globalization and linking up the insecurity of international commodity markets, foreign exchange markets, money markets and stock-markets

When foreign trade is substantially liberalized, money markets are deregulated, more and more of the assets of the country are securitized and traded on the stock-market, and capital is allowed to flow in and out of the country with little hindrance, the risks of all the markets become linked. Disturbances in one market can cause mayhem in any of the other markets and lead to instability in the whole economy. In India, except for the fact that there are still some restrictions on movements of capital into and out of the economy, all the other licences permitted to free-wheeling private interests have been accorded since the onset of reforms.

In India up until 1991, the banking system was closely regulated by the Reserve Bank of India (the central bank) and the Ministry of Finance, and the money and capital markets were segregated. Banks were not allowed to hold shares of private firms as part of their statutory holding of liquid assets against their liabilities. The Reserve Bank of India laid down two aggregate constraints on the operations of commercial banks. The first was a minimum cash reserve ratio (CRR); that is, of cash to liabilities, and the second was a legally stipulated minimum ratio of the value of approved securities to the total liabilities of banks – the statutory liquidity ratio (SLR). There was also a distinction between the so-called term-lending institutions such as the Industrial Finance Corporation of India (IFCI), the Industrial Development Bank of India (IDBI) and the Industrial Credit and Investment Corporation of India (ICICI) and the commercial banks, which were supposed to extend mainly short-term credit. The rates of interest paid by banks on various classes of deposit and the rates of interest charged by them on different categories of loans were also specified. There was also a regulation that at least 40 per cent of the credit extended by the commercial banks would be given to the socalled priority sectors such as agriculture, small-scale industry, transport operators and so on, at rates of interest which were lower than those charged to other borrowers.

Issues of new capital through the stock-market were also regulated by an official Controller of Capital Issues. Banks could act as underwriters of capital issues but would not hold equities as major assets: in any case that would tend to infringe the requirement of keeping a minimum SLR as officially stipulated. Foreign investors were not usually allowed to hold more than a small percentage of equity in an Indian company.

From 1991, most of the regulations, controls and devices of segregation between the money and capital markets, and between Indian and foreign investors, were eased if not removed altogether. Banks were allowed to set their deposit and lending rates within certain limits, the requirement of setting aside 40 per cent of the credit for priority sectors was eased, and because of the perception that reducing the fiscal deficit of the government would lead to lower borrowing requirements of the public sector, by 1997 the SLR had been reduced from 38 to 25 per cent (RBI, 1997). The CRR was also reduced to 10 per cent in a move to increase the liquidity of the banks in a regime of generally high interest rates. From May 1992, foreign institutional investors were allowed to participate directly in the Indian stock-market. Already in 1987, public sector banks (i.e. the major part of the banking sector since all major banks had been nationalized) had been allowed to set up mutual funds for subscribing to bonds and equities. Non-banking companies were allowed to mobilize funds through deposits and other schemes, and other non-banking financial companies (NBFCs) were permitted to operate in the capital and money markets. Banks and NBFCs were allowed to raise money through certificates of deposit in India and abroad (by means of the so-called global deposit receipts or GDRs). Under the neoliberal regime, money market mutual funds – not necessarily linked to banks – were allowed to be set up in the private sector as well. In order to allow companies to tap new sources of funds, and potential investors everywhere access to profit-making opportunities, many new stock exchanges were set up, covering all major cities and regions.

The logic of financial liberalization

The rationale behind all these moves was partly allocation-oriented and partly oriented towards promotion of entrepreneurship and thrift.[1] It was believed that higher rates of interest on deposits with banks and other financial intermediaries would encourage people to save more. At the same time, freedom to set rates of interest on the parts of banks and NBFCs would encourage competition and better allocation of the savings mobilized between the capital and money market agents. The unification of capital and money markets was also aimed at on the same grounds of better allocation of resources and faster growth. Finally, the Government of India had already been offering attractive rates of interest to foreign and non-resident Indian depositors on foreign currency deposits. Their privileges were further strengthened, and in a bid to attract both foreign direct and portfolio investment, foreign investors were allowed to enter many sectors of the economy which had earlier on been closed to them, and they were allowed to hold progressively larger shares of equity in such firms. The current BJP-led central government has allowed foreigners to hold 100 per cent equity stake in most sectors of industry and services, including infrastructural facilities. A programme of progressive privatization of major public sector corporations such as the State Bank of India, Indian Oil Corporation, Oil and Natural Gas Corporation and Bharat Heavy Electricals was set in train. From 1992 foreign institutional investors were allowed to buy and sell shares in the market, and their permitted stakes have been hiked progressively over the years. In the USA and Britain, the unification of the money and capital markets was already occurring in the 1980s. Large transnational clearing banks, merchant banks and mutual funds had become used to operating in both money and capital markets on their own behalf and on behalf of their clients. It was believed by policy-makers that these banks and fund managers would invest in the Indian money and stock-markets if they were allowed to have the same freedom of operation in India as they enjoyed abroad. (In fact, the origins of the so-called 'bank scam' of 1991 to 1992 may be traced back to 1987, from when some of the transnational banks abused the new facility extended to them of the right to manage portfolios of stocks and bonds for their assets, and the Reserve Bank of India authorities turned a blind eye to these abuses in order not to offend the potential foreign investors.)

Reaping the harvest of poorly regulated financial liberalization in India

When the Government of India adopted the step of abolishing official regulation of capital issues by companies, and indicated that further measures liberalizing industrial and financial regulation were in the offing, it started a boom in the stock-market, and the share prices of many companies doubled and trebled within a few months. This share market boom collapsed around May 1992. It was revealed soon after that the boom had been fuelled by a small group of bull operators who had been financed mainly by a few foreign banks such as the Citibank, ANZ Grindlays Bank, Bank of America, and major public sector banks such as the National Housing Bank and the Bank of Baroda, often in violation of the central bank regulations and prudential norms. A sum of at least Rs.5,000 crores (Rs.50 billion) lent by the banks to brokers in the stock-market remains unaccounted for even now. It is symptomatic that M.J. Pherwani, the then Chairman of the National Housing Bank, who had been a key player in the extension of the jurisdiction of the stock-market (having recently chaired two high-powered committees relating to it, appointed by the Reserve Bank of India: Misra, 1997, p. 353) died under suspicious circumstances as soon as the so-called 'bank scam' came into public view. The lesson of this piece of history is that if government regulation breeds corruption, so does the operation of private interests. Only an official watchdog with sufficiently strong penal powers can check the worst abuses committed by unscrupulous dealers and bankers. However, since then, with some fluctuations from time to time, the share prices moved south, and 1998 witnessed new troughs reached by the share market. In 1999 to 2000, with a boom in technology and entertainment stocks, the index moved upwards (Table 14.2), but with the collapse of the information technology-led boom in advanced countries, Indian share prices moved downwards again.

The averages of the share prices conceal very large fluctuations within the year. Between April 2000 and April 2001, the Bombay Stock Exchange Sensitive Index (Sensex) moved from around 5000 to 3100 (Reserve Bank of India, *Annual Report 2000–2001*, Chart V.9) and by September 2001 it had moved down to 2918. These movements in share prices were triggered by various events such as budget announcements that seemed to give more indulgence to speculators and tax-dodgers, by the announcement of disinvestment of the government in yet another profitable public enterprise, and by deliberate manipulation of the stock-market, some of which may have been initiated by persons close to the Ministry of Finance. For example, in early 2001, around budget time, the United Trust of India (UTI), India's oldest and biggest mutual fund, which is owned by the government or other public enterprises, was directed to invest in a whole host of companies, including those that were not listed on the stock exchange. At the same time, a stockbroker who was close to the powers in the central government began manipulating stocks. The result was a boom in the stock-market, its collapse when big players with inside knowledge sold their stakes at the top of the boom, and huge losses sustained by the UTI. The UTI was unable to meet its obligations under many of its schemes and thousands of small investors, including pensioners who had put their life savings into the UTI, were left in the lurch.

One of the assumptions, quite falsely based, behind financial liberalization was that a major chunk of new finance for investment in the private sector would come from new equity issues. Table 15.2 shows how mistaken this assumption has turned out to be. Joint-stock banks mostly still in the public sector continue to be the main sources of funds for private enterprise, and of most of the public enterprises as

Table 15.2 New capital issues by non-government public limited companies, India 1989 to 2001 (figures in Rs million for columns 2 and 3)

Year	Ordinary shares	Total	Index numbers of prices of industrial securities	Bombay Stock Exchange Sensitive Index
(1)	(2)	(3)	(4)	(5)
1989–90	12201	65099		
1990–91	12843	43122	500.3	
1991–92	19162	61931	776.2	
1992–93	99526	198034	1142.3	
1993–94	99597	193303	1051.3	
1994–95	174144	264167	1537.3	
1995–96	118774	159976	1169.6	
1996–97	61014	104095	1146.8	3469
1997–98	11624	31383	1061.0	3813
1998–99	25627	50131		3295
1999–2000	27525	51533		4659
2000–01	26416	49241		4270

Source: RBI (2001), Table 66.

well. Again, on the mistaken assumption that enforcing the Basle capital adequacy norms is to restore the health of financially fragile banks and keep the others healthy, the government has tightened credit for most of the domestic economy, and this has aggravated the recession in the economy.

Coming to another index of an active globalization process, namely inflows and outflows of foreign direct investment (FDI), the reformers expected that they would be strongly stimulated by the neoliberal reforms. I note in parenthesis that the growth of no sizeable economy outside the Atlantic seaboard, let alone the growth of a subcontinent such as India, has been supported to any significant extent by private capital inflows. As it turned out, the FDI inflows were also rather feeble for India as compared, say, with China, Singapore or Malaysia (Table 14.3). We also see from Table 15.3 that except for the years 1997 to 1998 and 1998 to 1999, the inflows of FDI have been lower than those of portfolio investment. The latter flows have been volatile as we would expect, with movements of hot money, and have been a major factor in influencing the movements of share prices in India. Some of the FDI inflows have been directed towards acquiring controlling shares in Indian companies and have not added to the productive capacity of the economy. It is indicative of the mimetic mindset of the Indian policy-makers that with all the negative evidence available about the effects of a rampaging market for corporate control, the latest *Economic Survey* of the Government of India reports the progress of such a market in India in wholly positive terms (GOI, 2002, par. 4.23). Table 15.3 demonstrates further that private transfers, which are primarily remittances from West Asian countries of Indian workers labouring there, far outweigh the FDI and portfolio investment combined. Government policy depends on those remittances as a stabilization device, and squanders them through accelerated

Table 15.3 Foreign investment inflows and private transfers into India, 1990 to 2001 (in US$ million)

Year	Foreign direct investment	Portfolio investment	Total of direct and portfolio investment	Private transfers
1990–91	97	6	103	2068
1991–92	129	4	133	3783
1992–93	315	244	559	3852
1993–94	586	3567	4153	5265
1994–95	1314	3824	5138	8093
1995–96	2144	2748	4892	8506
1996–97	2821	3312	6133	12367
1997–98	3557	1828	5385	11830
1998–99	2462	–61	2401	10280
1999–2000	2155	3026	5181	12256
2000–01	2339	2760	5099	12798

Sources: RBI (2001); GOI (2002).

expenditure on military heads and burgeoning central government administration and communalist public theatre.

4 Volatile markets, insecurity, communalization and further concentration of wealth in India

In an earlier study, I analysed the volatility in foreign exchange markets, and the way the Reserve Bank of India (RBI) was seeking to manage and contain that volatility (Bagchi, 1999/2000). Currently, the RBI is following a policy of sterilizing the net inflows of foreign exchange as both a device for controlling inflation, and as a means of keeping a tight leash on expansion of base money and credit. This has not obviated day-to-day fluctuations in the foreign exchange and the need, on the part of RBI, to use various kinds of intervention in the foreign exchange market (Ghosh, 2002). The high rates of interest in the Indian economy continue to attract deposits from non-resident Indians, but at a severe cost to the Indian economy, and burdening the economy and the joint-stock banks with a high repayment cost. Ironically enough, these inflows have not been used to bring down the foreign debt of India, and the country is incurring a large cost in service and repayment obligations.

The stagnation of the economy, combined with expansion of the financial sector, the tapering off of central government investment to mitigate the regional differentials in industrial and agricultural growth and in infrastructural facilities have converged to enormously increase regional imbalances, the inequalities between town and country, and between income and wealth classes. The currently governing parties at the centre have used deliberate provocation of communal conflicts between Hindus and Muslims, occasionally whipping up war hysteria by citing the issue of cross-border terrorism as a way of mobilizing votes and illegally exercised muscle power and lapping up further public resources for public benefit. The latest example of these ways of managing politics and amassing funds for the operators in and around the government is the ongoing carnage in Gujarat. Given the currently prevailing hostility of Western governments to Muslims in general and their resounding inaction in redressing the violence unleashed on the Palestinians by the Government of Israel, the ruling coalition at the centre need fear little except mild verbal reprimands from the part of the international community that matters. Their decision to put up an expert engineer in the making of nuclear-powered missiles is an index of their cynical confidence. Moreover, how can Western governments seriously displease a government which, through its active privatization exercise and its willing submission to most of the diktats of the WTO, seems determined to push funds towards the TNCs and foreign financial bodies? Market fundamentalism and religious or racist fundamentalism are comfortable bedfellows everywhere, and India's rulers enjoy the comfortable glow of approval from their counterparts from the White House to the Kremlin. There are protests by peasants, workers and egalitarian democratic forces within India against most of their policies, but as yet they have made very little impact on the globalizing and corrupt, war mongering policies of the federal government and its allies in many Indian states.

Note

1   The theory of financial liberalization and development of a market for corporate control is composed of many strands. The first is the theory of mergers and take-overs developed by Marris (1964) and Manne (1965).The second is the fallacious theory of 'financial repression' developed by McKinnon (1973) and Shaw (1973). The third is the theory of the firm developed in Jensen and Meckling (1976), as an entity in which the equity-holders are seen as the sole stakeholders. For a demonstration that financial markets are necessarily rationed markets and that there is nothing peculiar about the so-called 'financial repression', see Stiglitz and Weiss (1981) and Gertler (1988); for a critique of the Jensen–Meckling theory, see Bagchi (1997); for demonstrations of the very mixed nature of welfare outcomes of actual mergers and take-overs in the USA and Europe, respectively, see Ravenscraft and Scherer (1987) and Bishop and Kay (1993).

References

Bagchi, A.K. (1992). 'Transnational banks, US power game and global impoverishment', *Economic and Political Weekly*, 27(22) (30 May): 1133–1136.
—— (1993). 'Transnationalisation en Asie du Sud', in S. Amin and P. Gonzalez Casanova (eds), *Mondialisation et Accumulation*, Paris, L'Harmattan: 199–238.
—— (1994). 'Globalising India: the fantasy and the reality', *Social Scientist* (Delhi), 22(7–8): 18–27.
—— (1995). 'Employment and economic reforms in India'. Background Paper for the ILO *World Employment Report 1996*, Geneva, International Labour Office.
—— (1996). 'Fluctuations in global economy: income, debt and terms of trade processes', in Sunanda Sen (ed.), *Financial Fragility, Debt and Economic Reforms*, London, Macmillan: 73–102.

—— (1996). 'Structural adjustment in South Asia and Latin America: stabilization, liberalization, growth and employment'. Background Paper for the ILO *World Employment Report*, Geneva, International Labour Office.

—— (1997). 'Economic theory and economic organization, 1. A critique of the Anglo-American theory of the firm structure, Occasional Paper no. 165, Centre for Studies in Social Sciences, Calcutta.

—— (1999/2000). 'Globalisation, liberalisation and vulnerability: India and the Third World', *Economic and Political Weekly*, 6 November; also published under the title 'Globalizing India: a critique of an agenda for financiers and speculators', in J.D. Schmidt and J. Hersh (eds), *Globalization and Social Change*, London, Routledge.

—— (2000). 'The past and the future of the developmental state', *Journal of World Systems Research* (http://csf.colorado.edu/jwsr), XI (2) (summer/fall): 398–442.

Bishop, M. and Kay, J. (eds) (1993). *European Mergers and Merger Policy*, Oxford, Oxford University Press.

Business Standard (1998). 'US-64 equity exposure 68 per cent', *Business Standard* (Calcutta, 8 October).

CAC (1997). *Report of the Committee on Capital Account Convertibility*, Mumbai, Reserve Bank of India.

Chandrasekhar, C. P. and Ghosh, Jayati (2002). *The Market that Failed: A Decade of Neoliberal Economic Reforms in India*, New Delhi, LeftWord Books.

Dasgupta, A. and Mookherjee, D. (1998). *Incentives and Institutional Reform in Tax Enforcement: an Analysis of Developing Country Experience*, Delhi, Oxford University Press.

Datta, B. (1992). *Indian Planning at the Crossroads*, Delhi, Oxford University Press.

Freixas, X. and Rochet, J.C. (1997). *Microeconomics of Banking*, Cambridge, MA, MIT Press.

Gertler, M. (1988). 'Financial structure and aggregate economic activity: an overview', *Journal of Money, Credit and Banking*, 20(3): 559–588.

Ghosh, S.K. (2002). 'RBI intervention in the forex market: results from a tobit and logit model using daily data', *Economic and Political Weekly*, 37(24) (15 June): 2333–2348.

Government of India (2002). *Economic Survey 2001–02*, New Delhi, Government of India, Ministry of Finance.

Jensen, M.C. and Meckling, W.H. (1976). 'Theory of the firm: managerial behaviour, agency costs and ownership structure', *Journal of Financial Economics*, 3: 305–360.

Keynes, J.M. (1936). *The General Theory of Employment, Interest and Money*, London, Macmillan.

McKinnon, R. (1973). *Money and Capital in Economic Development*, Washington DC, Brookings Institute.

Manne, H.G. (1965). 'Mergers and the market for corporate control', *Journal of Political Economy*, 73: 693–706.

Marris, R.L. (1964). *The Economic Theory of 'Managerial' Capitalism*, London, Macmillan.

Misra, B.M. (1997). 'Fifty years of the Indian capital market', *Reserve Bank of India Occasional Papers*, 18(2 & 3): 351–383.

Nayyar, D. (1996). *Economic Liberalization in India: Analytics, Experience and Lessons*, Hyderabad, Orient Longman.

Ravenscraft, D.J. and Scherer, F.M. (1987). *Mergers, Sell-offs, and Economic Efficiency*, Washington DC, The Brookings Institution.

Reserve Bank of India (2001). *Report on Currency and Finance, 2000–01*, Mumbai, Reserve Bank of India.

Sachs, J. (ed.) (1989). *Developing Country Debt and the World Economy*, Chicago, IL, University of Chicago Press.

Shaw, E.S. (1973). *Financial Deepening in Economic Development*, New York, Oxford University Press.

Stiglitz, J.E. and Weiss, A. (1981). 'Credit rationing in markets with imperfect information', *American Economic Review*, 71(3): 393–410.

Swaminathan, M. (2000). *Weakening Welfare: The Public Distribution of Food in India*, New Delhi, LeftWord Books.

Tarapore, S.S. (1998). 'Hosannas for capital control', *Business Standard* (Calcutta), 9 October.

Telegraph (1998). 'Govt., public sector banks pledge support to UTI', *Telegraph* (Calcutta), 14 October.

Tversky, A., and Kahneman, D. (1974). 'Judgment under uncertainty: heuristics and biases', *Science*, 185: 1124–1131.

UNCTAD (1997). *Trade and Development Report 1997*, Geneva and New York, United Nations Conference on Trade and Development.

—— (1998). *Trade and Development Report 1998*, New York, United Nations Conference on Trade and Development.

WDR (1996). *World Development Report 1996*, New York, Oxford University Press for the World Bank.

16 Conclusion

The theory and practice of the Chinese Model

Tian Yu Cao

1 The emergence of the issues

China's reform originated directly from the comprehensive negation of the Cultural Revolution. With this as the turning point, the Party reflected on and comprehensively re-evaluated the theory and practice of the Mao Zedong era. The rejection of the mass political campaigns that reached a peak with the Cultural Revolution has had two direct consequences. The first is that the Party has learned the importance of strengthening democracy from within the Party and improving the legal system; the second is that it has decided to switch the focus of its work from ideological and political struggles to the economy, raising the slogan of building a socialist and powerful country through the modernization of industry, agriculture, science and technology, and national defense.

Deng Xiaoping's modernization plan

Deng Xiaoping defined the "Four Modernizations" and the construction of democratic and legal systems as the self-improvement, rather than the abandonment, of socialism. This concept of socialist modernization is naturally different in essence from capitalist modernization. At the same time, he also emphasized that building socialism with Chinese characteristics mainly involves the market economy and opening to the West; this was different from the socialism characterized by the planned economy and confrontation with the West. Therefore, how to theoretically understand and practically evaluate the new Chinese model of modern development becomes an issues worth studying.

Modernization is a process aimed at realizing modernity. Modernity is a concept that has widespread and complex connotations. Its contents go far beyond the "Four Modernizations," which are technical and economic in nature and, even including democracy, is not enough to encompass its meaning. It involves various institutional arrangements in economic, social and political life, and also includes certain value systems based on a particular set of ethical doctrines and cultural traditions. If we want to evaluate the theories and practice of the Chinese model, we should first review the concept of modernity.

Modernity within the frame of liberalism (i): Its basic elements

Historically, the development of the technological economy touched off by the scientific and industrial revolutions, along with the emergence of a series of social phenomena such as secularization and urbanization, marked the fact that Western societies had entered into the process of modernization. But conceptually, the principal elements of modernity are to be found in institutional arrangements and value systems.

First is the market economy which is characterized by free competition. As an embodiment of economic rationality (division of labor and efficiency), it promoted economic development and technological progress. At the same time, it demanded a series of political, juristic, and ideological changes to guarantee its operation. The most important of the changes instituted were the efficacy of business contracts and individual freedom as the basis of the labor market.

Although democracy is the "best shell" (in Lenin's words) for capitalism, there is no logically necessary connection between democracy and the market economy. In the history of Western thought, the two have not developed simultaneously. After the era of classical Greek democracy, the idea of democracy, as one of the main elements of modernity, emerged as an offshoot from yet more fundamental values of liberalism.

Starting from the Renaissance, with the development of commerce and trade, the rise of cities and bourgeois, humanism emerged, freeing the secular individual from the shackles of theology. The first person who laid the theoretical foundation of individual freedom was John Locke. Locke believed that the property created by individual activities is the foundation of individual dignity and responsibility. Therefore, private property is the foundation of individual freedom. Kantian ethics defined autonomous individuals as the final end of human activity, not the means. From the high perspective of dialectical philosophy, Hegel defined modernity as the realization of subjective freedom.

The emancipation and development of individuality discussed here, even if they are rooted in private property, logically are not necessary in conflict with some forms of collectivism. After all, individuals are always in certain social relations, especially in those of classes and nations. The collectivism manifested in class and national struggles are inevitably the necessary means to strive for individual liberation and development. But it is only a means, not an end.

Ethically equal autonomous individuals give vitality to social life; their human and civil rights, and the right to engage in political activities, must be protected. On the basis of these values, democracy has gained a certain status in modernity, as a special mode of power-sharing and as a system contributing to the universal realization of individual rights.

Another important element in modernity is rationality. It includes instrumental rationality, which is unrelated to axiological goals but is manifested in the development of science and technology, the organization of industries, and public administration. It also includes value rationality in the pursuit of, for example, individual freedom and emancipation, democracy, justice, or national interests. But critical rationality is even more important, which judges all things and behaviors in terms of ultimate ends. Critical rationality is perhaps the most fundamental and vital element in the concept of modernity. It is precisely this element that drives modernity forward and brings about its self-improvement.

Another related concept is nationalism. The idea of nationalism, based on blood ties, territory, history (myth), language and writing, culture or religion, has its roots in pre-modernity. The nationalism of modern nation states, rooted in a certain market and mandated to protect it, is historically an important constituent of modernity. Of course, colonies and dependencies may be frequently involved in modernization, to a certain extent, by the metropolitan countries. However, without an independent nation state as its foundation, no society can achieve modernization in the true sense of the term.

Modernity in the frame of liberalism (II): Its historical trajectory

The above elements are abstracted from a particular mode of modernity that was first realized in the historical development of Western capitalism. To clearly understand their real meaning, therefore, we have to return them the social and historical context in which they were realized. In so doing, we will find two types of problem in the capitalist mode of modernity.

The first type is related to the market. First, in the market relations between capital and labor, the nominal equality of two sides expressed by their contractual relations cannot cover the reality of capitalist exploitation and control over labor. Workers in their activities of selling their labor are not free, and are not equal to the capitalists. Second, market competition and the concept of the "survival of the fittest" inevitably cause polarization within society as a whole. The serious economic inequality hollows out to a great extent the real content of legal and political equality. The system becomes democratic only nominally, and individual development and freedom in a positive sense become privileges that only some people can enjoy.

Since capital in a capitalist society is nothing but alienated labor, an alien force, its nature is to pursue profit and expand without limit, the economic vigor brought by individualism and market competition is manifested mainly in pursuing growth rather than meeting human needs for survival and development. One result is the plunder of limited natural resources and the destruction of the ecological environment; another is that the desire for material goods (inspired by the consumerism that is necessary for capitalist development) suppresses spiritual and intellectual development, distorting human nature itself. Market competition causes greed and fear to corrode social psychology and the social ethos. Apart from this, as Marx pointed out, blind forces in the market cause periodic economic crises, and with every crisis the situation of labor sinks further into misery.

Capital's need for controlling labor and its demand for expansion have greatly promoted the development of instrumental rationality, but are not conducive to and have even suppressed the development of critical rationality.

The second type of problem is related to international expansion of capital. Even though the age of naked colonialism and imperialism is over, the 1990s witnessed the beginning of a new wave of globalization. Because its nature is the expansion of capital, it still has serious problems: many so-called "fair" procedures that assure free competition actually benefit only the stronger side, and they contradict and conflict with the long-term goals of developing the national economy in backward regions of the world.

On the international stage, as the liberal modernity in the developed Western countries showed up in the form of colonialism and imperialism (complementing them were fascist modernity in later developing capitalist countries and the comprador-dependent modernity in colonies and dependencies), it contrasts with the revolutionary nationalism that has pursued freedom, independence and liberation in many of the backward countries in the East. But in the age of globalization, when transnational capital vigorously promotes globalization in backward regions, the needs of nativization cause Western liberal modernity to pick up some of the social, political and cultural features that are specific to the region.

However, no matter that it is the revolutionary nationalism which emphasized collectivism in the past, or the contemporary "multi-modernity" that has distinctive features specific to particular social, political and cultural contexts; all of them are in essence merely responses to Western modernity. In their basic institutions and values, none have been able to transcend Western liberal modernity. The very existence of the "opposing-the-West-to-join-the-West" type of nationalism, and of "multi-modernity" that seeks to join the Western mainstream with a non-Western self-identity, has fully demonstrated the powerful vitality and taming force of liberal modernity.

Modernity in the frame of liberalism (III): Its potential and limitations

Although the capitalist forms of modernity have the two problems discussed above, one should not overlook the fact that the basic value of universal emancipation of individuality, which has embodied the ideals of the development of humanity and of human emancipation, along with the notion of critical rationality based on these values, have endowed liberal modernity with great potential for self-improvement, which is clearly vindicated by the improvement of human and civil rights, the development of social democracy, the construction of the welfare states, the abandonment of imperialist and colonialist policies, the self-reflection on and self-criticism of past and present situations, and the pursuit of social justice and global justice. But all of these pluses cannot cover up another fact, namely that liberal modernity has insurmountable limitations that stem from the internal irresolvable contradictions in its theoretical foundations. What are these contradictions and limitations?

The first prerequisite of liberalism is that private property, as the basis of individual dignity and moral responsibility, is sacred and inviolable. Any type of violation, even one that stems from the public will formed through the democratic process, is considered immoral and intolerable. Thus all unfair distribution of property that has taken shape in the past is eternized. Any reforms and improvements can at best, even in principle, only redistribute national income (as we see in the welfare states), and cannot touch the foundation of private property, namely the control of the process of production. Because production finally decides distribution, this type of redistributive justice cannot eliminate the source of social injustice. In addition, because of the powerful resistance from those who own property, most liberal social philosophers are not optimistic about maintaining and improving redistributive justice, particularly since the end of the Cold War.

However, without touching on the first prerequisite of liberalism, all other values of liberal modernity, such as individual autonomy and democracy and the critical rationality based on these values, cannot penetrate into the core area of economic life, and private property, as the basis of individual dignity and moral responsibility, cannot be distributed fairly. In other words, the universal development of individuality, as the basic pursuit of modernity, cannot be truly achieved within the frame of liberalism. Its achievement requires an alternative, non-liberal modernity.

The Chinese model and alternative modernity

Since the Opium War when the Western powers forced China to open its doors, China, whose peasant society has cherished the equalitarian ideal of "fearing inequality, not poverty" for thousands of years, with its political expression of "étatism" (limiting what the rich and powerful could take for themselves with the imperial power) being a historical tradition, has been seeking a path to modernity which is different from that taken in the West. However, what is expressed in *On Great Harmony* by Kang Youwei and Sun Yat-sen's *The Three People's Principles* is the basic demand for equality and modernization in a nationalist sense. The "May Fourth Movement" which advocated democracy and science against imperialism and feudalism showed its liberal colors through its goal of "opposing-the-West-to-join-the West."

Because the success of the October Revolution in Russia opened up a new path, political development after the May Fourth Movement created a new historical tradition, i.e. the victory of the Chinese revolution in 1949 and the following thirty years' theories and practice of Mao Zedong. Mao Zedong critically inherited the historical traditions of egalitarianism, nationalism, and étatism, grafted Marxist ideology, Leninist party structure, and Stalinist ideas and practice concerning the construction of socialism on to China and nativized them, trying to break a path to modernity of China's own, different from those in the West or the Soviet Union. This path was eventually rejected and abandoned due to the failures of the Great Leap Forward and the Cultural Revolution.

Deng Xiaoping's modernization project is a new stage along the Chinese path. Deng Xiaoping inherited Mao Zedong's étatism and nationalism, although he also tried to practice them in a less doctrinaire way, with more individual freedom and tolerance for social activities, and with communication and cooperation with the West in the fields of economy, politics, culture and military. But Deng Xiaoping's originality lies in his abandonment of the planned economy, the basic tenet of Mao Zedong and traditional socialism. He took the market system as the underlying institution for China's economic modernization, while at the same time trying to bring the market economy into the framework of socialism. Thus he introduced an alternative modernity that is different from liberalism as well as from traditional socialism.

The traditional leftists are suspicious and critical of the Chinese model Deng Xiaoping advocated. They believe that the internal logic of the market economy would inevitably lead China to capitalism – not capitalism of the usual type, but rather a dependent form, characterized by the dominance of officialdom and compradors. At the same time, the liberals also attack the Chinese model. In their view, a distinctive Chinese path that emphasizes placing China outside the "mainstream of human civilization" (i.e., the institutions and culture of liberal modernity) could only intend to and result in prolonging the present political autocracy. And without democracy and rule by law, individual freedom and liberation and the free development of a market economy would be only empty words. Therefore, how to understand the theory and practice of the Chinese model has become the focus of the present ideological and even political struggles in China.

2   Theory

Alternative modernity: The principle of universality and institutional arrangements

In the pursuit of such an ultimate value as the free development of autonomous individuals, in the hope of rationally organizing social life, and especially in the emphasis on the development of a critical rationality that judges all according to adopted values, the alternative modernity that the Chinese model has represented and pursued has no essential difference from the liberal modernity. What is different is merely that the former is more universal and more thoroughgoing than the latter. In other words, the Chinese model requires the freedom for all to develop his or her individuality and ability through appropriate institutional arrangements; any current social arrangement that protects only the "free" development of some people or prolongs historical injustice must be corrected. This means, first, that institutional arrangements which differ from capitalism must be made at the core of economic life, namely in the control of production and the corresponding distribution of social wealth.

Such a thoroughgoing principle of universality, although it differs from egalitarianism in its respect for individuality and individual responsibility, rejects in principle any form of structural inequality. At the same time, it challenges the basic theoretical premise of liberalism (the notion that private property is sacred and inviolable), and differs from and conflicts with liberal modernity on a series of derivative social goals, political and economic policies, and even cultural values.

But the Chinese model also takes the market economy as its underlying institution for economic modernization, although it has historically developed only within the framework of capitalism and is taken by the liberals to be the major model of social organization according to the liberal principles. Thus how to judge the Chinese model, in terms of its social content (socialism or capitalism), its political content (the economic functions of the state apparatus and labor organizations and their relationship to the free market), its dealings with transnational capital, and its relationship to the two traditionally opposing ideological systems (liberalism and socialism), becomes a difficult issue but one worth investigating in political economy and social philosophy.

The goals

The Chinese model expects to develop productivity through the advancement of science and technology and the improvement of the market. This is relatively simple, and has achieved considerable success already. It allows some segments of the population to become rich first, but its goal is prosperity for all. It relies on market forces, but also retains the power of the government to regulate the market (especially the labor market) and to implement macro-planning. It shows great concern for the goal of increasing growth fourfold, but takes into account population pressures, social stability and the welfare of the masses, and is willing to cut back on growth if necessary. Politically, the socialist direction of the market is guided by a powerful state authority; at the same time, this authority must be empowered through democratic processes in order to retain legitimacy and sustainability, and complemented by the rights of labor and other social stratums in establishing their own independent organizations and participating in economic democracy and social negotiation for protecting their own interests. Culturally, individual development and consumerism should be coordinated with goals of social responsibility, social justice, and social integration. Can these goals, which traditionally belong to the market society and socialist society respectively and apparently at odds with each other, be achieved at the same time? This is the most challenging issue in the theory of market socialism.

Theoretical foundations (I): Market logic (or its structural features)

Traditional socialism regards the market as a social form of the spontaneous division of labor. The blind force in the market is the result of alienated labor, which in turn results in the further alienation of human nature. Only by transcending market logic and overcoming the alienation of labor can mankind be emancipated and the free development of the human nature be possible. In fact, the market itself is only a mechanism whereby the division of labor and cooperation may be realized through competitive exchange. As to who gets the profit and how to deal with the winners and losers in the market economy, the answers to these questions are essentially conditioned by other social institutions in which the market is operating.

Traditional liberalism holds that the market is the most efficient form of economic activity, the best mechanism for information processing required by the division of labor for economic cooperation, the best model of social self-organization, and the highest form of economic rationality. But the information entering the market is not symmetrical to all parties involved, whose strengths and positions in the market (especially the relationship between capital and labor) are not symmetrical either. Such an unsymmetrical market relationship makes it possible for exploitation and domination to occur within enterprises and to take shape through contract relations in the labor market, although the roots of exploitation and domination do not lie in market exchange, but rather in the disparity of market relations under certain social and historical conditions.

At the same time, when a pure free market processes incomplete and unsymmetrical information, efficiency will inevitably coexist with distortions (and thus waste). The waste and destruction (creative destruction) caused by competition are themselves a type of distorted expression of the vitality of the market economy. The inevitable result of free competition is the instability of economic life (serious polarization and social turbulences). In particular, a subject involved in market relations faces alienating market forces that he or she cannot control and thus experiences a lack of security.

Whether the market is free is not determined by the market itself, but rather by a society's political and economic arrangements and cultural orientation. In this sense, the market may be regarded as a neutral mechanism that promotes the division of labor and cooperation, and socializes production, labor, capital, and knowledge. Its vigor and its inherent tendency to cause social polarization are both determined by its essential attribute (competition). Whether a society can take full advantage of its vigor and avoid disastrous social polarization depends on the way in which a society regulates the market. One can also see evidence of the limberness of the mechanism of the market itself, or its adaptation to the social, political, and cultural environment, from historical changes of the capitalist market relations, such as the formation of a property rights market; the socialization of capital or its social usage; the transfer of production control from the capitalists to the entrepreneurs and management; and the achievement of workers enjoying a status of being human capital and thus being entitled to a share of the profits. Therefore, at least in principle, the market system and socialism are not incompatible. Their integration may result in a new form of social organization.

Comments

It is necessary to add the following perspectives. First, the self-organization of the market is not the only manifestation of economic rationality. The actual economic experience in both East and West has shown that the market on the one hand, and macro-planning and public administrative management on the other, can complement each other, making the results of rational organization of society and the economy even better.

Second, the market requires only a system of legal protection; it is not inevitably tied to a democratic system. In addition, in general, the political indifference brought on by greed and fear (which accompany market competition), and the radical mood caused by competition and polarization are not favorable to the construction of democracy. The developmental states that promoted the market economy successfully after World War II mainly adopted a "new-authoritarian" political system. Their democratization afterwards was promoted by forces outside the market, especially by the labor and student movements.

Third, the disparity in the market relations caused by the unjust initial conditions led to the breakup of fair market contracts from genuine social justice. This comment also applies to the fair rules of WTO and other international credit organizations. To achieve real social justice in a country, a region, or in the world, we need to go beyond not only market relations, but also the limitations of liberalism. Neo-liberalism, which asserts that the market is the embodiment of rationalism, democracy and justice, is an ideology without theoretical justification.

Theoretical foundations (II): Socialism

Although socialism is not egalitarianism, it cannot tolerate structural inequality. The social democracy that tries to achieve social justice through redistribution is different from real socialism: the historical experience of Western societies showed that it was not intended or able to eliminate structural inequalities.

The concepts of public ownership and planned economy had been thought of as the main characteristics of the socialist economy, but ownership can never determine the nature of a social system. State ownership can exist in a state-capitalist economy; the shareholding system may be regarded as social ownership, although up until now it has basically existed as a form of corporate capitalism. Ostensible public ownership cannot assure economic equality when the actual control in the field of production, and thus the profit distribution, is in the hands of a minority who are separated from workers and a democratically formed social body.

The state makes general arrangements of the national economy through the macro-plans and other measures to regulate the operation of the market. This is a necessary, but not a sufficient condition for a socialist system: social democracy within the liberal framework also has planning and regulations, although a completely planned economy is impossible, even in the Soviet Union.

A powerful state apparatus is decisive in assuring the socialist nature of the market economy. Any society with a legal system in place can establish market order and assure fair competition. But the structural inequality in economic and social life can be totally eliminated, and the socialist nature of the whole system assured only when the state is able to make necessary arrangements in the field of production; to promote economic democracy, so that the goal and direction of production are in accordance with socialist values and goals, and the surplus, or profits, can be distributed fairly according to the contribution of the main factors of production (labor, technology, management, and investment).

However, socialism cannot mirror étatism. Individual freedom, and human and civil rights must be assured, and should not be intervened in by the state. The daily, micro-economic activities should be managed by enterprises and the market, and should not be intervened in directly by the state. The government should vigorously fund the development of social causes such as culture and education, science and technology, medical and health care, and so on, but the actual work should be organized and pushed forward by non-government professional agencies. In politics, the legitimacy of the state authority must be based on the empowerment of democracy, and cannot be manipulated and controlled by the privileged stratums, in order to contain autocracy and corruption. At the same time, the independent civil organizations should have the political right to protect their own interests in a legal way. On the other hand, the leading role of the socialist party is irreplaceable. The Party should not replace the administration, to direct and take care of everything; instead, it should direct government activities, lead public opinion, educate the masses, and confront the ideological hegemony of global neo-liberalism intellectually and theoretically with socialist principles. The party in power, when it is empowered through a democratic process, should assure the socialist direction of the economy, politics, and cultural life.

The most essential characteristics of the socialist culture are: exploring individual and human liberation as the ultimate value of modernity in its most universal and thorough form; judging and evaluating all existing institutions and cultures, making appropriate institutional arrangements, and developing corresponding philosophical, economic, political and cultural theories on the basis of that value. Therefore, socialist culture, as the most thoroughgoing form of critical rationality and the best demonstration of human spiritual creativity up until now, becomes the source of inspiration in conceptual and institutional innovations.

Changing tracks

Crucial to the Chinese model is the transference of the planned economy to the track of the market economy, replacing administrative intervention, and privilege and monopoly with fair and free market competition, and maintaining and improving the socialist nature of the whole social system, so that the alternative modernity that is higher and more thoroughgoing than the liberal modernity may be realized.

The existing market system has been established and developed within the capitalist framework. Therefore, the most difficult theoretical issue we face as we change tracks is how to separate and remove the capitalist form of the market from the market itself, and then to integrate the market into the socialist framework.

The efficiency and vitality of the market system derives to a great extent from the clear property rights of the subjects who participate in market activities. Only clear property rights can assure those factors, such as risk, management, loss and return that lead to efficiency and vitality function well, but what the state and collective enterprises lack in the traditional planned economy is exactly the clarity of property rights. Therefore, instituting clear property rights has become the main content of China's changing tracks. Of course, the change of tracks also allows for the establishment and development of private enterprises in the market system, as well as allowing a certain number of foreign enterprises to enter the domestic market. However, although those aspects are important in economic life, they will not affect the socialist nature of the whole economic system.

The simplest and ready-made method to clarify property rights is privatization. However, with the privatization of the property rights of enterprises, the controlling power, the rights of making claim to surplus (profit) and distributing them, all fall into the hands of a minority, especially when the management holds the majority of stocks. This way, domination and exploitation within an enterprise are inevitable, and the social nature of enterprises (whether socialist or capitalist) grows ambiguous.

However, it is not necessary to privatize in order to make the property rights clear. The modern system of Western enterprises is able to separate management from ownership – why cannot the socialist state or collective enterprises do the same? This separation does not affect the final control of the enterprises that the state, as the representative of the public, or the collective owners hold, but it does enable enterprises to conduct normal market activities. Under normal circumstances, the owners do not exercise their right to final control, as long as they are satisfied with their claims to a certain percentage of surplus, or profits, shared with management, technology, labor, and other main factors of production. But the final control by the state or collectives over enterprises in the Chinese model assures that democratic control and management of production and the reasonable distribution of profits according to the main factors are much easier to put into practice in this case than for private enterprises to do the same.

Another important issue about China's changing tracks is how to control the operation of a market with socialist principles from outside the market. Market competition causes social polarization; bankruptcy and unemployment are inevitable consequences. Capitalist welfare states provide workers with unemployment relief and training for re-employment. In the socialist market economy, on top of these measures, every worker also has the right to a share of the income stemming from the state property rights because of his or her contributions to the generation and accumulation of the social wealth. Moreover, socialist countries should also replace "market competitivity" with "efficiency of the system," establish many labor-intensive enterprises, aiming not at profit or economic growth, but rather the protection of employment; they should also consider reducing working hours and averaging employment, so that the cost of changing tracks will not fall disproportionately on the more vulnerable segments of the population. This way, the overall efficiency of the socialist market economy will be higher than the unstable free market economy, even if the efficiency and competitiveness of some individual enterprises may not be as good as the best ones in the free market. Therefore, at least in theory, the change of tracks does not necessarily mean that we must accept exploitation or tolerate social polarization.

Nationalism

Although the Chinese model has clear traces of its particular history, culture, and tradition, what it represents is not nationalism in a cultural sense.

The age of globalization is marked by great expansion of transnational capital, with global powers controlling the rights to making and interpreting the rules of the game in international economic life. Under such circumstances, if China as a developing country lacks national consciousness and blindly connects its track to the West, it will inevitably be partitioned by others at will and will not be able to free itself. But if China refuses to take part in globalization and isolates itself, as a giant country, it may be able to maintain its independence and self-reliance, but it would not find itself in a favorable position for technological and economic modernization. The Chinese model differs from the above alternatives. According to this model, China should participate actively in globalization with a clear sense of national identity; it should interact with transnational capital with a goal of developing domestic economy based on domestic enterprises and backed by a powerful government, which implements appropriate industrial policy and development strategy; it should try to use its funding, equipment and market channels, and learn from it in the fields of science, technology and management, in order to upgrade China's industries and modernize its own technology and economy.

The reason why the Chinese path to modernity that fully engages globalization carries a nationalist tinge is in part responsive. The reason why transnational capital demands that China opens its door is to have access to China's huge market and to exploit its cheap labor, not to develop China's economy and add a powerful competitor. Therefore, the long-term strategic goal of transnational capital, led by the United States, is to contain China's development economically, politically, militarily, and diplomatically, and prevent it from becoming a world power. This strategy will manifest itself unavoidably in various aspects of Sino–Western relations, although sometimes it is obscured by the complexity of the situation. Facing the ostensible offers of friendship that try to conceal actual hostility, the rise of a national consciousness and the emergence of nationalism in China's path to modernity is inevitable. However, nationalism in this sense has no necessary connection with the alternative modernity that China tries to achieve; it is merely a reprint in China of the nationalism that appeared in Western history and has no substantive difference to the nationalism of the developmental states in East Asia and Latin America. The goals of those states are the same as those of the West, although their practice may differ.

However, the nationalism of the Chinese model does have one aspect that is voluntary and closely related with alternative modernity. The highest achievement of Western modernity is accomplished in the United States. Is it good to turn China into the United States? The liberals think that it would be too wonderful to be achievable. Although the United States has its own problems, they believe that it is better to first follow its steps. However, Sun Zhongshan, Mao Zedong, and Deng Xiaoping disagreed and pursued an alternative form of modernity. The Chinese seek a world in harmony and human emancipation, which are far more thorough and universal values than those pursued by the United States. For this reason, every measure that China takes to embody this alternative modernity will inevitably be faulted and pressured by the capitalist world. The emergence of the confrontation between nationalism and cosmopolitanism (or the "mainstream" of civilization) is actually the confrontation between two types of modernity, and it is also the first step for the alternative modernity to spread worldwide and to become a universal principle. The impact on China of the global confrontations and conflicts results in the struggle between the leftist nationalism that adheres to socialism and liberal cosmopolitanism.

Distinctive features of the Chinese model

The Chinese model is essentially different from social democracy and traditional socialism, although they overlap in some aspects. It differs from social democracy in its pursuit of an alternative modernity, which transcends the logic of capital expansion inherent in the latter's ideology, with its final goal being a thoroughly humanist one: it aspires to implement the principles of equality and fairness in the core of social and economic life, i.e., the democratic control of assets (and thus production) and fair distribution of surplus, in order to assure, in terms of resources, the free development of each and every individual. It differs from traditional socialism mainly in its use of the market system in the economy; politically, in its commitment to democratization, to a new mode of Party's leadership, and to the establishment of a civil society. It adopts the positive achievements of human and civil rights and democracy from liberalism, and breaks the statist tradition of replacing administration with the Party and with a system of patriarchy.

3 Practice

The practice of the Chinese model (reform) started in the late 1970s with the ideological liberation movement and the re-evaluation of the Mao Zedong era. The liberals tried to use ideological liberation to completely reject Mao, but they failed. The efforts made by the traditional leftists to defend Mao also failed. In fact, the struggle over this major issue involved what should be taken to be the guiding thought for reform, and this was itself part of China's path to modernity. So what are the legacies of Mao Zedong?

The legacies of Mao Zedong

The thought and practice of Mao Zedong were the product of special historical conditions: the final victory of the revolution after long-term domestic military struggles; a concern about being surrounded by hostile external forces after the victory of the revolution; and an anxious desire nationwide to become rich and strong in order to catch up with and surpass the advanced nations. It combined the historical traditions of the nation and communist revolutionary tradition with the basic doctrines of Marxism and the rigid dogmas of the Soviets. The era spanned the brilliant successes in the area of nuclear bombs, missiles, and satellite technology, along with miserable failures of the Great Leap Forward and the Cultural

Revolution. Its heritage includes insightful but undeveloped ideas such as the idea of "letting a hundred flowers blossom and a hundred schools of thought contend," and that of struggling against bureaucracy and privilege; along with lost opportunities to build a new democratic society, to oppose individual cults, and to develop a democratic legal system following the Twentieth Conference of the Soviet Communist Party. They are complicated and intertwined, and hard to summarize, but in general, Mao's thoughts and practice had three major components: developmentalism, nationalism, and socialism.

Mao Zedong's concerns of developing heavy industries first, launching the Great Leap Forward campaign, putting forward a goal of a high level of accumulation, implementing the policies that concentrated on the production of grain and steel, and implementing the mass line in the course of economic development. He exemplified the characteristic anxiety of a backward nation that is eager to catch up and surpass the advanced countries, and finished with a very rough form of developmentalism. Mao's rough form was derided and rejected, but his developmentalism has been carried over into reform in various forms.

In his opposition to the two superpowers, Mao Zedong never retreated and never surrendered. He had the courage to struggle and achieve victories. Surrounded by hostile external forces, Mao led the Chinese people towards self-reliance and encouraged them to do all they could to make the country strong. Despite the serious setbacks from the Great Leap Forward and the Cultural Revolution, China achieved amazing accomplishments in the fields of industry, agriculture, science and technology, national defense, and education and health care in under thirty years, and laid solid material and human foundations for further development. People usually connect Mao's nationalism with isolationist and closed-door policies, but the alliance with the Soviet Union in the 1950s and the normalization of relations with the United States, Japan, and Europe at the beginning of the 1970s were Mao's decisions. The "isolationist" and "closed-door" policies were imposed for a period of time by the outside enemies, and were also necessary to protect revolutionary achievements and national dignity. Meanwhile, economic, political, and diplomatic relations with the Third World countries were much closer than they are at the present time. In general, Mao's nationalist heritage has not met with any serious challenges in China's reform.

The most controversial aspect of Mao's heritage is his conception of socialism. The power of the Chinese Communist Party was not imposed by outsiders but is the result of a lengthy armed revolution of the Chinese peasants. The agricultural socialist ideal of modest prosperity, universal harmony, and egalitarianism that the peasants pursued imbued the ideals of the Party's cadres at all levels. But at the same time, the power of the leadership of the Chinese revolution was tightly controlled by the Communist Party which was in turn guided by Leninism as interpreted by Stalin, along with various doctrines of the Third International. Mao's model of socialism included aspects of egalitarian and agricultural socialism, together with some aspects of Stalinism that were not thoroughly criticized. In the fields of ideology and politics, Mao was extremely rigid and dogmatic, trying to control the direction of social development by ceaselessly launching political campaigns, His stances in fact betrayed an anxiety for survival and victory that is characteristic of "one-country socialism" and obviously exaggerated the risks of the hostile environment at home and abroad.

In the fields of politics and the economy, the difference between Mao Zedong and Stalin lay in Mao's mass line and his opposition to bureaucratic authority; this included positive factors such as democratic participation, and negative factors such as the neglect of legal systems and rejection of plans. Although ultimately the mass campaigns were only the special means he used to do politics, the mass line, the four "big freedoms" (big criticism, big opening, big character poster, and big debate), and the idea that "revolts are justifiable" had indeed broadened the arena of political activities, and provided a certain legitimate basis for democratic participation, and thus had become a special kind of political heritage.

Mao's model of socialism, as an expression of revolutionary modernity pursued by a backward country, boasts the following main achievements: although the government was not established by election, it was not corrupt; although there was no procedural democracy, masses of workers and peasants could enjoy substantial democracy to some extent; it was committed somewhat to meeting the basic needs of the majority and controlling polarization; it also achieved great accomplishments in organizing economic, social, and cultural life. The main weaknesses of the model were that it seriously limited individual freedom and lacked a constitutional democracy and legal systems; and that in the command economy based on the will of government officials, there was no vitality of the market economy, nor the order and balance of the Soviet type of planned economy, and resources were hugely wasted due to a series of disastrous mistakes. Although money worship was rare, power worship was rampant.

The guiding ideology of Deng Xiaoping

The ideological liberation movement was a serious struggle, but Deng Xiaoping controlled the situation quickly. He opposed the liberals' complete rejection of Mao's legacies, but also pushed aside the resistance by Mao's loyalists to his profound and far-reaching revisions of Mao's political line (not including the Party's structure and the political system) and economic policies (especially agricultural policies). He integrated the ideological liberation movement into the process of the reform that he defined as socialist self-perfection.

The guiding ideology of the reform of Deng Xiaoping springs from three sources. First, he represented the cadres and intellectuals who were hurt during the Cultural Revolution, and determined to eliminate any possibility of ever experiencing the Cultural Revolution again. To this end, he proposed the "four cardinal principles" (persistence in following the guidance of Marxism–Leninism–Mao Zedong thought, the leadership of the communist party, the socialist path, and the proletarian dictatorship), abandoned Mao's "four big freedoms" and big democracy, promoted the legal system, and criticized mass campaigns of Mao's style. To some extent he inherited the Chinese étatist political tradition along with the cultural tradition of state worship in the past thousands of years.

Second, history has demonstrated that the imperial authority gained legitimacy in the eyes of the peasants when their demand for egalitarianism was seen to be met in the authority's limiting the annexation of land by the despotic gentry. Similarly, Deng Xiaoping's call to "rule by laws" gained support because it was associated with another slogan "prosper together." Although Deng encouraged some people to prosper before others, the egalitarian appeal of a long history has continuously conditioned the practice of reform, and theoretically becomes the core of his conception of socialism.

Third, in order to completely reject the theoretical foundation of the Cultural Revolution, namely that "class struggle is central," and to give concrete content to the goal of the reform, Deng redefined the goals of socialism as "developing productive forces, eliminating exploitation, and achieving prosperity together," and thereby had successfully shifted the Party's focus of engagement.

In the beginning the development of productive forces was expressed only in developmental slogans such as "the Four Modernizations" and "quadruple production," but soon the focus had moved to the key issue of how to improve economic efficiency. There were several ways he could choose to replace Mao's economic model: return to the Soviet model and improve the planned system, imitate and practice the Yugoslavian model of workers' self-governing, or follow the line of reforms in Eastern Europe and introduce the market elements. The contract system of responsibility that separates the right of operation from ownership and integrates the operations of the collective and individual peasant households in rural reform provided Deng with further inspiration. The economic reform in the 1980s was actually a process of groping for and moving towards the market system until Deng made his "journey to the south speeches" in 1992 and the Party's Fourteenth Congress. From then on, the development of the socialist market economy has become the core in the theory and practice of the Chinese model.

The global expansion of transnational capital and the ideological pressures from neo-liberalism

We need to emphasize that China's reform has proceeded under heavy pressure from the global expansion of transnational capital and from the ideological fashion of neo-liberalism at home and abroad. At the start of China's reform, neo-liberalism began to prevail in Britain and the United States. This new ideological fashion identifies the market economy that is free of government regulation and allows the free movement of transnational capital with efficiency, growth and welfare, with the mainstream in the development of human civilization. Since the dramatic changes in the Soviet Union and Eastern Europe, the great advances in information technology, and the rapid expansion of financial capital at the beginning of the 1990s, this ideological fashion has spread throughout the world and has had a major impact on the orientation of economic policies in many countries. China's reform conducted under an open-door policy naturally is not an exception. When China joined the WTO, the impact of this ideological trend on China's reform entered a new stage.

Resistance and driving forces

The different attitudes towards reform inside and outside the Party are based both on actual interests and ideological concerns. There is no clear logical connection between one's attitudes towards economic and political reform. In political reform, aside from building a legal system, there is inertia within the Party so far as promoting constitutional democracy is concerned.

The leftists, who hold the traditional views about the planned economy, the state's functions, and the market logic in particular, naturally oppose or have doubts about the market-oriented reforms. Those who had enjoyed privileges in the planned system may instinctively resist the reform. When the employees of the state-owned enterprises, who enjoyed job security before the reform, find their vested interests threatened, their incomes relatively decreasing, or their jobs being eliminated without proper compensation, or could not find employment, would naturally turn to a traditional conception of socialism and challenge the direction of the reform and its legitimacy. These forces are mutually supportive, and have rigorously conditioned the practice of reform. Once the economic situation turns severe without being handled well, these forces, from the top to the bottom, might even join together to threaten political stability. After all, the heritage of Mao Zedong and the specter of the Cultural Revolution have not disappeared in the collective memory of people in and outside the Party, and can be opportunistically mobilized.

As far as the driving forces are concerned, the reinterpretation of the market and socialism is a necessary support to the reform. At the same time, the actual effects of reform, including the increase in the standard of living, have laid a broad foundation for support from the masses. Some functionaries in bureaucratic apparatus, under the circumstances of lacking strict regulations and supervision, take full advantage of opportunities the "change of tracks" has brought to them to seek rents or even to directly appropriate public assets. Thus, centered around these functionaries, there formed, by way of corruption, a quick-rich stratum that is characteristic of the changing tracks period. This stratum has both political and economic strengths. It is mixed with the reform faction, but also maintains close connections with transnational capital. It is a fertile ground for the seeds of comprador-dependent capitalism in China. The neo-liberal dogmas become their tools to turn the change of tracks towards crony privatization.

In general, reform forces prevail in practice. But the ideological orientation of neo-liberalism and the actual interests emerging through crony privatization have turned some of the practice away from the original theoretical principles.

The main records

Politically, the establishment of the legal system is progressing most rapidly; the actual power of the People's Congress increases; the grass-roots election is promoted; and the concept of human and civil rights has spread gradually. Individual freedom has improved and the limitations on social activities have lessened. But reform towards constitutional democracy has not yet been put on the agenda. Without further theoretical breakthroughs and thereby forming a consensus that would prevail in the Party, it seems unlikely to achieve anything soon.

Economic reform started in rural areas. The disbandment of the communes, the contract system of responsibility linked to production, and the institution of two-level management have caused agricultural production to develop rapidly and has improved peasants' lives. This reform has achieved some breakthroughs in the theory of property rights, and is an inspiration for the basic model of the socialist market economy. But in practice, the reform is not that different from the imperial policy of distributing land equally to farmers and the policies of compromise throughout history that have met the farmers' demand to divide the land evenly. Of course, because of the persistence of public ownership of the land and no possibility of buying and selling it, the social consequences of land annexation and monopoly are avoided, while rural households are assured the right to use land. This practice has great social and political importance because of China's large rural population and its dependency on land as the ultimate safety net. However, a series of mistakes were made around the issues of peasants moving to the cities (management of the household registration system), agriculture investment, grain prices and tax, and policies that resulted in major setbacks in public education and health care have made those problems in agriculture, in rural areas and about peasants increasingly serious since the beginning of the 1990s. Some of the great accomplishments achieved at the beginning of the reform, and even earlier, during the Chinese Revolution, have been lost.

The reform in the cities that aimed to stimulate the vitality of enterprises and to establish a normalized market system has achieved much. In addition, the degree of opening up to the world is quite impressive: the rapid development of foreign trade and the huge size of foreign investments (with the introduction of capital, technology, management, and accompanying job opportunities) have greatly promoted the rapid development of China's economy, and attracted worldwide attention. But a serious problem has arisen with measures introduced at the early stages of the reform, which allowed enterprises to draw up production contracts and more rights and profits, and enabled a dual-track price system. The original goal of those measures was to promote the vitality of enterprises, and some results were positive. But one result that cannot be ignored is that in some regions and sectors the state capital differentiated into the monopoly capital in various departments. The inequality in resource appropriation in the planned system was thus turned into inequality of incomes, providing the corrupt officials with rent-seeking opportunities. This was not only morally unfair, but also pro-voked political protests. In terms of economic rationality, these corrupt acts also made fair competition impossible in the market. The root of the problem may be identified as the administrative privileges that have been attached to the old planned system.

In the in-depth reform of the economic system, the way to handle those admin-istrative privileges has raised an even more serious challenge. Here, the so-called in-depth reform of the system refers to the reform of state enterprises, aiming at clarifying property rights. Theoretically, the issues of the vitality of state enterprises and social justice may be jointly settled through the separation of the management of enterprises from the (state-owned) property rights, and the sharing of profits by the state and various sectors (labor, technology, and management) in the state enterprises. But in practice, due to the vested interests of officials and the ideological pressures of neo-liberalism, the reform has degenerated into a wave of crony privatization which has resulted in losses of state assets, causing many workers to lose their jobs in the process of system-changing, annexation of property, bankruptcy, and reorganization. This form of privatization, because the initial arrangement of property rights was extremely unfair in enterprises' system-changing (e.g., allowing the management sector to hold the majority of shares with bank loans and to own the hugely devalued assets of the state enterprises, while common workers were forced to take extremely low severance pay and to give up their jobs), is nothing other than direct plunder of public assets by the people in power, and has thus posed the most serious challenge to the socialist nature of the reform.

The main problem in cultivating the market system is not technical, such as how to regulate the capital market, although these problems are difficult and complicated to handle. The biggest problem is the labor market and its extremely unsymmetrical relationship between powerful capital (especially foreign capital) and vulnerable labor (especially migrant laborers from rural areas). The state should have regulated the labor market and supported employees' efforts, according to socialist principles, to organize unions to protect their own interests by ensuring a minimum wage, maximum work hours, labor protection, participation in management, and profit sharing. But many local governments simply allow the capitalists to exploit workers. They even tolerate the sweat-shop factories (including some foreign enterprises) to exploit workers through extra-economic means.

Many strategies for development have achieved remarkable results. These include those for the development of coastal areas and Special Economic Zones, as well as export-oriented strategies, taking comparative advantage to participate in the international division of labor, and joining the WTO. The state has paid enough attention to acquiring advanced foreign technology, supporting research and development, upgrading the industrial structure, and developing a knowledge-based economy. Naturally, export-orientated strategies will exacerbate regional imbalance, but this problem can be remedied by developing the inland areas (the northwest area). Upgrading the industrial structure will aggravate unemployment, but China is large enough to properly address this issue by increasing its internal demand and developing its domestic market.

In recent years, efforts to increase internal demand and develop the domestic market have not been successful. Is the goal of development growth, or full employment? The latter is an essential condition for the increase of internal demand. These different goals determine different industrial policies and different directions in investments. Capitalism typically focuses on growth (capital expansion) and does not seek full employment. In fact it requires a certain amount of unemployment as industrial reserves to force employed workers to give in. Socialism is different. The aim of prosperity for all (as a prerequisite for the universal development of individuality) dictates that full employment is a basic goal of economic development, even if it requires sacrificing the growth rate. The main reason to reject privatization of the state enterprises as an economic solution is that this would deprive the state of the power to decide industrial policies and control the direction of investments.

How to evaluate reform since the Fourteenth Party Congress

The historical contribution of the Fourteenth Party Congress of 1992 was to incorporate the market economy into the socialist ideological system and thus to legitimize it. Subsequently, the development of the Chinese economy has attracted worldwide attention. Many people at home and abroad believe that this development is in fact the restoration of capitalism, governed by the ideology of neo-liberalism. The rightists have applauded it (although they continue to demand political reform to move towards a multi-party system); the leftists have attacked it. But what is the reality?

In history, it was capitalism that promoted the development of the market economy to its peak. Because some of the social, political, and cultural conditions conducive to the capitalist characteristics of the market remain in China, the market economy that has greatly developed in China since the 1990s inevitably has strong capitalist tendencies. First, the original social economic systems of China include aspects of the Soviet systems and those of Mao; to some extent they tend towards state capitalism. Because the democratic rights of workers had no institutional protection at that time and during the period of reform, it was impossible for them to effectively supervise the people in power. Thus a new property class may be created through crony privatization. Second, the slogan "Development is the first priority" may prevail over the goal of "Prosperity for all," and more attention may be paid to growth and the market's competitive capacity than to the overall efficiency of the system and people's welfare. These ideas are somewhat manifested in government's industry policy and wage policy, which have deviated from socialist ideals and betrayed capitalist inclinations. The reality is that some people do prosper, but "common prosperity" becomes an empty phrase. In addition, transnational capital has penetrated the Chinese economy through globalization and has had a comprehensive and profound impact – in terms of ideas of operation and modes of management that are conducive to the capitalist characteristics of the market – on the development of China's market. Third, as commercial advertisements and mass media have entered daily life, culturally, consumerism and money worship have also corrupted the socialist faith and values. When most people have lost their socialist faith and are pursuing material self-interest, the operation of the market cannot but have a capitalist nature.

However, by changing the external environment it is possible to render the market a place for equal and fair competition. For example, crony privatization can be cut off by democratization, lopsided developmental goals conducive to capitalism can be limited by the final goal of socialism, and the socialist cultural setting for enterprises and spiritual civilization can be mobilized to confront the trend of setting profit-making and consumerism as first priorities, and thus to assure the socialist direction of the market economy on the micro-economic level (operation of enterprises and individual motivation). It is difficult, but not impossible, to achieve all these goals. Reform is still in progress and people are still making efforts. It is not yet time to draw any final conclusions.

The outlook

Whether the practice of the Chinese model can eventually realize an alternative modernity, and not take on some version of liberal modernity, does not completely depend on its past history. Although social development frequently shows path-dependency (historically conditioned), it is not fatalistic: at every turning point, it is also path-breaking. The expectations emerging from the present situation form the foundation for conceiving the future. Without this kind of conception, no future would be created. At the same time, it is the perspective of the present situation that makes it possible for us to re-evaluate our historical heritage and its implications for the future. So, what is the current situation?

The most remarkable feature of the current situation is the rapid development of the economy. But potentially, a crisis could emerge at some point which would render the situation apparently unstable and insecure. The rapid pace of development is due mainly to market forces and proper macro-control, to the ideal environment for investments that has attracted many foreign investors, and thus created new jobs and opened up new international channels of operation and sale. However, at present the market is neither normal nor fair: there is a monopoly system left over from the planned economy, which causes unfair competition; there are unfair market conditions that vulnerable laborers cannot but accept. The most important issue facing China is whether effective policies of macro-controls, after having joined the WTO, can endure the pressures from the neo-liberal ideology that is supported by the transnational capital. The ideal environment for investment (a stable political situation, cheap labor, low costs of resources and environment protection measures, and the absence of trade unions) sacrifices the environmental and labor interests, and depletes limited natural resources. The plunder of the resources and environment will make the development unsustainable; sooner or later the exploitation of the sweat-shop factories will cause opposition. All these issues are the deep roots of a potential crisis.

The second feature of the current situation is that the political conditions are relatively stable; the political environment is opening up and relaxing; democracy as the core value of political culture has been reinterpreted and acknowledged. But at the same time, the price of stability involves the suppression of democracy and the concealment of social contradictions. The reform is a huge adjustment of social interests. The contradictions and conflicts it has caused will make stability unsustainable if they cannot be fairly solved through democratic channels.

If, after more than twenty years of reform, the characteristics of traditional socialism gradually fade away, and nationalism and developmentalism are overwhelmed by globalization, then the distinction between the special type of socialist developmental states, originally required by the Chinese model, and the existing type of developmental states, will be increasingly obscured.

Facing up to the current situation should not shake our determination in reform. But we also have to re-evaluate the gains and losses, figure out our direction, and solve some major problems.

First, we should safeguard the socialist achievements that revolution and reform have accomplished, including, politically, independence and sovereignty; economically, public assets; and in terms of social development, the accumulation of human capital, and so on.

Second, we should re-examine and give play to the special advantage of backwardness the Chinese revolution enjoys and the comparative advantages in China's development, and pay special attention to socialist ideas. As a rational weapon for critiquing the current situation, the socialist ideology is the source for intellectual and institutional innovations.

More important is political reform, including the construction of socialist democracy and reform within of the Communist Party itself. Although this issue is sensitive, we should not shy away from it, because without thinking about the future, we cannot achieve anything desirable.

What is democracy? We should not simply identify it with the multi-party system, nor can we assume that it is fully covered by certain working styles, such as "connecting with the masses" or being "multi-voiced." The concept of democracy is as complex as the concept of property rights. It has many components. We can and should break it down into these components and gradually build the democracy according to the time and situation.

Democracy is essentially an egalitarian model of power distribution. Its realization requires certain conditions. The biggest failure of Western liberal democracy is that the procedural democracy that was legally fairly designed has no meaning for people whose economic status cannot allow them to exercise their legal rights.

Therefore, the first and most important step in building a socialist democracy is to implement economic democracy. Workers should not only have their voices heard on issues concerning the organization of production in the workplace, but also, as a whole, they should have the right to participate in the management, decision-making, and profit distribution of the enterprises, and to receive a due share of the profits, which implies the elimination of exploitation.[1] The practice of economic democracy requires the support of the state, but does not require changing the whole current political system. Therefore, it is feasible in principle.

Parallel to this is democratic supervision. This issue is particularly urgent right now. The institutional corruptions can hardly be contained by policies and decrees. Only through broad supervision by public opinion and authoritative supervision by the masses can transparency and fairness in the change of track be assured. Constructing a system of democratic supervision should in principle be easier than the practice of economic democracy.

The core of building a socialist democracy is to institute constitutional democracy. Constitutional democracy may be divided into several components. One is the legal protection of various rights of freedom such as human and civil rights. The independent and autonomous associations and organizations are also very important. Various social strata and interest groups need to form a consensus, through consultation and negotiation, to protect their own rights and to enable the reform to move forward in a relatively smooth way.

The two points above refer only to the constitutional freedom (or rights) that people should enjoy, and do not touch on the ultimate source and distribution of political power. The core and theoretical foundation of socialist constitutional democracy can only be the sovereignty of the people. Theoretically the sovereignty of the people can take various forms: election, recommendation, consultation; one-party, multi-parties, or no party. Which model is most suitable to the Chinese situation remains to be explored. However, one thing is clear: any efforts to build the socialist constitutional democracy should be based on the reform of the Communist Party itself. The socialist constitutional democracy will not be realized if the old models of Stalin and Mao Zedong remain; that is, if there is only one voice and no democratic process within the Party; the administration is directly controlled by the Party, and there is no legal system in society at large. But it would not be helpful in building socialist constitutional democracy if the Party is to be transformed into one member in a multi-party system, according to the liberal principles and taking social democracy as a model. The reasons are simple. The multi-party system will only pave the way for economically powerful, privileged strata and interest groups to control political power if it is put in place before economic and social foundations of socialist democracy are laid down. The obvious illustration of this is the evolution of Russian politics after the disintegration of the Soviet Union.

The status and roles of the Communist Party in the constitutional democracy need to be clearly expounded in the new socialist political culture. Since an alternative modernity cannot be realized without a powerful socialist state, steering the direction and laying down the guiding principles of governing for such a state are the Party's first priorities. In addition, as the party in power, the members and organizations of the Party must serve society and the people, so that they can play the leading and pioneering roles in building democracy. The Leninist party structure is justifiable during wartime. But the structure needs to be reformed because it is not favorable to the free development of Party members' individuality and of the democratic spirit within the Party and in the society at large. Many Party members died heroic deaths, one after another, in the struggles of the long period of time after the establishment of the Chinese Communist Party. Their heroism and idealism were undeniable, relations between the Party and masses were in harmony, and a broad foundation of support existed. Such a party with such ideals should be able to transform itself in order to adapt to the new historical tasks in the new historical conditions, under the efforts of the new leadership following the Sixteenth Party Congress.

Political reform is the necessary guarantee of the decisive success of economic reform. But economic reform itself has its own difficulties. The greatest difficulty is how to handle the structural dependency of the market economy on capital investments and entrepreneurship spirit. Without capital investment and entrepreneurship spirit, the vitality and efficiency of the market system cannot be realized. In all versions of market economy up until now, the functions of capital investment and entrepreneurship are handled by capitalists and entrepreneurs. New ideas need to be developed for handling the two functions in order to establish a socialist market economy.

One of the proposals for economic democracy is that the capital of the state enterprises, as the main body of the socialist market economy, remains to be controlled by the state, not to be privatized (it will not conflict with the ongoing development of private and foreign enterprises). However, this type of state capital is not able to collect necessary investments for projects such as research and development for the new advanced and high-tech industries and new trades for the creation of employment, because the profits of enterprises must be distributed fairly among the main factors of production. If the funding comes mainly from private investments, the socialist nature of the whole economy will lose its material foundation. Here, it is worth exploring if the huge social pension fund under democratic control, in addition to the state taxes, may be used to avoid dependency on private investments.

The entrepreneurs who have enterprising spirit, ability to act, and actual control of the use of capital are very important for maintaining the dynamics and vitality of economy under the circumstance that the operation and ownership of capital are separated. Their activities should be encouraged and rewarded properly. But if an unreasonable incentive system allows them to take most of the profits, they will form a new exploiting class that is different from the traditional capitalists. They not only grab the profit that belongs to the state capital, they also control and exploit various other strata (workers, management, and technicians) that perform other functions in enterprises. Once that happens, even though the capital of an enterprise remains publicly owned, the enterprise is capitalist in its real nature.

This problem may be solved from two directions. Institutionally, the distribution of profit in an enterprise must be reasonably decided through democratic consultation among the members of various departments (labor, technology, operation and management, development and entrepreneurial decision-making) in the enterprise, and cannot be decided by what the entrepreneurs might say. In terms of guiding principles, entrepreneurs' contributions should be encouraged mainly by honoring them socially, treating extra-salary rewards only as supplementary incentives, which should not be too far away from the average level of incentives enjoyed by most members of the same enterprise. Otherwise, we would only encourage greed, the seizing of profits which others deserve, fraud, fraudulent accounting (as in various company scandals in the United States), and ultimately harm the operation of enterprises. The problem can be solved if the Party members dare to become socialist entrepreneurs, or if the Party encourages entrepreneurs to become Party members and strive for the development of the socialist market economy. The solution also requires a certain social ethos that is the result of education, literature and arts, and public opinion and media. It will be hard even for the entrepreneurs who are Party members to be persistent in the socialist ideal in such a materialistic and consumerist atmosphere.

The final issue concerns China's position in global integration. Although some groups of people worship the United States and incline towards cosmopolitanism, identification with the Chinese nation and patriotism remain a mainstream consensus. To be sure, in the development of the national economy and protection of the national interests, many strategic and tactical issues remain to be explored and clarified. But it is worth emphasizing that the nationalist component of the Chinese model is different from other forms of nationalism due to its pursuit of an alternative, socialist modernity. Facing the tight encirclement of global capitalist forces, firm nationalist and socialist stands are mutually supportive. In this sense, the Chinese position may be regarded as the first sign that an alternative modernity is entering the world. It takes the future universal development of its own as its immanent horizon. It will not content itself with effectively applying instrumental rationality (for example, science and democracy) but is actively promoting conceptual and institutional innovations under the guidance of critical rationality. Therefore, the nationalism of the Chinese model goes far beyond the anti-imperialist and anti-feudalist forms of nationalism with their slogan of science and democracy in the May Fourth Movement.

The development of critical rationality requires universal education that enables everyone to acquire the capacity to reason and criticize independently; it also requires the social conditions of free debate and communication so that the rational capacity may be practiced and developed. In the long run, the formation and completion of the two conditions have practical consequences that are important not only for economic development (a knowledge-based economy) and the improvement of human quality (ability to innovate), but also conform to the ultimate goal of socialist and communist values.

Note

1   The "Constitution" of the Anshan Steel and Iron Corporation, written in Mao's era, in which workers' participation in management was proposed, has been despised because, some assert, it was nothing but empty words. Procedural democracy has not changed the monopoly of political power by the rich in the United States, and is thus meaningless to the poor, which explains why only a small fraction of the population care to vote. However, this does not mean that procedural democracy is not a good ideal. The same reasoning applies to "workers' participation" and other ideas, policies, and guiding lines that did not fulfill their promises in Mao's era. Of course we should go beyond Mao and continue to move forward. For example, the Constitution of the Anshan Steel and Iron Corporation does not mention that the workers have rights to share the profits of the enterprise; it thus separated workers' income from their contributions to the enterprise and the performance of the enterprise itself. This way, workers were forced to contribute their share of the profits to national savings, although only in a disguised way, without having the right to participate in decision-making about and control over those profits. As mentioned above, this problem may be solved through economic democracy.

Index

agriculture 12–13, 19, 30–2, 57–8
Allen, Franklin 180
Amin, Samir x, 20, 123, 147, 210, 215, 259, 290
Amsden, A.H. 248
Anderson, Perry x, 20, 187
Anti-Rightist Campaign 13–14
Asian Financial Crisis 248
Asian-pacific Conference of China (1996) 25–6

Bagchi, Amiya Kumar 279, 289
Balassa, Bela 265
Blackburn, Robin x, 215
Braudel, Fernand 162–3

Calabrese, Michael 185
California Public Employees Retirement Systems (Capers) 185
Cao, Tian Yu x, xii, 16, 18, 156, 259
Campos, J.E. 249
capital 54, 58–9, 160
capitalism 2, 131, 311; actually existing 18, 20; anti-market 162–3; clean-path 18; crony 20; definitions of 201–2; entrepreneurial 203–6; grey 180; Marxian insights 190–1; paths through 117–18; and socialism 12, 115–16, 202–3; and stock markets 205–6; three functions 200–1
Chinese Communist Party (CCP) 11, 14, 23, 24, 28, 46, 56, 96, 100, 152, 227, 230, 232, 314
Chinese Economics Association 34
Chinese miracle, advantage without restrictions 98; compared with Eastern Europe 98–9; end of unfairness/inefficiency 97–8, 100; and July 1st Speech (2001) 99, 100; two stages of 97–100

Chinese model 297–8; changing tracks 302–3; distinctive features of 305; evaluation of reform since Fourteenth Party Congress 312–13; and global expansion of transnational capital 308; goals of 299; guiding ideology of Deng Xiaoping 307–8; and ideological pressures from neo-liberalism 308; legacies of Mao Zedong 305–7; main records 309–12; market logic 299–301; nationalism 303–5; outlook for 313–17; in practice 305–17; resistance/driving forces 309; socialism 301–2; theory 298–305; and transference of planned to market economy 302; universality/institutional arrangements 298–9, *see also* market socialism
Ch'u, Wan-wen x, 259, 262
Chubais, Anatoly 163–4
Clark, J. Maurice 169
class struggle 26–7, 266
Cold War 63, 80–1, 179, 223, 267
Communist Youth League 229
comparative advantage, actualization of 268; and cheap labour 264–5, 266–71; and class struggle 266; and collective bargaining 266; concept of 264; cultural tradition 273; definitions/terminology 266; and economic reform 271; endogenous/exogenous factors 269; human capital 267, 269, 273; and international division of labor 275; national independence/security 272; and open policy 270; potentially vast domestic market 273; and privilege of historical backwardness 275; public control over national economy 273; and public finance 275; re-evaluation of position 274; and welfare institutions 274

Cui, Zhiyuan 272
Cultural Revolution 24–5, 50–1, 71, 81, 82, 227, 305–6, 307

Dai, Yi 42
democracy 100, 227–8, 312–14; and citizen participation 13; and issue of fairness 110–14; Maoist view 13–14; and political reconciliation 121; and political reform 13–15; procedural/ economic 4; and process of changing tracks 118–23; US path vs Prussian path 114–18, 122; and values, rights, obligations 14; Western models 5
Deng, Liqun 43, 49
Deng, Xiaoping 11, 19, 23, 25, 35, 37, 38–9, 48–52, 76, 88, 98, 113, 125, 153, 226, 237, 293, 297–8, 304, 307–8
Diamond, Peter 175
Dittgen, Herbert 222
Du, Runsheng x, 19, 58, 105, 123, 124

economic democracy, challenges to 198–200; and foreign capital 208–9; and free trade 209–10; model of 192–4; problems facing 206–8; reforms leading to 196–8; and social control of investment 194–6; transition to 210–13; and workplace democracy 194
economy, absorbing/withdrawing cash 106–10; anti-marketization movement 119–20; assembly line of primitive accumulation 106–10; capitalism/ socialism debate 115–16; and Chinese miracle 97–100; and collectivization 123–5; compared with Eastern Europe 98–9, 107–8, 114, 119, 121; and credit loss 108; and debt crisis 109; fairness vs radical change 110–14; and living off interest 111; and mourning the old days 113; and peasant demonstrations 112–14; and private enterprise 89, 90, 96, 99–100, 109–10; and privatization 112, 120–1, 122–3; and property rights 89–97, 107, 120; prospects of post-commune age 114–18; public/ private assets 108–9; and social transformation 101–5; and stock market 106–8, 111; Stolypin's Reform 111, 115–16, 117, 118, 120, 121–2, 123; Vichegrad path 121
Election Law of the National and Local People's Congress of the People's Republic of China 231

Feenstra, Robert 265
Fei, Xiaotong (also Fei Hsiao Tung) 167–70, 167–72
Financial Investment and Loan Program (FILIP) 176
flexible specialization 169–70
Friedman, David 168

General Agreement on Trade and Tariffs (GATT) 238, 240, 241, 256
General Policy in Transitional Time (1953) 24–5
Gerschenkron, A. 246
Gesell, Silvio 165–6
globalization 2, 76, 312; and capital flow 256; challenges of 221–2; changes in trend of 242–4; and Chinese reform/open-up policies 226–8; and citizenship 222; and communication 153; and de-stratification 222; definitions of 153, 219; and dependency theory 239; and direct foreign investment (FDI) 243; and domestic politics 225–6; economic factors/theories 220, 245–7; future prospects 244–5; and governance 223–4, 225; historical perspective 152–3; impact of 219, 222, 225–6, 238; and insecurity of international commodity markets/foreign exchange markets 284–9; and internal interventions 225; international perspective 222–3; and labor flow 243–4; meaning of 238; motivating force of 255–6; and multinational territories 220–1; and nation states 219–20; neo-liberal explanations for 238–9, 244–5, 247, 256–7; and non-governmental organizations 224–5; and post-War growth 258; as process/ policy 277–9; revisionist school views 239, 247–50, 257; and skill premium 244–5; subclasses 277; trade, investment, integration 255; and trade/economic growth 256; and transformation of global system 239–42; and undeveloped countries 245–50, 257–8; and the United Nations 222–4; and World Trade Organization 251–5, 257, 258–9
Gorbachev, Mikhail 28
Gorton, Gary 180
Gosh, S.K. 289
governance, and direct election/local

autonomy 231; effect of globalization on 223–4, 225, 235–6; and emergence of civil society 229–30; and establishment of legal system 230; and government/enterprise separation 232; and local government innovations 232–5; and Party/state separation 228–9; and political development 230
Great Leap Forward 25, 305
Gu, Mu 31

Heckscher–Olin hypothesis 264
historical materialism 189–90
Hobsbawm, Eric 179
Hu, Angang 267
Hu, Qiaomu 49, 52
Hu, Sheng 49
Hu, Yaobang 30, 36, 49, 52, 63
Hua, Guofeng 50

India, changes in foreign trade/payments regime 280–1; as developmental state 279–80; economic reforms in 279–84; financial liberalization in 281–2; foreign trade/national income ration 278; and global recession 278–9; globalization/financial markets link 284–9; and logic of financial liberalization 286; poorly regulated financial liberalization in 286–9; restrictions/regulations in 279; volatile markets, insecurities, communalization, concentration of wealth 289–90
industrialization, and capital accumulation 54–5, 57, 59; domestic restrictions 54–5; and large-scale production 55; and multi-system economic structure 58; and resource capitalization 58–9; and resources 54; Soviet transformation 55; strategic transformation under changing international conditions 56–7; and the system 54; third path system 59–60; and withdrawal of government from rural areas 57–8
International Monetary Fund (IMF) 46, 73, 246, 257
International Treaty of Economic, Cultural and Social Rights 227

Jia Ran 33
Jiang Qing 51
Joyce, James 166–7

Kangxi dynasty 42

Keynes, John Maynard 159, 165
Khan, Azizur 272
Klaus, 96
Korean War 56–7, 80

labor-capital partnership 160
Lassale, F. 171
Lenin, V.I. 51, 115–16, 117
Li, Qiang 272
Li, Xiannian 31
Li, Xin 49
Li, Yimang 31, 34, 37
Li, Yining 98, 111
liberal socialism 159–61
liberalism 299–300
Lin, Bao 29, 51
Lin, Chun
Lin, Zili 36
Liu, Shaoqi 24, 25
local governance, and administrative efficiency/honesty 235; and administrative services 233–4; and cadre selection/power restriction 234–5; and political transparency 232–3

Mao, Zedong 13–14, 19, 24, 25, 29, 50, 51, 64, 124–5, 228, 229, 298, 305–7, 309
Maoism 131–3, 136, 138, 144
market economy 11, 36, 118, 119; acceptance of 37–8; establishment/development of 5; Stolypin-type 104
market socialism 299; assessment of 131–3; and catch-up policies 140–1; and central planning 129, 130–1, 133–6, 140, 146–7; and competition 302; concept of 128–9; current initiatives 143–4; debates on 131; and domestic market/employment 311–12; and economic growth rate 136; and economic reform 310–11; and fairness 301; and free market liberalism 128, 130; future of 213–14; and grass-roots election 309; and human/civil rights 309; importance of education 146; and individual freedom 309–10; and labor mobility 134–5, 155; and legal system 300–1, 309; limitations 129–31; Maoist phase 131–3; and market opening 140–3; micro-/macro-economic changes 135; and national/global contradiction 130; and neo-liberalism

141–2; and new middle class/new rich 137; operation of 303; positive aspects 144–5, 146–7; and priority given to light industry/service sectors 136–7; problems/dangers 145; and reform movement 133–6, 144–7; and regional inequalities 131, 139–40; and rural inequality 137–8; and self-organisation of market 300; and separation/removal of capitalist form 302–3; as social not socialist 129–30; and state industrial sector 143–4; transition to 214; and urban/rural gap 131–2, 138–9, *see also* Chinese model

market society, and market/social rules 80; and the Cold War 80–1; and economic inequity 82–3; emergence/formation of 74–5; and free/non-free labor market 78; and influence of business class 76; and maintenance of economy 83; and market expansion 79; and globalization 76; and opening up to outside world 82; and participaory/procedural democracy 83; and political arrangements 75–6; and privatization 79–80; reform/ open-door policy 80; and relaxation of residence registration system 77–8; and Sino-Vietnamese war 81–2; and state 'do-nothing' policy 80; and state/society interaction 79; and trade protection 83; and urban/rural reform 76–7

Marx, Karl 114, 117, 151, 171, 247

Marxism 2, 11, 29, 33, 51, 55, 170; and addressing basic needs of society 206–8; and age of socialism 210–13; background 188–9; and economic democracy 192–6; and entrepreneurial capitalists 200–6; and foreign capital 208–9; and full employment/ entrepreneurial activity 198–200; and historical materialism 189–90; and nature/dynamic of capitalism 190–1; and raising cultural/education level of population 206–8; and reform 196–8; and trade 209–10

May Fourth Movement (1919) 23

Meade, James 159–61, 164–5

Meidner, Rudolf 183

Mill, John Stuart 158–9

modernity 293–4; alternative 297–305; basic elements 293–4; historical trajectory 295–6; potential/limitations of 296–7

modernization 1, 2; as all-encompassing 9; China's path to 3, 5; differing views of 2–3; East/West influences 17–18; and foreign experiences 16; historical perspective 152–3; and historical/ cultural heritage 16; imagining alternatives 16–20; and intellectual ferment 16–17; Maoist period 17; models for 18; and need for state/ private investment 9; plan for 293; and principal contradiction/principal aspect 19; problems concerning 9, 154–5; Reform Era 17; and reform of system 153–4; and societal forces 154–6

Munnell, Alicia 175

nationalism 2, 303–5

neo-liberalism, and ageing society 178; background 61–2; and contract system 66; and creation of market conditions 66; and crisis of legitimacy 68; definition 62; and demand for democracy 71, 72; and double-track price system 66; and the end of history thesis 73; and expansion of domestic/ international markets 73; and formation of interest groups 69–70; and globalization 238–9, 244–5, 247, 256–7; hegemonic status of 61; ideological emancipation/ enlightenment 63; ideological pressures from 308; and income 67; and interest groups 70; and neo-authoritarianism 70; as new dominant ideology 74–5; as oppositional 71; and price reform 67; and property rights 66; and rural/urban reform 64–6, 67–8; and the social movement 62–74; and social protection/justice 69; and social welfare structures 67; state tensions/conflicts 68, 71; and student movements 63–4; and tax structure 67; and wide social mobilization 71–3

Nichols, Donald 266

Nixon, Richard 25, 57

open-door policy 5, 32, 35, 57, 58, 80, 81

Organization Law of Village Committees of the People's Republic of China 229

pensions, and ageing society 177–8; background 175; challenges 176; democratization of 185–6; and ethical/socially responsible investment

184; pay-as-you-go (PAYGO) system 176–7, 178; problems concerning 178–81; proposed reforms in 178; provision for 175–6; share levy proposition 182–5; solutions to 181–6; and tax advantages 181–2, 183–4

petty bourgeoisie, and anti-market capitalism/real estate 162–3; art of socialism 166–7; and financial reform 165–6; and landownership system 157–8; and liberal socialism 159–60; and modern enterprise system 158–9; and post-Fordism 167–72; Russia vs China 162–3; and shareholding cooperative system 161–2; socialism vs oligarchy capitalism 163–4; and topsy turvy state share ownership 164–5

Piore, Michael 168–9

Plaza Accord (1985) 241

politics 13–15, 20, 41–2, 75–6, 121, 225–6, 230, 232–3

post-Fordism 167–72

private enterprise 89, 90; acceleration of 96; and Party member ownership 99–100; scale of 109–10

privatization 79–80, 96–7, 112, 120–1, 122–3, 303

property rights 303; agricultural sector 12–13; combined system 11–13; and delimitation 93–5; and household contract 12; and landownership system 157–8; legal aspects 95–6; and management rights 66, 94; modes of 92; paradox of 95; and privatization 96–7; and public ownership 11–12, 39–40; reform of 92–7; and small and medium enterprises 91–2; state 89–91; and state employees 92; strange phenomenon of 107; three-tier structure 170–1

protest movement *see* social movement (1989)

Proudhon, Pierre-Joseph 157–8, 165–6, 171

Qianlong dynasty 42

Qin, Hui 272

Qing Dynasty 153

reform process 64; and agriculture 30–2; and class struggle 29; commodity economy 35–6; and communist ideological education 42–3; and contracting output to households 34; and Cultural Revolution 25–6; current stage of 38–40; and decentralization of power 33; developing scope for 32–6; development zones 35; discussion on 48–52; education, science, technology 34; essential/non-essential social systems 40; financial 58; foreign comparisons 33–4; goal/direction of 49–50; historical background 26–8; improved economic system 23–4, 29–30; Initial Stage of Socialism 35; insitutional changes 49; internal factors 23–6; and market economy 37–8; Marxist theories 33; merits/demerits 43–4, 48; national-democratic revolution 23, 24; periods of 48–9; philosophical issues 44–6; and political system 41–2; problems concerning 50–1; and production 28–9; and proletarian dictatorship 24; and public/private ownership 34, 39–40; rural/urban 32–3, 64–6, 76–7; schisms in 49, 50; socialist revolution 23, 24–5; special economic zones 34; stages of 51–2; township/village enterprises 34; transition stage 24–5, 40–1; Wenzhou model 34; world context 26–8; and WTO participation 46–7

Regulation of Town and Township Enterprises (1997) *see* South Jiangsu (Sunan) model

revisionist school 239, 247–50, 257

Riskin, Carl 272

Root, H.L. 249

Sabel, Charles 167–72

Sanerkellens, Pierre de 223

Schweickart, David x, 18, 50, 215

Sen, Amartya 78

Shao Yanxiang 270

shareholding-cooperative system (SCS) 161–2

Sharkey, William 169

Sino-Vietnamese war (1979) 81–2

Smith, Adam 247

social movement (1989) 88; complex structures of 69–74; historical conditions of 62–9; impact of 62; multiple demands of 69–74

social transformation, and class division 101–5; extent/nature of polarization 101–5; and financial assets 103; move from populism to oligarchy 101; and

rich/poor disparity 101, 102–3;
    urban/rural gap 103–5
socialism 55, 299, 301–2; actually existing
    18; balanced with capitalism 12; and
    capitalism debate 115–16; with Chinese
    characteristics 10–11; and combined
    property rights 11–13; and democracy
    of constitutional government 13–15;
    development/improvement of 10;
    function of 11; humanist 3; Initial Stage
    of 35, 40; and internal limits of
    capitalism 3; market 18, 19, 20; and
    market/state relationship 3–4, 11;
    Marxist/revisionist difference 55; and
    social justice 3, 19
South Jiangsu (Sunan) model 88–9
Southern Jiangsu model 34
special economic zones 34, 35, 153, 231,
    270, 311
state, do-nothing policy 80; industrial
    sector 143–4; interaction with society
    79; investment 9; market relationship
    3–4, 11; property rights 89–91;
    separation from party 228–9; share
    ownership 164–5; society
    relationship 151–6; tensions/conflicts
    68, 71
State Council Commission on Economic
    Structural Reform 34
Stelper–Samuelson theorem 265
Stewardship Fund 184
Stiglitz, Joseph 175
stock markets 88, 164–5, 205–6
Stolypin's Reform 88–91
student movements 63

technology 9, 10, 32
Tiananmen Square (1989) 72
trade unions 154, 229
*Treaty of International Human and Civil
    rights* 226, 227

Unger, Roberto M. 167–72, 170
United Nations 46, 81, 222–4

Wade, Robert 271
Walesa, Lech 96
Wan, Li 32–3
Wang, Daohan 32
Wang, Hui x, 20, 120, 154, 155
Wang, Huide 51
Wang, Xiaoqing 270
Wei, Jingshent 52
welfare systems 100, 118
Wen, Tiejun xi
Wenzhou model 34
Westernization Movement 154
Women's Federation 229
World Bank 41, 46, 246, 247, 257, 272
World Trade Organization (WTO) 1, 13,
    73, 83, 142, 236, 238, 257, 258–9, 290,
    308, 311, 313; China's participation in
    46–7; and conflict between fair
    competition/development 252; and
    difficulty of defining fair competition
    253; and foreign trade/investment
    policies of far east 253–5; impact of
    China joining 251; and protected policy
    leeway 252; and September 11th
    251–2; and taking initiative to
    participate in making regulations
    251
Wu, Jinglian 106, 111
Wu, Lengxi 49

Xiong, Fu 49
Xue, Muqiao 32, 36

Yao, Yilin 31
Ye, Jianying 52
Yu, Guangyuan xi, 48, 50, 51, 52, 53, 152
Yu, Keping xi, xii, 237

Zhang, Jingfu 32
Zhao, Ziyang 48
Zhou, Enlai 51
Zhou, Siyuan 42
Zhu, Houze xi, 20, 155–6
Zhuo, Jiong 36

Printed in the United States
by Baker & Taylor Publisher Services